A SPECK ON THE SEA

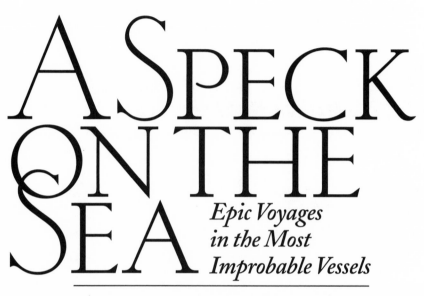

A SPECK ON THE SEA

*Epic Voyages
in the Most
Improbable Vessels*

WILLIAM H. LONGYARD

International Marine / McGraw-Hill

Camden, Maine • New York • Chicago • San Francisco • Lisbon • London • Madrid
Mexico City • Milan • New Delhi • San Juan • Seoul • Singapore • Sydney • Toronto

The **McGraw·Hill** Companies

1 2 3 4 5 6 7 8 9 0 DOC DOC 0 9 8 7 6 5 4 3

Library of Congress Cataloging-in-Publication Data
Longyard, William H.
    A speck on the sea : epic voyages in the most improbable vessels /
William H. Longyard.
       p.   cm.
    Includes bibliographical references (p.   ) and index.
    ISBN 0-07-141306-5 (hardcover)
    1. Seafaring life. 2. Adventure and adventurers. 3. Sailing. 4. Rowers.
5. Sea kayaking. I. Title.
    G540.L776 2003
    910.4′5—dc21   2003007479

NOTE: Neither the author nor the publisher encourages any unsafe form of
sailing, rowing, or voyaging. It is recommended that all boaters comply with
all U.S. Coast Guard regulations and recommendations concerning boat
handling, safety, and cruising. Neither do the author or publisher endorse or
warrant as fit for any purpose any of the designs or services by naval architects or companies identified.

Art on facing page: William Andrews's finest hour, his arrival in Spain
in 1892 just as the nation was celebrating the quatercentennial of
Columbus's first voyage to the New World. That Andrews gladly accepted the accolade as the "new Columbus" hinted at a character flaw
that would later prove deadly.

To my sisters

Cheryl Fulton and Margaret Mather

and

my wife

Pam

CONTENTS

INTRODUCTION: WHY WOULD ANYONE
CROSS AN OCEAN IN A SMALL BOAT? *1*

1. THE FOGBOUND PAST: 63 AD–16TH CENTURY 7
   Inuit Kayakers Get Lost ◆ Saint Brendan the Non-Navigator
   ◆ Diego Méndez Saves Columbus

2. TWO DESPERATE ESCAPES:
   THE 17TH AND 18TH CENTURIES *21*
   William Okeley Rows for His Soul ◆ Captain Bligh Saves Souls

3. VICTORIAN VENTURERS: 1865–1876 .... *42*
   God's Paddler, John MacGregor ◆ Three Jeers for the *Red,
   White & Blue* ◆ Inflated Dreams: The *Nonpareil* ◆ Vanishing
   Beauty: The *Vision* ◆ The *John T. Ford*: A Tragedy in One Act
   ◆ The *City of Ragusa* Saga ◆ Paul Boyton Floats to Glory and
   Coney Island

4. THE PATHS OF GLORY: 1876–1900 .... *67*
   Alfred Johnson's *Centennial* ◆ Take Your Wife, Please:
   The Crapos ◆ Nathaniel Bishop Leaves His Cranberry Bog
   ◆ Tanneguy de Wogan: The Paper Paddler ◆ The Andrews
   Brothers ◆ Norman and Thomas's *Little Western* ◆ The Little
   Tub That Could: *The City of Bath* ◆ Bernard Gilboy Leaves
   Home ◆ Andrews Solo ◆ The *Mermaid* vs. the *Sea Serpent* ◆
   The *Christopher Columbus* Gets Soaped ◆ Norwegian
   Clammers Row for the American Dream ◆ Fingerless
   Blackburn ◆ Till Death Do Them Part

5. A WORLD TO CONQUER: 1900–1920 .... *122*
   The Man Who Didn't Circumnavigate ◆ The Egg That Didn't Go
   Over Easy ◆ *Yakaboo* and a Poet, Too ◆ Stiff and Frozen Upper
   Lips: Shackleton and Worsley ◆ The Mystery of Hope Cove

6. LOVERS AND OTHER LOSERS: 1920–1930s *146*
   Franz Romer: Canoeist or Kayaker? ◆ *Liebe* Story: Paul and
   Aga Müller ◆ Leaving Latvia: The Rebell Yell ◆ Ivy League
   Vagabonds

7. **BIG FEAT, LITTLE NOTICE:** THE 1940s *173*
Three Men in a Rubber Raft ◆ Navy Hero Poon Lim: Thanks,
Now Leave ◆ Jack Schultz: Like Father, Like Son ◆ Like
Father, Like Daughter ◆ Postwar Hopes: The *Nova Espero*

8. **GOOFY AND GALLANT:** THE 1950s *193*
Jeeps Can Cross Anything, Including Oceans ◆ Once
More for *Nova Espero* ◆ Sweet *Sopranino* ◆ Dr. Bombard's
Bombast? ◆ Escape from the Foreign Legion but Not
the Sharks ◆ *Trekka*: Boy Makes Good ◆ By Log Across
the Atlantic ◆ *L'Égaré* Earns Its Merit Badge, Sorta ◆
Dr. Lindemann Crosses in a *Real* Kayak ◆ What's a Nice
Balloon Like You Doing on an Ocean Like This?

9. **DOING YOUR OWN THING:** THE 1960s *228*
The *Craig* and the River Goddess ◆ Kenichi Horie Brings
Shame and Glory to His Family ◆ Young John Riding vs.
the OSTAR Geezers ◆ Robert Manry Fights Suburbia on the
Atlantic ◆ The West Wight Potter Story ◆ The Birth of the
"Capsule" Boat ◆ The First Great Rowing Race ◆ Francis
Brenton: Transoceanic on the Cheap ◆ William Willis:
Have Hernia, Will Travel ◆ Jet Jockey Makes an *April Fool*
of Himself ◆ The Shagadelic Rower

10. **THE PURSUIT OF HAPPINESS:** THE 1970s *264*
By Lugger to Australia ◆ Aoki and Van Ruth ◆ David
Blagden Tames a *Willing Griffin* ◆ There's No Place Like
Home, Thankfully: Shane's *Shrimpy* ◆ Bas's Boat ◆ Webb
Chiles in an Open Boat ◆ Mexican Minimalist Mariner
Carlos Aragón ◆ Spiess Girl

11. **THE GOLDEN DECADE:** THE 1980s *279*
New Technology ◆ Don't Forget the Catamarans: The *Rag
Tag Fleet* ◆ Starkell and Sons: Epic Canoeists ◆ Sven the
Swede: The Edison of Small-Boat Builders ◆ Three Men Duke
It Out for Who's Smallest ◆ The 500 Days of Serge Testa ◆
Ed Gillet Kayaks and Kites to Hawaii ◆ French Impressions

12. **RECORDS AND REDUX:** THE 1990s *306*
Stephen Ladd *Squeak*s through a War Zone ◆ "Ant" Steward
Does It in the Open ◆ We're Great, But Don't Tell Anyone
◆ Friends and Foes: Vihlen vs. McNally ◆ Delaging the
Question ◆ Gvodev and Glasnost ◆ Lecomte Swims for Love

13. **NEW FACES AND OLD: THE NEW MILLENNIUM** *324*
It's a Girl! ◆ Elvis Has Left the Marina ◆ The Humpback
Kayak ◆ The Glory of Spain on a Sea-Doo

CONCLUSION: **TO SEA, OR NOT TO SEA:
THAT IS THE QUESTION** *330*
A Final Warning Before You Go

APPENDIX *334*
Rowers and Other Strangers ◆ Other Notable Voyages

NOTES *343*

BIBLIOGRAPHY *353*

ACKNOWLEDGMENTS *361*

ART SOURCES *364*

INDEX *366*

WHY WOULD ANYONE CROSS AN OCEAN IN A SMALL BOAT?

THIS BOOK IS ABOUT REMARKABLE WATERBORNE VOYAGES made in surprisingly small boats, generally, but not always, boats under twenty feet in length. Just as any good small-boat skipper knows never to cleat off a sheet lest he or she be blown over by a sudden gust, we won't encumber our narrative with an exact size limitation. After all, the length of a boat isn't the only determiner of its size, though it is commonly thought to be. To take two examples from this book, boats like Gerry Spiess's ten-foot sloop *Yankee Girl* were much larger volumetrically than, say, Ed Gillet's twenty-foot kayak *Tofino*. So by our definition a "small boat" is one less than about twenty feet long, but also one that is pushed to the extremes of its design limitations to complete a journey that spans great distances, often whole oceans.

Inevitably we ask: Why would a person make a hazardous long-distance voyage in a small boat? Why would a person risk his or her life, fortune, or future to achieve a feat that might, and often did, lead to death? Was it worth the years, the money, or even a life? What separates those who cast off from those who stay in port? Who are these adventurers?

Our sailing adventurers can be classified into eight categories. To be sure, human beings are complex creatures who do things for many reasons, not usually for just one, but, broadly speaking, our sailors took to the seas for one of these eight reasons.

The first and most elemental reason is *survival*. The Inuit kayakers who washed up on the coasts of Scotland and Ireland fifteen hundred years ago fully intended to return to their dwellings by sundown on the day they were blown over the horizon and lost their way. They weren't looking for the north*east* passage. Nor did Captain Bligh ask to be disembarked from the *Bounty* in midocean. The great William Okeley did choose to put his rickety folding rowboat into the dangerous Mediterranean under the nose of his Algerian oppressors, but he and his compatriots saw their undertaking as a last roll of the dice before they too suffered the same cruel fate that had befallen so many Europeans in Algeria.

Another motivation has been simple *curiosity*. What *is* over the horizon? Who can stand on the shore at the Pas de Calais and look across to that thin white coastline of Kent and not want to go there immediately and explore? What was it like to be an Irish fisherman in the sixth century and find a dead Inuit in his kayak washed up on your beach and know that he had to come from somewhere just beyond your fishing grounds—but where? How far? Would you have stuck to your daily routine of fishing to support your family and village or would you have summoned up the courage to tell your friends that you would go a-rovin' and find out for yourself where the alien came from? It would have taken as much courage to be different from your clan as it would have to strike out away from shore into the unknown. Was an Irishman in a skin boat the first European to intentionally sail away west? Or was it a Norseman in a clinker-built longship? Curiosity is a spur to all cultures. Christopher Columbus was probably motivated primarily by curiosity—he was a true explorer at heart. To be able to satisfy his curiosity he had to tell others that he wanted gold and land, but it wasn't avarice that drove him.

Money, however, is another motivation for some of these adventurers. The spectrum of money-chasing sailors ranges from poor, deluded Paul Müller, who claimed he wanted to earn just enough money from his voyage so he could buy a farm and marry Aga, to William Andrews, whose financial killings in Atlantic City were never quite enough to satisfy him and whose gold lust led to the literal killing of his naive child-bride Mary South in the most irresponsible voyage chronicled in this book.

The fourth major motivator is *fame*. There are two sorts who seek fame—those who have no public reputation and would like one, and those who are known to the public but want to keep or enhance their name recognition. Fame can be a powerfully addictive narcotic to those who experience even a little of it. The fame junkie often finds himself trapped in a cycle of always looking for the next "hit," knowing that the next hit has to be a little bigger than the last one to have an effect. Each stunt has to be more outlandish, and always more dangerous, than the last one. The inevitable conclusion to these games—which benefit only the media tycoons—is disaster or death for the players. Too many of our sailors completed a successful hazardous voyage only to be lost on the next, slightly more risky, one. Joshua Slocum, Si Lawlor, and William Willis are sad examples. Probably the most determined fame-seekers are those who fight to make records. Chief among these are Hugo Vihlen and Tom McNally, who are absolute tigers in their quests to hold the record for the smallest boat to cross the Atlantic. So far each has sought the record in a gentlemanly and sensible way—if the word "sensible" can be used to describe any of these voyagers! Struggling to keep a record is really trying to be immortalized. It's carving a stone that says "I was here" and expecting all eternity to read it. That is a dubious expectation.

There are also *sociopolitical* reasons to make record passages. Pauls Sprogis, aka Fred Rebell, wanted to show the governments of Russia, Germany, Australia, and the United States that he would accept no limits on his freedom to move about this world as he saw fit. What this ocean tramp wanted was political freedom for the "forgotten man," and his voyage was partly a tribute to that credo. If only for this Sprogis deserves to be long remembered and held in esteem by mariners, and all people, the world over. His suffering, both physical and mental, left us a poignant gift—the example of courage to stand up and fight against bureaucratic monoliths even when we fight them alone. The elusive Gladys Gradely seems to have sailed to prove a point, too. When maritime historians track her down and bring to light the truth of her voyage, it may be that this historical shadow made her own bold political statement with her Edwardian escapade. Was she a feminist who wanted to show that women were just as capable as men when it came to courage and beating the odds? If so, why did she disappear after apparently having conquered the veritable Mount Everest of sailing challenges? Did she choose to remain quiet and savor her victory by herself, or was she forced by outside pressure—a domineering husband or father—to hide her news and immediately return home? The trail of this mystery is cold after all these years, but not frozen.

Sailing is a *technical challenge* as much as anything else, and many skills must be mastered to achieve a successful long-distance voyage in a small boat. Some people are attracted to this aspect of sailing, just as some people like to solve complex math equations or finish the London *Times* crossword puzzle on the tube ride into the City from Kew. Boatbuilding, knot-tying, meteorology, sail-handling, navigation—all these demanding skills go into record voyaging, and learning them is a pleasure in itself. John Guzzwell, John Letcher Jr., and even the obsessive Ben Carlin seemed to be motivated by the enjoyment of technology as much as anything else. For them, conquering the oceans was a series of technical hurdles to be jumped over: solve the engineering problems and you've made your voyage. There can be as much beauty in the harmony of numbers as there is in an ocean sun-

An accident to Baron de Wogan's trigger finger led him to the joys of kayaking *en papier* (see chapter 4).

set for some, and the chance to test skills and theories in the real-world laboratory of ocean sailing is just one more inducement for people like them.

The seventh motivation, a more primitive one, is that ocean voyaging is a *personal test*. As society increasingly separates people from their natural instincts and herds them into politically correct corrals, there are always some who seek ways to avoid such restrictions and express their innate urges. The quest for a rite of passage from youth to adulthood seems to have motivated Kenichi Horie. In orderly, subdued postwar Japan, a healthy, hearty young man felt out of place, and the voyage of the *Mermaid* can be seen as opening fire in the generational wars that were to rage in the 1960s. Horie's defiance of the Japanese authorities and his flouting of the cultural rules that hammer into the psyches of all young Japanese the notion of extreme obedience must have been like a tonic to his fellow young countrymen. For himself, the voyage changed the boy into a man. Similarly, when John Riding disregarded the limitations set on him by the OSTAR (Observer Singlehanded Transatlantic Race) committee, he was proving to himself that he deserved membership in "the old boys' club" that organized competitive ocean sailing had become, even in those early years. Misbegotten Mary South likely was motivated by a quest for adulthood, too. Trapped in a humdrum life in a small farming community on the flat, dreary New Jersey shore and living dutifully in her parents' house with little prospect for any excitement, she must have seen William Andrew's newspaper ad seeking a bride to accompany him as the providential deliverance she had long prayed for, finally a chance to be a woman with her own life instead of her mother's obedient daughter. In this case the common predicament led to a tragic ending.

Finally, there is the *quest for purpose*, the motivation that writers from Shakespeare to Hemingway to Springsteen have all written about so passionately, hauntingly, and beautifully—the harrowing quest by men and women to find the indefinable *something* that makes this world and a person's life worth living. Why suffer the slings and arrows of the outrageous fortune that human existence throws at us only to be unavoidably eaten by the shark of death at the end of it all? Isn't there one thing a man or a woman can do to say—not to other people, but to the Universe or to Fate, "I was here and I achieved something grand against all odds and in defiance of you; I had my moment"—? Can a person find "a moment when the world seems right" and thus find peace in his or her own soul, a feeling that life isn't all just a foreordained joke, with someone else getting the last laugh? This most complex of all motivations surely drove Robert Manry to slam shut his goddamn desk drawer at the *Plain Dealer* for the last time while still only in his forties and head out to cross the mighty Atlantic Ocean in a converted lake dinghy. It's what gave Bernard Gilboy the quiet determination and personal certitude that enabled him to abandon his wife and children and his expanding little grocery business in Buffalo and head back to the fearsome Pacific. The more his bourgeois lifestyle thrived, the more his soul died. He *had* to go. Francis Brenton, Shane Acton, and Webb Chiles forswore the comfort of the modern world repeatedly so as not to be seduced from their quests for personal fulfillment. There was something about the ocean—the process of sailing and constantly challenging Fate—that made the twentieth-century conveniences that most men seek seem *not* worth it. At sea they were on equal terms with life, while ashore life had the upper hand, and they had to play its game. To cross oceans was to have a brief victory—and a brief victory was more than most other men would ever have in this world.

It might be said that for some of our adventurers life posed the question: To sea or not to sea? They, like Hamlet, chose life.

Art on facing page: Inuit kayakers caught in storms were sometimes blown off course to Europe, where they arrived barely alive. Thinking they came from India, the Romans called them "Indians."

THE FOGBOUND PAST

63 AD–16TH CENTURY

♦ INUIT KAYAKERS GET LOST   ♦   SAINT BRENDAN THE NON-NAVIGATOR
♦ DIEGO MÉNDEZ SAVES COLUMBUS ♦

IT IS IMPOSSIBLE TO SAY WHO MADE THE FIRST GREAT LONG journey in a small boat. Probably it was some poor prehistoric tribesman who, swept off his feet during a great spring flood, grabbed onto a floating log and was unable to get to land until many miles, if not days, had passed. Perhaps he was swept from the Andean foothills in Bolivia and found himself deep into the Amazon jungle before he could get to shore, if he ever did. Maybe he was swept out into the Atlantic and died. Maybe his log flowed out the mouth of the river but was later caught by the current and swung around, finally landing him on the coast. Far from home, far from the safety and customs of his own tribe, he must surely have become the captive of whatever local tribe found him. They would have been as startled and frightened by the appearance of this stranger as he would have been of them. His fate would not have been kind. Or was he on the Ganges or the Tigris or the Yangtze? Perhaps one day a young tribal renegade decided the only way to escape his clan's restrictive traditions was to leave and see what was over the horizon. Perhaps this prodigal adventurer intentionally found a log and used it to escape. Modern sailors have done that. Human motivations don't change, just the means of conveyance.

The big blue ocean was an unknown quantity to the ancients, so surely the first small-boat voyagers navigated, or just drifted, by river flow. Likely the first "overseas" trip in a small boat was made in the Mediterranean, perhaps by an Egyptian, gale-blown far from shore in a reed boat. The fog of history only lets us speculate; we cannot know with certainty any more than we can know which one of these daring travelers first realized he could find his way home by following the stars.

The first evidence of long-distance small-boat travel may have been found in Scotland (North Uist) and Ireland (County Down), where archaeologists have located first-millennium sites that contain Inuit-style tools. These Inuit would have had to come from the west coast of Greenland, a thousand miles away. The sites seem to indicate that there were groups of Inuit present, and if that is the case, then they probably did not arrive in individual kayaks, but in *umiak*, larger, undecked boats that the nomadic Inuit used until the twentieth century as something of a family station wagon to move wife, children, and household goods from one seasonal campsite to the next. They were definitely ocean-worthy vessels because they were also used to hunt whales. Did one or more make a nearly transatlantic west–east crossing a thousand years ago?

Why would an Inuit group intentionally venture to the east? Or were they blown off course during a routine seasonal relocation? Actually, if the tools found in Scotland and Ireland *are* Inuit, they were probably brought back by Viking travelers who were exploring Greenland, led by Erik the Red after his three-year expulsion from Iceland for murder. His pioneering journey resulted in six hundred Norse settlers moving to Greenland in the 980s. Perhaps returning Norse settlers brought back with them some Inuit implements that they either found there or bartered for.

It seems unlikely that Inuit umiaks traveled long distances, but there is some tantalizing evidence that they did reach Europe and the British Isles during the first millennium and up through the Middle Ages. In his *Natural History: Book II* Pliny the Elder cites Cornelius Nepos, who reported that dark-skinned non-Europeans landed in Germany in 63 AD.

Christopher Columbus reported seeing the corpses of two "Chinese" in 1477 off the coast of Galway, Ireland, when he was, he claimed, on a voyage from Bristol to Iceland. He wrote:

> *Men have come hither from Cathay in the Orient. Many remarkable things have we seen, particularly at Galway in Ireland, a man and a woman of most unusual appearance adrift in two boats.*

Columbus's Cathayans (Chinese) must certainly have been Inuit, who had similar Asian features. This sighting, though, helped change the course of history because it further convinced the Italian navigator that the Orient lay not that far across the ocean. If two kayaks could span the distance, surely European caravels could.

———◆———

While in Galway, Columbus, who had an insatiable thirst for seafaring narratives and cartographical information because of his off-season profession as a map and book dealer, must have learned of the Irish *immrama* (rowing tale) that concerned Galway's local saint, the sixth-century cleric Brendan.

Brendan was born about 484 in County Kerry and became an ordained priest when he was about twenty-eight. He was a tireless prose-lytizer who spent the next thirty years establishing religious communities, first in southwestern Ireland, but later in Wales, Scotland, and even Brittany. Brendan's boundless energy and personal dynamism led many to visit him at his monastery in Ardfert, Ireland, where he was often asked to speak of his wide-ranging travels, travels that had to be done in boats.

Though the pious priest himself died in 577 in Annaghdown, his legend had not yet been born. That would happen over the next three hundred years as the tales of Brendan's travels were mixed with factual nautical accounts of Irish fishermen and the fictional sagas of the voyages of two legendary Irishmen, Mael Duin and Bran. By the late ninth century *Navigatio Sancti Brendani Abbatis (The Voyage of Saint Brendan the Abbot)* had been written; this work (in Latin), purported to tell the true tale of how Brendan, at an advanced age, was visited by an angel who told him that God would allow him to go to the Land Promised to the Saints. Inspired, Brendan has three *curraghs*, boats with wood ribs and covered with one-quarter-inch-thick cow hides, made and sails off to the west with seventeen fellow clerics in search of this promised land. Along the way, they encounter Satan, who tempts them with a chalice, giant sheep, an island inhabited by birds who were once angels but fell out with God, and other spectral sights.

After three months of voyaging the holy pilgrims haven't reached their destination and return home, where Brendan's foster mother tells him that they failed because their boats were made from slaughtered animals. Brendan and his crew now build a larger boat, of wood this time, and set sail again, but with a crew of sixty. After many harrowing adventures over the course of seven years they pass through a great fog bank and reach the Land Promised to the Saints. Brendan sees a paradise where milk and honey flow freely and returns home to spread the joyous news.

Even today, more than a thousand years after the story was first set down on vellum, some insist that the story has some historical basis and that perhaps Saint Brendan *did* find the Land Promised to the Saints and that it was *really* Newfoundland or maybe even Connecticut.

The best clue to sorting out the whole Brendan legend is the *fact* that the earliest recorded versions of the story appear at the *same time* that Viking raiders were attacking the west coast of Ireland. Though many sources give credit to the Vikings for first venturing to Iceland, Greenland, and the New World, it is entirely possible that the Vikings were inspired to explore farther west after hearing about land in that direction from Irish fishermen—fishermen who first realized there must be something out there when they encountered lost Inuit kayakers. Did the Irish ever visit these places themselves? Probably not. The odd twist in the Brendan saga provides a telling clue. This clue is the surprising break in the story when Brendan returns home and forsakes the traditional Irish curragh in favor of a wooden boat—the type the Vikings were using. The switch to the high-tech longboat, brilliantly employed by the Norsemen, seems like a cultural admission that the world had changed and that the future of sea power lay in clinker-built wooden craft, not traditional Irish curraghs. It may be Gaelic pride, however, that caused the bard of the Brendan

Irish missionary Saint Brendan in a very un-Gaelic clinker-built vessel and looking for the Land Promised to the Saints. Did he find it?

saga to retain for Ireland at least the *priority* of western exploration. After all, the saga declares that the Irish got there first—before the Vikings.

Thus *The Voyage of Saint Brendan* does seem to be evidence that the early Irish knew about land to the west. Probably their fishermen, who had occasional encounters with kayaks, passed this knowledge to the Vikings yet wanted to retain for themselves some measure of glory— even though the Vikings had the technology to get there and they didn't. To believe that Abbot Brendan reached the New World is a stretch. If he had, he would have brought back detailed descriptions that his acolytes would have passed on, or recorded, rather than just the scanty details found in the narrative.

One researcher who believed that Brendan did reach the New World was Tim Severin, a university-trained historian who, during

1976–77, completed a transatlantic journey in a 36-foot skin boat built in much the same way that sixth-century Irish shipwrights made their boats. Severin recorded his remarkable trip in *The Brendan Voyage*, in it claiming that particulars in *The Voyage of Saint Brendan* jibe very closely with fact. For example, the Islands of Sheep are perhaps the Faeroe Islands, and the "thick white cloud" seen just before paradise is perhaps the fog typically found on the Grand Banks off Newfoundland. For these reasons and others, Severin believed that Brendan *must* have made the voyage to the New World.

What Brendan supporters should remember is that the texts of the Brendan saga that we have today were written three hundred years or more *after* Brendan's death and that they likely incorporate facts gathered after the saint's lifetime, perhaps even details reported by returning Viking mariners. Severin's epic voyage in a small skin boat, though a great feat of both empirical scholarship and gutsy seamanship, no more proves that Saint Brendan was the first European to see the New World than did Thor Heyerdahl's equally impressive *Kon-Tiki* voyage prove that South Americans populated Polynesia.

But whether Brendan actually saw the Land Promised to the Saints mattered little to Christopher Columbus when he learned of the saga in Galway in 1477; it only mattered that there were more clues to a land to the west. It *had* to be China, he thought. Fifteen years later, of course, he reached Terra Nova, which he mistook for China. Columbus made four trips in all to the New World, and an event during the last of these provides the first concrete record of an epic voyage made in a small boat. It was a voyage that saved Columbus's life.

In May 1502 Columbus led four caravels out of Cádiz harbor on his fourth and final journey to the New World. The Spanish government had not wanted him to go, and he was told beforehand that he would not be allowed admission to Spain's main Caribbean port, Santo Domingo on Hispaniola. A combination of Columbus's iconoclastic visionary behavior, poor governing skills while in charge of Hispaniola during a previous voyage, and his often wildly inaccurate reporting of the facts of his voyages had finally caused the government to break most of its professional relationship with him. Only Queen Isabella showed continued friendly feelings for the fifty-one-year-old admiral, who was increasingly plagued with arthritis.

In late June, while approaching Santo Domingo, he knew from long experience that a hurricane was imminent. Despite the prohibition, he sailed into Santo Domingo and requested permission from Governor Nicolás de Ovando to ride out the impending storm safely in harbor. He also warned the governor not to dispatch the thirty-ship treasure fleet to Spain. Ovando refused Columbus's request to put in and sent the treasure fleet on its way. Columbus sailed to the lee side of the island just in time to escape the worst of the hurricane that indeed developed. Of the treasure fleet, one ship made it to Spain, four limped back into Santo Domingo, and all the others were lost, along with five hundred hands.

For the next six months Columbus sailed along the eastern coast of Central America, searching for the mythical passage to the Indian Ocean. He never found it, but he did find gold, so much gold that he thought he had stumbled onto King Solomon's mines. He established a trading post at the mouth of the Río Belém (which he named for the biblical Bethlehem, and which is in present-day Panama). Relations with the local native tribe were cordial enough to begin with, and the two groups traded trinkets for gold. However, some of Columbus's men began to sneak off the ships at night and either rape, or barter for sex with, some of the local women. Tensions grew, and what made matters worse for the Spaniards was that the river level had dropped and their ships, now trapped behind a sandbar that spanned

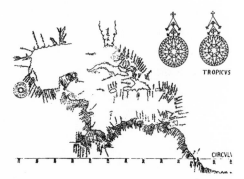

Spanish map from 1523 showing the lands touched on Columbus's fourth voyage. Shipwrecked on Jamaica, he had to contend with warlike natives and a mutinous crew.

the river, couldn't put to sea. There was no way out. Soon the Spanish could see canoes full of native warriors traveling across the river and proceeding up the coast to a local village. Were they war parties assembling for an attack?

At this juncture, one of Columbus's crew offered to perform a very brave act. Diego Méndez was a gentleman adventurer who may have put up some of the money to help finance the expedition. In some archives he is cited as the admiral's secretary, though it seems more likely that he grew into that role rather than signing on as such.

Méndez volunteered to take a skiff up the coast to reconnoiter the natives' movements. Once within sight of the encampment, he saw to his consternation that as many as one thousand natives had gathered there, an overwhelming force if it came against the Spaniards. Columbus's total force numbered 136. Méndez screwed up his courage and brazenly proceeded *alone* to enter the camp. He was told that the warriors had assembled in preparation for a war against two other tribes. Skeptical, Méndez returned to his boat, anchored just offshore, and rode watch on the war camp all night, thus acting as a trip wire to prevent any sneak attack on the landlocked Spanish flotilla. A few days later he compounded his bravery by boldly entering the village of the local chieftain Quibian. The village was festooned with the heads of hundreds of dead tribal enemies killed during recent fighting. In fact, Quibian himself was wounded in the leg with an arrow that had not been gotten out. When Quibian's own son tried to accost Méndez, he coolly whipped out a pair of scissors, a comb, and a mirror and instructed another Spaniard with him to give the boy a haircut. This inspired bit of cosmetology placated the hot-tempered youth for some reason and saved Méndez' own life.

While all this was going on, another problem that had beset the ships since leaving Spain had to be dealt with. All four of the caravels were rotting from the keels up because of shipworm attacks. One ship was in such bad shape that Columbus initially planned to leave it in the river with a garrison crew while the other three were towed over the sandbar the next time the river rose after a rain. In fact, three of the ships did manage to just scrape over the bar as planned. A small crew with provisions was left on the fourth, the *Gallega*, with orders to try to reestablish trading ties after the other ships departed for Hispaniola.

From his second reconnaissance, Méndez came to the conclusion that war was imminent. He returned to Columbus before the ships left and told him to prepare for battle. He was right. Several skirmishes followed in which the Spanish held off the natives, but about a dozen of their men were killed, and many were wounded, including Columbus's brother Bartholomew. The situation became untenable, but now they had to rescue the garrison crew, stranded on the other side of the sandbar. Again Méndez stepped forward to save the situation. Having noted that the natives' dugout canoes drew less water than his own skiff, he rafted two of these canoes together and over the course of two days lifted the entire garrison crew and its equipment over the sandbar to safety.

The thankful survivors quit Río Belém on April 16, 1503, only to face an open-water voyage in ships that were seriously deteriorating. One of them, the *Vizcaina*, was so rotted that she was abandoned and the crew split between the remaining two, the *Capitana* and *Santiago de Palos*. Even so, they couldn't make Hispaniola because of leaking, and when the pumps could no longer keep up with the water in the bilges, Columbus ordered that the ships be run aground at present-day Saint Ann's Bay, Jamaica. But because Jamaica was known not to have any gold, Spanish ships never put in there. Consequently, Columbus and his crew were stranded.

The Jamaican natives were at first helpful to the Spaniards, trading food for trinkets and allowing the free use of two local streams for freshwater. But once again members of Columbus's crew committed criminal acts that raised tensions. Columbus had to get word to Hispaniola quickly and summon a rescue party. For the third time Diego Méndez stepped forward with a plan.

Méndez successfully traded a brass helmet, a shirt, and a cloak with a local chieftain for a large dugout canoe. To this, he attached a keel, mast, and sail. With a mixed crew of Spaniards and natives, he proposed to sail and paddle to Santo Domingo, a distance of nearly four hundred miles. But not long after setting off his canoe ran into a storm and he put to shore, where he was attacked by hostile natives. With most of his party killed or missing, he returned to Columbus's base, determined to try again.

Méndez' new plan provided for a second canoe to escort his own. Bartolomeo Fieschi, captain of the abandoned *Vizcaina*, would command this second canoe, to be crewed by six Spaniards and ten native paddlers. The first canoe would have a similar complement. The six Spaniards on each boat would allow three always to be awake—three armed Spaniards being enough, it was presumed, to control ten unarmed natives, whose loyalty was suspect.

Sometime in August 1503 Méndez led his motley flotilla out again on a final desperate bid to secure help, as before, against all probability of success. After coasting along the hostile shores of Jamaica and then crossing nearly two hundred miles of open ocean during hurricane season, the brave Spaniard finally sighted the hills of Hispaniola. What eventually stretched into a four-hundred-mile voyage was in fact the first intentional long-distance open-water crossing in a small boat ever recorded.

Méndez immediately went to Governor Ovando to request that a ship be sent to rescue his shipmates. The governor scoffed at the notion of rescuing his archnemesis Columbus, and it took Méndez seven months of persistent diplomacy to change the governor's mind, but meanwhile Columbus's men had staged a mutiny and were at war with each other on Jamaica. It wasn't until a year later, in June 1504, that a small caravel Méndez chartered picked up the survivors and brought them back to Hispaniola.

Columbus was sent home to Spain, never again to see the New World he had helped discover. When he died in May 1506, his loyal gentleman adventurer friend was at his bedside. Méndez went on to

Brilliant, daring, and loyal, Spanish aristocrat Diego Méndez used a dugout like this one to make the first recorded great small-boat voyage. He risked his life in an attempt to save his hero, Christopher Columbus.

serve the Spanish crown in various administrative posts and eventually became the chief justice of Hispaniola. His will, dated June 19, 1536, is a remarkable testament to what a small boat meant to him. It reads:

> *Item—I order that my executors purchase a large stone, the best that they can find, and place it upon my grave, and that they write round the edge of it these words :—"Here lies the honorable Chevalier Diego Méndez, who rendered great services to the royal crown of Spain, in the discovery and conquest of the Indies, in company with the discoverer of them, the Admiral Don Christopher Columbus, of glorious memory, and afterwards rendered other great services by himself, with his own ships, and at his own cost. He died. . . . He asks of your charity a Paternoster and an Ave Maria."*
>
> *Item—In the middle of the said stone let there be the representation of a canoe, which is a hollowed tree, such as the Indians use for navigation ; for in such a vessel did I cross three hundred leagues of sea ; and let them engrave above it this word :*
>
> *"CANOA."*

Columbus's first voyage opened the floodgates to European exploration of the New World. It wasn't long before ships ranged up north from the Caribbean, notably the fishing boats of the Basques, then the French and Dutch, who all sailed in northern waters. Predictably, contact was established with the Inuit, and from the 1570s on ship captains often tried to kidnap Inuit men, women, and children and bring them to Europe to be put on display as novelties for paying audiences. Martin Frobisher was guilty of two such outrages, in 1576 and 1577. Several Inuit kidnap victims even toured Europe, though most died shortly after contact with Europeans, probably because they had no immunities against European diseases.

Kayaks were also taken during these encounters, and some of these still exist in museums in Britain and the Netherlands. Over the years historians have debated whether or not any of these kayaks, or kayakers, arrived in European waters of their own volition, were blown off course, or were the victims of self-serving kidnappers. The kidnapping "trade" went on for nearly 150 years before the Dutch government in 1720 issued a decree prohibiting it by Dutch whalers. This has caused some historians to speculate that the increased sightings of kayakers in European waters at this time were due to ship captains off-loading their captives before they reached home ports and the law. Perhaps they kept these men on board until the last moment to use as whale scouts.

Martin Frobisher skirmishes with Inuits in 1577 in the first battle between Native Americans and Europeans since the Viking era. The fight was the result of miscommunication on both sides.

But the timing doesn't quite fit. Even before the decree by the Dutch Staten Generaal kayakers appeared often around the Orkney Islands in the 1680s, and one even paddled into the River Don near Aberdeen about 1728; his boat has been on display at Marischal College there for three hundred years. A mummified kayaker, still in his boat, was picked up in the Skagerrak between Denmark and Norway as early as 1607.

In 1693 the memoirs of the Reverend James Wallace, of Kirkwall on Orkney, were published. They contain this reference to kayakers, whom he mistakenly refers to as "Finnmen":

> Sometimes about this country are seen these men they call Finnmen. In the year 1682 one was seen in his little Boat, at the South end of the Isle of Eda, most of the people of the Isle flocked to see him, and when they adventur'd to put out a Boat with Men to see if they could apprehend him, he presently flew away most swiftly. And in the year 1684, another was seen from Westra, and for a while after they got few or no Fishes for they have this Remark here, that these Finnmen drive away the fishes from the place to which they come. These Finnmen seem to be some of those people that dwell about the Fretum Davis, a full account of whom may be seen in the natural and moral History of the Antilles, Chap. 18. One of their boats, sent from Orkney to Edinburgh, is to be seen in the Physitians hall, with the Oar and Art he makes use of for killing Fish.

Were Inuit intentionally making epic voyages of one thousand miles across the raging North Atlantic in fragile skin-covered kayaks? Some doubt that a skin boat could last for what must have been at least a two- to four-week voyage without becoming waterlogged. They say that a skin boat needs to be regreased every two days. However, anthropologists who have studied Inuit culture have shown that Inuit only greased their kayaks' skins once per hunting season. A finicky boat that needed attention every few days would be too marginal a craft to have been used as long and as well as the Inuit used their kayaks.

More importantly, though, is that those who are skeptical about Inuit transatlantic voyages during the late seventeenth century apparently have not taken into account that Europe was gripped by a mini–Ice Age during this time; ice-core samplings have proven that its worst years

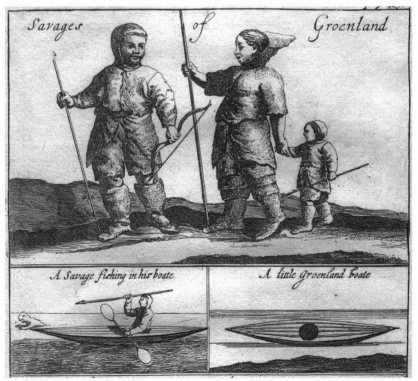

Many Inuits died shortly after they were brought to Europe because their immune systems were not prepared for European diseases. This fated family is seen in a 1732 English print.

were from 1680 to 1730—precisely the time of numerous sightings of kayakers around the British Isles. In light of this, what seems most likely is that because these kayakers were forced to travel farther offshore from Greenland to find food in the colder waters of these years, they may have gotten lost or fatigued and sought temporary refuge on ice floes. While on an ice floe a kayaker might have eaten, slept, and even regreased his hull. These floes drifted east with the current and began to melt, and the kayaker then had to relaunch. Seeing seagulls he may have followed them to land—but the land was not Greenland. It was Scotland, or the Orkney or Faeroe Islands.

There is no known modern kayak voyage from the west coast of Greenland to Ireland or Scotland—that is to say in a "normal" un-modified sea kayak. Though many great kayaking voyages have been undertaken in the last two decades, a voyage in an "off-the-shelf" boat of, say, twenty feet with a beam of less than twenty inches (typical Inuit dimensions) would be incredibly dangerous. Would it prove anything? No more than the Severin or the Heyerdahl voyages—but what an adventure!

Art on facing page: In 1639 Algiers was a walled city as large as London. White slavery fueled the African city-state's economy in the seventeenth century.

TWO
DESPERATE
ESCAPES

THE 17TH AND 18TH CENTURIES

◆ WILLIAM OKELEY ROWS FOR HIS SOUL ◆ CAPTAIN BLIGH SAVES SOULS ◆

PERHAPS THE TWO GREATEST SMALL-BOAT VOYAGES EVER made were led by two Englishmen, both named William, one a religious pilgrim and nonsailor and the other one of the best seamen the seafaring nation of England ever produced. The first was a slave, and the second an alleged slave driver.

William Okeley feared God and hated King Charles I and Archbishop Laud, the two most powerful men in 1639 England. Together with like-minded Puritans, Okeley decided to obey God's calling, quit what he saw as his morally bankrupt country, and sail to an island off the coast of Nicaragua where he and his band of fellow pilgrims hoped to found a truly godly nation.

The ship *Mary*, probably no bigger than the *Mayflower*, was hired to transport them to this island, called Providence. She departed Gravesend in June but wallowed around the English Channel for six weeks waiting for fair winds. When they came she headed west and made good progress for six days. God had different plans for the seventh day.

Just outside the English Channel the *Mary* ran into three Turkish warships that were hoping to capture small merchantmen, their hulls already crammed with prize loot and enslaved sailors. *Mary*'s captain debated fighting or running, and at first chose to fight, but at the last minute, when he realized how ineffectual his six guns would be against the combined firepower of the Turks, he decided to run. It was too late. The Turks were on him in a flash and after a few quick cannon broadsides a boarding party swung in to finish the job. Six of the *Mary*'s crew were killed and many more injured. Okeley survived unscathed, "Jesu be praised," but was clapped in irons and forced into the nauseating hold of one of the enemy ships, where he endured a voyage of a month and a half to Algiers. During the long voyage he heard many rumors about conditions in an Islamic country. Life was cheap, he was told—he might be killed instantly on nothing more than the whim of a local pasha.

Upon arrival Okeley and his fellow captives were taken to the ruling viceroy's palace, where every tenth men was given to the potentate as his share. The rest were then taken to the slave market to be sold. At the market Okeley was poked and prodded to test his fitness. Prospective bidders pried his jaws open, as if he were a horse, to examine his teeth. As it turned out, he was pronounced fit and quickly sold to a Tagarene—an Algerian moor of Spanish descent—who took him to his house.

When the Tagarene's father saw that his son had purchased a Christian slave, the old man berated his offspring and slapped Okeley. Okeley, the religious zealot, made a gesture with his hands as if he were sewing. This, he and his captors knew, was a mockery aimed at Mohammed, whom the Christians of that time considered to be nothing more than a "cobbler." The old man became enraged and pummeled Okeley, and the more the Englishman tried to deflect the blows, the more angry the old man became. Finally, to mollify his father, the Tagarene drew out his long knife and came at the defenseless Okeley to settle the point of honor. Just then the Tagarene's wife entered the room and parted the theological combatants. She reminded her husband that killing the slave would not profit anyone and that the beating was punishment enough. Okeley later recorded: "I was but a martyr to my own folly . . . when the body is a slave, the reason must not expect to be free."

For six months Okeley accepted his role as slave and performed household chores. After this he was required to assist his master's men who were fitting out a twelve-gun warship for a speculative pirate trip around the Mediterranean. For a few weeks he helped, but when he was then told that he must join the corsair, he suffered a moral crisis—could he in good conscience take part in a voyage that might endanger *Christian* lives, he who had been on a religious pilgrimage in Christ's name when he was captured? However, his mind was made up for him by his owner, who told him that he would go or die. He went. For nine weeks Okeley played the part of an Algerian corsair, though he always hoped they would not encounter another ship. Finally, his ship came upon a hapless "Hungarian-French" warship, which it took, though with little booty to show for the effort. They then returned to Algiers.

What happened next may seem very odd to those uninformed about the white-slave trade in North Africa during those years, but because of the lack of a good profit from this voyage, Okeley's master was forced to put him out into the Algiers streets to earn a living,

Christian slaves were hobbled as punishment for trying to escape. This involved breaking all the bones in the feet with as many as three hundred blows from a club.

not as a free man, just at liberty within the city walls. He was required to earn two dollars per month payable to the Tagarene, though he was free to keep anything he earned over that. Thus after nearly a year in captivity Okeley found a measure of freedom. Like most other cities in the "civilized" world at that time, Algiers was walled, yet it was large— its walls were three miles in circumference, the same as London's. The city was full of wonder and, as Okeley was to find out, danger and opportunity, as well.

Okeley commended his fate to his god and set out within the guarded and gated confines of old Algiers to make a living. To fail would mean death. A bit of good luck soon came his way when he chanced to meet another English slave, who also was required to earn a monthly levy for his master. This man operated a bric-a-brac stall in the marketplace, selling all sorts of odds and ends from small quantities of food and liquors to used bits of metal. He offered to take on Okeley as an assistant and teach him his trade. For his first business deal Okeley bought a small bundle of tobacco leaves, which he and his new partner cut and diced for smoking. They quickly sold out, turning a small profit. Similar deals, including retailing wine, built up the "company" funds, and soon the two had become reputable merchants who could even buy on credit from the local Algerian businessmen.

Okeley's contribution to the partnership must have been mostly his charisma, because it was only after he joined the other man that the business thrived.

Security, routine, and the easy access to wine caused Okeley's partner to lose interest in the business. Okeley pressed on and soon was able to rent a cellar to use as a warehouse. Over the next three years he came to know several other Englishmen in similar straits, and together they pooled their extra cash each month to pay the levy of an enslaved English preacher, so he would not have to work in the streets and could instead minister to his small English congregation. This employment of Devereux Spratt to help with their spiritual salvation was to lead to their earthly salvation.

Though life in Algiers had become bearable for Okeley and his small cadre of friends, as foreigners (and Christians at that!), they were always under the watchful eye of Algerian spies and constables under order of the viceroy to make sure that none of them escaped the city. The penalty for trying to escape was death, though first-time offenders were usually "just" tortured as a warning because it was hoped that an income-producing slave could be dissuaded from further attempts to escape rather than being wastefully killed.

Okeley witnessed many cases of torture and death in the city, including a Spanish friar who was beaten with a lash until near death and then burned at the stake. Thieves who had their hands chopped off were required to wear their newly cut-off hands on a string hanging from their necks. A young Dutch slave was staked to the ground and had his arms and legs smashed to bits with a sledge hammer, his death cries barely audible over the cheers of the crowd. Though free in a limited way, the Englishmen knew that it was only a matter of time before their turn to deal with the fickle and cruel Algerian law would come.

This happened sooner than expected. Because Okeley and his friends were sober, trusted slaves, they were allowed a certain amount of freedom outside the Algiers city wall. They were allowed by the authorities, for the sake of maintaining good health, to walk a one-mile promenade that stretched from the city toward the sea. On one of these walks Okeley and a new business partner, John Randal, walked a little farther than permitted. The men were seized by a constable and returned to the city, where they went before a judge, accused of attempting to escape. They forcefully pled their case and were let off with a stern warning. Okeley's master, to make sure the Englishman couldn't run away, ordered that Okeley work as a cloth weaver under close supervision. Randal wasn't so lucky. His master wanted to make sure he didn't try any further escapes and so had his feet subjected to three hundred blows from a baton, which broke all their bones. He hobbled for months.

Okeley knew now that he must escape. He felt that he was becoming like the Israelites held captive in Babylonia who "forgot Canaan and dwelt with the king for his work" (I Chron. 4:23). But next the Tagarene who owned Okeley suffered a business collapse when his latest pirating expedition failed, and he was forced to liquidate to pay off creditors. Okeley was put up for sale and by a stroke of luck was bought by a gentlemanly old landowner whose estate was a few miles outside the city walls. He allowed Okeley to pursue his merchant trade and kept a fairly loose rein on him. Okeley grew so fond of the old man that as the months passed his determination to escape weakened. What was the difference between paying a levy to this old man and paying taxes to the king of England? Business was good in Algiers; he had nothing in England. England was now embroiled in civil war—good Christians were killing one another. England was cold, Algiers was temperate. England was where he was trying to escape from when he was captured. Why go there? Why go back? Why not stay in a place where he was appreciated? His owner liked him and treated him well, even allowing him to return to his market stall, and he had an amiable circle of English friends. Why go home? The answer was that it was *home*; the call of the sceptered isle could not be ignored. But how to escape?

In June 1644 William Okeley convened a secret meeting of English slaves, all trusted friends and members of Spratt's congregation, in his rented storage cellar. He swore his six fellow plotters to secrecy and then proposed to them perhaps the most fantastic means of escape ever proposed to desperate men—a folding rowboat, to be built right under the noses of their captors. Okeley's personal charm must have been enormous; it had helped him survive the rages of his masters, succeed quickly as a merchant, even escape sentencing by a judge. Now he must have turned it on full to talk the six men into risking their lives in a boat they would have to make in the heart of heavily populated Algiers, carry out through the city gates past the guards, launch from the beach without being seen, then row through the breakers, and finally—if they got that far—row more than one hundred and eighty miles to the Spanish island of Mallorca. Okeley's persuasive powers melted all objections, and the entire group signed on that night.

The boat would be built in that very cellar. His plan was to build it in pieces, no piece over six feet long, and most much shorter. It was to be twelve feet in length. To make it fold, and therefore portable, it would be made from planks that would be joined with two nails. The first nail was to act as a pivot, while the second, to be inserted on final assembly, would fix the plank's position. The keel would be made in two pieces and the ribs in three—one floor with starboard and port vertical pieces hinged to it. The men worked as quickly and quietly as possible in the after-business hours. The frame pieces were made by so many hands that after only a few nights' work the boat was ready for covering. Covering a twelve-foot boat would have taken many board feet of expensive wood and, worse, would have involved a lot of cutting and hammering to fix it to the ribs—noisy work that would have attracted outside attention. Even if all that could have been done in secrecy, the boat would not then have been portable.

Okeley's solution was brilliant. He proposed to use for his boat's "skin" the coarse fabric that he used to make cheap ready-to-wear clothes for sailors, which he sold at his stall. The fabric, in a double layer, was quickly attached in long strips, carefully cut and temporarily tacked in place, and then the seams were sewn. As with coracles back home, the English slaves coated their boat with a noxious concoction of pitch, tar, and tallow.

The process of coating the boat nearly killed Okeley. To ensure secrecy he had ordered that all the openings leading up to the street from his cellar be stopped up with rags. The coating compound had to be liquefied in earthen pots over a small flame, but this gave off a pungent cloud that overwhelmed him in the sealed room. The other men hoisted their leader up and out into fresh air, where he revived. He reluctantly agreed to open the cellar door so the coating of the skin could continue. It took two nights to complete the job, and no one bothered to investigate the odor.

Now that the boat was made, including seats and paddles, it was disassembled and folded up. The men conferred about the best way to get the pieces out of the city. According to their plans, one of their members, a bricklayer, carried the long keel pieces outside the city walls with his tools and hid them in an agreed-on spot. Others took the shorter rib pieces and other fittings. The skin, the bulkiest single part and therefore most difficult to conceal, was taken out one day by a launderer who had permission to go to the water's edge to wash clothes. He stuffed the carefully folded skin into a large laundry bag and for good measure put a pillow on top. He walked right past the guards at the city gate without attracting attention.

Okeley himself took on the job of spiriting a sail they had made out to the rendezvous point. Sure enough, as fate and bad luck would have it, the very spy who had caught him and Randal before saw Okeley carrying the bag through the city gate and tailed him. Okeley almost panicked because he couldn't think of an alibi—he felt that guilt was written all over his face, but saw no way out. Just then he saw another Englishman washing clothes at the water's edge. Kneeling beside him, Okeley pulled the sail from the bag and began to "wash" it, spreading it on a rock to dry. No doubt disappointed, the spy ambled off back to town.

When Okeley told his coconspirators of the spy, their determination weakened, and they discussed for the hundredth time the pros and cons of their dangerous plan. Talking revived their courage, and they fixed a time for departure, the sooner the better—an hour after dark on the last day of the month, June 30, 1644.

Each by his own means was able to get out of the city that day and lose himself in the crevices and gullies that led down to the sea. How their hearts must have pounded as they tried to estimate, without watches, when the sun had been down for an hour. Every little sound from the hills around them and from the seashore below them must have filled them with a quiet terror. With great courage one by one they rose and crept through the shadows to the rendezvous.

As they gathered to assemble their boat some murky figures were seen approaching. The men froze, but the figures passed by in the night, not realizing how close they were to such a remarkable undertaking. Nothing more was heard, and the Englishmen began to assemble their boat. First they fixed the ribs onto the keel by tying them in place with stout cord. A fig tree trunk was added to stiffen the keel, while some saplings were bent along the sides to help define the shape from stem to stern. Next the skin went onto the skeleton, and the boat was built.

Okeley later said it reminded him of a funeral to see the boat carried a half mile down to the shore on the shoulders of four of his friends. Because there had been no time to test it, they didn't know what to expect. Would it even be watertight? They carried it into the surf and some way out so that it wouldn't be holed by an unseen rock, and then one by one they clambered in over the side. Disaster—the twelve-foot boat wouldn't carry seven men. There was hardly any freeboard, and it was shipping water at an alarming rate. One man immediately lost heart and begged out, and after a little discussion, another man volunteered to leave. Now the boat floated with some margin of safety. The remaining five, John Anthony, William Adams, John Jephs, a third John (surname unknown), and William Okeley, began to paddle for their lives. Too much of the night had already gone and the sun would be up soon. A northerly wind made the sail useless.

At daybreak the escapees were dismayed to see the city walls staring them in the face—they had made barely any progress against the tide and damnable opposing winds. It would be an easy trick for an Algerian boat to pluck them out of the water if they were seen. But they weren't, and inch by inch they crawled over the horizon northward, away from Algiers. Though they had no compass, Mallorca was a straight shot north across the Mediterranean, and it shouldn't be that hard to find if they could just keep following wave patterns during the noon hours. At other times it would be easy to guide themselves by the sun with a pocket dial they had brought and at night by the polestar.

Because of the danger of being caught carrying food outside the city gates—an obvious sign of escape plans—they had taken only a few hunks of bread and a little water in leather bags. The

William Okeley implores God for protection while attempting to escape Algiers in a folding rowboat. Manna from heaven came in the form of a sleeping turtle.

bread had been soaked during the launch and salt water in the bilges caused the water bags to leach tanning chemicals into the freshwater. They rowed on, battling wind and waves, stroke after stroke. When they paused to rest the wind immediately drove them backward, and they had to reearn the distance. Their water soon ran out. The hours lengthened into days, and they knew they couldn't make their goal with their failing strength. It all seemed hopeless, like a foolish dream. On the evening of the fourth day they gave up. As they bobbed dejectedly up and down on an uncaring sea, God provided their means of deliverance, as Okeley said later. One of the men spotted a sea turtle asleep floating near the boat. They hauled it in, cut off its head, drank the blood, and ate the other parts. It restored them, and they could resume rowing.

The next morning they were even more lucky: they saw land. Mallorca! It took them until ten o'clock on the evening of their sixth day at sea to reach the island. As they did, fate had one last twist waiting for them—a Turkish warship that crept by in the darkness just yards away. The men cowered at their oars and held their breaths. Had anyone on the corsair spotted them? No, their boat was too low to be seen in the evening gloom, and they went undiscovered. They were able to land in the darkness, safe at last, "Jesu be praised."

Because one of Okeley's men spoke Spanish, they were able to relate their incredible adventure to the Mallorcans and receive help from the local governor. He sent them on to Spain, and from there they returned to England. After his return William Okeley remained in England. Somehow his missionary zeal had cooled, and he grew fond of the country that God had once told him to leave.

Captain William Bligh was ordered to sail from England to Tahiti in December 1787 to obtain breadfruit to feed slaves in the West Indies. Chosen over another young but promising naval officer, Horatio Nelson, thirty-three-year-old Bligh skippered HM Armed Vessel *Bounty* first to Cape Horn, but, unable to make way against the terrible wind, bore off and proceeded to the Cape of Good Hope.

After a short stay at the cape, Bligh and his crew of forty-three spent five more months cooped up on the relatively small *Bounty*, heading east. The *Bounty*, originally built as the collier *Bethia*, only 91 feet and 215 tons, had much of her limited interior space reserved for the potted breadfruit cuttings that were to be taken from Tahiti to be re-planted on Saint Vincent and Jamaica, where it was hoped they would propagate future crops. The crew, including the officers, were packed in like sardines, which made a rough journey all the more difficult to endure.

Captain William Bligh was a ge-nius at navigation but a failure at people skills. The *Bounty* mutiny wasn't the only exam-ple of his subordinates re-belling against his heavy-handed leadership.

Ten months after leaving England and 27,000 miles later, the *Bounty* finally arrived at the island paradise of Otaheite (now Tahiti) where the men found the weather mild, their work negligible, and the women willing. To them it was paradise found. Bligh lingered for six months in this antipodal Eden, perhaps longer than he should have. Had he succumbed to its temptations, as had his men? According to the log kept by the ship's medical officer, venereal disease was common among the crew. Bligh had the mind of a mathematician: logical, orderly, and unwavering. He knew his duty, expected others to know theirs, and dealt swiftly with those who fell short of his high standards. Had this island of tropical delights become a siren that caused this rigid, unsensuous man to neglect the execution of his orders to sail promptly?

For whatever reason, Bligh dallied long enough in Otaheite for his crew to grow used to its charms and comforts. Many had native lovers, and some had children on the way. Bligh had to bully them to get them back on the ship for the return voyage, which began on April 4, 1789. It didn't take long before the journey unraveled into mutiny.

On April 26, Bligh noticed that coconuts were missing from a storeroom. He questioned several of the crew about the theft, including Fletcher Christian, his acting lieutenant, a man with whom he had

sailed twice before and with whom he had a close professional relationship. In fact, Christian, about twenty-six at the time of the mutiny
to Bligh's thirty-four, was something of a protégé of his captain, who
now had become his interrogator. He rankled under the examination,
blurting out, "I hope you don't think me so mean as to be guilty of steal-
ing yours." Bligh, highly skilled in seamanship but much less so in leadership, retorted, "Yes, you damned hound, I do."

These two men, both young, capable, ambitious, and proud, could
not remain on the same ship together for a six-month, or longer, voyage
back to England. One of them would have to go, and whereas Bligh had
alienated the crew with his heavy-handed bullying, Christian had the
loyalty of key crew members who were willing to act. In only one day he
secretly organized a takeover of the ship, promising a return to Otaheite
and its women to those who signed on with him. About eleven did, only
a quarter of the crew, but enough. In the early morning hours of April
28, 1789 (just ten weeks before the French Revolution), he committed
the most famous mutiny in history.

The mutineers' plan was simple: they raided the gun locker and
used its muskets and pistols to threaten those members of the crew who
had not joined them. They took the sleeping Bligh last, tying his hands
behind his back and marching him topside with the others. At the point
of a bayonet Christian told him to remain silent, but Bligh tried to negotiate with his captors. At first the mutineers intended to place the
members of the loyal crew into a small cutter and set them adrift, but
when it was pointed out that the cutter's planks were rotten, they relented and ordered the larger launch lowered.

Into this were forced eighteen members of the crew and lastly Bligh.
Some still on the *Bounty* wanted to join Bligh but because of their
needed technical skills were restrained by the mutineers. The nineteen
castaways were given supplies and provisions, including canvas, ropes,
sails, twenty-eight gallons of water, 150 pounds of bread, and some rum
and wine. Bligh was given a quadrant and compass, but Christian ex-
pressly forbade the softer-hearted members of his crew to pass down
either a sextant, timepiece, or chart. He told Bligh that with the equipment and food they had given him he ought to be able to get his boat

to the nearby island of Tofua (now part of Tonga). All the while his fellow mutineers jeered at their hapless former crewmates, bobbing up and down in a twenty-three-foot launch that could boast only seven inches of freeboard. For the boat to last even an hour without being swamped, let alone reaching Tofua, was a dubious proposition.

Just before the launch was released to its fate, additional supplies were lowered—pork, clothes, four cutlasses, and a sextant. But when Bligh asked for firearms he was laughed at. One of the last things Bligh heard, other than the laughing and some cheering as the *Bounty* filled her sails and moved off, was one crewman on board who said, "I'll be damned if he does not find his way home . . ." That's exactly what Bligh intended to do, though he had no charts or nautical almanac, and their only timepiece was a pocket watch.

Who other than Bligh would have been optimistic about what had happened to the nineteen men who found themselves in the crowded

Captain Bligh demands firearms from Fletcher Christian but only receives old cutlasses. This dramatic scene illustrates the beginning of the greatest single small-boat voyage in history. No man alive at the time could have achieved what Bligh did without a map, and with only his memory of charting the South Pacific with Cook to guide him and his eighteen fellow castaways.

launch in the middle of a wide blue sea? Bligh not only claimed to be hopeful but acted accordingly, immediately ordering his men to row northeast toward Tofua. He intended to increase his store of supplies there, and then head west to the Dutch colony on East Timor some four thousand miles away—and all without a chart or proper navigation equipment. How could any man in that boat have thought other than that Bligh had lost touch with reality? Sail four thousand miles across the Pacific Ocean in a nearly swamped boat and find a small island in virtually uncharted water, without a map, relying solely on Bligh's recollections from a previous voyage? It couldn't be done. Oddly, when times had been good, his worst character flaws had manifested themselves. Now, in this desperate hour, Bligh's prodigious reasoning skills were to come to the fore and give him and his men a fighting chance.

That night Bligh reached the first of his goals. They hit Tofua dead on and anchored in a lee cove. At daylight the sailors awoke, landed, and cautiously picked their way through the interior of the island, looking for water and food. At least they were back on dry land, but, as Bligh warned them, the Tofuans might be hostile. They found no islanders that first day, but neither did they find food or much water. As they were forced to stay another day, Bligh ordered some men to sleep on shore and some in the boat, ready to pull away at the first sign of trouble. Bligh himself slept little that night, but at daybreak all was quiet. A foraging party finally made contact with islanders, some of whom had met British sailors from other voyages before. They agreed to trade water and plantains for trinkets.

On the next day, May 2, a large party of Tofuans arrived at the cove where the launch was anchored. Bligh did his best to show outward confidence, even though he was vastly outnumbered by the natives and had no firearms. All day long more and more islanders came to the cove while Bligh was busily engaged in conversation with their chief, who ostensibly was friendly. However, Bligh didn't fail to notice that the natives were slowly encircling his party, moving ever closer to the launch. Some even began to beat small rocks together rhythmically—as if to signal their fellows to be ready to attack. Bligh likewise used subtle clues and gestures to try to position his men to make a break for the launch. Tensions built when a few natives crowded near Bligh, who had to brandish one of the cutlasses to clear a path to the boat, still anchored in the cove. The game continued for hours.

As the sun lowered on what should have been an idyllic island scene, Bligh and half his men were still on the beach, nearly surrounded. The Tofuans' intent was clear, though their chief still tried to distract Bligh and separate him from his men. The tempo of the rock beating increased. They were at an impasse, and it only remained to see who would make the first move. It was Bligh, who ordered his shore party to proceed directly to the boat, on the double. Their sudden move froze the Tofuans, waiting for an order from their chief. His hesitation gave the Englishmen their chance. Bligh himself bravely brought up the rear and was the last to climb into the boat just as the Tofuans recovered from their momentary daze and began to hurl rocks—their only weapons—at the Englishmen. Desperately, Bligh's men tried to row out of the cove, but they were held fast by the anchor, which was fouled on the bottom. There was a confusion of orders and John Norton, the young quartermaster, jumped from the boat, past the restraining hands of his crewmates, and went to retrieve the anchor. They had only to slash the anchor rode with one of the cutlasses to free themselves, yet Norton tried to save the anchor. It cost him his life. Enraged Tofuans brought him to his knees with their missiles and then beat him to death. The now-freed launch pulled away from shore as its crew, furiously rowing, watched in horror and pity the brutal murder of their comrade.

Breaking through the surf, Bligh and his men still weren't safe. A war canoe manned by stone-throwing warriors shot after them from the beach. Just as it was about to close in, Bligh, thinking quickly, tossed over the side some of their spare clothes. The Tofuans stopped paddling and turned to collect the scattered garments—items that were rare and valuable in their society. The launch lumbered away into what was now total darkness—and safety. The precious little water and food they had gotten on Tofua weren't worth the price of John Norton's life, but they had learned a valuable lesson that would save them later.

In the darkness of the night and the vastness of the great ocean, Bligh plainly told the men that their only hope lay in reaching the

Dutch colony on East Timor and that they could not count on resupplying on the many islands along the way. The islanders, as they had just seen, were friendly only at the point of a gun, and the party had none. They had to make the provisions—the bread, pork, water, and wine—already on board last eight weeks, the time Bligh estimated it would take to reach East Timor. That meant that each man could have only one ounce of bread and one quart of water per day—slow starvation rations. Fish and birds might be caught en route, but that was uncertain. In short, the situation was desperate, but not hopeless.

Whatever these men had thought of Bligh's captaincy on the *Bounty*, they knew now he was their sole hope for survival. It would be his experience, intelligence, and iron will versus the mighty Pacific Ocean in a nearly four-thousand-mile-long roll of the dice.

It was very cold that first night out, but a favorable wind allowed them to hoist the two lug sails on the ketch-rigged boat. Despite being overburdened the craft moved along smartly, and by the noon sight on the next day they had made eighty-six miles. A gale blew up, and the boat was shipping too much water, so Bligh ordered the men to lighten it as much as possible. By jettisoning the rest of the spare clothing, rope, and sails they gained a little precious freeboard—seven inches total. Even so, at least one man was always bailing. Under a reefed foresail they made ninety-five miles the second day. Once again they spied an island, but they did not consider landing. The following day as they passed another island, which Bligh reckoned to be Fiji, two large sailing canoes came after them and stayed in pursuit the rest of the day. They managed to elude the native craft but were reminded just how dangerous the rest of the voyage would be.

The days ticked off slowly, and each morning when they awoke the crew members considered themselves lucky. The weather was either squally or blew a full gale. They were cold, constantly bailing, and always hungry. Bligh devised a scale from two coconut halves to weigh each portion of daily bread, one pistol ball's weight of bread per meal per man. One of the men fashioned a cloth screen attached to the gunwales; this raised the freeboard enough to allow them some relief from constant bailing and the ever-present threat of sudden swamping.

The continual gale weather brought blessings as well as dangers. The wind kept the boat moving at a good clip in a northwesterly direction, while the attendant rain showers provided much needed water. During one storm they managed to collect twenty gallons. Another benefit to the bad weather was that the men were not exposed to the tropical sun. Though cold and often shivering, they at least were not sweating away precious water or suffering from sunstroke.

On Monday, May 11, the seas were so high and confused that it took two men bailing to keep the ocean at bay. The high seas and the constant cold sapped their strength, and one by one their resistance wore down. Yet that day they managed a record run of 102 miles. The next day they made only 89 miles, but when they saw man-o'-war birds they knew they were close to land. Bligh shared with the men his knowledge of the local hydrography in order to raise their spirits and let them know that each hard day brought them closer and closer to their goal.

On May 16 the winds were from the south, which greatly concerned Bligh because he feared being blown toward New Guinea, the home, he knew, of particularly aggressive peoples. He tried to sail on a reach to the west, but the continuing high seas threatened to capsize the boat whenever it presented its beam. He was forced to run with the sea—directly toward New Guinea.

The worst days were now upon them. Some in the crew grumbled about the short rations and unavoidable nuisances. Up to this point the men had been remarkably understanding and cooperative, but now the cracks were showing. The rain and gales made it impossible to get dry or warm, and with so many in the launch it was also impossible to stretch out into a comfortable position. Bligh recorded in a daily log that he hardly slept during the weeks of this ordeal. Adding to the danger was a near miss with a water spout and a terrible lightning storm that began on Monday, May 18, and went on all through the next day. On Wednesday Bligh wrote that his fellow sufferers "seemed half dead." On Friday, May 22, the winds were so high that the launch surfed along the steep rolling waves. It made a remarkable 130 miles in twenty-four hours, the record run for the voyage. In fact, the launch's average daily distance covered was about a hundred miles, about the same as the *Bounty's* herself!

With the crew at its breaking point, Bligh rationed out two gulps of rum to each of the nerve-shattered men on May 23. It seemed to stiffen their resolve once again. That night the winds abated, the gale blew out, and the sea was calm. As if to say that the men had passed muster and could now have liberty, nature presented the sun in all its golden glory on Sunday, May 24. It was the first sunny, warm day the men had seen in fifteen days. They were now just halfway to East Timor.

Taking stock of the situation, Bligh told his crew that he had to cut their bread ration because he felt they wouldn't have enough if the search for the Dutch colony on East Timor proved fruitless and they had to go on to Java. Surprisingly, they agreed to give up their noon morsel. That they would do this speaks well of Bligh's leadership. Whatever he had been on the *Bounty*—tyrant, bully, martinet— he was proving now to be one of the greatest seamen ever. There was literally no other man alive who could have achieved what Bligh had thus far, so few having been to the South Pacific. But there were more weeks ahead, including crossing Australia's Great Barrier Reef—without a chart.

On Monday, May 25, the crew caught a noddy and ate it for lunch. Later that day they caught a booby, and Bligh ordered that the three weakest men be given its blood to drink. More birds were caught in the following days. Tree branches were also spotted in the water, along with water snakes. These were good omens that they were approaching land.

At 1:00 A.M. on the morning of May 28, the helmsman cried out that he heard breaking waves. Bligh immediately ordered him to bear off to the northeast. He had no intention of daring the Great Barrier Reef in the darkness. In the morning they approached the reef again and picked their way through it. They spotted an island and decided to risk a landing.

Bligh ordered into effect his standard island watch system, half to stay with the boat and the other half to go ashore to forage. For the next two days the men feasted on oysters, berries, heart of palm, and freshwater. Bligh even made an oyster stew with bread and pork strips, using a magnifying glass to start the cooking fire. As the men tramped around the island they found abandoned campsites that signaled the presence of others in the area. They kept their eyes out for trouble, but none came.

After two days of rest Bligh noted the improved condition of his men. But his old temper flared when he found that someone had stolen pieces of pork. He ordered that the pork be divided on the spot so it could not be pilfered again. Even more valuable than the pork, the bread was safely locked in the carpenter's tool chest. That afternoon, as they were preparing to depart, twenty armed aborigines suddenly appeared and charged them. The party managed to row out to sea in time to avoid the attackers, and as they rowed between several small islands they saw others hiding in wait. Had their party been scattered on shore, many, if not all, might have been killed.

Bligh and his men knew this territory as New Holland (Australia). Mile by mile they worked north past chains of islands to starboard, with the mainland to port. During this coasting natives could be seen on shore beckoning them to land. Bligh declined. Finally, spotting an island with a large hill, he decided to land to scale it so as to survey the region. As the launch made to shore, a crew member incredibly tried to incite another mutiny! Bligh would have none of it and challenged the man to a duel there and then. The man's anger waned, but more trouble lay ahead.

On June 1 they landed on yet another island, this time to forage for food. Troublesome crew members began to build a fire, which Bligh had forbidden due to the threat of being seen. The illicit fire got out of hand and caught the island's scrub grass, creating a huge billow of smoke. In another incident a selfish crew member frightened a flock of birds that the crew was trying to snare, so that not one was caught. Bligh was rightly furious. They had come too far to get careless now when the goal was so close.

With oysters, clams, and even sea snakes supplementing their diet, most of the crew appeared in better shape during the six days they worked their way around the northern tip of Australia. However, some were still frail, including Lawrence Lebogue, an old tar toward whom

Bligh felt kindly. He gave this man and some other sufferers spoonfuls of wine as a restorative. It seemed to help.

Once again on the open ocean, the launch was hit by variable seas. During the next week the men's condition deteriorated quickly. They were slow to respond to questions and many had a faraway look in their eyes. Doses of wine helped, but Bligh knew they were again at their limit. He was astounded when the boatswain told him that *he*, Bligh, looked worse than the rest of the crew! Bligh ordered that the worst-off men be given an extra ration of water, himself excluded.

On Friday, June 12, the incredible happened—they made Timor. Bligh wrote of his triumph:

> *It is not possible for me to describe the pleasure which the blessing of the sight of this land diffused among us. It appeared scarce credible to ourselves that in an open boat, so poorly provided, we should have been able to reach the coast of Timor in forty-one days after leaving Tofoa [Tofua], having in that time run, by our log, a distance of 3,618 miles; and that not withstanding our extreme distress, no one should have perished in the voyage.*

The next day the launch landed at a hut on shore. A guide was hired to direct them to Coupang (now Kupang), the Dutch colony, which they found on the morning of June 14. As Bligh wrote, since leaving Tofua not one man had died, and all reached Coupang safely, where they were kindly received by the Dutch governor, who did everything he could to aid them and help them return to England via the Dutch port of Batavia.

On his arrival home Bligh wrote his account of the *Bounty* mutiny and subsequent miraculous escape. He remained a hero for two years until some of the *Bounty* mutineers were captured and returned to England, where they gave their version of events. Bligh was then, probably rightly, seen for the ham-fisted commander that he was. His subsequent career as a naval officer, and then as a governor in Australia, continued to bring out the worst in his character, and he was often held in contempt by those who worked closely with him. But not one of those seventeen men who made it safely to Coupang would have had it not been for Bligh's leadership and skill. Many, including this author, consider Bligh's exploit in the launch to be the greatest single feat of maritime navigation in history.

———◆·◆———

A curious footnote to the *Bounty* saga is the story of the ship the British Admiralty dispatched to round up the mutineers after Bligh returned to London and reported the incident. This ship, the *Pandora*, lost two small boats while searching for Christian and his men in the South Pacific. One of the boats virtually duplicated Bligh's journey to Coupang. The *Pandora* herself was lost on the Great Barrier Reef, and four boats with the survivors also made it to Coupang. Although these are impressive survival stories, it would seem unfair to compare them to Bligh's feat because all the *Pandora* craft were well armed, provisioned, and were crewed by men who knew of and had Bligh's example to follow.

3

VICTORIAN VENTURERS

1865–1876

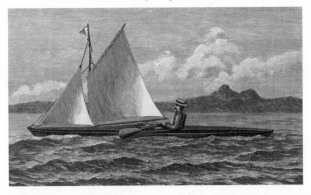

◆ GOD'S PADDLER, JOHN MACGREGOR ◆ THREE JEERS FOR THE *RED, WHITE & BLUE* ◆
INFLATED DREAMS: THE *NONPAREIL* ◆ VANISHING BEAUTY: THE *VISION*
◆ THE *JOHN T. FORD*: A TRAGEDY IN ONE ACT ◆ THE *CITY OF RAGUSA* SAGA ◆
PAUL BOYTON FLOATS TO GLORY AND CONEY ISLAND ◆

NEARLY THE ENTIRE PLEASURE-BOATING INDUSTRY CAN BE
traced back to a versatile nineteenth-century Briton, John "Rob Roy"
MacGregor. His enthusiasm for boating was nearly as strong as his evan-
gelical religious convictions, and he spent a lifetime preaching the joys of
both. He started by introducing the world to kayaking and then widened
his scope to demonstrating the pleasures of gentlemanly yachting under
sail. He made legions of converts to boating; probably the number of
his converts to his religious faith was considerably smaller.

Two developments set the stage for MacGregor's pioneering efforts. One, the circular saw blade, which made possible cheap wood planking, was invented around 1813 by an unlikely figure, Tabitha Babbitt, living in the Shaker community of faraway Harvard, Massachusetts. According to tradition, as she was spinning one day and watching two men wrestling with a pit saw, ripping logs into planks, she was struck by the waste of time and energy in the reciprocating motion. The thought suddenly occurred to her—a spinning wheel with teeth. The resulting circular saw did to sawyers what the powered loom had recently done to weavers: it put most of them out of business and dramatically lowered the price of the product. Cheap planking and the second development, cheap sailcloth, meant that boats could be built for pleasure, rather than just for commercial or naval use.

John MacGregor undoubtedly was not aware of his first great adventure on the water. At the age of two months, he was aboard the *Kent* with his parents on their way to a new post for his father, who was in the army. It was March 1, 1825, and the close-reefed East Indiaman, carrying 641 people, was in dire trouble in the Bay of Biscay. As a strong gale knocked the ship onto her rail again and again, smoke suddenly came pouring out of the hatches. The crew and passengers, mostly soldiers and their families en route to India, desperately fought the fire belowdecks, with no success. The ship was doomed, but there were not enough ship's boats, and, in any case, launching the few there were into the tempestuous sea seemed futile. At that moment sails appeared on the horizon, drawing steadily closer—the brig *Cambria*, which had spotted the blazing *Kent* and was racing to the rescue. The boats were launched, and after many trips five hundred people were transported to the brig. Those who were lost, too afraid of the water to jump in and swim for the boats, were actually killed when the *Kent*'s powder magazine blew. Passed from his mother's arms to a sailor, the first soul rescued was infant John MacGregor. Meanwhile, his father, Major Duncan MacGregor, had helped lead the fire fighting and rescue efforts and had tried to persuade the terrified people to jump for

Art on facing page: The most influential small boat in history, John MacGregor's 1866 *Rob Roy*. This boat inspired more copies and imitators than any other boat in history.

their lives. He was one of the last to be rescued before the overloaded *Cambria* slowly pulled away.

The same dedication to helping his fellowman that his father exhibited during the *Kent* disaster, John MacGregor was to show his entire life. He was an outstanding student in all subjects, especially math and science, but he equally excelled at sports like boxing, mountain climbing, and shooting. He had a quick mind and a great sense of humor, as revealed in his many articles published in *Punch* magazine. He was also an accomplished artist, and his diaries and letters are crammed with images drawn during his wide-ranging voyages. These travels took him to North America, Scandinavia, Russia, Italy, Greece, Turkey, and the Holy Land—where he wrote rhapsodically of his nearness to Jesus. But he saw violence when he was in Paris during the Revolution of 1848.

When not traveling, MacGregor found time to work for charitable organizations such as the Protestant Alliance, Ragged School Union, Shoeblacks, *Band of Hope Review*, Slavery Question, Palestine Exploration Fund Committee, London Scottish Volunteers Militia, and Lawyer's Prayer Union, the last of which was connected with his training for the bar in London after he attended Trinity College, Cambridge. He was a human dynamo of hard work, good intentions, and moral role-modeling. Though perhaps today his idealism seems naive—at one point he even preached on street corners in London—this criticism wilts in light of the many positive outcomes his work brought about and the total sincerity and altruism in it all. London's poor, especially young boys, directly benefited from MacGregor's efforts.

At age forty MacGregor decided to spend more time on himself and indulge an idea that had occupied his busy mind since he had first seen Inuit in Canada many years earlier. He would build a planked version of their timber-and-skin hunting kayaks. He had the boat built for fifteen pounds Sterling in June 1865 at Searle's boatyard in Lambeth, across the Thames from his bachelor digs in the Strand. It was fifteen feet long with a thirty-inch beam, a typical clinker-built boat except for its low lines and deck. It had oak frames and planking and a cedar deck and weighed eighty pounds—ninety including double paddle, mast, and lug sail. This might seem hefty now for a kayak, but it was nothing compared to the weight of other small boats of the day, including wherries and punts.

After a few trial paddles on the Thames, MacGregor, in his usual grandiose style, announced that he would embark on a tour of Europe in his tiny boat, which he named *Rob Roy* after his famous ancestor— the eighteenth-century Highlands clan hero Rob Roy MacGregor. His tour began on July 9, 1865 (just three months after the end of the American Civil War). He paddled on the Thames down to Sheerness, crossed the Channel via ferry to Oostende, and paddled for a few days on the Meuse and the Rhine. At that time, shipping odd-sized cargo on the growing railroad system was common, so he had little trouble sending his kayak, for a small fee, to wherever he wanted to paddle. In Germany he proceeded to the Main, the lower Rhine, and then to the Titisee in the Black Forest. When he couldn't arrange rail transport, he hired ox carts and porters and moved his boat to the nearest water. During the months of this summer tour he slept in small hotels, private homes, and even barns. He ate with the locals, preached Protestantism to them, and proudly showed off his wooden creation, including the little Union Jack he flew from the kayak's mast. Life was good and God *was* an Englishman!

MacGregor loved the attention he got from the Continentals wherever he brought his revolutionary kayak, but those back home were not forgotten. Every day he posted reports to London that newspapers published, to the delight of young would-be sportsmen. The *Rob Roy*, the first kayak ever built in Europe, was the portent of things to come—recreational boating. MacGregor's 1865 tour spawned a huge appetite among his countrymen to undertake similar trips. His tour continued on the Danube above Ulm, then Lake Constance, the Swiss lakes, back to the Rhine, and on to France, where he paddled the Mulhouse Canal, the Mosel, the Meurthe, and finally the Marne to Paris. On October 7, he returned to London on a rising tide up the Thames and was greeted with adulation by his many friends, both old and new.

A few months later, in January 1866, his travelogue *A Thousand Miles in the "Rob Roy" Canoe on the Rivers and Lakes of Europe* appeared in bookshops. This is the most important book in all of small-boating history. It launched thousands of "ships" and continues to do so to this day. The first edition quickly sold out and was reprinted many more times. How did MacGregor spend the profits from his work? He donated every penny to the Shipwrecked Mariners' Society and the National Lifeboat Institution and continued to live modestly in his bachelor flat in London near Temple Bar.

In the summer of 1866 he conceived the idea of the Canoe Club, which held its first meeting at the Star and Garter Hotel in Richmond (after more than 135 years both the Canoe Club and the Star and Garter are still in existence). The Canoe Club, with MacGregor as its captain, attracted many young, aristocratic sporting blades of the day and eventually royal patronage. It organized regattas, tours, and races. MacGregor, again to set an example, decided to go on another kayaking tour of Europe, this time around Scandinavia. That summer's voyage was chronicled in The "Rob Roy" on the Baltic, another classic in maritime literature. The Rob Roy of this book, however, was a different boat, only fourteen feet long and twenty-six inches wide, weighing a third less than the earlier one, only sixty pounds, close to a modern kayak's weight. MacGregor had learned the lesson many small-boaters learn the hard way—less is more, especially when you have to portage your craft, or at least hire porters, as was his usual practice.

MacGregor decided to extend his street-corner preaching to his watery travels, so he began taking religious tracts on his kayak trips and distributing them to peasants along the way, especially Catholics. For this type of activism MacGregor, and other young men like him, were called "muscular Christians," a somewhat ambiguous term, though MacGregor, we may assume, was proud of it.

Then an opportunity that must have seemed heaven-sent came his way, an opportunity to carry his proselytizing even farther. In 1867 he was so famous for his boating activities that Napoleon III, hoping to inspire French youth to healthy pastimes, invited him to bring to an Exposition Universelle in Paris a delegation of English "canoeists." MacGregor readily accepted but resolved to take more than just small boats and their owners to France—he would carry the message of "muscular

Christianity" right into the heart of that "popish" nation. He would do this by sailing, alone, what he thought was the smallest practical boat from England up the River Seine to Paris. Such a solo voyage, across the turbulent English Channel, was unheard of at the time, and for that reason MacGregor felt that by accomplishing it he would greatly increase the audience to whom he could preach his spiritual message, accompanied by his religious tracts.

The new small boat, again called the *Rob Roy*, wasn't a kayak or canoe in the modern sense of the word, but rather more like a catboat hull—21 feet long by 7 feet wide and 3 feet deep. She was rigged as a yawl, with gaff mainsail and jib forward, and lug mizzen aft. MacGregor devised a sleeping and cooking cabin nine feet by three feet just abaft the foremast, with a little three-foot-square steering well just forward of the mizzen mast. He cleverly planned on using a large spray skirt attached to the rim of this

Crossing the English Channel single-handedly in a small boat wasn't easy then, or now.

well during bad weather. Structurally, the boat employed the best construction of the time, too—double planked, with varnished mahogany over yellow pine.

The sail across the English Channel from Dover to Boulogne in August was a much trickier proposition for a sailor then than it is today. MacGregor had no GPS, no depth finder, no radio, and the weather in the Channel at any time of year is unpredictable, unsettled, and often foggy. Yet it was hardly an ocean crossing in drama or danger. He made it safely, then coasted his way west toward Le Havre and from there up the Seine to Paris. His nautical and religious missions were executed with enthusiasm, with the usual optimistic letters to newspapers, confident introductions to people of importance, well-attended speeches and lectures, and dissemination of free religious tracts. He lived on board the yawl the whole two weeks at the Exposition and then sailed back to England to even greater fame. A few months later his book *The Voyage Alone in the Yawl "Rob Roy"* began a craze for small-sailboat ownership that continues to this day. He donated the profits

MacGregor in mufti. In this garb he enthralled Victorian audiences with his stories of his kayaking adventures on the River Jordan.

from that book to training ships for impoverished boys.

In three years, and with these three voyages (and a kayaking tour of the Holy Lands in 1868), John MacGregor single-handedly popularized the sport of pleasure boating. He made people around the world realize that waterways and even oceans belonged to them. People could sail without a heavy ship that required rocks for ballast, topgallants for speed, first mates, and bankers or queens for financial backing. The world of water belonged to those plucky enough to sally forth, even if alone. Epic voyages in small boats *were* possible.

John MacGregor made boating a leisure pastime, rather than just something for fishermen and other professionals. He demonstrated its healthful, recreational promise to a growing generation of office-bound, increasingly middle-class, young Victorians. And he did this all without the thought of material profit for himself. He loved the adventure, he loved the acclaim, but mostly, it seems, he loved his fellowman and sharing his great love of life and life's possibilities with him. Recreational boaters the world over owe him their thanks.

When MacGregor arrived at the Exposition Universelle in Paris, he examined two other small boats that had undertaken epic voyages on a scale that even he hadn't dreamed of—two American craft that had crossed the Atlantic Ocean. The first was the *Red, White & Blue*, which reputedly had made the voyage from Sandy Hook, New Jersey, to Deal, Kent, the previous summer, 1866. This boat was an odd mixture of future and past technologies. On the one hand it featured an innovative sheet iron riveted double-ended hull, entirely galvanized to prevent corrosion; yet on the other hand it was rigged as a three-masted square-rigger! So authentic was its rig that it even had studding sails. All this was contained in a boat with a length of just twenty-six feet and a beam of six feet, one inch.

Why the odd rig? The boat was the conception of a New York boatbuilder, O. K. Ingersoll, who was trying to sell all-metal lifeboats and thought the novelty of the rig would attract more press attention. Why he didn't think that a transatlantic crossing *alone* would be sufficient to convince shipowners of his lifeboat's value isn't obvious. Along the gunwales he had painted "Ingersoll's Improved Metallic Life Boat." The crew of the *Red, White & Blue* consisted of the professional seaman John M. Hudson and his mate Frank E. Fitch—and a dog, Fanny. They left New Jersey on July 9, but only two days later were spotted by the pilot boat *A. T. Stewart*, hove-to in a strong contrary wind twenty-five miles off the coast. On July 11 they were seen by a schooner off Barnegat Bay, but then they were not seen again for twenty-five hundred miles, until they made the English Channel.

THE MINIATURE SHIP "RED, WHITE, AND BLUE"

Currier and Ives produced popular prints of important ships of the day, though usually not small fries like the *Red, White & Blue*.

When they reached Deal on August 15, they had every reason to expect a hero's welcome, but they got much less. Soon after they had told the story of their thirty-five-day crossing, which they claimed averaged eighty five miles per day, skeptics noted that this was a nearly impossibly good record for such a small, unhandy boat. Further, the weather for the crossing had been bad, and there was at least one report of the boat hove-to. How could they have made up so much lost time? Compounding their credibility problem was their log book, which seemed suspiciously untidy. To some it appeared that it had been written afterward.

Hudson and Fitch intended to make a profit from their voyage by displaying the *Red, White & Blue* at the Crystal Palace, the great exhibition hall south of London. Thinking to make the boat more presentable, they repainted its galvanized hull black, with a contrasting gunwale stripe; they also tarred its ropes. Alas, all this beautifying effort had the effect of confirming to their critics that they had something to hide.

The display at the Crystal Palace was a failure, and so was their attempt to win over the French the next year at the Exposition Universelle. Few tickets were sold, and the two Americans were the butt of jokes. MacGregor, though critical of their lack of professionalism and thirst for commercial profit, examined their boat, their log, and their stories very carefully, both in England and in France, and concluded their voyage had been genuine. His endorsement might have meant something if the mate of the *William Tapscott*, an American named Kennedy Childs, had not just told a reporter that his ship, which had departed New York, had stopped in early July and picked up the *Red, White & Blue* and transported it over to the English Channel, where it lowered it again off the Scilly Islands. The *William Tapscott* was known to ply this run regularly, taking Irish and Mormon immigrants to America and bringing back cargo. However, Childs's story doesn't ring completely true, either—reporters were known in those days to pay for good stories with nothing more than a drink at a bar or by picking up the tab for a few nights' lodging in a sailors' flophouse. In any case, the average transatlantic run for a ship was about thirty-five days. Furthermore, Captain Bligh had shown eighty years earlier that he could get a hundred miles per day from a smaller lifeboat, with less sail area, though he had had generally favorable winds.

What really happened? MacGregor, who was there and spoke to the men involved, seems to be the most reliable witness. Hudson and Fitch knew their business, sailing, not marketing, and undoubtedly sailed the boat over without help. The *William Tapscott* was a 195-foot cargo hauler with a substantial sail area, and a large crew, and any conspiracy would surely have been witnessed and exposed by more than just one of the crew members. (Interestingly, the *Tapscott* met her own end sinking in the English Channel in the early 1890s.)

———•◦•———

The other boat that MacGregor saw at the Exposition Universelle was even stranger than the *Red, White & Blue*. This was the *Nonpareil*, also a lifeboat—or, more precisely a life raft. Built by the Life Saving Raft Company of New York as the Perry's Monitor Life Raft, it was made of three cigar-shaped bladders twenty-five feet long and twenty-six inches in diameter. The bladders themselves were made from gutta-percha, a resin much like rubber but from a species of tree found only on the Malay Peninsula. The advantage of gutta-percha over rubber is that it's less brittle when dry. To protect this material from sunlight and from objects in the ocean, the *Nonpareil*'s builders covered the bladders with close-fitting heavy duck cloth.

Seven stout ten-inch planks were transversely mounted on top of the raft, attached to three longitudinal deck planks. The middle of these deck planks extended five feet aft, where it supported a rudder. A flimsy deckhouse, really a pup tent, gave the crew some protection from the weather. Driving this contraption was a two-masted rig. From the foremast were flown a dipping-lug foresail and a jib, and on the mainmast was a gaff-rigged mainsail. Provisions were kept in a locker lashed to the planks under the tent, along with some barrels of water and two spare bellows for emergency inflations.

The captain of this lumbering beast was John Mikes, who in August 1866 made a remarkable amphibious landing of twenty-five American troops at Greytown, Nicaragua, using a Perry's Raft launched from the steamer *Santiago de Cuba*. Mikes had no doubt of the eventual success of his proposed transatlantic crossing and told the New York newspapers so. Ironically enough, less enthusiastic was the president of the Life Saving Raft Company, William C. Thompson. Thompson wrote tersely to the *New York Times* that though he wished Captain Mikes success, his company was in no way sponsoring the expedition and in fact had tried to dissuade Mikes from making the attempt. Thompson noted that the previous year he had refused Captain Hudson's request to borrow a Perry Monitor for his intended transatlantic crossing.

The inflatable life raft *Nonpareil* was undoubtedly a ship with no equal at the time.

On June 4, 1868, the crew, John Mikes (captain), George Miller, and Jerry Mallene, departed from the Battery and headed out of New York Harbor. Unlike their predecessor, the *Red, White & Blue*, they spoke to many ships as they battled their way across the Atlantic and finally arrived at Southampton fifty-one days later. Though they were hove-to seven times during the crossing, Captain Mikes told reporters that the crew felt entirely safe the whole voyage and claimed that they had never even gotten wet. When John MacGregor saw the raft he scoffed at its practicality, as he had the *Red, White & Blue*. Members of the Royal Yacht Squadron were more charitable and hosted Mikes and the crew to a fine dinner when the *Nonpareil* was towed over to Cowes.

Mikes would need all the free meals he could get—his U.S. sponsors had left him stranded in England without funds. Despite some public notoriety and the attention of Charles Dickens, who went to see the boat on display at the Crystal Palace, Mikes was unable to pay his bills and soon found himself arrested as a debtor.

The record isn't clear how he got out of prison, but by December he and Miller had returned to New York, where they told the story of the *Nonpareil*'s crossing, including how the kerosene stove caught fire and nearly led to disaster, how they rigged a dripping water can to measure time after their watch stopped working, and how passing ships helped reprovision them when supplies ran low.

As a practical life-saving tool, the *Nonpareil* was obviously inadequate. Deflated and folded, it weighed one ton. Unfolding, inflating, redecking—all that would have taken hours. On a pitching, sinking ship in a storm, it would have been impossible to deploy. The *Nonpareil*'s voyage nevertheless stands out as an important contribution to smallboat voyaging in that it was one more piece of evidence that great voyages could be made in small craft.

———◆●◆———

Sadly, despite these two transatlantic successes there were two dramatic failures at this time. In June 1864 the *Vision*, with a waterline length of only fourteen and a half feet and a beam of four feet, ten inches, left New York bound for England. She, too, sported a silly rig, this time brigantine. Under the command of New Yorker J. C. Donovan, who funded the voyage through a public subscription, and crewed by William Spencer and a dog, Toby, she quickly sprang some timbers and had to limp along to Boston for repairs. The next month she attempted to cross the ocean, but after leaving Boston was never seen again.

Vision dropped from sight soon after leaving Boston in the summer of 1864.

———•·◆·•———

The *John T. Ford* was a wooden miniature Grand Banks pinkie that attempted the Atlantic crossing in 1867. This story, too, ends in tragedy, one tied to one of the greatest losses in American history.

In 1867 the people of Baltimore enthusiastically supported the plan of four local men to sail across the Atlantic and demonstrate the civic pride of Baltimore at the Exposition Universelle in Paris. Through private donations a twenty-four-and-a-half-foot ketch was built at the Walker & King Boatyard, internally ballasted, with a full deck and a cutout in the center for the crew to get below out of the weather, and heavily canvassed. The boat was named after a prominent figure in Baltimore who had championed its construction and was glad to have the positive publicity the voyage might lend to his political ambitions; he was running for mayor that year in a tight contest.

The plan was to reach France in stages—first Halifax, then Ireland, and finally Le Havre and the mouth of the Seine. Captain Charles W. Gold, a Baltimorean who was the driving force behind the effort to build the boat and fund the voyage, brought with him two gentleman sailors, John Shaney and Captain Riddle, the latter formerly of the Fourth Maryland Infantry, as well as a boy, Edmund Murphy. They departed Baltimore on June 22, 1867, to the hails of an enthusiastic crowd assembled at the Pratt Street wharf. Innumerable large and small craft provided escort down the Chesapeake Bay as they made their way to the Atlantic.

A leisurely ramble up the Atlantic seaboard brought them to Halifax, where Gold reprovisioned and recrewed for the leg to Ireland. He dropped off Shaney and Riddle—brave men probably, but perhaps not good sailors—and hired mates Shering and Armstrong; Murphy remained. They departed on July 16, rather late in the season for a transatlantic attempt, but made good progress and spoke with many ships along the way. The Atlantic would not be trifled with, however, and lashed out at them on August 5, when the seas erupted and a huge swell overturned the boat, though the ballast immediately righted the boat.

Shaken by the frightful experience, the four mariners took stock of

Citizens of Baltimore crowd the docks in 1867 to witness the departure of the *John T. Ford*. A public subscription funded her voyage, but a blunder made in desperation doomed her not far from her goal.

their situation. Their only losses were some of the freshwater and the oil supply they used for cooking and for lighting the compass. All things considered, they had gotten off lightly. What they did next may be inconceivable to someone who is at home, warm and dry, comfortably ensconced in an easy chair, but to these men—cold, hungry, and suffering from shock—it seemed the right thing to do. They pulled up the wooden floorboards holding the ballast in place and burned them to dry themselves, warm their food, and "obtain light for the compass."

Two weeks later, on the night of August 19, the Atlantic exacted its revenge for the blunder. A heavy gale raged, with nasty variable winds rolling around the compass. A cross sea flung the boat about until it finally turned turtle. The unrestrained ballast fell free and crashed around under the deck. Nevertheless, the *John T. Ford* righted itself again and again—capsized, righted, capsized, but finally remained capsized. The men scrambled out of the cockpit and held onto the slippery hull in the raging, frigid sea, all that night clinging to whatever line or fitting they could reach. The gale roared on, but they knew they were not very far off the coast of Ireland. If they could only hang on.

They survived the night, and with the morning came the hope of being sighted and rescued by a passing ship. At noon, with the seas still turbulent, they saw a sail, but the other ship didn't see them and disappeared. The mate Shering became unhinged at the disappointment and after asking the others to pray with him, shook their hands, kissed a picture of his wife he took from his pocket, and slid into the sea. The boy Murphy was the next to go. As the day wore on he lost the strength to hold on and asked Armstrong to tie the two of them together. Armstrong did, with his belt, but somehow the boy still wasn't made fast, and a big swell swept him away that evening. Now it was Gold's and Armstrong's turn to be washed off. Gold was quickly sucked away from the boat and as he went down cried, "God help my poor wife and family."

Armstrong fought frantically to regain the upturned hull and succeeded. For four nights and three days he clung to life, though barely, as he had no food or water. He managed to tie a scrap of canvas to the end of an oar to signal a ship if one came near enough. He couldn't afford not to be seen again. On August 23 the *Aerolite* of Liverpool saw the tattered flag and rescued Armstrong. He was eventually taken to London. On September 6 the hulk of the *John T. Ford* washed up at Tacumshane, Ireland. For all it had been through, its condition was surprisingly good.

The fates of the *John T. Ford* and its crew were flashed around the world via telegraph on the new transatlantic line. It hit particularly hard in Baltimore; especially devastated was the rising politician who had hoped the success of the voyage would help erase any lingering negative connotations his name might have with Baltimore voters. Most of them, and the rest of America, still associated John T. Ford with the theater he owned a few blocks from the White House in Washington—Ford's Theater—where President Lincoln had recently been assassinated.

———•◦•———

One of the most intriguing mysteries connected with the small-boat sailors is the true identity of the owner of the first small boat ever to make a round-trip voyage across the Atlantic. This man seems to have used the Italian name "Di Costa" in some contemporary press interviews, but the Croatian "Primorac" in others. The Croatian-Italian border was in a state of political flux in the late 1860s, and that may have had something to do with the change in names. Adding to the confusion was the press's spelling of the name as "Primoraz," "Primorec," "Primorez," "Primorca," and other variants.

The most believable account of the early part of this story comes from Irish sea captain John Charles Buckley, though it is at great variance with the widely reported account by Croatian historians—who themselves have at times also claimed that Columbus sailed from *Croatia* on his voyage of discovery in 1492!

Buckley was an interesting character who by the time of the voyage had led a remarkably full life, though he had not yet reached middle age. He was born in Kilteely and enlisted in the Second Dragoon Guards when the Crimean War started. Evidently this unit didn't see enough action to suit his tastes, so he joined the Royal Navy, where he rose to the position of signal officer and participated in the bombardment of the Russian fort at Sveaborg in 1855. After the war he served aboard ship in the Far East but left the navy in 1857 to become a merchant mariner. Giving up the sea for a time, he returned to the army and became an infantry sergeant in the Royal Limerick Regiment. While stationed with that regiment at the School of Musketry in Hythe on the south coast of England he earned the Silver Medal of the Royal Humane Society for rescuing two fellow soldiers from drowning in the ocean. Two years later he joined the Pope's army in the Italian wars of unification, fought in the battles of Castelfidardo (1860) and Spoleto, spending time as a prisoner of war in Geneva. For his service to the

Catholic cause he was awarded a knighthood in the Order of Saint Sylvester. After his military career ended he took to the sea again and rose by his early thirties to become a ship's captain.

He is quoted as saying that he and Primoraz (as he spelled it) had been friends for some time when they joined to attempt to sail a small boat across the Atlantic. He said their motivation was purely for the adventure, though some accounts say Primoraz made a £1,000 bet that he could do it. Buckley reportedly found an old lifeboat in a marine salvage yard in the Liverpool area and showed it to Primoraz, who agreed it was suitable; the boat was then purchased. It seems likely that Primoraz was the financial backer of the trip, hence the name of the boat, *City of Ragusa*—Ragusa, the city on the Dalmatian coast, is now Dubrovnik. This probably was Primoraz's way of asserting his ethnic and cultural pride, denied expression for years by the repressive Hapsburg Empire, which at that time held sway over the area. It seems likely also that this is why Primoraz began to use a common Croatian name and abandoned the Italian "Di Costa." Perhaps he had used Di Costa for business purposes to avoid the cultural bias of his Austrian overlords against Slavs.

Primoraz/Di Costa was a bit of an eccentric, though an inspired one, and he determined to sail the twenty-foot lifeboat across the Atlantic against the prevailing winds. The few transatlantic crossings that had been made thus far were near-run things, even though they had favorable west–east winds. A small boat simply couldn't make a three-thousand-mile voyage in the face of the winds, it was thought by old salts along the Mersey. The Croatian mariner, however, had a plan. He and Buckley decked the *City of Ragusa* over, installed a low cabin, and fitted her with two masts, ketch style. What Primoraz did next made history. Evidently inspired by the lighter-than-air dirigible experiments then taking place in France, where inventors like Henri Giffard had installed giant propellers driven by small steam engines on their primitive dirigibles, he mounted a six-vane propeller-windmill on his mizzen mast. This above-water propeller was connected by bevel gears and a drive shaft to a stern-mounted two-bladed water propeller. With this arrangement he believed that he could easily convert head winds into rotary power and forward thrust. Brilliant, but practical? Not really. Such a large windmill on a small boat would have endangered the crew. Further, the boat had barely more than a foot of freeboard, and if it rolled just a little too far or a nearby swell grew a bit too large, the windmill blades would have clipped the water, breaking or bending them, thus creating an unbalanced flywheel condition that in a matter of seconds would have ripped the whole contraption off the back of the boat and would likely have holed the hull itself.

A picture in a contemporary issue of *The Illustrated London News* shows this boat under way, sails furled and powered only by the windmill, with Primoraz/Di Costa walking along the deck. The system seemed to work in moderate conditions, but such conditions could not be expected on the Atlantic. Knowing this, Primoraz had the rig dismantled and settled for a more "normal" crossing with traditional sails on both masts. Primoraz and Buckley displayed the boat before their departure, both at the foot of the Wellington Monument in Liverpool and as part of the Italian Cirque, presumably a touring carnival.

With Buckley in command and in view of a crowd of hundreds, the *City of Ragusa* departed Liverpool June 2, 1870, bound for New York, but a leak through the propeller shaft's stuffing box forced them into port at Cork. They left Cork on June 17, 1870, and for the next twelve weeks they zigzagged toward their goal, averaging a mere thirty-one miles per day because of strong headwinds. Compounding the dreariness of the tacking was the poor engineering that had gone into refitting the lifeboat as a sailboat. Wind loads on the masts warped the hull just enough to cause constant leaking through the planks. Both men spent much of their time bailing. Though originally intending to sail directly to New York, they arrived in Boston on Friday, September 9, eighty-four days out, having made the first east–west crossing of the Atlantic in a small boat.

Their arrival in Boston was widely hailed, and the boat was taken out of the water and put on display at the fair grounds, where anyone could see it for twenty-five cents. Buckley's forty-eight-page log book was published and sold for a quarter a copy by the *Pilot Press*, a semiofficial organ of the Catholic Diocese of Boston. The skipper was, after all, a

The *City of Ragusa* crossed the Atlantic twice without the windmill gear despite claims otherwise. The gear was used only experimentally at Liverpool before departure.

Catholic war hero. Oddly, the cover doesn't show Buckley's name, nor does it give his partner's name. Why does Buckley, the keeper of the log, refer to his fellow crewman three times in the book as Pete, when the Boston and New York reporters called him Nicolas? Obviously, Pete is an anglicized version of Pietro. This bolsters the theory that Buckley and Primoraz had known each other for years—perhaps even having met when Buckley was serving in the Pope's army in Italy—and that the name change to Nicolas Primoraz only came later—when Pietro Di Costa was ready to assert his cultural identity and take his perhaps true name of Nicolas Primoraz (more correctly, Nikole Primorcu).

After a month in Boston the boat was put back in the water and during October and November 1870 it was sailed down to New York City. Buckley left at this time, and Primoraz captained the *City of Ragusa* back across the Atlantic, accompanied by New Zealander Edward R. W. Hayter. They departed New York Harbor on May 23, 1871, and made Liverpool on July 10 after a speedy sail through mostly stormy seas.

But what had happened to Buckley? Had he been paid off sometime the previous fall and sailed back to Europe aboard another boat, perhaps as a mate? Much research is still needed on the *City of Ragusa* voyage, though actually, few people in England or Croatia today know anything about their record-setting countrymen. The twin voyages of the little *City of Ragusa* mark the first time a small boat sailed east to west across the Atlantic and the first return trip in a small boat. These are significant accomplishments for a boat and crew about whom so little is confidently known.

The fate of the boat is known, though again with some uncertainty. One report suggests that after its return to Liverpool, the *Ragusa* was taken across the Mersey River to the town of Birkenhead and installed on the large lake at the park where it floated for many years until it rotted and sank. According to another more credible account, the boat was displayed at the boathouse at Birkenhead Park for a time and then moved to the garden of a hotel in Rock Ferry, where its owner (Primoraz?) took up residence. When he left the hotel he offered the boat to Birkenhead, which accepted it again.

Paul Boyton was a mariner without a boat, even a small boat. Yet he is one of the most interesting nautical characters to appear on the world stage in the decade following the American Civil War.

Boyton was born in Dublin in 1848, but by 1863 he had emigrated to the United States, where he joined the Union Navy at age fifteen. After the war he became one of the early salvage divers, but then he lost all his equipment in a shipwreck near the Mexican Gulf coast and briefly became a mercenary soldier in the revolution in Sonora. From 1867 until 1869 he co-owned a shop in Cape May, New Jersey, where people bought coral, shells, and other nautical objects to decorate their homes. He also rescued weekend swimmers as an unofficial lifeguard, gaining a local reputation for his lifesaving prowess. When a fire swept Cape May and consumed his shop along with many others, he decided to seek high adventure again. He found it in France, where Napoleon III's army was being trounced by Bismarck's Prussians. Boyton joined the fray as a franc-tireur, a French infantry irregular, and saw combat in 1870–71. When the Prussians pushed the French back into Paris,

Boyton, who was inside the city walls, became entangled with the short-lived Paris Commune—a nasty little civil war among the French holdouts in besieged Paris. Only his quick wits saved him from being a victim of this brief reign of terror.

Returning to New Jersey from his European adventure, Boyton became a lifeguard for the Camden and Atlantic Railroad Company, which put him in charge of the lifesaving station at a new resort town they were developing at the eastern terminus of their track. As captain of the Camden and Atlantic lifeguards at Atlantic City, Boyton, not surprisingly, showed his men how to perform their duties by personally rescuing seventy-one souls.

Hemmed in by the New Jersey Pine Barrens, Atlantic City, in those preboardwalk, precasino days, was too small for a hard-charging bull moose like Boyton. He knew his destiny lay beyond and that, if only he could find it, it would be grand indeed.

What he came upon was an inflatable rubber suit designed to save the lives of imperiled mariners, the invention of Clark S. Merriman from the land-locked state of Iowa. Merriman had patented a thirty-five-pound multichambered floating suit in 1869, but he sorely needed someone who could show the world that it could save the lives of sailors and others trapped on sinking ships. There was no better salesman than Paul Boyton, a man with a gift of gab, a lust for life, and the pluck to take great, calculated risks.

Boyton conceived a frighteningly bold plan to make the world take notice of the Merriman suit. He planned to stow away on a ship bound for Europe and, 250 miles from the U.S. coast, to spring from his hiding place wearing his suit, leap over the rail, and then paddle to shore with a specially designed paddle. He had already experimented off the Jersey coast to prove he could paddle a course in Merriman's india-rubber cocoon.

In early October 1874 the U.S. steamer *Queen* was about two hundred miles out of New York City bound for Liverpool when Boyton slid onto the deck from the lifeboat in which he had been concealed. He inflated the five air chambers in his suit and prepared to hurl himself over the side. He had a canteen of water, brass horn, food for ten days, ax, knife, compass, signal lights and rockets, and of course his wooden double paddle. Once in the water he would float on his back and paddle toward the New Jersey shore. Certainly there could be no better demonstration of the Merriman suit's effectiveness!

Just as Boyton was about to leap, the skipper of the *Queen*, Captain Bragg, appeared and demanded that he identify himself and declare his intentions. Bragg at first thought Boyton a lunatic, but Boyton's coolness and force of personality soon convinced the skeptical captain otherwise. For his part, Bragg talked the proto-frogman into forgoing that night's attempt, instead waiting until the ship was closer to shore. But the next shore was several thousand miles away in Ireland. Bragg sweetened the deal by promising not only that he wouldn't arrest the daredevil, but that he would allow Boyton to dine with the officers for the duration of his stay. Boyton wisely accepted.

On October 21 the ship was thirty miles off the Irish coast, and Boyton could wait no longer. At nine that evening he cheerfully bade farewell to his host and to the passengers who had assembled to witness the unprecedented stunt. Down into the sea he went with his inflated suit and with a few paddle strokes pulled away from the ship and struck out for the country of his birth. Within two hours a gale was blowing so fiercely that more than fifty-six ships were lost that night in waters off the British Isles.

But Merriman's suit, with Boyton in it, was not among those lost. Boyton's sheer guts and indefatigable will enabled him to muscle thirty miles to shore and then another ten or so to Cork. The Irish at first wouldn't believe his story, which sounded like blarney, but after it was confirmed, he became a national hero—a "son of the sod" had returned triumphant!

Boyton took Europe by storm. He demonstrated the Merriman suit in waters in Ireland and England, including the Thames, and by spring 1875 the press was clamoring for him to be the first to attempt to "swim" the English Channel. Boyton flicked his great moustache, tossed back his large head, and gamefully accepted the challenge.

His first attempt to cross the Channel was from Dover in April 1875. A steam tug escort was to keep him from getting run over by other Channel traffic. The effort ended just eight miles from France, when the captain of the tug forced Boyton to give up: delays in starting had caused them to lose the advantage of the tide, and the weather was worsening.

In this 1875 print Boyton is seen conquering the Thames River with his gear and in various activities: using an umbrella as a sail, smoking, having tea, reading the paper, waving a flag, sending a signal flare, and doing what he did best—blowing his own horn. The ax (center) was for warding off sharks.

Boyton's second attempt was successful, however. He left Cape Griz-Nez on May 28, using not only his paddle, but also a small gaff-rigged sail, with its mast inserted into a socket on his left boot. For twenty-four hours he paddled and sailed, battling currents that warped his straight-line course into a series of huge U-turns, thus making a twenty-six-mile route nearly forty. He finally arrived at South Foreland, near Dover, to stupendous acclaim and a new international reputation. Queen Victoria promptly sent her congratulations and then ordered Merriman suits for the crew of HMY *Victoria and Albert*, the royal yacht. President Grant sent a cable. Everyone in England clamored for Boyton to speak at their dinners, and, being an extrovert, he was only too glad to oblige. Feted, bemedaled, lionized by the press, and financially successful for the first time in his life, Boyton had hit his stride.

His success was well deserved. An inflatable garment is the most micro of all microboats, and Boyton's first Channel crossing was hailed as a marvel of its age during an age of weekly marvels. Nor did Boyton fumble the opportunity. In fact, he enlarged upon it for years to come. He embarked on a worldwide tour to demonstrate and sell the Merriman suit. He paddled or "swam," as newspapers of the day often called it, down the Rhine in Germany, the Rhône and Seine in France, the Tiber and Po in Italy, the Danube in Austria and Hungary, and many other European rivers. He crossed the straits of Gibraltar and Messina and the Bay of Naples out to the isle of Capri. For his bravery, and novelty, he picked up more than forty medals and citations from appreciative local governments. Jules Verne even wrote a novel, *Tribulations of a Chinaman*, inspired by Boyton's exploits.

Back in the United States, Boyton-mania reached fever pitch. Books were written about him. A cigar was named after him, capitalizing on the fact that for warmth he often puffed on a cigar during his "swims." Dressed in full garb he was featured on an early baseball card. He published his derring-do autobiography, *Roughing It in Rubber*. His heroic escapades down the Hudson, Connecticut, Ohio, Mississippi, Missouri, and Yellowstone Rivers were front-page news around the nation. In all, he claimed to have traveled 25,000 miles in the prone position.

In 1880, Boyton improbably combined the utility of the Merriman suit with his zest for guerrilla warfare: he volunteered to fight for the Peruvian navy during the Ten Cents War, a war among Peru, Chile, and Bolivia for control over the enormous quantities of guano (bird droppings useful as fertilizer and munitions oxidizer) that had accumulated over the centuries on the countries' mutual frontier, the Atacama Desert. To try to end the Chilean blockade against Peru, Boyton slipped into the water one night, towing a 125-pound mine. His plan was to attach it to the side of a Chilean warship, swim away undetected, and wait for the bomb to go off. Ultimately, his efforts as an early Navy Seal were unsuccessful, and the Chileans won the war. With Chilean takeover of Peru, Boyton was now a marked man. He was soon captured and imprisoned to await execution, but a plan evidently hatched by his brother on the outside allowed him to escape and swim out to a ship waiting for him on the coast.

Back in the United States, Boyton repeated his stealth attacks against ships when he placed a mine on the side of the British warship *Garnet* in New York Harbor at the behest of some Irish Fenian friends. Fortunately for the British, he used a dummy bomb. It was the possibility of what *might* have happened that thrilled his Gaelic blood.

In his forties, Boyton bought a New York City bar and tried to settle down to the role of affable publican, but he found a bar too small a stage for his appetites and abilities. He had one more razzle-dazzle left in him: he invented the amusement park.

Boyton had honed his showmanship skills during his tenure as the world's foremost "swimmer." It is no exaggeration to say that Boyton's deeds led many in Europe and America to try swimming themselves, though without the inflatable suits. Before Boyton, the water had always been feared and avoided. Capitalizing on his gift for pleasing crowds, Boyton began a small traveling carnival in which he featured live seals and, of course, himself paddling around in the Merriman suit. This little carnival act was successful on both sides of the Atlantic, ultimately resulting in his opening Paul Boyton's Water Chutes in 1893 on Chicago's South Side. The first enclosed, one-price amusement park in history, it was a hit.

What worked in Chicago could work in New York, so two years later he opened Sea Lion Park, a sixteen-acre park with rides and a midway, at Coney Island. The rides included a water slide, Shoot-the-Chutes, and later a roller coaster that featured a complete loop, the Flip-Flap Railroad. Paul Boyton, more than anyone else, made Coney Island the leisure-time relief valve that the hordes of tenement-confined immigrant New Yorkers turned to during the first half of the twentieth century.

Art on facing page: Alfred the Great: Danish immigrant Alfred Johnson pioneered solo long-distance voyaging. Design features on *Centennial* set the pattern for most record-seeking small boats for the next fifty years.

THE
PATHS OF
GLORY

1876–1900

◆ ALFRED JOHNSON'S *CENTENNIAL* ◆ TAKE YOUR WIFE, PLEASE: THE CRAPOS ◆
NATHANIEL BISHOP LEAVES HIS CRANBERRY BOG ◆ TANNEGUY DE WOGAN: THE PAPER
PADDLER ◆ THE ANDREWS BROTHERS ◆ NORMAN AND THOMAS'S *LITTLE WESTERN*
◆ THE LITTLE TUB THAT COULD: *THE CITY OF BATH* ◆ BERNARD GILBOY LEAVES HOME
◆ ANDREWS SOLO ◆ THE *MERMAID* VS. THE *SEA SERPENT* ◆ THE *CHRISTOPHER
COLUMBUS* GETS SOAPED ◆ NORWEGIAN CLAMMERS ROW FOR THE AMERICAN DREAM
◆ FINGERLESS BLACKBURN ◆ TILL DEATH DO THEM PART ◆

LIKE PAUL BOYTON, THE UNITED STATES OF AMERICA WAS
full of self-confidence and bursting with pride in the year 1876. And
why not? It had reached its one-hundredth birthday, having beaten off
all foreign powers, settled manfully, though bloodily, a civil war, and

staked out its territory from sea to shining sea. The people of the nation felt that their country had "arrived."

In order to "celebrate myself, and sing myself," as America's most noted poet of the time, Walt Whitman, joyfully wrote, the country decided to host a grand international exhibition and strut its stuff. It would show those great powers of Europe just what the former colony had achieved economically, technically, agriculturally, and even sociologically.

The Centennial Exhibition, as it was called, opened in Philadelphia, the site of the signing of the Declaration of Independence, in May 1876 and was scheduled to run until the fall of that year. It featured exhibits ranging from new inventions like the telephone, typewriter, elevator, and zipper to great displays of zoological specimens like the Smithsonian Institution's own four hundred meticulously painted plaster casts of marine life. There were displays of new guns, household goods, huge steam engines, machine tools, and even a somewhat enlightened for its day ethnology exhibit that respectfully presented objects from the daily life of the American Indians, as they were called. This exhibit assumed ironic dimensions when later that summer some Indians at Little Big Horn in the west showed General George Custer and his Seventh Cavalry that the white man was not invincible, in spite of all his Yankee ingenuity.

Unknown to the organizers of the exhibition, a twenty-nine-year-old Danish immigrant who lived in Gloucester, Massachusetts, was formulating plans that summer to steal the show. Alfred Johnson was a halibut fisherman who sailed out of Cape Ann each season for the Grand Banks. There he worked as a doryman, dropping his trawl lines from a two-man dory. A dory is a simple slab-sided boat with V'ed sides. The shape allows dories to be stacked within each other on a schooner's deck. The mother ship goes out to the fishing grounds, deploys a dozen or so dories, and awaits their return each evening with that day's catch.

Johnson was just one of thousands of men similarly employed—a man low in the hierarchy of maritime economics. Blond, blue-eyed, tanned, and fit, Johnson had dreams of making a name for himself though financially humble. Some months earlier he and a dory mate, while working yet another long, hard trick on the Banks, began to discuss small-boat crossings, including that of the *Nonpareil*. Johnson's partner suggested there was no reason a dory like the one they were in couldn't make the crossing. After all, dories went over the side routinely in all kinds of foul weather. Hadn't they experienced gales, blizzards, fogs, and long separations from the mother ship? Hadn't they survived cold, wet, loneliness, and physical privation? It was all the same to them—it came with the job. So what was an Atlantic crossing but just a long series of working days strung together?

Johnson mulled those thoughts over for some weeks, then when he heard of the forthcoming Centennial Exhibition, a plan crystallized. He would cross the Atlantic alone in a modified dory and on reaching England quickly ship the boat back to Philadelphia, where he would gain fame, and hopefully some cash, by putting the boat on display. He would call his dory *Centennial* in honor of the nation's birthday and paint it red, white, and blue in a final flourish of patriotic élan. The crowds would love it and pay to see it. Oh, would to God his days hauling those halibut lines might end soon!

The *Centennial* was like most other dories in hull form but differed from them most notably in that she was decked over, though simply so, without a cuddy. Into her deck were let two hatches, the larger one midships for stowing supplies and perhaps for ducking into in bad weather, and the smaller one aft for sitting while steering with the tiller attached to the rudder, which hung from a narrow transom. Her sail plan, too, was simple, but effective. Johnson gave her double headsails, a jib and a staysail; thus the twenty-foot boat sported a short bowsprit. She had a gaff-rigged mainsail that could be lowered and a square sail's yard that could be hoisted quickly when steady west winds blew (the square sail was the pre-yachtsman's version of a spinnaker). And that was it—no stormsails, no trysails, no self-steering vane. It was a simple dory with a simple rig and a simple sailor. Johnson even eschewed any standard methods of navigation. He used a log only twice on the voyage, relying mostly on a crude dory compass—a card on a spindle, not suspended in liquid. For a chart he had a rudimentary map of the North Atlantic. He decided he needn't worry much about compass deviation and would rely mostly on his experience, knowing where the sun should rise and set each day, which would tell him his latitude. He had to stay north in the shipping lane, but not so far north that he might encounter icebergs and fog. He convinced himself that anywhere he hit Europe, from Ireland to Spain, would be just fine, though his avowed goal was Liverpool.

Johnson's departure from Gloucester was as low key as his boat was simple. Who was he to brag to the other hardy fishermen of America's oldest fishing port that he would be the first to conquer the Atlantic alone, and in such a small boat? Humility in sports, and solo sailing, is a wise practice. He slipped out of port on June 15, 1876, and crept his way up along the coast of Maine, then Nova Scotia. With the Grand Banks still to clear, he had hoped to rely at least somewhat on his compass, but found that it had been so far thrown off by the iron pigs he had lashed to the floor for ballast that he decided to put into Shag Harbor, Nova Scotia, to reposition them. For three days he puttered around with the ballast, carefully securing the pigs in new locations. Later events would reward his diligence.

On June 25 Johnson screwed up his courage, hoisted the sails, and set out on the real voyage. He was alone on the Atlantic, looking back once more as the little village of Shag Harbor receded over the horizon. (The village wouldn't reappear on the world stage for nearly another hundred years, in 1967, when residents and officials alike claimed that a sixty-foot UFO had landed in their harbor and submerged into the murk, never to be seen again.) For thirteen lucky days Johnson sailed east, shaping his course on the corrected compass and his empirical knowledge as a doryman of the sun's position at sunrise and sunset. Just over four hundred miles out from Nova Scotia he was struck by his first gale, a strong one from the southwest. The boat responded well, but the waves were powerful, and with only a foot of freeboard his deck was constantly awash with green water. He deployed a sea anchor, but still the ocean swells broke freely over the rails.

A sailor can be sure that anything that can be broken will break during a gale. The coaming surrounding the midships hatch had some kind of flaw in it, and when a particularly strong wave swept the deck it split the wooden plank and a chunk of the coaming floated away, allowing gallons of seawater to spill in under the hatch and ruin some of Johnson's supplies. He held his position in the aft cockpit, calculating that not enough would be spoiled to defeat the venture. He would bail it out as soon as possible, and the *Centennial* would go on. When the gale died down, Johnson, battered yet bold, bailed out his bilges as best he could through the cramped hatch and once again hoisted sail. He took his seat in the cockpit and headed east toward the next adventure. That came about a few days later when he was hailed by a bark out of Mexico, bound for Liverpool. The captain drew up to Johnson and neatly backed his sails, coming to a full stop midocean. In excellent English he offered to "rescue" the American sailor. Johnson explained his purpose, at which the sly skipper scoffed and winked. He offered to hoist the *Centennial* on board, let Johnson work his way across, and then discreetly lower the two close to the Irish coast. After all, no one in his crew spoke English, so who would tell the tale? Johnson virtuously declined the offer but did ask his position, getting a fix from the other mariner, who gave him a bunch of bananas in parting.

The *Centennial* jogged on until July 16, when a strong west wind struck her reefed sails and sent her barreling along the waves. Her flat bottom and V'ed sides allowed her to fairly plane down the front of the waves as Johnson kept a firm hand on the tiller. In the other hand he gripped the sheet, which led through a bronze traveler mounted on the deck behind the cockpit. If he could just maintain this speed he would sight Ireland in no time.

The wind did hold—that is, until August 2. While Johnson was speaking with the brig *Maggie Gander* just three hundred miles off the coast of Ireland, off Cape Clear, the ocean swell rose prodigiously, and the winds also came on with a roar. It had been Johnson's careful practice to unship his mast at night or if bad weather threatened. He did so now and carefully lashed it to the deck. How a lone sailor, tired, cramped, suffering from sunburn and sores, could manage those long spars on an unkeeled dory on a heaving sea by himself, with no one at the tiller, defies a modern sailor's comprehension. The only possibility is that Johnson's mast was fitted into a sturdy tabernacle (hinge) and could simply be folded backward; there is some scant photographic evidence

With his mast folded down on the *Centennial*, Johnson fights off a shark with a boat hook. There is less exaggeration in this picture than one might suppose.

for this. However he accomplished it, after stowing the spars, Johnson set his sea anchor and hunkered down into his cockpit to see what would happen. This one was going to be bad, he knew.

The iron pigs in the bilges must have squealed at the strain as the little boat was tossed around in the confused sea, but they didn't break free, unlike those on the *John T. Ford*. Johnson's sea anchor was only partially effective, however, without a mizzen sail, or jigger, to help steady the boat and keep it pulling down wind, heading into the wind. In addition, the dory's rudder was probably unshippable. The sum of these factors was that the *Centennial* skidded around in the roiling water and never settled, as a properly rigged boat does behind a sea anchor. But this was over a hundred years ago, and Johnson was pioneering the art. His foresight in placing and securing ballast carefully, and his using a sea anchor at all, are a tribute to his skill as a seaman.

Skill sometimes means nothing to the sea, however. After several hours of being kicked around, the *Centennial* met a wave that wouldn't be denied. It rolled her over, pitching the redoubtable Johnson into the brine. Again, good planning saved him: he had tied a rope around his waist as a lifeline. When he popped to the surface, the *Centennial* was at the other end of the stretched line, bottom up. He couldn't swim through the frightful seas, so he pulled himself back to the boat hand over hand, using the tether. But how could he right the slippery, slab-sided hull in a raging sea? What could he grab onto? Why hadn't his ballast already righted the boat? Until he could come up with a plan, Johnson heaved himself onto the flat upturned bottom and, bracing with his arms and legs, held on for dear life.

It next occurred to him that if he could wrap the hull with a stout rope, he could stand on one side, lever backward, and "unwind" the hull upright. His lifeline was too thin to bear that kind of strain, but he thought of an alternative: one of the halyards. He felt around until he found one, grabbed it, dove under the boat to the opposite side, tossed the line over the boat, and swam back to the first side. Next, he pulled himself out of the water with the halyard and climbed up on one side of the bottom of the boat. He heaved on the line, leaning as far back as possible. The boat wouldn't budge. He tried again, and again failed. Nearly exhausted, and in the cold water for twenty minutes by now, he pulled one last time and with the help of a wave on the opposite side, he broke the suction between the gunwales and the water. Finally, the boat flipped over. He had done it. The pigs now did their work and kept the boat bottom down.

The next day the worst of the storm had passed, and Johnson assessed the damage. His situation was grim. Most of his food was ruined by salt water, as were his clothes and bedding. His little stove was gone, so he couldn't heat what food he had left. And it was raining. Johnson did the best he could, trying to straighten out his gear. He hoisted his mainsail again (the square sail had been lost), and headed in the direction he thought would take him to Ireland.

Four unhappy days later his luck turned when he spoke with the brig *Alfredon*. The captain generously offered him aid in the form of water, bread—it never tasted better to Johnson—and, almost as good, his position. He was only a hundred miles out now. Two days later he got another fix, from the *Prince Lombardo*, and, feeling better, decided not to land in Ireland but press on to Liverpool. He turned up Saint George's Channel but on August 12 decided at the last moment to land for a much-needed breather. He found the tiny harbor of Abercastle nestled in a little cove on the Welsh coast and sailed the *Centennial* up onto its pebbly beach. When he landed he had completed the first verifiable solo crossing of the Atlantic Ocean in a small boat. This undisputable achievement was deservedly accomplished by a brave, careful, quiet man of modest means. It was a remarkable feat of boatmanship and raw courage.

Four days later, Johnson finally arrived in Liverpool and then realized his ultimate goal was unattainable. The Centennial Exhibition was winding down as the end of summer approached, and by the time he got home the crowds would be mostly gone. There was no point in hurrying, and there would be no money awaiting him at home, only the halibut line. He shipped the boat to the exhibition anyway, while he headed back to Massachusetts on a Boston-bound ship. In the end, life wasn't as bad as he feared. At home he soon had a commission to skipper a Grand Banks fishing schooner, which freed him of ever having to haul a line again. Sometimes life is fair, aye.

———◆◆———

Across Massachusetts, to the south from Gloucester, on the southern shore fronting Buzzards Bay is another great New England fishing town, New Bedford. A local laborer at a salvage and junk shop read about Alfred Johnson's epic voyage that summer of 1876 and vowed to do the same thing, but in a *smaller* boat. That would not only give him the record for smallest boat crossing but also bragging rights that he was certain he could turn into real cash, unlike the laconic Johnson. After all, being a lowly employee in someone else's junk business had as much long-term appeal to him as halibut fishing had to Johnson. He wanted his share of the American dream.

This entrepreneur was Thomas Crapo, ex-whaler, ex-diver, ex-U.S. Navy (sailed with Farragut), ex-U.S. Army (in the thick of the fighting around Vicksburg), and ex-ship's mate, not to mention a recently failed fishmongering business. Certainly a man could make some money from voyaging if he played his cards right.

Crapo set out to design his version of the perfect small cruiser, and what he came up with was much like Johnson's *Centennial*. Though Crapo later called it a "dory," it had more in common with the speedy whaleboats he had crewed in as a youngster. The boat, which he named *New Bedford*, was nineteen feet, seven inches long (intentionally a half foot less than Johnson's boat), with a beam of six feet, two inches; it sported a split rig with leg-o'-mutton triangular sails, had no bowsprit, but had a hatch and a cockpit, as in Johnson's boat. It was thirty inches deep and drew thirteen inches when loaded. The *New Bedford* differed from Johnson's boat in two important ways: it was a true double-ender (the *Centennial* had a small V-shaped transom like a dory) and it was basically a clinker-built whaleboat, making it stronger than Johnson's dory. Crapo was afraid of whales, having observed their power at the beginning of his maritime career, so he wanted the strongest small boat possible in case he ran into one.

His craft was built by a friend and professional whaleboat builder, Samuel Mitchell, who had a yard on nearby Fish Island in the Acushnet River. Crapo must have visited it often during construction and when it was finally finished in early May of 1877, he wrote: "I was positive my little boat could live where a large vessel could, and I scanned her with a longing akin to love."

But the boat was not the only love of his life. Five years earlier he had married the youthful Joanna Styff, whom he had met during a voyage to Marseilles. When Joanna learned of his plan she put her foot down and told him that under no circumstances would he make that voyage alone—it was too dangerous. She insisted that he have a first mate along to help him, and who better than she? Even descendants of the Crapo family are not sure what happened next. How stiff was

Thomas's resistance? What was Joanna's ultimatum? What were her true reasons for going, and why did he persist in his desire to go alone? Isn't it likely that Joanna really loved Thomas and wanted to be with her man, come what may? She knew she could be of at least some use to him, if merely as a lookout when he was asleep.

Actually, Joanna was capable of a lot more and earlier in their married life had proved it. During one frightful passage from Florida to England, the brig *Kaluna*, with Thomas as first mate and Joanna a passenger, was overtaken by a hurricane. Pandemonium broke out aboard the ship as gigantic waves smashed into the vessel, ripping out spars, shattering the ship's boat, and staving in the after cabin. The binnacle light was washed away, and in total darkness the helmsman could not steer a course. Certainly the brig would founder without a course. At that moment in stepped Joanna, undaunted, holding a lamp she had brought from below. All through the storm's fury she held it over the binnacle so that a course away from the tempest could be maintained. Though the ship pitched and rolled violently, often down to her rails, Joanna never flagged or abandoned her post. Like Florence Nightingale, this lady with the lamp saved the ship and proved her mettle.

So why was Thomas reluctant to take her? Of course he argued that the boat was very small, with only so much room for provisions, and he simply couldn't squeeze another person in. Joanna must have insisted that she was small, there were two hatches, and that she didn't eat much. What else she said is unknown, but finally Thomas relented and agreed that she could accompany him—but only as a passenger, not allowed to steer the boat. This proviso has also puzzled historians, but there is a simple explanation for it, too. Crapo had envisioned a solo enterprise and probably feared that if he had help at the helm, his voyage might not seem as meritorious as Johnson's one-man effort. After all, this was a business venture to Crapo, and public perception meant everything. Would Joanna's presence diminish the acclaim he hoped to garner? Would the public consider him a cad for endangering the "little lady?" At least if he kept her out of the cockpit and did all the steering himself, he could still claim it as a kind of solo voyage, with only an unskilled, nonactive "passenger."

This desire to make a record passage had to be the reason that he chose not to use the best resource he had, his wife. She could have spelled him at the tiller and kept the boat under way whenever he chose to sleep. As it turned out, he only slept four or five hours a night and was often exhausted. His fatigue nearly cost them both their lives later, yet during the entire voyage Joanna, the stout-hearted sailor's wife, was confined to the forward hatch away from the tiller and the sheets. Her enforced inactivity probably added two weeks, and needless danger, to the trip.

The townspeople of New Bedford were all abuzz when word finally got out that Thomas *and* Joanna Crapo were off on a transatlantic attempt. If Thomas had wanted publicity, he certainly had it now. Newspapers from as far away as New York sent reporters to get the story as May wore on and the departure date drew near. The eminent *New York Times*, after calling Thomas a "bold and reckless" man, opined about their chances: "Perhaps for the first two they may be happy; but about the third day the writer is afraid that a sun burnt nose does not add to his wife's attractiveness, and she, on her part, will ask herself if it is possible for a woman to respect a man who uses tobacco. Such little differences will surely arise, and the remedy of a temporary separation being impossible, a week—but a small portion of the forty days the voyage is to take if all goes well—will probably land them in the middle of a considerable 'row.'" Secretly Thomas may have wondered if the reporter wouldn't be found to be prescient.

They departed New Bedford on May 28, 1877, to the cheers of a large, encouraging crowd. Just before leaving, Thomas, ever the businessman, sold many souvenir photographs of the boat. The coins he gathered into his pocket felt as good as ballast. This departure turned out also to be the one and only shakedown cruise. Thomas had been simply too busy to test the boat before, what with Joanna pestering him, the supplies to collect and load, the crowd to deal with, and finally the photos to sell. Something had to give, and it was the testing of the boat.

But new wooden boats have to be in water so they can swell and close any gaps in the planking. The still-green *New Bedford* hadn't been in the water long enough to swell, and sure enough she now leaked like a sieve. Too embarrassed to turn back, Crapo steered her out of the port, weaved his way through Buzzards Bay and the Elizabeth Islands and finally made Nantucket Sound. He had to put into port fast, as she already had shipped a foot of water into the bilges. His "passenger" must have been bailing like mad. That evening they sheepishly sloshed into Vineyard Haven on Martha's Vineyard. Crapo put on a brave face, and while Joanna hawked dozens of photos of the boat, he quietly searched out a tinsmith and ordered a bilge pump made quickly. The good people of the town hailed them as heroes—though they had voyaged little more than fifteen miles—and

Joanna Crapo standing by her man during their record-setting voyage though he would have preferred she stayed home.

put them up at the best hotel for the night. The next morning, amid another throng of well-wishers, they took their leave and skirted the south shore of Cape Cod until they arrived at Chatham. There, decently far enough away from the view of their hometown friends, they emptied the five hundred-pound boat in order to have it hauled. The leaking had become serious, and there were no more repair stops between Cape Cod and Britain.

First, the hatches had to be fixed; they leaked badly and were cumbersome to use. A local carpenter was hired to remedy their faults. Next, two hundred pounds of pig iron was taken on, as Crapo had found the boat too tender as originally loaded. Finally, he ordered a painter to slather on a "good thick coat" of paint, which he hoped would help seal any remaining planking seams. All was in order on June 2 and after restowing their provisions and gear they set out for good at two o'clock, accepting a helpful tow out to deep water.

Finally, they were alone. For the first time, the enormity of the undertaking seemed to strike Crapo. As he wrote later, "From this time until our arrival we were to undergo what we had never dreamed of." For the next twelve days they made good progress east by north and spoke with a few Grand Banks fishermen. On June 14 their first gale rolled in, not a big one, and it only lasted a day, but enough to show Crapo that the sea anchor he set out wasn't up to the job. He would need a bigger one, and soon, before they were struck by a serious storm.

Like Alfred Johnson, his predecessor, Crapo didn't worry much about navigation. In those days there were so many ships plying the Atlantic trade routes that one could reasonably count on crossing paths with at least several each week. Ships were spotted in the distance almost every day. Therefore Crapo's navigation plan was simply to ask passing ships his position. Fog, occasional heavy seas, and whales all bothered the captain and passenger of the *New Bedford*. Though he published a ghost-written book of the voyage sixteen years later, Crapo seems not to have kept an accurate log, perhaps because that was too much like real work, and so the dates recorded in his book don't always jibe with the records of the ships he spoke with. Why didn't he assign the duty of log-keeping to his "passenger"? Again, perhaps because then he might not be credited with being the sole crew member?

About three weeks into the voyage, when over eleven hundred miles out, the Cunard liner *Batavia* spotted them in a gale. Crapo was busy manhandling the sea anchor line, trying to ease the tension on the bitt as the boat slid up and down the wave crests. Thinking they were a lifeboat, the liner came to the rescue, only to be turned away politely. Crapo was in command and needed no help, not his wife's and not a Cunard captain's! At least he needed no help until the twenty-sixth day of the voyage, when he and his wife were both becoming exhausted. The help came in the form of the German bark *Amphritite*, bound for Québec. When she came up to the *New Bedford* the captain offered the Crapos a chance to come on board, but they declined. However, the captain's wife pressed the offer, and their resistance melted. After almost four weeks at sea the chance to stretch their limbs, wash, and eat a full, sit-down meal was a heaven-sent respite. They spent forty-five minutes soaking up the luxury before reboardng their boat.

On the evening of July 2 Joanna Crapo once again saved the boat, though it was a near thing. Thomas had gone to sleep and assigned her the watch. She had been awake too long already and, probably bored from so little to do, was heavy-eyed. About eleven o'clock, despite splashing both fresh and salt water on her eyes to try to stay awake, she fell asleep. Two hours later she woke with a start and looked up. A huge steamer was bearing down on the *New Bedford*. She cried out to Thomas, who jumped up, saw the steamer, grabbed a lantern, and waved it frantically while standing on the deck clutching the mizzen mast. Instantly the ship veered off and the little boat was saved. Though it would be easy to criticize Joanna for falling asleep at her post, it would be fairer to say that if her husband had allowed her to steer the boat and keep it moving during her watches she would never have fallen asleep.

A few days later Joanna became seriously ill. It is uncertain what her ailment was, but shortly before, on July 7, she had indulged herself with a rich meal offered by the passing steamer *Denmark*. Was it food poisoning or, as some have speculated, a touch of scurvy? Still hundreds of miles away from the Irish coast, these were worrying days for the Crapos, especially when Joanna said she didn't care whether or not she lived to see land. There was nothing to do but press on. Thomas's wish to sail alone and his earlier arguments with his wife must have eaten at his conscience now as he remained at the tiller, his wife a few feet away, perhaps hovering near death on the high seas.

Joanna's condition stabilized, though she still felt awful, but she was determined to stay with her husband, flatly refusing when the German bark *Astronom* offered to take her off on July 16. She would stick with Thomas to the end. Shortly after the bark sailed off, the boat's rudder head split, but in the heaving sea of a moderate blow Crapo couldn't replace the rudder with his spare. The sea tossed the *New Bedford* around like an "eggshell," to use Thomas's own word. The motion must have been horrible for Joanna and her retching stomach.

On July 21 they finally sighted the Scilly Islands but were unable to make landfall. Instead, they made for Penzance and landed at Newland at eleven o'clock in the evening. The self-assured Thomas swung into action to make the hazardous voyage pay off. While Joanna recovered under a doctor's care in Penzance, the entrepreneur, now captain of the high seas, organized a tour around England for the *New Bedford*. For six solid weeks it was displayed to appreciative paying audiences at the magnificent Alexandra Palace north of London. From there they went on to Liverpool, Oldham, and Brighton. Big crowds came to see the boat, and even ex-President Grant planned to drop by when it was in Brighton, but at the last moment could not come.

Flush with cash for the first time in their lives, the Crapos embarked for New York on January 4, 1878, on the steamship *Canada*, whose captain offered to take the *New Bedford* aboard free of charge. In New York they continued to reap a cash crop when they exhibited their boat first on Broadway and later at Gilmore's Gardens, the predecessor to Madison Square Garden. They followed their New York run with a tour as part of a traveling circus that visited many eastern and midwestern states. Finally, at the end of that year they used their earnings to buy the schooner *James Parker* and settled down to coastal trade in New England.

A few years and a few boat trades later they owned the brig *Manson*, carrying the *New Bedford* aboard as a skiff. In 1898 the *Manson* went down, taking the historic little whaleboat with her. With the loss of the *Manson*, Crapo was financially back to square one. Approaching sixty years old, what could he do to regain his fortune? It occurred to him that another small-boat stunt might do the trick. To that end he had a ridiculously small nine-foot boat built, which he dubbed *Volunteer*. He set off from New Bedford for Cuba in the spring of 1899. If he hoped to tap into the patriotic fervor of America in its war with Spain over the Caribbean island, then he was too late—the war had effectively ended the previous fall. Desperate, aging, and out of step, Crapo still headed south. On May 3, 1899, he departed Newport, Rhode Island. Later, his body was found washed up on the beach near Charleston, South Carolina, likely the victim of a gale he should never have been in.

Joanna Crapo, the first recorded woman to sail across an ocean in a small boat, soldiered on alone (she and Thomas had no children). She wrote an epilogue to the book *Strange, But True* that her husband had had ghost-written back in 1893 and reissued it. For years, until her death in 1915, she continued to sell copies of this sad memoir to eke out a living.

The little nine-foot *Volunteer* that Thomas Crapo lost his life in may have been inspired by the boats used a few years earlier by a New Jersey cranberry grower named Nathaniel Bishop. Bishop undertook two noteworthy small-boat journeys between 1874 and 1876, and the books that he wrote chronicling them inspired thousands of others to undertake similar journeys. In that respect, he did for American waterways what John MacGregor had done for European waterways.

Bishop was assailed by wanderlust at a young age. When he was only seventeen he sailed from Boston to Montevideo, Uruguay, and marched by foot a thousand miles across the pampas and over the Andes. As the scion of a family of successful pioneer cranberry growers in New Jersey he could afford further explorations. In his midthirties he decided to attempt a long voyage by canoe from Québec to Florida. With a hired Jersey waterman named David Bodfish he began the voyage on July 4, 1874, in an eighteen-foot wooden canoe-rowboat. The two progressed smoothly down the Saint Lawrence, the Richelieu River, Lake Champlain, and finally the Hudson River. All the while, though, Bishop complained about the excessive three-hundred-pound weight of the canoe, which they sometimes had to portage. When he reached Troy he learned about a revolutionary new method for making light boats—laminating strips of manila paper together over a mold. He ordered from Elisha Waters's small workshop a paper canoe, rigged for rowing, which, when completed, weighed only fifty-eight pounds. Delighted, Bishop named her the *Maria Theresa*, dismissed Bodfish, and resumed his journey alone down the Hudson. (Waters, incidentally, would later exhibit his paper boats at the Centennial Exhibition, along with the *Maria Theresa* itself.)

In 1874 it was possible to cut across New Jersey via the Delaware and Raritan Canal rather than down the Atlantic coast of New Jersey and past Cape May. Bishop chose the canal route, reaching the Delaware Bay and then skirting the Eastern Shore of Maryland, but he was soon out of the Chesapeake Bay and along the Outer Banks of North Carolina. He continued south to Florida and then west on Saint Mary's River across to the Suwannee River and then the Gulf Coast. Bishop had many adventures along the way, including a capsizing, encounters

Nathaniel Bishop's paper canoe gets the once-over from an imposing Florida gator.

with alligators and a panther, and most interestingly, his meetings with the impoverished people of the post–Civil War South. Though often desperately poor and uneducated, they always showed Bishop great respect and hospitality. He was humbled by their humanity.

The next year Bishop put the paper canoe away and set out in a "sneak box," a beamy, flat-bottomed duck hunter's boat then common in the swamp lands of southern New Jersey. This voyage saw him row twenty-six hundred miles from Pittsburgh, at the head of the Ohio River, down to the Mississippi—where he heard of Boyton's voyage that year—down the "Big Muddy" to New Orleans, then along the Gulf Coast to Cedar Keys, Florida. He described his trips in two books, *The Voyage of the Paper Canoe* and *Four Months in a Sneak Box*, classics of the genre and memorable as well for their cultural observations of a vanished time in America's history.

Nathaniel Bishop's voyages resounded in Europe as well and in particular inspired one French nobleman, Tanneguy de Wogan, who had read the French edition of Bishop's book. De Wogan was about to embark on a hunting trip to Scotland in 1884 when he accidentally cut his trigger finger. Canceling the trip, he happened to visit a boatbuilder in Paris who mentioned a new kind of boat they were experimenting with made from paper using the American (Waters) method. De Wogan seized upon the idea and ordered a kayak built *en papier*, sixteen and a half feet long with a twenty-five-inch beam and a skin thickness of only one-eighth inch; it weighed just fifty-five pounds, though its payload was 275 pounds. He proposed to explore the rivers and lakes of France in the boat, hoping to promote healthier sports activities for French youth so that they would be physically fit for the next conflict with the Kaiser's army. The humiliation of the Franco-Prussian War still boiled de Wogan's blue blood (his father was a baron).

Tanneguy de Wogan is plucked to safety in the English Channel by fishermen.

He named his sleek craft *Qui Vive?* — "Who goes there?"—the sentinel's challenge. He took it on a ramble down the Rhône, Rhine, and Danube Rivers and across several lakes, including Geneva and Constance, but finally had to be rescued when he ventured into the unforgiving English Channel. (It's a great shame that his book *Voyages du Canot en Papier* has never been translated into English as Bishop's was into French.)

◆ ◆ ◆

In 1877, piano maker William Andrews of Beverly, Massachusetts, read of the Crapos' voyage, considered his own life, which had become monotonous, and thought that he would like to undertake a transatlantic voyage, too. Why should the Atlantic frighten him? After all, he had faced down Johnny Reb in no less than twenty-five battles, had been wounded three times, and still had the courage to take up the flag and lead the charge when called upon to be the regimental color bearer—

the single most dangerous job in the infantry. War might be hell, but life in the Chickering piano factory was boring for the thirty-four-year-old father of three. Yes, to sea it would be. But there was a problem. Except for one trip to the Grand Banks years earlier, Andrews had almost no nautical experience. His twenty-three-year-old brother, Asa Walter Andrews, on the other hand, was like a fish, spending all his time on the water in boats. William would ask Asa Walter to go along.

Agreeing on a June departure date the next summer, the two commissioned a dory from Higgins and Gifford of Gloucester. Just as Crapo had chosen his boat to be a half a foot shorter than Johnson's, the Andrewses, aiming for the record, made their boat a half foot shorter then Crapo's—nineteen feet long, six feet seven inches wide, and twenty-seven inches deep. The *Nautilus*, as they called it, was flat bottomed and had half-inch-cedar lapstraked sides. Again mindful of Crapo's boat, the *Nautilus* was fully decked with two hatches and was equipped with a sea anchor attached to three hundred feet of rope. As an improvement on their predecessors' practices the brothers intended to set a stormsail to help ease the boat during gales.

These images of William Andrews (left) and Walter Andrews (right) appeared in the 1880 book, *A Daring Voyage Across the Atlantic by Two Americans, the Brothers Andrews.*

The Andrewses adopted an unusual rig, a semi-loose-footed lateen sail with a full-length luff yard, about twenty-five feet long, but on the foot only a short club boom about eight feet long, attached to the clew end of the foot. The Andrewses wanted to use the lateen rig because of its utter simplicity and no need ever to go forward. Yet the long yard must have been a handful in a seaway, and the sail must have been very difficult to reef. (William apparently liked it, however, because on a later voyage he used the same rig.) For downwind runs they had a square sail. The boat had no buoyancy tanks or flotation devices of any kind, except for *one* life belt!

Provisioning followed the common practice: canned food and water barrels—sixty gallons in six kegs, enough, they thought, to last sixty days. They would heat their food with either an oil or an alcohol stove and as they finished each water barrel they would refill it with seawater as ballast. Navigation was to be by secondhand quadrant and oil compass, but these were mostly backup. The brothers fully intended to hail ships, as their predecessors had, and beg a position.

On June 7, 1878, the Andrewses departed City Point, Boston, at 3:00 P.M., cheered on by a big crowd and many reporters. The hurrahs had hardly died down when they ran into their first gale that night. First, the cover for their binnacle light blew overboard. They couldn't see the compass now, to steer. Next, their one and only navigation light was smashed, so other ships couldn't see them at night. William later related, "Shortly after, something very serious happened, and then we concluded to return and repair damages." What the "something very serious" was he never revealed, but it must have been embarrassing for someone. By morning they were near land again and that evening made for Beverly, and home. William's wife was shocked when he appeared at the door.

With repairs done, they made a second departure on June 12, waved on by a smaller crowd at Beverly. After a thirty-mile run the first day, the winds moderated and died altogether on June 14. Exhilarated by and keen for their big adventure and already behind schedule, with good cheer they manned the oars and made "a fine white ash breeze" until the wind returned. On June 20 they hit the Gulf Stream and reeled off a healthy fifty-mile run. Only two days later a gale hit them, but thanks to their sea anchor and long cable they weathered it well, although William remarked, "I don't want to see anything worse while in the *Nautilus*." The Andrewses' normal practice during gales was to let out the sea anchor and then unship the rudder. The next three days were spent mostly hove-to in the heavy blow, and William nearly met his end when the boom struck him in the head. When things got really bad on June 24, they poured cod-liver oil onto the water to see if it would calm the sea, but the results were negligible except that every seabird for miles around caught wind of the smell and came to investigate. Their greatest fear was that if they didn't get moving soon they would be blown onto Sable Island off Nova Scotia, with its treacherous sands. Luckily, by afternoon the next day the wind slacked off enough for them to set out again under reefed sail. It was a wild ride, but at least they were putting space between them and Sable Island.

A few nights later they found themselves among a shoal of whales, which caused them great con-cern. William especially was afraid of them because they would often use the wooden hull of the dory as a back-scratching post. He decided his only defense was simply to go to sleep and put them out of his mind. He told his brother not to wake him unless a whale was coming directly at the boat with its mouth open.

The unusual club-footed lateen sail on *Nautilus* worked to perfection.

On July 8 they reached the halfway point of the voyage, but it had been nearly two weeks since they had shot the sun with the quad-rant. They knew their position only from passing ships. It wasn't un-til July 13, after eighteen days, that they were able to calculate their own position with a sighting. On the thirty-fourth day of the jour-ney there was a weird episode. William, while keeping a weather eye on some whales that were following the boat a little too closely for his comfort, heard a noise in front of the boat and quickly turned to see what had caused it. "I was startled to see what appeared to be a part of a huge monster in the shape of a snake." This "monster" was black, with a body about fifteen inches in diameter. It had leapt out of the sea into the air and was descending when William caught a glimpse of the last dozen or so feet of the body. He called to Walter, who was below in the forward compartment, but Walter saw noth-ing, though he reported hearing the splash.

So what was it? Other sailors have made similar reports in modern times, so perhaps there are giant snakes in the ocean that have not yet been captured. Either that, or the strain of the voyage was playing tricks on William's mind, especially since, at the time, his fear level was high because of the unwanted close attention of the dreaded whales.

The next night it was unfortunately real when Walter started coughing up a lot of blood. This continued through the night, but there was nothing they could do. His poor health caused William great concern, but at least they were nearing their goal. Providentially, a kindly ship captain they encountered gave Walter a bottle of medicine called "friar's balsam," a concoction, available even today, formulated from the resin of the benzoin tree. It alleviates the symptoms of bleeding gums and ulcers and was immediately effective for Walter.

July 26 found them on the Great Sole Bank just off the English coast, but the shoal waves were short, steep, and driven into a crazed condition by gale-force winds. William poured more of the stinking cod-liver oil on the water, threw out his anchor, and hoped for the best. Two stormy days later they spotted Bishop's Rock and finally on July 31 landed at the coast guard and lifesaving station at Mullion Cove, Cornwall. They reached Le Havre on August 8, the smallest U.S. boat ever to arrive there. (Walter died shortly after returning to the United States, possibly of tuberculosis or lung or stomach cancer.)

Two summers went by before another attempt was made on the Atlantic. Again, Gloucester, Massachusetts, was the point of departure, but this time the daredevil captain wasn't a New England Yankee but a British professional mariner, Frederick Norman, who had recently crewed aboard the American warship *Trenton*. Norman and his friend George Thomas of Halifax, Nova Scotia, hatched a plan to buy a small boat with their savings (something few sailors ever had) and give the "Western Ocean," as the British then called it, a go. In Gloucester they bought a sixteen-foot decked boat, a little cutter, in fact, christened it *Little Western*, and provisioned it for the trip.

They departed Gloucester June 12, 1880, cheered on by nearly everyone in town, it seems. After a week of steady sailing they spoke with the Cunard liner *Gallia*. However, the next day, June 21, *Little*

Western was reported as having lost sixty miles because of strong contrary winds. Had Norman and Thomas forgotten to bring a sea anchor, or had it been lost? They muddled through despite the setback, and on July 26 spotted Land's End. *Little Western* arrived at Cowes on the Isle of Wight two days later, having traveled twenty-five hundred miles in only forty-six days. They now held the record for the smallest boat to achieve the west–east crossing.

After a tour of England, displaying their boat to paying crowds, the two men decided to try for an even more important distinction in the summer of the following year. They departed the then-new Thames Embankment in London, announcing that after sailing the Channel they would cross the Atlantic east–west, against the prevailing winds. If successful, it would be the greatest small-boat voyage since Johnson's five years earlier.

Seventy-five grueling days after they rode the tide down the Thames, they reached Halifax, Thomas's hometown. It had been a hard-fought wet slog, but they averaged a very respectable thirty-seven miles per day (one and a half miles per hour) while fighting against the wind and currents. On September 16 they completed the circle by arriving at Gloucester, the first sailors ever to cross the Atlantic both ways in a boat smaller than twenty feet and the first to sail it east–west in a boat under twenty feet.

◆ ◆ ◆

The same year the *Little Western* completed her east–west crossing, another Briton, John Traynor of Bristol, attempted a west–east crossing along with a Norwegian mate, Olsen, in an eighteen-foot cutter-rigged dory with a five-foot beam, outfitted much like the first transatlantic small boats. The *City of Bath* had two hatches and water ballast. The crew slept under a sliding hatch in a sort of cabin lit by two portholes.

Traynor left the Kennebec River in Maine July 7, 1880, but after his boat suffered damage during a gale he put into Trepassey, Newfoundland, to repair a leak. According to one contemporary press report he and Olsen didn't leave Newfoundland until July 29 and arrived at

Falmouth, England, on August 24. Their boat was reported to Lloyd's by several ships along the way, so there is no doubt about the authenticity of the voyage.

With Atlantic voyages now becoming almost routine, a quiet grocer from Buffalo, New York, was the one who raised the bar, and significantly so.

Bernard Gilboy was a soft-spoken, dutiful son of Irish immigrants who had settled on the shores of the Niagara River in Buffalo. Educated at the local parish school, he usually did what his parents told him to do. His parents must have been very proud when, at a time when the average laborer earned five dollars a week, young Gilboy managed to save one hundred dollars with the avowed intention of buying a pocket watch. But when he had that sum, at age seventeen, he quietly announced that he wasn't buying a watch but instead was using the money to leave home. He wanted to join the navy. A few days later the quiet young parishioner told a fib to the navy recruiter, saying he was twenty-one. Thus he embarked on a three-year naval career, serving on several ships until he was mustered out in 1872.

The serious countenance of a serious voyager: Bernard Gilboy. Like Alfred Johnson, he deserves more recognition than he ever received.

From the sketchy evidence, it seems he next showed up on the West Coast, based in San Francisco and working as a seaman aboard various steamers. Again, sketchy but compelling evidence indicates that in 1877—the year after Johnson's first transatlantic small-boat voyage—Gilboy mirrored him with an open-boat journey from British Columbia (probably Victoria), to Hawaii! This stupendous achievement has to rank as one of the bravest of all the journeys reported in this book, yet Gilboy was so soft-spoken and self-effacing that he hardly discussed it during his lifetime, mentioning it in an offhand way once to a reporter and on rare occasions to his children later in life.

Sailing alone halfway across the *Pacific* in an open boat in the 1870s! At least Atlantic mariners could count on help from the many ships they were sure to meet along the way. Most of them traveled crowded sea lanes where help with navigation, emergency supplies, or rescue was at hand. That steady stream of sailing ships and steamships traveling back and forth across the North Atlantic was a dependable safety net. But Gilboy had nothing to count on except what was in his boat and in his head. What Gilboy accomplished was done entirely on his own. And he never sought recognition or remuneration for it. As with saving the hundred dollars for the watch, it was the *accomplishment* of the deed that meant all to him. He was the quiet man.

Upon returning from Hawaii, Gilboy went home to Buffalo to digest his ten years of life at sea. His family fervently hoped he would go no more a-rovin' and to this end introduced him to a friend of his twin sisters. Romance blossomed and Gilboy married Catherine Whalon, settling down to the life of a grocer in Buffalo. Business was good, his wife bore him a child, the tattoo of an anchor on his left hand began to blur as he gained a few pounds—but, alas, the Siren sea called. That city by the bay in particular beckoned. After two years he had had enough. He sold his business for a profit and told his family he was moving back to San Francisco to, as he said, open another business there. He would send for them "later." One wonders how often this former Catholic school pupil went to confession?

Back in San Francisco he worked at a shoe factory to earn money while the real object of his return was being built. That was an eighteen-foot two-masted schooner-rigged double-ender whose hull shape owed much to Columbia River salmon boats. Gilboy must have seen the raw power of the Columbia on his previous tour of the west and calculated that a boat tough enough for the Columbia's brutal fury could probably handle the occasional Pacific storm. It was a perceptive bit of deductive reasoning. This time he was going all the way across. Next port of call—Australia!

The boat, built by Burns and Kneass in 1882 for about four hundred dollars and christened *Pacific*, featured a watertight partition six feet from the stern and two hatches, again following the practice of his mentor, Johnson. The aft hatch opening was the steering cockpit, with handy compartments for daily necessities like navigation tables and sextant. The forward hatch covered the food and water needed for five months of voyaging; it was to be opened only once a week, at which time stores for the coming week would be transferred aft to the cockpit. The stability of the boat would be aided by a hefty 1¾-ton chunk of iron attached to the keel. Like Johnson, Gilboy intended to unship the masts in a real blow and so had his builder fashion sealable mast holes.

Gilboy had mostly kept his intentions secret, though he told a few close friends, and so there was no crowd to see him off when he tried to depart on August 17, 1882. He later said that because it was late in the year for leaving and thus he hadn't had time for sea trials, he didn't want anyone around if he had to return to port to make adjustments. Though quiet, he had a certain amount of pride, too.

By bad luck he found the customs office had closed for the day, so he postponed the trip until the next day. Finally, on August 18 he was away. His biggest concern early in the voyage was that he would get run down by a ship if he were caught in the fog so common along that coast. He soon devised a system: he would sleep only in the early morning hours from four until eleven, when the sun was up. Gilboy was a disciplined, organized man who did what he said he would, and through rigid control he managed to sail, sleep, eat, and make progress in an orderly fashion despite the rigors of the journey.

Sailing into September, Gilboy encountered contrary winds and sometimes made as little as twenty-five miles a day. This was worrying because he had provisioned for only five months, and each slow day lengthened the voyage. To supplement his supplies he caught and ate flying fish, squid, and turtle. The remnants of these meals attracted a curious shark, who decided that *Pacific*'s rudder made a nice backscratcher. Gilboy let it have its way, even though he carried a double-barreled shotgun and a pistol.

Gilboy's choice of a schooner rig was a good one, as was the heavy keel. He could easily set his sails to any condition, even though that meant sometimes going forward. In heavy weather he hove-to, using sail trim and a sea anchor—a large one on a heavy, long line. In better weather he could trim the sails in such a way that the boat would steer itself and he could sleep away the miles. This self-steering was accomplished *seventeen years* before Joshua Slocum amazed the sailing world with his self-steering techniques aboard the *Spray*.

On October 27 he crossed the equator behind schedule, but still making reasonable progress. Another shark began to bother him, but this time Gilboy wasn't as tolerant. He shot and jabbed at it with a trident, but it, or its kin, kept nuzzling the boat while picking off the little fish that had taken to swimming under it. Gilboy knew that if a shark charged the boat or chomped on the rudder, disaster might result. He had lunged at them so many times with the trident that they had learned to stay away if they saw his shadow. He couldn't spend all his time fending off the persistent sharks because he had to sleep in the daytime to look out for ships at night, so he devised a very simple anti-shark weapon—a spare shirt. He hung this from some thin line near the tiller so it cast a shadow on the water. The sharks thought he was on duty when in fact he was sleeping.

Ninety days out, on November 17 he spoke with the barkentine *Tropicvance* out of Tahiti, bound for San Francisco. This was his first human contact, and the only one he would have for the *entire* trip. Even after ninety days alone and confined to his small world, Gilboy didn't ask to be taken aboard, where he could have stretched his legs or washed his face or had a proper sit-down meal. He simply asked the captain to confirm his position. The captain also had a load of fresh fruit passed down to him and promised to report him on arrival in San Francisco. Everything continued to improve for Gilboy. The trade winds blew from the east and he was in a helpful current. Some days he could count eighty-five miles run under his keel. On December 8 he spotted land for the first time, the island of Eua. Things were looking good.

Then, on December 13, after crossing the 180 degree West meridian (directly opposite Greenwich, England), a heavy swell crested exactly under *Pacific*'s rudder. He threw his weight against the tiller to keep control, but in a flash the boat broached and turned turtle. Gilboy found himself under the boat but calmly surfaced and climbed onto the hull. The heavy keel didn't immediately roll the boat upright because the cargo in the forward hold had fallen onto the submerged deck and was acting as a counterbalance. Contributing to the resistance were the submerged masts and sails. Gilboy could hear the heavy water kegs rolling around inside the boat and feared they might spring a plank. Despite the imminent threat, Gilboy coolly removed his oilskins and flannel shirt and wrapped them around his precious watch. He hoped they would protect the timepiece just long enough for him to dive under the boat and fetch the sea anchor line, which he could then use, just as his hero Johnson had used a halyard, to "unwind" the boat.

Even after he found the line and looped it around the hull it took him another hour to haul the boat upright because of the weight of the spars and rigging below. Once the boat did come upright he slashed at the halyards, rigging, and sheets to unship the sails and masts, fearing another roll, but before he could finish the *Pacific* rolled again, keel up for the second time. This time with less underwater resistance, the boat was quickly righted, but when Gilboy had a chance to survey the damage he found that many of his provisions, already low, were spoiled and that, worst of all, his compass was gone. That meant he wouldn't be able to steer a reliable course at night or in bad weather, further lengthening the trip and increasing the food shortage.

Alone in the middle of the Pacific Ocean, with over fourteen hundred miles to Australia, Gilboy, with no helpful steamship on the horizon or the likelihood of one, began to bail out the hundreds of gallons of water in his hold. It took him about eight hours of backbreaking effort with a large square sugar tin to bail out the boat. Surveying the damage in the morning light of December 14, *four months* into the solo journey, Gilboy received another blow when he found that his mizzen mast, rudder, and watch, which he had carefully wrapped in his oilskins, were gone. His only hope now was to employ his iron self-discipline and will as he never had before. This was the critical moment: either give in, or dig in. He dug deep within himself to find solutions.

His first job was to restep the foremast. Then he spliced the lines he had cut trying to unship the two masts the night before. That done, he tackled his worst problem: no rudder. He had no spare, so he improvised: he lashed one of his twelve-foot oars to a spare boom. The other oar he used in a highly imaginative way as a jib foot for his mizzen sail. It proved quite effective, to his surprise, and showed just how sound his reasoning even under what he knew were survival conditions. He couldn't afford one more mistake in problem solving, or execution. His life now depended on his twenty-foot steering oar contraption and his jury-rigged mizzen mast. He still had fourteen hundred miles more of Pacific Ocean to cross, and without further mishap. Dead tired, he hove-to as best he could and went to sleep content in the knowledge that he had solved his most serious immediate problems and had already formulated a plan to deal with future ones. He was wrong.

The next day started promisingly, sunny with a nice touch of trade winds to move the boat along, and Gilboy spread out his clothes and ropes on deck so they could dry in the warmth. About five o'clock, though, his bad luck returned. Hearing a thump under the boat, Gilboy quickly looked over the side and saw an enormous swordfish swimming away from the hull. It had rammed the boat with its sword and holed it! He popped open the forward hatch to find ten inches of water already in the bilge. The fish had punctured a garboard plank. It would have been all over for Gilboy if the fish had split the plank when withdrawing its sword. Trying not to think of what could have been a final blow, Gilboy thought instead of a solution and quickly found a piece of lantern wick that he stuffed into the gushing hole. Immediately the flow lessened to a trickle, so he closed the hatch, returned to his cockpit, and set up his hand bilge pump so he could pump while steering. He had to do this for the rest of the voyage. Could it get any worse? he wondered, as he hoisted his sails and set off again.

As Christmas approached the days grew longer in the Southern Hemisphere and the weather became reliably moderate. Squalls were infrequent, and soon Gilboy began to spot reefs and small islands. The log of his journey seems confused about dates and locations around this time, but he may have been near Matthew Island, south of New Caledonia. His greatest concern now was a critical shortage of food and water; he still had a thousand miles to go before the Great Barrier Reef.

Wednesday, January 3rd, 1883. I have to-day four pounds of beef, one quart of alcohol, and ten gallons of water left.

To supplement his dwindling rations he caught seabirds, which were now frequent visitors. Even on the days he had fresh meat and juices to give him renewed energy, the continual worry about food and water and the lack of human contact must have played tricks with his mind. This accounts for the imprecision that crept into his log. He wouldn't allow himself to despair or become maudlin, though he knew that the chance of meeting a ship that could resupply him was virtually nil.

> *I lived on hopes, and tried to console myself by repeating the old proverb — "Dark is the hour before the dawn."*

The food situation worsened, and the week of January 7–13 he subsisted on two pounds of canned beef, three birds, and a few flying fish. He was losing strength, and that caused him to make another critical error on January 15. He lost his steering oar through sloppy rope-handling in the early evening—he had used a stiff cotton line to tie the oar to the boat, and its inflexibility had allowed the shaft to work free. Too fatigued to think through this latest problem, he simply went to sleep. The next morning he evolved a solution by making a new rudder from one of his unneeded mast tabernacles and two locker doors. It worked perfectly and was much easier to handle than the oar sweep. It is strange that he hadn't thought of it a month before.

By January 21, having failed to catch a bird or any fish, he fell to the last resort of most famished sea survivors—picking barnacles off the hull and eating them. Two days later he shot a bird with his pistol, but though it fell into the sea only twenty feet from the boat, he was too weak to maneuver the boat to pick it up. Eight days later, having survived on only a few very small flying fish that fell into his boat overnight, he finally began to give up hope. He was down to a gallon of

Gilboy only spoke with one other ship during his 7,000-mile passage from San Francisco to Sydney. He is seen here at the helm of *Pacific* after his recovery from near starvation and typhoid fever.

water and two teaspoons of alcohol—and no food. With failing strength he hung his head over the side of the boat, let it steer itself, and wondered how long it would be before he died.

A sad hour later he saw a sail. Immediately he altered course and ran before the wind on a line to intercept the ship. He waved his umbrella, ran up a flag, fired the last six shots of his pistol, and frantically motioned for the ship to heave to. They didn't see or hear him. Soon the ship pulled ahead of the *Pacific* and showed its stern, but just then it tacked and came around. A lookout had spotted Gilboy.

Moments later he was aboard the schooner *Alfred Vittery*, bound for Queensland, Australia. The captain ordered the *Pacific* lifted into the davits and extended to Gilboy every courtesy. The American sailor had been at sea 162 days and was a mere 160 miles shy of Sandy Cape, off Queensland. The *Pacific* had traversed seven thousand miles of open ocean without having once landed, and having spoke with another ship only once.

Arriving in Australia, Gilboy spent several weeks recovering and then exhibited the *Pacific* in Sydney. During this time he wrote and published a log of his extraordinary voyage, but he failed to gain the widespread acclaim his voyage should have earned him. In this respect, too, he was like his role model, Alfred Johnson. In fact, many thought his voyage was a fool's venture. Back in San Francisco the newspaper *Daily Alta California* snorted:

> *The dory* Pacific *is reported as arrived safely in Australia. Her only occupant gives a thrilling account of his perilous trip. He arrived, as above, and the fools are not all dead yet.*

Five years after Gilboy's outstanding solo effort, William Andrews picked up the Atlantic gauntlet again in an attempt to wrest the small-boat record from Norman's *Little Western*. His brother Walter having by then died of his illness, Andrews could manage the voyage in an appreciably smaller boat, and so had a three-quarters replica of his

Nautilus built. It was only fourteen feet, three inches long, and two feet deep, with a five-foot beam. She carried the same sail plan, though scaled down, which meant her lateen sail's yard was seventeen feet long, hung on a diminutive eight-foot mast. The sail on a modern Sunfish isn't much smaller. Imagine crossing the Atlantic on a Sunfish!

Andrews had secured the backing of newspaper magnate Joseph Pulitzer for his latest attempt. Pulitzer, a Hungarian immigrant and human dynamo, had purchased the *New York World* only five years before and was determined to *make* news when there wasn't any to be had. He wanted stories that would interest his middlebrow, often immigrant, readers; what they liked most were tales of derring-do where "the little guy," someone like themselves, did something great by taking on a big challenge and winning. Andrews's proposed voyage fit that bill. The Massachusetts piano-maker-turned-sailor banked more sponsorship money when a theatrical promoter paid him handsomely to name his little boat *Dark Secret* after a potboiler drama then making the theater circuit.

On the day of departure, June 18, 1888, Andrews rushed to stow his gear into the newly built boat, another product of Higgins and Gifford in Gloucester. With the trumpeting of the voyage by the *World*, more than twenty thousand people showed up at Point of Pines, Boston Harbor, to see the tiny boat on its way, and Andrews was kept busy rushing back and forth, trying both to load the boat and give quotes to journalists. When all was finally ready a local brass band blew rousing renditions of "Yankee Doodle Dandy" and "God Save the Queen," the latter in tribute to the fact that the *Dark Secret*'s destination was Queenstown, Ireland, which of course was under the titular rule of Queen Victoria.

Despite the airy blasts from the trumpets and tubas, Andrews's sail remained limp in the fog and dead calm. Somewhat anticlimatically, he had to be towed out of the harbor by a steamboat. More days of desultory conditions followed, and it wasn't until nearly a week later that the boat finally crawled over the horizon out of sight of the coast.

This was a bad start for what became a dismal, soggy escapade. Day by day Andrews tried to make progress, and with a lateen rig he ought to have been able to move along smartly even with somewhat unfavorable winds. Instead his boat just bobbed and yawed along. The hull was built from half-inch cedar planks that leaked, and the keel was a high-tech hollowed-out oak affair with internal water ballast and a two-hundred-pound iron shoe that was detachable at the turn of a screw. It is most likely that the boat's poor performance was caused by its small sail area versus weight, plus the fact that the rig had never been "tuned" for the hull. The centers of lateral resistance and lateral effort were probably too close to each other, which is why the boat could not hold a course. Andrews was guilty of not conducting sea trials, but, as we've seen, he wasn't alone in that omission—even the great Gilboy was guilty of that. If Gilboy had been on the *Dark Secret*, however, perhaps he might have been able to tune the rig while under way. He was a better sailor and understood sail trim more intimately than Andrews ever would.

Aggravation turned to agony when soon into the voyage Andrews's blankets were swept overboard, and he was forced to sleep under salt-encrusted sails during the cold North Atlantic nights. Even worse, the boat was so small and unsteady that he usually had to forgo heating his meals because the stove was unmanageable with all the motion.

After two months of miserable dawdling along, Andrews called it quits, just over halfway to Ireland. His spars were damaged, the boat leaked, and he was cold, hungry, and spent. On August 19 the New York–bound bark *Nor* picked him up, and for the first time in sixty-two days he enjoyed a warm, dry berth. He didn't care what Joseph Pulitzer, safe and dry in his Manhattan offices, would think about his quitting.

It took three years for William Andrews to dry out and catch Atlantic fever again, but by 1891 he had. Having found sponsorship once more, he dramatically announced that he would race anyone across the Atlantic in a small boat. The winner was to receive five thousand dollars (the price of an above-average house in those days) and a silver trophy. Andrews stepped up the dramatic tension by announcing that if he reached Europe, he would have his boat shipped to Japan and sail her home from there!

Taking the challenge was Josiah W. Lawlor, who had in 1889 famously skippered F. L. Norton's *Neversink* water-ballasted thirty-six-foot lifeboat across the Atlantic to Le Havre. "Si" Lawlor was an outstanding candidate for the race because, as everyone knew, his father was the noted naval architect Dennison Lawlor, who had designed hundreds of ships, including very fast schooners and nearly two hundred steamships. He would design and build his son's boat. Andrews relied once again on Higgins and Gifford.

Both boats were built to identical dimensions, though in detail they varied greatly: fifteen feet long, five-foot beam, two feet deep. Andrews's, named *Mermaid*, carried an unusual combination rig incorporating a sliding gunter yard above a gaff. Though finicky and top-heavy, this innovative rig allowed additional sail to be set with minimal moving about on deck. In typical Andrews fashion it seemed clever, but, as the saying goes, "too clever by half." Trying to avoid the sluggishness of *Dark Secret*, he didn't ship any ballast other than his provisions and relied on a centerboard, rather than a keel, for lateral resistance.

Lawlor's boat, the *Sea Serpent*, on the other hand, was ballasted and boasted a simpler sprit rig, but it too had a fussy technical sail contrivance consisting of a laced-on upper sail that filled the triangle between the sprit and the mast in what was then known as "lobster-boat style." Undoubtedly this was so that the sail could be scandalized (reduced in area) quickly—but what about relacing while bobbing on a small boat in large ocean swells? Dennison Lawlor, who knew how to squeeze every last knot from a wooden boat, fudged the *Sea Serpent*'s dimensions by adding a bowsprit. This boat's sail plan was, in the end, better balanced and with a lower center of effort than *Mermaid*'s. Andrews was a master at publicity and self-promotion, but he hadn't mastered the concepts of small-boat design.

The rules of the race were simple. The first man to reach any port in Europe from the starting point in Boston would be the winner. Lawlor announced that he would take the traditional northern route, while Andrews—again, too clever by half—stated that he would pioneer a more southerly route for small boats, one that would take him past the Azores and on to Portugal. That route was shorter, less tempestuous, and—considering his previous cold slog toward Ireland— warmer. Since his boat had a centerboard and a longer-boomed main, the slightly more quartering winds would also help with speeding her along, as opposed to the more westerly winds of the northern route.

Because of variable winds, the official start of the race on June 17, 1891, was delayed until June 21. Winds continued to be light, so both men landed, with Lawlor departing late the following day and Andrews the morning after that. Such would be the tempo of the "race." Andrews had boasted of a fifty-day crossing, but his judgment again proved in error. It was Lawlor on the northern route who made the best time and, being in the shipping lanes, was often reported in Boston by inbound ships. He made Coverack, Cornwall, on August 5 without much incident other than falling off the boat two times—saving himself each time with a lifeline—and later fending off a shark that was munching on his bow by tossing an exploding yacht salute timed with a fifteen-second fuse into its mouth. In only forty-five days his little boat skimmed across the ocean, a real testament to his seamanship and his father's design. (Sadly, the elder Lawlor would die within the year.)

Andrews, meanwhile, was stuck in the doldrums of the southern route and having a bad time once again. After eight weeks at sea he had gotten to within six hundred miles of the Spanish coast when he ran into a terrific gale. He unshipped his rudder, threw out his sea anchor, and dove under the deck for protection. He closed the sliding hatch over his head and held on. The *Mermaid* skidded dangerously around its sea anchor. It eventually presented its side to a large wave, which rolled it over, Andrews somersaulting along with it inside his wooden cocoon and then finding himself in the capsized hull. Breathing deeply inside the air pocket, he managed to slide open the hatch, which was below him, and then swim outside. To his horror he found that when the *Mermaid* had turned turtle her centerboard had slammed home into its trunk so he had nothing to grab onto as leverage to upend the boat. For thirty long minutes he clung to the side and took stock of the situation. His only hope was to get the centerboard out, and he dug frantically at the end of the blade with his fingernails. Millimeter by millimeter he worked the board up from the trunk, all the while trying to maintain his balance on the unstable hull in huge seas. Eventually he got enough out to grasp it, but even then he was afraid it would slip away, slam home once again, and shatter the trunk, thus sinking the boat. But it didn't. He got the whole board out and then pulled against it for all he was worth. In a moment the boat began to right itself, and then popped around, bottom down. Now a grim sight appeared: the deck was devoid of fittings, including mast and rigging, and the interior was likewise nearly empty. With virtually all of his supplies lost, he was adrift.

With no recourse but to survive as best he could, Andrews went back into the hold and slid the hatch closed again. Wet, hungry, thirsty, and battered, he collapsed. He may have been unconscious as long as four days. On August 20 an Antwerp-bound steamer, the *Ebrus*, spotted the drifting boat and stopped to rescue him. He was physically shattered, and it was only after he had been aboard the steamer two days that he could get out of bed.

———♦——

The following year, 1892, Lawlor, the winner, and Andrews, the challenger, agreed to another Atlantic run, though each would leave when ready. Their mutual destination would be Spain. Both men wanted to ride the celebratory mood of the European discovery of the New World four hundred years earlier by Christopher Columbus. With that in mind Lawlor named his new boat after the Genovese explorer, while Andrews accepted the sponsorship of the Enoch Morgan's Sons Company, which wanted to promote their soap product, Sapolio.

Sapolio was the strangest of all Andrews's boats. Only fourteen and a half feet long, five feet five inches wide, and three feet deep, it retained the gunter-gaff rig of the *Mermaid*, but mated it this time with a wood and canvas collapsible hull that had a full keel—apparently Andrews had enough of centerboards, which would not make a boat self-righting! But why a collapsible hull? To save weight? If so, then the full keel canceled that advantage. Perhaps Andrews thought the novelty of the design would attract more attention, and he was correct. The *Sapolio* was apparently meant to collapse top to bottom, and in that respect it was like the folding kayaks developed by "Blondie" Hasler for the "cockleshell heroes'" raid against enemy shipping at Bordeaux fifty years later during World War II. According to one account, the deck had to be removed before the hull was folded up. In final form the hull was only about four inches thick and could be carried under the arm. Whatever the collapsing method, this design feature was a frivolous "Andrews-esque" notion. On the serious side, he did add a bowsprit similar to the one on his rival's previous boat, and this undoubtedly better balanced the rig, so at least in one respect he was learning. He also went back to using ballast, in the form of 350 pounds let into the keel.

Lawlor departed in his *Christopher Columbus* in the late spring and was never heard from again. Andrews left Atlantic City, Boyton's old stamping ground, on July 20, late in the sailing season. His route was designed to take him near the Azores, and unlike the previous year he sailed his course with little incident. After thirty-seven days he landed at Terceira, Azores, where he spent three days resting and resupplying. He made Portugal three weeks later, after a close encounter with his much-hated and feared whales—a pod of feeding finbacks came barreling by his boat, mouths agape, causing him to get "shaky in the knees."

Although William Andrews's *Sapolio* was the first folding boat to cross an ocean, Franz Romer's Klepper, which made the crossing thirty-seven years later, is often mistakenly credited with the record.

Andrews finally arrived September 27 at Huelva, Spain, to a grand reception. For the next few weeks he was feted by the Spanish government and hailed as a modern-day Columbus. There were enough glowing reports in the local newspapers about his valorous adventure to make even him forget those hungry whales that had made his heroic knees so shaky.

Just a dozen miles inland from where William Andrews launched his sailing career lived and toiled one of America's most successful authors of the 1890s, Horatio Alger Jr. of Natick, Massachusetts. In books like *Ragged Dick; Or, Street Life in New York*, and *Paul the Peddler; Or, the Fortunes of a Young Street Merchant,* Alger promoted the notion that if a young man worked hard enough, no matter what the circumstances of his background, social class, or other perceived handicaps, he could succeed in America. This was the "can-do" philosophy of pulling yourself up by your own bootstraps. Give a man an opportunity and let him take it from there. It was *opportunity* that drew millions of immigrants to the American shore.

Two such immigrants were Norwegian-born George Harbo and Frank Samuelsen. Harbo had come over at age nineteen in 1884, hoping to earn enough money so he could marry his sweetheart and start a family. He found menial work clamming on the Jersey shore. Nine years later Samuelsen, a merchant mariner of some skill, decided that he had enough of the sea rover's life and wanted to give America a try. In 1893 he too arrived on the Jersey shore, where he met and befriended Harbo. Harbo by that time had risen from clammer to harbor pilot, but the life of a pilot for ships coming into the various ports of New Jersey from Sandy Hook around and up to New York City was competitive, politically charged, and often dangerous. With a budding family to tend, he gave up that career and returned to clamming in a boat he built himself. He invited Samuelsen to join him.

They worked the rivers and creeks along New Jersey's "shoulder," the Atlantic Highlands (Harbo lived in a town of the same name). Digging for clams was backbreaking work. The men would row out to the tidal flats, thrust long-tined pincers into the mire, and feel around for the shellfish. Squeezing shut the tool and withdrawing it from the suction of the sand was a torturous daily workout for the biceps and back muscles. Samuelsen, a powerfully built man, though five years older than Harbo, was more suited to the work. With a family to feed, the younger man kept up with him through sheer willpower, though his mind was always racing ahead, looking for the next opportunity. Somehow he had to find the key to success in America and leave the desolate

Jersey shore. This challenge stumped even the best of Alger's heroes in 1890s America, in the grip of an economic depression rivaling in impact and duration the better-known slump forty years later.

Every ethnic group that came to America had its heroes. Irish and Italian immigrants had recently flexed their political muscles by having days designated officially recognizing theirs, Saint Patrick and Columbus. The hero of Norwegian immigrants, like Harbo and Samuelsen, was still alive and currently making news with his Arctic exploits. He was zoologist-explorer Fridtjof Nansen, who in 1888 had almost unbelievably crossed the unexplored frozen interior of Greenland on skis—a mode of transportation few in America at that time had even heard of.

Now, in the summer of 1895, Nansen was presumably stuck somewhere in the Arctic pack ice in his ship *Fram*, drifting, if everything went according to plan and the ice didn't crush the ship, north toward the Pole. The world was as yet without radio and so no one yet knew that Nansen had found the *Fram*'s northerly drift too slow and had in mid-March left the ship with one crew member, F. Hjalmar Johansen, and set off with sleds, dogs, and two kayaks in a bid to reach the Pole before the end of summer. Nor did anyone know yet that after reaching 86°14′ N, the closest anyone had ever gotten to the Pole, they had turned back because of dwindling supplies. Nansen was a risk-taker but not a fool. He and Johansen had no chance of ever reaching the still-drifting *Fram*, so they made toward Spitzbergen. By sled and on foot and with dogged determination they forced themselves southward through the cold, racing against their dwindling food supply and the shorter days. One hundred and thirty-two days after quitting the *Fram*, they sighted land again and established a winter base camp on one of the islands of Franz Josef Land, a Russian archipelago in the Arctic Ocean. They survived the dark and frigid Arctic winter by shooting polar bears and huddling in a rock and walrus-hide shelter they built. In May 1896 they set out once again south, this time using the kayaks they had made on board the *Fram* before leaving—lightweight single-seaters built from bamboo and sailcloth. Once during their retreat south they lashed the pair together, catamaran style, and fitted a square sail.

Fridtjof Nansen and F. Hjalmar Johansen weave through Arctic ice floes in their homemade kayaks that they rafted together in a desperate race south to beat the looming winter. Angry walruses slowed them down.

Certainly no small boat had been that far north before or endured the temperature extremes and buffeting from ice floes that Nansen and Johansen's kayaks did. Two months later, and after a bull walrus attacked Nansen in his kayak, holing it, at Cape Flora they luckily stumbled on the British explorer Frederick Jackson, who transported them home on his ship *Windward*. By coincidence, a week after their arrival the crew of the trusty *Fram* sailed into port. All of Scandinavia went wild for Nansen, but especially the Norwegians, who were then trying to extricate their country from Swedish control.

But in the summer of 1895 Nansen's final victory over the polar region was still a year away, when one day, while clamming, Harbo told his friend and partner Samuelsen that he had an idea about how they could better their lives and quit clamming. He proposed that they be the first men to row a boat across the Atlantic. *Row* a boat! Harbo had reasoned that both men were fit enough because of their daily workout with oars and clamming tongs and, as Alfred Johnson's trawling partner had once reasoned, what was an Atlantic crossing other than just a long string of working days tied together? His big friend was easily persuaded. Something had to be found to get them out of the clam beds and moving up the economic ladder in their adopted country. Surely if they rowed across the Atlantic fame would come their way, and putting their boat on public exhibition would earn them great wealth. They agreed to have a boat built that winter and row across the next summer. As they told their children in later years, they figured that, like Fridtjof Nansen, they would bring more acclaim to Norwegians the world over.

The two men tried to secure sponsorship for the voyage, but lacking Andrews's gift of gab they got only a vague promise of aid from Richard K. Fox, publisher of the somewhat racy, lowbrow journal, *Police Gazette*. Fox, a younger, Irish version of Joseph Pulitzer, promised the two clammers that if they named the boat after him, on successful completion of their journey he would award them medals from the *Police Gazette*. He promised that his journal would avidly follow and report on their progress (why not?—it was a good story at no cost to him) and that with such great publicity their tour on returning was bound to be a commercial success.

Honest, hardworking, but not very savvy about business, the two men nodded and left Fox's office without even getting tram fare out of him. Thus their boat, a typical New Jersey double-ended surf boat, was named the *Richard K. Fox*. It measured eighteen feet long, was five feet at the beam and was clinker-built of white cedar. In her ends were set two galvanized cork-filled buoyancy tanks. For added safety, two grabrails ran along the bilges on the outside of the hull so that in a capsizing the men would have something to pull on to right the boat. A custom-fitted canvas skirt was sewn that fit closely over the gunwales, with two openings so the men could row even in bad weather. Rowing would be done by three pairs of ash oars and two pairs of spruce sweeps. The boat was provisioned with a hundred pounds of tinned biscuits, two hundred and fifty eggs wrapped in seaweed, nine pounds of coffee, tinned meats, and thirty gallons of water for each man, as well as wine, beans, vegetables, and more. The provisions weighed more than the hull! They would navigate by quadrant, though it is likely they planned to beg positions along the way, as their predecessors had.

On June 6, 1896, they made ready for departure at Castle Garden on the southern tip of Manhattan. Members of the quality press were there shoulder to shoulder with the tabloid press, like Fox's *Police Gazette*, to record the moment. Many onlookers shouted insults and Bronx cheers (also known as raspberries) at the two rowers, predicting cruelly that they would never see land again. Even reporters made elegiac farewell comments. Several newspapermen were asked to certify and sign a document stating that they had examined the boat and found no masts or sails of

The humble *Richard K. Fox* was nothing like the man for whom it was named, but everything like the poor immigrants, George Harbo and Frank Samuelson, who bravely rowed it across the Atlantic.

any kind. This done, Fox's private launch towed the rowboat out past the Narrows to the edge of the open sea.

Undeterred by their callous send-off, Harbo and Samuelsen rowed toward the horizon and faraway Europe, intending to reach Le Havre and then row up the Seine to Paris. Things went pretty well for the first week, and they averaged forty-five miles a day, which wasn't bad considering that most of the sail-powered boats described in this book averaged about the same. On June 13 they narrowly avoided being rammed by a steamship, but dodged her, only to find themselves caught in their first big gale, with twenty-foot waves, the very next day. To ride this out they shipped their oars and deployed a sea anchor. It held their bow to the sea, but at their next sighting they reckoned they had lost twenty-five hard-earned miles during the blow. On June 16 the German steamer *Fürst Bismarck* stopped to "rescue" them, an offer they politely declined.

After only ten days they had made good an impressive five hundred miles. But because of southerly winds, they found they had drifted farther north than they intended and were in fact on the Grand Banks. The weather remained good, however, and they rowed for nine straight days until June 27, when another gale tossed them about. They took this latest blow with equanimity. Harbo and Samuelsen were the perfect team for such a perilous journey because they knew each other well, having spent years together on a small boat eking out a living on the Jersey shore. They knew each other's moods, jokes, soft spots, and just when to acquiesce.

Like Nansen, Harbo and Samuelsen were careful planners, and among the most useful equipment they had on the boat were two mattresses filled with reindeer hair. These were warm and waterproof, so at least at night they could count on a good sleep. While one man slept, the other rowed and kept watch. Even during blows they kept rowing because movement gave them directional control, which allowed them to steer into the waves. They never had to worry about being in the "wind shadow" of a wave at a critical moment, as the sailors had.

On Independence Day, July 4, the worst gale of the trip sent swells warning that it was coming. Two days later, thirty-foot breaking waves thundered in from the west. They were going in the right direction, at least, and propelling the little *Fox* toward its destination, but at an unsustainable rate. With every wave the boat zoomed up the slope and then raced back down. It was all happening too quickly. If they slid down the face of a wave too fast, the boat would nose under in a trough and pitchpole. In an effort to regain control, they spun the boat around and began to row westward *up* the faces of the waves. This did give them control, but not for long. The seas continued to pile up and the thirty-footers grew until the waves were as tall as two *Richard K. Fox*es stacked end to end. At any moment if one of those broke over the boat the men could be crushed. It was time to deploy the sea anchor and hope for the best.

Hope wasn't enough. A sharp *crack* told them that the sea anchor line had snapped under the strain, and now the boat was at the mercy of the raging sea, its bow skidding left and right. At lightning speed each man threw a set of the stronger ash oars into the thole pins and started pulling for his life. They would have to row nonstop until the savage storm blew out because that was the only way to keep the boat head to seas and keep from rolling. It was night and pitch dark, so they couldn't see the direction of the waves—they would have to feel and hear the waves and use their best judgment. This was the supreme test.

By daybreak they had won their battle. Exhausted from rowing, bruised and sore from the impact of the wind and water on their faces, callused hands now open and bleeding, the men drew deep breaths as they saw the seas return to some sanity. A new sea anchor was the first order of business. When that was made and deployed and they had eaten, the weary adventurers rested. Two nights later they wondered if they were hallucinating when the wind suddenly stopped and they felt ice crystals on their faces. What was it? A few moments later, the ice melted and the wind returned. They realized they had passed behind an iceberg! They indeed had drifted too far north in the storm.

The next day brought another fierce gale. They stoically rowed on and through brute strength fought to keep the nose of the boat headed into every rising wave. Then, in the distance, several waves united into the tallest wave they had yet encountered. It came right at the boat and seemed to hover over it for a moment like an evil spirit. The *Fox* made a feeble effort to lift its bow and ride up it, but the wall was absolutely vertical. The mountain of liquid suddenly collapsed and Harbo and Samuelsen were engulfed in the deluge as if they had sailed under Niagara Falls. When each man came to the surface they found their boat capsized. It didn't have ballast other than the supplies, so they used the bottom handrails to right the boat. Clambering over the side they saw the damage wrought by the rogue wave. Most of their supplies were gone, as well as the new sea anchor. It was bad, but the raging storm didn't give them any time for self-pity. They unshipped oars again and fought to gain control in the midst of the fury. The battle wasn't over and neither they nor the sea were yet the victors.

After three days of combat the sea relented, and the men could finally take turns sleeping again. Samuelsen, the hardier of the two, told Harbo to sleep first. It was typically thoughtful. Never once did he blame his friend for getting the two of them into their present predicament. He had signed on voluntarily, and he took full responsibility for being there. Later, when Harbo awoke, he estimated their position and reckoned they were more than halfway across. The terrible westerly storm had actually vaulted them in the right direction, and they were now only about twelve hundred miles out. Burning as many calories as they did rowing, the men didn't have enough food or water to reach the nearest coast. They needed help.

Five days after capsizing their luck changed for the better, when, as they were rowing, Samuelsen spotted a sail away to the north. Taking a chance, they changed course and chased it. It turned out to be the Norwegian bark *Cito* bound for Pembroke, England. Its captain backed his sails on spying the little boat, again presuming a rescue, and invited the two men aboard. Surprise turned to admiration when they told him their story, and he gave them a meal, use of freshwater for a good sponge bath, and enough provisions for them to finish the voyage.

With this one chance meeting Harbo and Samuelsen were rejuvenated and confident they would succeed. In that sense, Horatio Alger's philosophy was correct. Their integrity, courage, and persistence were about to pay off. On August 1, after fifty-four days at sea, they rowed into Hugh Town, Scilly Islands, becoming the first men ever to row across the Atlantic. Six days later they were across the Channel at Le Havre.

And that's where the Alger-esque story ends, because despite their honesty, industry, persistence, and belief in the system Harbo and Samuelsen failed to attract paying crowds with their boat. They were a publicity flop. Unlike Boyton, Andrews, or even the crew of the *Red, White & Blue*, neither man had the flair for drama, the natural charisma, the gift of gab. What they had accomplished through the brawn of their backs and courage in their hearts remains one of the greatest sea voyages ever. It was on a par with Johnson's and Gilboy's. Yet they couldn't make it pay. Sometimes life isn't fair. From France they went back to England and flopped as an attraction there, too, then on to their native Norway, where they at least made a little news and a little cash. Finally they boarded a ship back to New York, where the most they got was the promised medals from the *Police Gazette*. The simple mariners had failed to get rich quick, but was that what Alger had promised his readers? Not really. Alger had promised stability, security, and mostly a sense of belonging and dignity for those who worked hard. He wrote about different versions of success, not just financial.

After their Atlantic escapade Harbo and Samuelsen returned to the Jersey shore to try again to find their niche in America. Harbo went back to piloting and eventually built a good business that provided financial security for his family; in that modest way he attained what Alger had promised. He was able to buy a home in Brooklyn, and his family came to realize the middle-class American Dream. At least, that is, until ten years later in 1908, when Harbo died suddenly of pneumonia.

After seeing his dear friend buried on what was still to him foreign soil, Samuelsen gave up on America and the American Dream, returning to the family farm in Norway. Life was slower there, less likely to provide material wealth, to be sure, but also less likely to cause the stress and loneliness he had all too often felt since leaving his native land. He lived there quietly as a dairy farmer until his death in 1946.

———— ◆ ————

William Andrews hadn't spent much time worrying about the American Dream, even during the depression of the 1890s. He had a government pension because of his Civil War wounds and had two successful transatlantic trips under his belt, along with two profitable books that he wrote about those voyages; in general, things were going well. In the summer of 1898 he made another Atlantic attempt, this time in a thirteen-foot canvas and wood folding boat named *Phantom Ship*. Delays over the summer caused him to make a very late start on August 24, and predictably his voyage ended with a midocean rescue after less than four weeks.

The next summer the middle-aged sailor tried yet again in the same boat, now called *Doree*, though a foot shorter thanks to quick work with a handsaw. As in the previous voyage, he had to be rescued midocean after only three weeks. He was found delirious in the bottom of the boat.

While Andrews was departing from Atlantic City on June 18, 1899, in his little twelve-footer, farther north a more serious sailor was heading out of Gloucester harbor for a transatlantic bid. Anyone who attempts the North Atlantic in a small boat is no ordinary sailor, but of all the extraordinary seamen to try it, this one was indeed the most extraordinary of all. He had no fingers.

In the winter of 1883, Howard Blackburn had been a Grand Banks doryman. That January he had signed onto the *Grace L. Fears* for a run up to Burgeo Bank off the southern coast of Newfoundland. It was incredibly cold, but halibut were to be had, and the money looked good.

The figure of Victorian respectability and success, fingerless Howard Blackburn dabbled in shopkeeping, gold prospecting, record setting in sailboats, and of course, bootlegging.

According to plan, on arriving at the fishing grounds the *Fears* put her dories over the side, and the little boats set their trawls, each a mile and half long with 480 individual hooks hanked on. Once the trawls were set, the dories returned to the ship to give the fish the better part of the day to take the bait. Plans changed when the captain thought he smelled bad weather moving in. By midmorning it had begun to flurry, and the atmosphere grew heavy. He ordered the dories out again to retrieve the trawls and told them to hurry back because of the threatening conditions.

Blackburn and his dory mate, Tom Welch, went out to their trawl and began to haul it in, killing a few halibut during the process and dropping them into the dory. The scattered snow turned to heavy snow, and they had trouble seeing the *Fears* in the gray gloom but could just make out her shadowy bulk. The wind died altogether as the men hurried on. They pulled up line, looked for a hooked halibut, killed it if they found it, or moved to the next hook. A few minutes after the wind died it suddenly roared back with a vengeance from the opposite direction. They were being blown away from the ship. Quickly they unshipped their oars and started pulling for the schooner. What should have been a few minutes' labor stretched to an hour. They put down the oars and listened for any sound that might reveal the *Fears*'s position—voices, a fog horn, blocks rattling—but all they heard was the eerie, relentless, howling wind. They were in the midst of a blizzard in a small dory somewhere on the Burgeo Bank and utterly lost.

They realized that any additional rowing might take them even farther from the ship, so they threw out the sea anchor and waited for the weather to improve, but it didn't. The snow ended as darkness fell, but the gale-force winds raged on. In the darkness they could see a light in the far distance; it was a signal lamp in the ratlines of the *Fears*. If only they could reach it, but the wind was against them and they couldn't make headway. With the sea anchor deployed, the nose of their dory dug into each sharp swell and flooded the boat, and though they bailed with wooden kegs, it was a never-ending battle and they were tiring. They pulled in the anchor and tried to row again, but now the wind pushed them farther from the *Fears* and the coast. It was useless to fight it, so they set a sea anchor and started bailing again. Blackburn momentarily took off his mittens while bailing and when he reached down to put them on again, they were gone. The seawater was like ice on his hands, but there was nothing he could do except keep bailing.

For two days they fought the wind and freezing water, but it was more than Welch could endure, though, like Blackburn, he was a strong, fit man. That second night Welch curled into a ball in the bow of the boat and some hours later froze to death. Blackburn, though he tried to save his mate and had once even prevented him from crawling overboard, now saw his chance to have mittens. He pried off Welch's, but when he tried to put one on, it wouldn't fit. His hands were bigger than Welch's, and they were swollen from encroaching frostbite. He knew his only hope was to row for the coast, but that was at least sixty miles away, and he had no water. His will to survive overcame all objections, and so he set to the oars and rowed.

The flesh on his now frost-bitten hands hung in black chunks, and soon pieces of his fingers fell away. He had to do something or else when his fingers were gone he wouldn't be able to grip the oars. He therefore cupped the palms of his hands and used them as sockets to pull at the oars. They would freeze that way, but at least they would work as long as Blackburn had the desire to live and keep them pulling.

His partner lying frozen to death in one end of their Banks dory, Howard Blackburn bails for his life.

He did. For three days he pulled and pulled and pulled. To stop was to die, so he pulled even when the wind pushed him back, even when his throat tried to strangle him from lack of water, and even when he could see nothing on the horizon but gray green waves and more bad weather. He mentally zoned out of his life at that moment and just rowed on as if he were an automaton. Row, don't think, row, don't feel. On the evening of the third day after Welch's death, Blackburn saw land: the Newfoundland coast. He landed and found an abandoned hut into which he crawled for the night. The next day he rowed up the Little River and found the rude shanty of a poor fishing family. Near starvation themselves from the harsh winter, they nevertheless took in the half-frozen man and saved his life, though he lost all his fingers and many of his toes.

That spring Blackburn was found alive at the remote shanty and brought back to Gloucester, where he received a hero's welcome and was the recipient of a generous public subscription to help him get his life back in order. Blackburn turned his misfortune into a tidy profit by opening a tobacco shop and later a saloon. His gregarious nature and ability to tell a good tale—and he certainly had one to tell—made him a local celebrity in Gloucester and his business flourished.

Money in the bank is one thing, but adventures in the bank of Life are something else, and so as he approached his fortieth birthday Blackburn decided he needed a few more. Gold had been discovered in the Alaska territory, so he formed a syndicate of avaricious Gloucester cronies, bought a schooner, and led them out west in 1897 in search of riches. Round the Horn they went in the *Hattie I. Phillips*, joining another forty thousand men who knew that they too would get lucky. Like most of the other gold rushers, the members of the Blackburn Expedition, as it was called, came home a year later, tails dragging and empty-handed.

Though profitless, the adventure had been a lot of fun for Blackburn, who felt cooped up in his saloon despite his rollicking band of local friends and backslappers who came every day to sip his spirits and enjoy his bonhomie. He wanted to do *something*. The summer of 1899 was full of small-boat news in Gloucester and all the way down the eastern seaboard. William Andrews was getting ready to ship out again, as was aging Thomas Crapo down in New Bedford. The press followed their plans closely, but were even more interested in another crusty New England salt, Joshua Slocum. Slocum, like Blackburn, had been born in Canada but moved to the United States, where he became a citizen. The summer before he had returned from an epic solo sail around the world in the thirty-seven-foot *Spray*, a boat that dated back nearly to the Revolutionary War. Considered by sailors in those days to be a "small boat," the old *Spray* and its captain would become famous that summer with the serial publication of Slocum's amiable and stirring narrative of the voyage, *Sailing Alone Around the World*, in *Century* magazine.

Blackburn must have missed the limelight as much as he desired a midlife fling. To satisfy both cravings he commissioned a thirty-foot gaff-rigged cutter patterned after a fishing boat common to the area called a "Gloucester sloop boat," but about two-thirds the size of an original. He christened her *Great Western*.

A gaff cutter for a man with no fingers? How could he make fast the halyards and sheets in those days before self-locking cam cleats? Blackburn still had thumbs up to the first joint, which allowed him to pinch a line, though just barely. To tie off a halyard or sheet he held the line between his stub thumb and palm, whipped the line around his fingerless hand, and then rolled the line around his body to take up a turn. He also used his feet and teeth to belay a line temporarily as he took it in. This method of sail handling was slow and didn't allow for great precision, but it did allow him the safety to hold the sheet with one hand and steer with the other, the best practice, as any small-boat sailor knows.

Because of his problems, he made a slow crossing. After departing from Gloucester on June 18, 1899, the same day as Andrews from Atlantic City, with the vague notion of some kind of race, Blackburn worked his way across, although it is obvious he didn't push the boat. For safety, he probably always traveled under reduced sails (a practice to be recommended to many sailors and one espoused by modern sailor Sven Lundin, whose remarkable adventures are chronicled in later chapters). Blackburn's thirty-footer, properly crewed, might have made the passage in forty days rather than the sixty-two it actually took before he reached King Road off Portishead, England. Still, the fingerless man had navigated and cooked and sailed across the wide Atlantic by himself.

Perfect sail trim was a Blackburn specialty despite his handicap. The *Great Republic* was the second small boat he piloted across the Atlantic alone, this one from Gloucester to Lisbon in just thirty-nine days.

Two years later, in 1901, Blackburn issued a challenge to anyone to race him across to Portugal. In anticipation of a race, and expecting Andrews to take up the challenge, he had built the twenty-five-foot *Great Republic*, essentially a smaller version of his previous boat. When no one came forward to accept the challenge, Blackburn continued on, anyway, telling a reporter that the pleasure he gained from voyaging made the hard work and inconvenience worth it. Out of Gloucester he sailed on June 9, 1901, and thirty-nine days later arrived in Lisbon after a relatively easy run. The same cannot be said for William Andrews's transatlantic attempt that year. He was about to go to the well once too often.

Howard Blackburn took the *Great Republic*, which had been shipped home, on an inland cruise of America as pioneered by Nathaniel Bishop from May 1902 through February the next year. From Gloucester he sailed down to New York, then up the Hudson to Albany, across the Erie Canal to the Great Lakes, through the lakes to Chicago, down the Illinois River to the Mississippi, down to the Gulf and around Florida, where he finally sold her.

No sooner had he gotten home to Massachusetts then he approached a Swampscott boatbuilder and ordered the construction of a seventeen-foot modified fishing dory. He was heading across the Atlantic again. This time he intended to make a round trip of it, sailing first to Le Havre, down the French canals and the Rhône to Marseilles, west in the Mediterranean, and finally home via the trade winds.

Blackburn hoped to make it a race between his dory *America* and the nineteen-and-a half-foot *Columbia*, skippered by German-American Ludwig Eisenbraun. Eisenbraun got out of port a few days before Blackburn, who left on June 7, 1903. Gales, a stoved-in hatch, and two capsizings convinced Blackburn to rethink his voyage. The *America* was a pretty little boat, but extremely tender. He had only just managed to save himself after the second dunking, and this all before he had even cleared the Maritimes. He gave up the first week in July and put in to Halifax, Nova Scotia.

Nor was Eisenbraun having an easier time with the Atlantic. Fierce gales drove him back to Boston, where he took on a crewman and tried again. On August 24 they arrived in Halifax, where he looked up Blackburn and the two exchanged pleasantries. Eisenbraun left his crewman there and departed again, even though it was late in the season. After a stop in Madeira, he finally made Gibraltar on November 20, 1903.

———◆◆◆———

A few years earlier Andrews had entered into a business relationship with "Captain" John L. Young, who owned the most famous amusement pier at Atlantic City. During the summer months Young's Pier featured a dazzling array of novelty acts to attract the resort crowds—an Italian military band under Signor Monoliti, a woman lion tamer, "negro" cakewalk dance contests, and even Gustave Whitehead's "flying automobile." Whitehead (or Weisskopf, as the German immigrant mechanic was known before his name was anglicized) was the man who some still say, incorrectly, made the first airplane flight even before the Wright brothers. Whitehead was paid to show his *No. 21* would-be airplane on the pier and make a flight, though, as usual, he failed to come through. It didn't matter to Young so long as the quirky inventor's machine drew in paying customers. Young's biggest attraction, quaintly enough, was his twice-daily hauling up of the fishing seines he lowered from his pier. Each day he personally pulled up hundreds of pounds of fish to be served in his restaurants on the pier. The turn-of-the-century crowd loved this simple spectacle.

Andrews, too, was paid by Young to become an attraction on the pier. Young realized that with the right promotion in the local newspapers people would pay each year to see Andrews preparing his little boat during the summer for that year's departure. The more people who came to see Andrews, the greater the sailor's take. Therefore it paid for Andrews to delay his departure, even though that meant a late-season start that would put him in danger of running into hurricane weather. So lucrative was the Young-Andrews alliance that the former piano maker earned as much as the highest paid sea captains in the country. Yes, he put his life on the line with each voyage, but the pay made it worth it to him.

In order to keep the crowds coming, Andrews and Young had to devise a new gimmick each year—somehow the voyage had to set a record or collect a new superlative. In 1901 either Young or Andrews struck upon the idea that Andrews would go that summer with a wife he would select from the women responding to an advertisement in newspapers. Andrews's first wife had died several years before, so why not find a young adventurous girl who wanted to have some fun? She would make the record books for smallest-boat transatlantic crossing by a woman.

Young's publicity machine spun into action, and eventually Miss Mary C. South from Pleasantville, New Jersey, was selected from among the other applicants. Women in those days had few outlets for adventure. They were stifled by society's expectation that they make respectable matches and then stay in the background of their husbands' lives. Wife, mother, then matron were all that was expected of them, or even allowed. For many young women this was a prison sentence, and perhaps especially so for Mary South, cooped up in her parents' home in Pleasantville in the flat, featureless farmland of southern Jersey, just over the causeway from Atlantic City. What did she know about William Andrews, other than that the newspapers had acclaimed him a great hero over the years? She knew nothing about sailing, so how could she know that real professional mariners scoffed at the "captain's" stunts? Let John Young and his paid stooge reporters for the local papers shout all they wanted about the vaunted Captain Andrews—the real salts knew better. But not Mary, who was young and wanted adventure. On August 18, at nine o'clock in the evening, Atlantic City's mayor, Franklin Stoy, officiated at her wedding to Andrews, with the largest crowd of the season in attendance on Young's Pier. The fifty-eight-year-old Andrews then announced that he and his blushing bride would depart for Spain on their "honeymoon cruise" on August 28.

As part of the attraction, Andrews himself built in front of the public on Young's Pier the boat he and Mary would take that year. Delays in receiving the wood from the lumberyard and the special canvas to cover the boat forced him to postpone their departure date into early September, Andrews claimed to the papers. Better weekly takes on the pier because of the addition of Mary to the crew may have had something to do with it, too. In fact, the departure was postponed many times through September, even after the thirteen-foot folding boat, the *Dark Secret*, was built.

Not everyone agreed with Andrews's pronouncements that it was still safe to depart that year. Experienced mariners privately and publicly warned him against beginning his voyage so late in the season.

Hurricanes or not, the approaching winter weather was bound to be appalling on the Atlantic, even on the southerly route to Spain. Andrews shrugged off all gainsayers. Even John Young, to his credit, told the stubborn New Englander he needn't depart that year. Young may have been speaking with the realization that he had already squeezed most of the profits out of the voyage that were to be had, anyway, or perhaps he spoke with genuine concern for the couple or perhaps with a tinge of guilt about young Mary. Whatever the reason, or combination of reasons, they didn't matter. Andrews would not be dissuaded, and Mary resolutely wanted to go along.

Unbelievably, the voyage was not begun until *October* 6, appallingly late in the season. It wasn't summer anymore; it was two and a half weeks into autumn. Bad weather had been the most recent causes of postponement, but Andrews wouldn't heed that warning sign. On Sunday, October 6, there was a little window of moderated weather, so, before a huge crowd to which Mary hawked as many as a thousand photographs of the pair in front of their boat, they finally set off at 4:25 in the afternoon. Captain Young and Mayor Stoy were prominently there for the send-off, as were Mary's parents and brothers from Pleasantville. Mary's mother convulsed in tears and grief at the parting, though the male members of her family knew she would be safely returned and told her so.

William Andrews and his bride, Mary South Andrews, departed on their fateful voyage in 1901 from Young's Pier in Atlantic City. The pier still juts out into the Atlantic even today as if pointing to Europe.

How wrong they were. After speaking with the ship *Durango* about a hundred miles out from New Jersey, whose captain later reported that Mary looked nearly sick to death, they were never seen again. The honeymoon cruise was over.

⇒ 5 ⇐

A WORLD TO CONQUER

1900–1920

♦ THE MAN WHO DIDN'T CIRCUMNAVIGATE ♦ THE EGG THAT DIDN'T GO
OVER EASY ♦ *YAKABOO* AND A POET, TOO ♦ STIFF AND FROZEN UPPER
LIPS: SHACKLETON AND WORSLEY ♦ THE MYSTERY OF HOPE COVE ♦

THERE ARE MANY REASONS WHY THE STORY OF CAPTAIN
John Voss's "circumnavigation" in a dugout canoe shouldn't be included
in this book, and the least of which is that he did not circumnavigate, as
he is often credited with doing. Another reason could be that his boat
Tilikum was thirty-eight feet overall, therefore not "small" by our definition—but this is a weak excuse because some of that length came from
the extended ornately carved figurehead, and in reality the *Tilikum* was
a small boat volumetrically, with a beam of only five and a half feet.

No, the best reason for not including the story of John Voss's note-worthy sail nearly around the world, despite the fact that so much has been written about him—and yes, he truly was a great sailor—is that the man was by most accounts a mean, ornery cuss who stole from Native Americans, exploited illegal aliens, robbed graves, ran from the law, and may have murdered one of his crewmen on board the *Tilikum* in a moment of lost temper. But much of this is debatable, so the least that can be done is to tell his story and let the reader judge.

Voss was born around 1858 in what was then southern Denmark, until Bismarck annexed it few years later, which is why Voss is sometimes said to have been born in Germany. His father ran a guesthouse, an occupation that seemed a little too tame for the stocky, quick-fisted son, so, in his teens, John Voss ran away to sea, serving first as a cabin boy. By the time he was forty he was a ship's master, but for some reason he gave up that occupation and reverted to his father's chosen career as hotelier, in Victoria, Vancouver Island, where he married. Evidence suggests that Voss had a taste for schnapps (as the Danes call aquavit) and other spirits, wasn't averse to a little hide-and-seek with the law over opium imports, had tried his hand at treasure hunting in South America, and had even been indicted by U.S. authorities for smuggling illegal Chinese immigrants into California. All his life Voss seemed beset by the desire to get rich quick, no matter the means, and likewise the habit of using people until they were of no further use, after which he would leave them.

In the spring of 1901 Norman Luxton, a thirty-year-old journalist, approached Voss to ask him if he could sail around the world in a boat smaller than Slocum's *Spray*. Probably around that time there were many old salts who boasted that they could outdo Slocum if only they had . . . if only . . . Voss, to his credit, or at least in pursuit of Luxton's vague promise of a five-thousand-dollar reward, agreed to do it, though in his autobiography Voss claims Luxton used the phrase "if we cross the three oceans." This doesn't quite ring true because Slocum had

Art on facing page: John Voss stands at the helm in the *Tilikum*, the dugout war canoe he sailed across three oceans, but not around the world. He never got chummy with any of his crew.

circled the world, and that would have been the standard to beat.

The two became partners, agreeing to split the reward money and the proceeds from a book deal that Luxton hoped to make after the trip. Voss went looking for a cheap small boat to use for the voyage, and what he found is shocking even today and even more so is the manner in which he acquired it. He found an ancient Indian log canoe lying un-used on the east coast of Vancouver Island near an Indian village. The canoe, made from the single trunk of a red cedar tree, looked pretty solid despite its age. When its owner, an old Siwash Indian, sauntered up, Voss offered him some rye in a flask. The lubrication aided negoti-ations, and soon Voss owned the boat. According to Voss, for good measure the Indian also gave him the skull of his father, who had built the canoe fifty years earlier.

To make the boat seaworthy, Voss added strakes along the gunwales to raise the freeboard, inserted one-inch oak frames every two feet, strengthened the floor with balks of timber, added an internal keelson and external keel with a three-hundred-pound lead shoe, and then shipped a ton of fixed ballast and four hundred pounds of movable bal-last, which could be used to trim the boat while under way. Next he added a deck and a five-by-eight-foot cabin. He rigged her as a three-masted schooner, with gaff-rigged fore- and mainsails and a jib-headed mizzen. The overall sail area was only 230 square feet, which speaks to Voss's experience, as does the low rig.

After a few weeks of sea trials, including a series of nocturnal raids on Indian burial sites to steal relics, Voss and Luxton started out from Victoria on May 21, 1901, but, like so many of the previous voyagers, they had to put into Fort Saint John, Vancouver Island, two days later to sit out contrary winds. They set off again on May 27, destination Pit-cairn Island, but bad weather fetched them up once more and they landed at the Indian village at Dodges Cove. Between robbing more In-dian burial sites, whaling with living Indians, fishing, hunting, and taking it easy, the two sailors killed five weeks and didn't put to sea again until July 6! Why did they do this?

According to Luxton, when Voss filed the papers to sail into American waters he falsely registered the *Tilikum* as the *Pelican*. Luxton claims that this was so the U.S. Revenue Cutter Service wouldn't arrest Voss, who was wanted for smuggling drugs and Chinese immigrants. It would be only a few miles after putting out from Victoria to American waters. If this version is true, it seems likely that Voss, who couldn't prevent a big announcement of his departure from being spread all over the Victoria papers, wanted a forgotten little backwater cove to hide in until after the heat was off and the Revenue Cutter Service had given up finding him in their area of authority. Curiously, after leaving Victoria in an untried marginal craft, Voss had no plans to go down the coast to San Francisco or San Diego before jumping off to the South Pacific. As this was not typical of the usually cautious, calculating, and crafty former sea captain, he probably had some reason for getting away from the American coast as quickly as possible—adding credence to Luxton's version of events.

Luxton was nautically illiterate at the beginning of the voyage. Along the way, Voss taught him the ropes, and soon the other man could steer a course, trim the sails, go forward to deploy the sea anchor, and in general be an able first mate. Even so, something came between the two men, and according to Luxton they argued so fiercely that at one point Voss threatened to throw him overboard. Luxton then took to pocketing a pistol just in case. By the time they reached Suva, the journalist had decided to quit and take a steamer to Australia. In a bar he found Voss a new mate, a Tasmanian. At thirty-one, Walter "Louis" Begent had already led an adventurous life. He was a qualified seaman, had knocked around the world a time or two, and had fought in the British army in the Northwest Frontier in India, where he was twice wounded. He was as tough as Voss—and therein may have lain the problem, *if* there was a problem. Opposites attract, likes repel.

There are two accounts of what happened next, but only one is from an eyewitness. According to Voss, Begent was at the helm one night about six hundred miles out of Suva when the binnacle light went out. Begent removed the lamp and passed it into the cabin for Voss to relight, but as he did so, a breaking wave rushed up from behind, catching him unawares. Voss cried out for him to grab hold, but it was too late—the wave washed over the boat and Begent was gone. In the strong following wind and waves, again according to Voss, there was nothing to do but drop the sails and throw out the sea anchor. There was no way he could round *Tilikum* up into the wind. His only hope was that Begent could swim to the sound of his voice, so in the darkness he called out again and again. When an hour later he hadn't shown up, Voss knew he never would. In the morning he lowered his Canadian flag to half-staff and continued toward Australia alone.

This exculpating version of events was later disputed by Luxton, who claimed that the two men probably quarreled and Voss, in one of his fits of uncontrollable temper, did what he had earlier threatened to do to Luxton—he threw Begent overboard. Luxton's sole basis for this version was the threat he alleged Voss made toward him on the first leg of the trip.

Would Voss, even in a fit of anger or a drunken rage, have thrown over the only other man on such a small vessel in such dangerous waters, especially when the other man was eminently qualified to sail the boat? That doesn't seem likely, yet temperamental people don't act rationally when enraged. Luxton was known to be sharp-tongued, and he was no saint with a bottle, either. Yet everyone knew that Voss had a short fuse, so perhaps Luxton was right. Further, wouldn't the experienced Begent have worn a lifeline, as Voss always did and claimed he told the younger man to do? The boat was small and the freeboard low, so being pooped by a following sea was an ever-present threat. Only a fool wouldn't tie himself in at the helm on the midnight watch. But even experienced sailors make simple, fatal mistakes.

The result was the same, no matter whose version of events is believed. Young Begent was drowned in the South Pacific while on his way home to his family in Tasmania, and Voss was now on his own. A further result was that when Begent went overboard he took the binnacle with him, and that same killer wave also carried away the uncovered compass. Like Gilboy before him, Voss was twelve hundred miles from Australia without a compass.

Voss used the sun and stars to shape a course to Sydney, where he arrived September 19. He claimed that he so enjoyed the sights of the city that he decided to stay for several months. According to Luxton, who met him there as they had agreed they would in Suva, his real reason for staying was to convalesce in a Sydney hospital from a disease he had contracted from an obliging native woman when the *Tilikum* landed in Samoa before arriving in Suva. Were Voss's alleged bouts of anger and irrational acts brought about by syphilis? Such behavior was common to sufferers from the disease, and in those days there was little effective treatment for it. If so, however, he would have had to have contracted the malady long before Samoa and may have suffered from it for years by then. His unstable home life, as shown by the fact that his wife left him shortly after his voyage began, lends credence to this supposition.

For the next two years Voss sailed leisurely on in the *Tilikum* with several different replacement mates—none staying very long. He went to Tasmania to pay his respects to Begent's sister, who bore him no ill will, then New Zealand, the New Hebrides chain, then into the Indian Ocean, to the island of Rodriques. What is undisputable about Voss, no matter what one thinks of his personal life, is that he was a great sailor. The narrative of his trip, *40,000 Miles in a Canoe*, is the quintessential primer on small-boat handling. He wrote this fully ten years after the voyage ended, when he gave up on Luxton ever publishing anything about the trip. Voss believed in multiple poles, so that no one sail would have to do all the work. A divided rig allowed for better boat balancing and kept the center of effort low; it was easier on the hull and required only simple materials. His shifting of sand bags in the cabin to balance the boat longitudinally is one more example of his great skill in a small boat. Finally, he provides lessons throughout his book on the proper use and handling of a sea drogue, or sea anchor, and how to use one to bring a small boat in to a beach through breaking waves. It is for his book that Voss mostly deserves inclusion in this narrative of small-boat adventures. He was a teacher who laid down the principles and practices of small-boat handling for all the generations to follow. His example, and his book, would launch a flotilla of small-boat adventurers in the decades to come. After all, the *Tilikum* was a log canoe! The magic was not in the red cedar but in Voss's mastery of the art of small-boat handling.

Three years and three months after it first set out, *Tilikum* arrived at Margate on the southern coast of England. After crossing the Indian Ocean Voss had landed in South Africa and then zigged across the southern Atlantic to Pernambuco, Brazil, before zagging back across to England. In England he officially declared the end of his "round-the-world" trip, profitably put his boat on display, was hailed as a hero in the mold of Slocum, and invited to become a Fellow of the Royal Geographical Society. Many articles and books over the years have trumpeted his great accomplishments and hailed him as one of the greatest sailors ever, crediting him with being the first sailor of a really small boat to circumnavigate the globe.

He didn't do it! Voss did not circumnavigate the globe in the *Tilikum* by any stretch of the definition. He was about 90 degrees short—one quarter of the way! Pernambuco at 34°47′ W was the closest he got longitudinally to Victoria, which is 123°21′ W. He would have had to round the Horn to complete the voyage, and he didn't. Captain John Voss was a great small-boat skipper, a leader in the field, but he *never* circumnavigated in the *Tilikum*.

When Norman Luxton returned to Canada, he moved to Banff and set up a trading store with the Indians. The former robber of Indian burial sites apparently repented his crimes, because over the next fifty years he became an early advocate of the preservation of the disappearing Canadian Indian culture. To that end he began a museum, now the Luxton Museum of the Plains Indians in Banff, Alberta, to house artifacts of their vanishing heritage.

———◆◆◆———

A few weeks before Voss put into the Channel port of Margate, another strange craft left the Norwegian port of Ålesund, heading out to sea. This boat was as advanced technologically as the *Tilikum* was simple. The *Uræd* (Unafraid) was an all-steel egg-shaped prototype lifeboat designed by her skipper, Ole Brude. Brude had spent ten years as a ship captain and had seen firsthand the horrors of passenger ships sinking.

Today it's hard to imagine that there could be so many sinkings and that passengers would still embark on voyages, but those were different days, and people accepted risk more readily because there were no alternatives. A quick review of the pictorial periodicals of the time, like *The Illustrated London News, The Graphic, Frank Leslie's*, or the good old *Police Gazette*, shows just how frequent were shipping disasters. These journals loved to report on sea calamities because they could print highly melodramatic images of women with outstretched arms beseeching the stormy heavens for deliverance from the god of the seas or a resolute, square-jawed Edwardian sea captain walking the bridge as the steamer goes down, after the boiler blew, taking him with her. What made for great paper pictures made for miserable real-life deaths.

Ole Brude's steel lifeboat, *Uræd*, lumbers westward across the North Atlantic.

Brude's goal was to make sea travel safer by making accidents survivable. The standard lifeboat of 1904 was little different from Bligh's launch of more than a century earlier. Boats like the *Nonpareil* and lifesaving suits like the Merriman-Boyton model were impractical novelties. The typical davit-slung lifeboat of the period was difficult to launch even in the best of conditions and liable to capsize when dropped into the sea under emergency conditions, as would be clearly shown eight years later in the *Titanic* disaster. Brude's goal was to create a foolproof boat that could be launched haphazardly, right itself, provide all-weather protection to its occupants, and even survive abuse if hurled onto a rocky coast.

Hence the all-steel egg shape. Eggs and honeycombs are nature's structural marvels. The eighteen-foot-long boat, with a cross section of eight feet, had a double bottom divided into four individual flotation chambers. A large trunk for a swing keel projected up into the cabin area, which had wooden benches around its perimeter. Brude claimed that in a pinch "about forty" souls could be squeezed into this cabin, though that seems optimistic. A toilet was provided for their relief. Ventilation and observation were through a little round conning house at the top rear of the shell.

In that it was a monocoque the *Uræd* was years ahead of its time, though the claims that it was the first all-metal lifesaving boat or even the first monocoque are not true. Patents had been applied for on those innovations years before in America and England; none of those boats, however, had all the design advantages of Brude's boat. Furthermore, Brude himself was inspired by his fellow Norwegian, Captain Donvig, who in 1900 had built an all-metal spherical hull that could carry twenty survivors. It had water ballast, a retractable ventilator at the top, a rudder, portholes, and a protective gunwale belt in case of collision. The boat was displayed to high praise at the Paris Exposition of that year, where it won a medal. It sailed on the Seine and later at Dover in England.

Brude improved on Donvig's design in several ways, but most importantly by giving his all-metal boat an egg-shaped hull that was more hydrodynamically efficient under sail than Donvig's ball. The second Norwegian designer also thoughtfully included a folding mast, so his boat could be sailed to safety if necessary. A standing lug, simple to handle, was included with each boat.

To prove the value of his lifeboat, Captain Brude and three sailors set off from Ålesund on August 7, 1904. Clearing the lovely green fjord, they directed their course southwest toward the Shetland Islands and arrived there after only two days. This was a promising start for a boat that strained the old rule of "if it looks right, it is right." The *Uræd* didn't look *quite* right, and as events bore out, it never sailed quite right—the old rule held.

After sitting out a ten-day blow in the Shetlands, Brude and crew were off again. Two weeks of good sailing followed, but then they ran into another gale. Brude ordered the mast folded down and a sea anchor deployed, attached to the heavy metal floating egg with no less than a half-inch-diameter steel cable, but the cable snapped. A makeshift replacement anchor was then deployed, which did the job. Brude claimed that even in these conditions the boat was so well ballasted (in addition to the steel swing keel they had five hundred gallons of freshwater in the lower compartments) that "a glass of water could stand on the table in very rough weather without falling down." This cable-busting wicked storm grew in intensity to hurricane force and lasted two days, but, according to the proud designer, "the *Uræd* behaved splendidly all the time."

Though the metal egg may have behaved well, the weather certainly didn't. On October 4 they were hit by such a terrific gale that it broke their eighteen-foot mast seven feet from the top and knocked down the stormsail. Brude calculated that the storm blew them three hundred miles to the east over the next four days. Another strong storm struck on October 14 that succeeded in wrenching away the sail, as well as driving them farther east. Late in October, approaching three months' confinement in the steel cocoon, they ran into their first snowstorm. Optimistic Ole later wrote about that day, "all was still going on well."

On November 17 they finally reached Saint John's, Newfoundland, and accepted a tow into the harbor. It had taken them eighty-seven long, wearying days of close confinement to make the east–west crossing.

Brude wasn't content to end the journey in the Canadian northeast. He knew that for the world to hear of his invention he would have to sail her into a major American port, Boston, his original goal. So they departed Saint John's on November 26, fighting northwest winds all the way down the coast. By Christmas they had only made Nova Scotia! The day after New Year's they ran into another hurricane, which bent the iron pole they had previously substituted for their broken mast. Three days later *Uræd* reached the approaches to Boston, but the weather was so bad that no tug would come out to tow them in. Finally on January 7 they made landfall near Gloucester. Here they repaired the mast and ate fresh food for the first time in five months. On January 16 they left the fishing village in the morning and arrived at Boston in the afternoon to a grand welcome.

Brude claimed that the voyage proved the strength of the egg design and was a complete triumph. He was half right. The voyage proved the boat was tough, but it also proved what an unwieldy craft it was. It was simply too big and cumbersome to be carried in sufficient quantities on liners of the time. Furthermore, it was expensive.

In all, twenty-two Brude lifeboats were built and put into service. One of them actually fulfilled its mission when on the night of April 22, 1917, the cargo ship *Giskø* was torpedoed off the Norwegian coast at Sognefjorden. The crew saved themselves with both a Brude lifeboat and a conventional one. That Brude boat is the only remaining example of the type in existence today and holds the place of honor in a museum at Ålesund near where the original was launched. Today the world's most advanced lifeboats use Brude's concepts of foolproof deployment, monocoque structure, and encapsulation. These "free-fall lifeboats" also bear a re-

The 1904 Brude boat is still the object of an international egg hunt. This sole surviving Brude's Egg lifeboat is on the water after a recent restoration in Norway.

markable resemblance to the *Uræd*, differing mostly in being made from composites and having engines for propulsion. Brude's egg was a noble experiment that landed sunny-side down.

In 1911 a young engineer with the heart of a poet built a sailing canoe and went on a sweeping five-month romantic ramble through the Lesser Antilles that has become a legend amongst small-boat sailors. He was Frederic "Fritz" Fenger, a Cornell- and MIT-trained mechanical engineer and naval architect. To be tied down to a desk was more than his wanderlust-struck soul could stand, so when he heard the call of the warm Caribbean Sea he responded. Fenger designed and had built a poet's version of a sailing canoe, which he dubbed *Yakaboo*, "good-bye" in one of the Polynesian dialects. She was seventeen feet long, thirty-nine inches wide, and planked out of quarter-inch cedar. Though at 147 pounds she would have been considered hefty even in her own day, Fenger was smart enough to realize that she would see hard use, encounter coral reefs, and be subjected to short, choppy seas. *Yakaboo* was built to last, he hoped.

Fenger's design breakthrough was the installation of a sliding daggerboard. He had read that Polynesian canoes were balanced by moving a daggerboard forward and backward through a slit in the bound-log hulls and thought that he could do something similar on his canoe. To that end he built a long centerboard trunk into his boat, but left the top off. The narrow daggerboard he used could slide back and forth, which allowed Fenger to balance the forces of the boat's hull and its two batwing-type sails exactly on the daggerboard blade. This obviated the need for a rudder and the attendant cables and pedals. He was doing on water what designers of tailless aircraft like the B-2 bomber do in the sky—reducing drag to increase speed. It worked brilliantly.

An engineer by training, but a poetic sailor by temperament, Frederic "Fritz" Fenger hikes out on *Yakaboo* somewhere in the Caribbean.

He planned to hitch a ride from New York City on a southbound tramp steamer to Grenada and from there sail fifteen hundred miles north along the Leeward and Windward Islands archipelago, ending his trip in the Virgin Islands. Arriving in Grenada in January, Fenger was eager to put his boat in the water and start, but then he learned from the locals that his assumptions about wind direction, sea conditions, tidal flows, and even sharks were all wrong. He had relied on charts bought in New England, and those didn't accurately describe the conditions he was about to encounter. He solved his problem by picking the brains of the locals, mostly the whale-hunting descendants of African slaves. Knowing the conditions firsthand, they told him how to manage the tricky currents and tide races. They warned him that the moon had a greater effect on wind and weather than most sailors realized. During the trip Fenger came to believe that, too.

On February 9 he finally shoved off from Saint George's and headed north. The *Yakaboo* was divided into three compartments, the fore and aft ones designed to be watertight. By his second day out he discovered that the forward compartment had sprung a leak and ever so slowly he was nosing into the sea. He landed, attempted a repair, and then went on to the northern tip of Grenada, where he landed again. By chance he met a European trader who owned a whaling station on the first island of the Grenadines, Île de Caille. He offered Fenger the use of his cabin there so that he would have time to repair his canoe, and, if he wanted, to go whaling. Fenger accepted the offer and was taken there by boat, with the *Yakaboo* as cargo. For the next few weeks he served as crew in one of the island's two six-man whaleboats, gladly going out with the native hunters chasing humpbacks.

After experiencing the thrill of catching multiton animals in a small boat, Fenger resumed his voyage in the canoe, now with a pet tarantula as mascot. *Yakaboo* sailed beautifully, but it continued to leak. Up through the Grenadines he went, each day trying to make his cranky boat keep its head above water long enough for him to fetch the next island. At night he camped on the beach and ate what provisions he had brought; he had an ample supply. Into such a small boat Fenger had crammed nearly two hundred pounds of food, camping gear, firearms, and photographic equipment, including a portable darkroom! In an era before boutique paddling outfitters he had made his own dry bags from muslin impregnated with linseed oil in the fashion of the early American balloon aeronauts. Painting boiled linseed oil on fabric is a primitive way of waterproofing it, but Fenger's bags remained dryer than his boat throughout the trip.

Other than sinking, his biggest fear was sharks. With only seven inches of freeboard, the same as Bligh had, he always feared that a shark might leap over the rail and attack him. To prevent that he kept a pistol handy in the cockpit and a wary eye out at all times. His fears seemed justified while heading toward West Cape on the island of Bequia he suddenly found himself surrounded by nineteen menacing fins, without enough ammunition to deal with them all. As he considered how many he could kill with his ax before they got him, one of them leaped out of the water, somersaulted in the air, and landed on its back. They were all porpoises.

That episode characterized his whole trip. Danger was always present, yet each day brought a new romantic interlude with different island locales and island people. Fenger lingered along his Caribbean trip and savored what each island had to offer—coconuts on deserted islands and unaffected natives on inhabited ones. He saw the islands before they had become kitschy aircraft "carriers" for inbound tourist jets and before the local people had become hawkers of trinkets to bored suburbanites seeking a quick winter tan or quicker weekend sin.

In all, Fenger and *Yakaboo* sailed five hundred hull-pounding miles from Grenada to Saba in the Leeward Islands. He reported that his deck was awash in seawater for all but about thirty miles. It was a much more demanding and wetter cruise than he had envisioned, mostly because of the opposing winds, currents, and tides. If he had not had the experience of the native boatmen to guide him, he wouldn't have gotten that far.

At Saba Fenger realized that his health was failing. He was light complected; his winter cruise had stretched all the way through the spring and into July, and he physically couldn't tolerate the heat or the ultraviolet rays of the sun any longer. He was laid low by attacks of sunstroke that worsened the farther he went. His growing illness and the fact that *Yakaboo* continued to leak forced him to give up the idea of attempting the 110-mile run from Saba to the Virgin Islands. Instead he shipped his boat to Virgin Gorda and after an attempt to sail the Drake Channel gave up because of the blistering sun. It had been a remarkable cruise in a well-designed, though evidently not well-built, boat. The narrative that Fenger left of the cruise, *Alone in the Caribbean*, stands with Richard Maury's *Saga of "Cimba"* as the most beautifully written of all the sea travelogues, and that's saying something because the sea has often wheedled fine tales out of its doting lovers.

In the years preceding World War I, there was a great race to see which country could plant its flag first on the two poles. American Robert Peary claimed to be the first to reach the North Pole in 1909, though that claim is now widely disputed, while Norwegian Roald Amundsen became the first to reach the South Pole in 1911, a claim that isn't. Britain was in the running for these honors, too, but its great explorer, Robert Falcon Scott, had been beaten to the South Pole by the Norwegian. The only remaining polar prize now was the crossing of Antarctica by land via the Pole, a journey of eighteen hundred miles across an unexplored frozen wasteland. One of the officers of Scott's South Pole expedition, Ernest Shackleton, was determined to be the first to do it.

Shackleton had the backing of the British government for his expedition, as well as of the Royal Geographical Society and the wealthy industrialist Sir James Caird. He made his preparations in secret and announced them only in January 1914 so he would have adequate time to select an able crew. His party would consist of eleven scientists and seventeen seamen.

In late July he, his crew, and their ship *Endurance* were in London and about to depart for Cowes to be inspected by King George V during Cowes Week, much as Boyton had stood inspection forty years earlier by George's grandmother Queen Victoria. Mysteriously, the king sent last-minute word canceling the rendezvous, and a few days later while at anchor off Margate Shackleton learned the reason from a newspaper. King George was about to declare war against his cousin Wilhelm, Kaiser of Germany.

Immediately Shackleton contacted the Admiralty and volunteered his ship and crew for naval duties. But Winston Churchill, then the First Lord of the Admiralty, who considered British polar exploration a useful way to project the nation's image as vigorous and resolute, ordered Shackleton to proceed with his expedition as planned. On August 8 *Endurance* cleared Plymouth bound for the Weddell Sea.

In late December 1914, after resting on South Georgia Island, they pushed south, but soon ran into pack ice. Nosing through the floating ice islands was slow going, but it was then the height of the Antarctic summer, so they felt confident of reaching land before the ice froze solidly around them. That wasn't to be. On January 22, 1915, within sight of land, their ship was surrounded and locked in the grip of a giant ice floe at 77 degrees South. That was as far south as they would go. They began a long, slow drift to the west that would last for the next nine months.

By October 1915 the ship had drifted twelve hundred miles across the frozen Weddell Sea, but her hull was being crushed by the relentless ice. When the planking could no longer stand the strain and began to burst open, the crew off-loaded as much cargo as their ship's three small boats could carry and prepared to make a desperate bid for survival. Their only hope was to pull the boats over the floes to find open water and then make for solid ground on an island outside the belts of solid and loose pack ice that surround Antarctica. Dragging the boats and their tons of supplies over the ice floes was brutal work. Their biggest fear wasn't falling through thin sections of ice so much as it was killer whales that might suddenly burst up through the ice and snatch one of them. They had seen huge holes in the ice where the whales had done this to grab a seal, and the men themselves had been stalked at times by the whales under the ice.

The farther north they marched, the less stable the ice became. One night while they were sleeping in their tents, a floe cracked directly under one of the tents and a man fell into the water and went under. In an instant Shackleton reached down and hauled him and his sleeping bag half full of water to the surface just as the two halves of the thousand-ton floe slammed back together. It was a near thing, but the man's life was saved by Shackleton's quick action.

On April 9, 1916, they got into the boats and, using oars both to row and to fend off ice, fought their way north. They had to make Elephant Island before the return of the Antarctic winter ice froze their boats in place and crushed them as it had done the *Endurance*, but getting through the floes and into the open water further taxed the exhausted crew. The winds blew at gale force and the seas ran high. All three boats were overloaded to the point of capsizing and were subject to constant inflows of seawater. The men had to bail constantly to stay afloat, which meant reaching into freezing seawater with buckets because the brass bilge pumps they had made from parts they'd ripped off the *Endurance* couldn't handle the job alone. Each boat was equipped with a mast and sails, which spelled the rowers when clear of the ice, but sailing meant that the lee rail was lower than before and even more water could come in. In addition, even in the open water they risked chunks of ice staving in a plank, and one boat suffered a hole above the waterline after striking a small berg. For four days they fought heavy seas and worried their way north to where they hoped Elephant Island would be. Shackleton had signed on Frank Worsley to skipper the *Endurance*, and it fell to this man now to navigate, using only the briefest glimpses of sun and stars to calculate their position. Worsley was a master at the art and brought up the island dead ahead. When he stepped on Elephant Island, Shackleton hadn't been asleep in the previous one hundred hours, but he remained awake to supervise the setting up of their camp and the safe beaching of the boats.

Over the next week the men shifted camp to a drier beach, but Shackleton and Worsley knew that to try to sit out the winter on the island would mean death. They had been subsisting mostly on seals and penguins, and the winter supply of them on the island was uncertain. They had to be rescued or die there. Since no one in the outside world knew where they were, they would have to go for help, but from whom?

Worsley had made contingency plans for this back during the long drift on the *Endurance*. There were three possibilities: Cape Horn to the northwest, closest at five hundred miles distance, the Falkland Islands north at six hundred miles, and last the South Georgia Islands northeast at eight hundred miles. Worsley and Shackleton both agreed it would have to be the last because they wouldn't be able to beat against the westerly gales and current in the Drake Passage. Although the farthest of the three, South Georgia was in the direction of the wind and current.

Only one of the boats was suitable for such a journey in the midst of the absolutely worst sea conditions on the planet, the British-built *James L. Caird* that Worsley had ordered made to his specifications by the Messrs. W. J. Leslie boatyard in London. The *Caird* was twenty-two and a half feet long and six feet wide. The two other boats were

Norwegian craft that came with the Norwegian-built *Endurance*, good boats, but a little smaller than the *Caird* and not true double-enders. Were Worsley's boat skills good enough to get the *Caird* to its destination? Shackleton admitted he knew nothing about small-boat sailing. It was up to Worsley to both navigate and skipper, and if he missed South Georgia the next stop would be Africa.

In preparation the *Caird* was modified by adding a deck made from scrap pieces of packing crates and sled runners. Its two flotation tanks were removed on Shackleton's orders, and more ballast installed in their place. This worried Worsley, as did the sail plan of standing lug, jib, and a small mizzen. He felt the mizzen sail meant that the boat would constantly work windward and would require constant compensating rudder correction, which in turn would rob them of speed and might make the boat more vulnerable to broaching. Overruling these fears was the fact that because of the short masts the boat needed more sail area and the mizzen was the only way to get it.

On the morning of April 24, 1916, Shackleton, Worsley, and four crewmen received a final load of supplies from shore and set off. There was a small break in the weather, and in the distance they could see a

The Shackleton expedition's photographer, Frank Hurley, captured the moment of launching the *James L. Caird* on a last-chance bid to find help 800 miles away on South Georgia Island.

gap in the ice that led out to the open sea. These facts, and the fact that it was Easter Monday seemed to them to be auspicious signs. Little did Shackleton know that on that very same day back in the country of his birth Irish nationalists had begun what would become known as the Easter Rebellion against their English rulers. Everyone, it turned out, was in for a time of it.

The first hour of the trip went well, and under sail they made about three miles. Then they ran into another belt of ice. Out came the oars, which again were used for propulsion and defense. When they reached the open ocean, the sea became hostile. Two men had to bail constantly while the others manned the oars or trimmed the sails. To prepare food two men had to wedge themselves against the sides of the hull and press on the Primus stove with their feet while a third hand managed the pot.

Howling gale winds assaulted their ears, while great dollops of frozen seawater stung their faces. Frostbite was nothing new, but in the rocking boat the only place to find any protection from the wind's bite was the forward covered deck. The winter gear they had brought with them at the beginning of the trip two years ago was now worn down to patched rags. Cold, salt-encrusted leather hides covered wool undergarments and every bit of it was soaked. When the clothes weren't frozen to their bodies, they were wet against them, and the only relief from the dank and frozen chill was sleep, but there was little of that to be had in a boat that tossed around its occupants as if they were dice in a tumbler.

When the winds were reasonable they could make good ninety miles or more in a day, but the winds usually weren't reasonable. It was the onset of winter in the Antarctic and the conditions were savage. Up a giant swell the *Caird* would be blown and then down the lee slope it would race. In the trough the sail would go slack and the boat would wallow, losing steerage, always a dangerous time in a small craft. On the top of the crest they were totally exposed to the killing winds, while down in the trough breaking waves poured in buckets of ice water. The continuous bucking motion of the boat, like an unbroken horse, made some of the men sick in addition to the agonies of the freezing temperature, wet spray, and lack of food. To make matters even worse they found that one of their water barrels had been holed and seawater had gotten inside, spoiling half their water supply.

Six days out saw them a third of the way along. With 238 miles behind them, it seemed they had a chance, but the weather was getting colder. It got so cold at night they had to take in the sails for fear of their freezing in place. The waves that broke over the boat left sheets of ice, adding tremendous weight to the improvised decking. Shackleton ordered the men, despite their misery and the great danger, to climb onto the slippery deck and chip it off. This vital work became a constant battle because with its heavy ballast, six men, and supplies for a month at sea the *Caird* was riding low in the water even without the added weight of the ice. Fortunately, the ship's carpenter had had the foresight to use one of the other boat's masts as a doubler for the *Caird*'s keel. He had bolted this timber in place to reinforce the keel the way Okeley had used a sapling on his folding boat for the same purpose.

Fighting the ice on deck became such a never-ending battle that someone finally had the idea to attach two of the oars to the mast stays, thus forming a makeshift guard rail. It made ice-chipping much safer, but no more enjoyable. But the weight of the ice still had to be reduced, as did the weight of the supplies in the boat. Two waterlogged, rotting reindeer-skin sleeping bags were jettisoned, which Worsley thought must have together weighed eighty pounds.

With the boat lighter, it rolled more, and the men were even less comfortable, if that were possible. Yet the strain on the boat from the pounding seas was all the *Caird* could bear, so lightening its load was paramount. They were lucky they did. On the ninth day out Shackleton was at the tiller and just happened to look behind him. He saw a bright line along the horizon, which confused him for a moment until he realized that the horizon was in reality a monstrous wave with a breaking top thundering right for the boat! He called out for all hands to hold on but was immediately submerged in the freezing broil of the rogue wave. By a miracle, or by Shackleton's insistence on extra ballast, the boat remained upright, though flooded. All hands flew to the work of emptying the ice water, and the boat was saved. However, when the worst of the water was out they found that the glass protecting the compass had been smashed. By good fortune the compass needle itself still seemed to indicate properly.

The next day the seas calmed and the sun came out. While the others laid out their frozen clothes and sleeping bags on deck to dry, Worsley was able to get his first sun shot in six days. By his calculations they were more than halfway there. When he reported this to the others their spirits soared, but now the earlier spoilage of half their water supply became an issue. They would have to outrace their water to South Georgia.

Parched and fading fast, they finally saw land after noon on May 8, fifteen days into the trip. It was Cape Demidov on the southwest coast. On approaching the shore they met breaking waves that marked an uncharted shoal, so they headed back out to sea to avoid a night landing. When the morning came they found themselves fighting for their lives against the fiercest weather Shackleton and Worsley had ever seen. They were blown down the coast toward Hauge Reef but managed to put out to sea once again and ride it out. That night the winds died down and suddenly a favorable wind sprang up that they rode into King Haakon Bay, where they landed the next morning.

Huge surf and a rocky shore confront the redoubtable *Caird* as she approaches the end of her terrifying gamble to reach South Georgia. Once landed, Shackleton learned he was on the wrong side of the island.

Having survived nine months drifting on unstable ice floes on board the *Endurance* and then marching over the crumbling ice floes to the edge of the Weddell Sea and then the journey to Elephant Island and now this most incredible journey of eight hundred miles through the ugliest weather imaginable—and to have finally arrived at South Georgia—the men found themselves on the wrong side of the island. They knew the whaling station they needed to reach was at

Stromness Bay on the *north* side of the island. There were two ways to get there: by relaunching the *Caird* and risking another bout of hurricane-force conditions, or by climbing the nine-thousand-foot mountains and crossing the seventeen miles of rocks and glacier fields without a map or any climbing equipment to reach the other side of the island. Shackleton choose the latter. Neither the *Caird* nor the crew could stomach any more sea battles.

Shackleton left the two weakened members of the crew in the care of a third member, and with Worsley and a third man set out to cross the island. Their thirty-six-hour trek is an epic of mountaineering as well as orienteering. On the morning of May 20 they thought they must be somewhere near the station, but in the fog and haze they didn't know which direction to descend. Shackleton then had an inspired thought. Looking at his watch he saw it was 6:30 in the morning. He told his companions to rest for a half-hour and thirty minutes later, exactly at 7:00 A.M., as he had predicted, the whistle blew at the whaling station calling its workers to their posts and guiding Shackleton's party to the station.

For the next three and a half months Shackleton tried to rescue his men left behind on Elephant Island. On his first attempt the Norwegian whaler *Southern Sky* was shut out by pack ice. The Uruguayan government then lent him the trawler *Instituto de Pesca*, but it too was unable to make headway against the ice. Concerned Chilean and British citizens now joined together to raise enough money to hire the schooner *Emma*, but when she was only one hundred miles away her engine gave out and she had to bear off. Finally, Chile lent the steamer *Yelcho*. With Shackleton aboard, she arrived at Elephant Island on August 30, a hundred and five days after the men had established camp there. Shackleton, in the bow, yelled to one of them on shore, "Are you all well?"

The reply came, "All safe, all well."

"Thank God," Shackleton said. Not one man of the twenty-eight had been lost despite all their harrowing adventures. Shackleton's leadership, and Worsley's seamanship, had saved them.

In his *Evolution of Singlehanders* D. H. Clarke tells of a day in 1941 when, while on leave from RAF flying duties on the Devon coast, he met an old fisherman who told him a strange tale. The fisherman said that one day in 1903 or 1904 he spotted a small clinker-built sailboat of about eighteen feet on the shingle at Hope Cove (part of present-day Torquay). Approaching the boat, he was shocked to find that its skipper was a twenty-something woman dressed in gray, physically worn out and covered with salt sores, filling a container with water from a little stream. He took her back to his cottage, where his wife fed and bathed her. While receiving this hospitality she told her hosts that she had just crossed the Atlantic, coming from America. The fisherman later gave to Clarke a photograph of the woman in front of her boat (taken before her departure from America); on the photo was the signed name "Gladys Gradely," or at least that's what the script looked like to Clarke. Years after the war, the photograph was among Clarke's belongings lost when his live-aboard boat sank. Since then, nothing more has ever turned up about a Gladys Gradely, who, if these facts are true, was the first woman in history to sail a boat alone across an ocean.

In July 1902 an equally mysterious Mr. and Mrs. Bradley crossed the Atlantic in the sixteen-foot *Jane Crooker*, landed in Dover, and then immediately set off for Antwerp. Their story appeared in the July 22, 1902, issue of the London *Times*.

> ACROSS THE ATLANTIC IN A SMALL BOAT
> *Last night a small covered-in sailing boat, 16ft. in length, arrived at Dover. The occupants, Mr. and Mrs. Bradley, who are stated to be on their honeymoon, had crossed the Atlantic from Nova Scotia. Mr. Bradley stated that some rough weather had been experienced, but the vessel had stood it splendidly. He left Dover again for Antwerp and will subsequently visit London.*

After the war, when Clarke came upon the *Times* piece, he speculated that somehow these two women voyagers were one and the same. "Gradely" might easily have been transposed into "Bradley," or vice versa. Also, the dates of the alleged voyages seemed too close to be coincidental. Other researchers thought this plausible, too.

Sometime later Clarke received information independently confirming the existence of the Bradley voyage. The Bradleys' boat was the *Jane Crooker*, and they took a dog along. But they couldn't have been the Gladys Gradely of Hope Cove.

Why had the Bradleys pushed on so quickly, though? In researching this book, picking up the trail of the nautical newlyweds, the only clue that could be found was that they may have hurried off to Belgium because the International Regatta at Oostende was beginning that third week of July. The regatta was mainly for large, fifty-ton racing yachts, but perhaps the Bradleys thought their little boat would be a great novelty. More than that hasn't been found, though research continues.

Gladys, though, is still completely elusive. Who was this strong-willed, talented, liberated Edwardian woman who made a historic journey only to duck immediately into the shadows of history? She probably came from an upper-middle-class family, since she could obtain a boat, provision it, and also have souvenir photos professionally made to pass out. She must have been a talented sailor to start with, so she probably came from a coastal town in America, probably New England, where sailing was common for both boys and girls. Her casual daring and lack of need for publicity—shown by the fact that she didn't end her trip at Hope Cove and head for the nearest telegraph office, as Boyton did—seems to say that all she wanted was personal satisfaction. Perhaps she came from a liberal-minded and well-educated family. The daughter of a Massachusetts or Maine preacher, perhaps? If ever revealed, the truth is likely to be completely different, but not less exciting. For now, the mystery of Hope Cove remains, but the lady has vanished.

→ 6 ←

LOVERS
AND OTHER
LOSERS

1920–1930s

◆ FRANZ ROMER: CANOEIST OR KAYAKER? ◆ *LIEBE* STORY: PAUL AND AGA MÜLLER
◆ LEAVING LATVIA: THE REBELL YELL ◆ IVY LEAGUE VAGABONDS ◆

IN 1915 FRANZISKUS ROMER ATTAINED THE AGE OF SIXTEEN.
Finally! Now he was old enough to leave his parents' farm at Dettingen on the shore of the Bodensee (Lake Constance) near the Swiss border and contribute his skills to the war effort. Across the lake he hurried
to Friedrichshafen, to the huge factory where the mighty zeppelins were
built, and there looked for work. Skills? He had none. Further, he found

that zeppelins were much like redwood trees—large, elegant, but for-ever in the making. That was work for women and old men, he grum-bled. He wanted action and adventure *now*, and if he couldn't find it in the air, then he would find it on the sea.

He volunteered for duty in the Kaiserliche Marine and was sent to serve on the Baltic Sea minesweeper *Adler* (Eagle). In late August 1917 the *Adler* itself struck a mine and went down, taking many of its crew with her. Romer gallantly tried to rescue others despite his own wounds; he was saved by a fishing boat and later commended for his bravery. After a long spell in a hospital his request to learn to pilot sea-planes was granted, so he went to the Naval Flying School, but the Armistice was signed before he could qualify as a pilot. Next he earned a coveted spot at the Seaman's School in Hamburg and there began his training to be a ship's officer. How proud he was when he earned his license and became a qualified officer for the great Hamburg-America Line (HAPAG). The Bodensee was but a pond compared to the many seas and oceans he now crossed.

It was all smooth sailing for Romer in 1928. He had a steady job, in fact, a career, he was seeing the world, he had married a girl named Maria, and all was well . . . except for that yearning that softly though steadily tugged at his heart. What had happened to the little boy who had wanted to fly zeppelins? He was now third officer on large, transoceanic passenger liners, but it was too routine for a twenty-nine-year-old at the height of the Jazz Age. He needed to *do* something. That desire for adventure still beat within him.

Do what, though? Charles Lindbergh was the hero of the hour, and young men and women all around the world went rushing off to emulate his great transatlantic flight. Romer, too, had sought spon-sorship for a record flight in 1926, a year before Lindbergh's *Spirit of Saint Louis* landed at Le Bourget in Paris. After the war, at his own ex-pense, he had earned his pilot's license, and in 1926 he tried to talk Junkers, the German aircraft firm that had pioneered all-metal aircraft, into lending him a plane to make the first airplane flight between

Art on facing page: Franziskus "Franz" Romer in his HAPAG uniform. He had hoped to beat Lindbergh across the Atlantic.

Hamburg and New York. They declined because they felt he was too inexperienced a pilot.

According to an interview Romer gave later, one of Germany's many folding-kayak companies heard about his desire to make a record journey across the Atlantic and proposed to him that instead of an airplane he take one of their boats. The company was Klepper, one of only two German folding-boat manufacturers that survived and are still making folding kayaks today.

The first practical folding kayak was produced in Germany in 1907 by Johann Klepper, a tailor in Rosenheim, just east of Munich. Twenty years later there were dozens of companies around the world spitting out the lightweight wooden-framed pleasure craft. Many of those companies were German, and on weekends every lake and river in the country saw paddlers who arrived by train with their kayaks folded into bags carried on board as luggage.

The kayak built for Romer was in no way an off-the-shelf model, as has sometimes been suggested. It was a one-off "super" folder, though it was never intended to be folded. Its length was nineteen and a half feet, beam thirty-nine inches, depth about eighteen inches, and though built in the traditional Klepper manner with straight-grain wood longerons and plywood frames, it was immensely strong. One picture taken during construction shows a man crawled up into the bow while the uncovered frame rests on two sawhorses, both of them *aft* of his feet. The key to the boat's exceptional strength was the use of nonstandard crossed diagonal bracing fore and aft of the cockpit. This type of bracing, called a "Long truss" (after the inventor) by bridge engineers, was not used in the cockpit sections of the boat, probably because the designer realized that a long, slender boat could survive on the ocean only if its hull was flexible. Thus the design allowed for some hogging of the hull to absorb uneven loading in choppy water. A biography of Romer written years after his voyage states that Romer *alone* designed the hull. This is highly unlikely. Neither Klepper the tailor nor Romer the professional mariner was a structural engineer, and this boat was simply too sophisticated for amateurs. Probably Romer laid out the general specifications for the boat but a competent engineer did the detailed design work.

Publicity photos of the boat, named the *Deutscher Sport*, show a mirthful Captain Romer in the cockpit with a double-bladed paddle in hand. Certainly Johann Klepper was trying to emphasize that this was a kayak that would make the voyage, but in reality it was ketch rigged and would be sailed, using sails Romer could handle from his cockpit. He would have to. Standing or moving around the boat was strictly forbidden. It was a kayak, after all, and, unlike Andrews's *Sapolio* folder, had only fabric decks. A pedal-controlled shoal-draft rudder was used for steering the chunky craft—chunky by normal kayak standards, that is. Its interior was so cavernous that when all the food, water, and equipment was stowed away, Romer had about three quarters of a ton of cargo on board, not including his own weight!

A unique feature of the design was the inclusion of internal inflatable gasbags, as well as external inflatable sponsons (air chambers). These bags could be inflated as needed from an onboard carbide gas generator that was likely taken from an old

Romer is dwarfed by the hefty kayak frame of the *Deutscher Sport*.

"brass-era" automobile. By 1928, cars used electric headlights, but just a few years before, headlamps had been powered by acetylene gas created inside a metal cylinder by slowly dripping water onto calcium carbide; a pipe from this cylinder led to the headlamps, which were then lit manually. Romer would have had to be very careful when lighting his Primus cooking stove near these bags, though Germans of the day seemed not to mind the close proximity of explosive gasbags to potential sources of ignition (they finally learned their lesson when the dirigible *Hindenburg*, built by Romer's boyhood heroes at the Zeppelin factory, blew up spectacularly over New Jersey only nine years later).

The Klepper-Romer internal bags, though filled with ordinary air, would later become standard on almost all modern folding kayaks, while the sponsons would be used on military kayaks employed by special forces after World War II. Another feature of Romer's boat seen on oceangoing kayaks many years later was a foot-operated bilge pump. The *Deutscher Sport* was then the most sophisticated small boat ever to attempt an Atlantic crossing (not the primitive Inuit skin boat that cinema audiences of the time were seeing in the first great documentary, *Nanook of the North*).

In March 1928 Romer took his boat, gear, and new wife to Lisbon, where he wisely did something few of our adventurers had done thus far—conducted sea trials. Satisfied with the boat, he made a short hop down to Cape Saint Vincent, where finally on April 17 he kissed his wife good-bye and began his voyage. Eleven days later he made the first of the Canary Islands, Lanzarote, where he spent four days recovering

Romer in front of the Klepper factory in Rosenheim just east of Munich.

from the stress of the first six-hundred-mile leg. On May 2 he set out for the capital of the Canaries, Las Palmas, arriving on May 10. A fever he contracted on the islands laid him low for the next three weeks, and he wasn't fit enough to put out until June 3, when he began the three-thousand-mile crossing to the Antilles. Considering how hard the first six-hundred-mile leg had been, what did he imagine the next three thousand miles would be like?

Most sailors consider the trade-wind route from the Canaries to the Antilles a milk run, nothing to it, but that wasn't Romer's experience. His woes began immediately when his foot pump broke and couldn't be repaired, so he had to bail with a one-gallon metal food tin. The problem with this was that the cockpit was so confined he couldn't easily immerse the tin in the bilgewater. Each dip required an elaborate contortion made all the more difficult because his leg muscles had atrophied from inactivity. The foresight to install the internal gasbags now paid off because without them the boat would have flooded and endangered his provisions. Nevertheless, Romer fought an endless battle with the bilgewater all the way across, though early on he reached a compromise—he accepted the fact that, due to the boat's framework, he would never get it all out. This compromise cost him in other ways, though. Sitting in a pool of seawater soon caused sores to appear along his legs and buttocks. As painful as these were, they were no worse than the blisters on his upper body caused by the constant exposure to the unrestrained tropical sun. His hat had been washed away, which left him totally at the mercy of the sun. It was as if he had become a Christmas goose basting in a roasting pan. The mist from the seawater in his boat rose to join the beads of salty sweat pouring out of him from the heat.

Fatigue was another problem. During the journey he was afraid to close his eyes because of the possibility of a wave knocking him over, or of being run down by a ship. Originally he had installed a closeable hatch over the cockpit with a yard-long snorkel-like air tube extending above it, a tube with a hole in the front to allow air in but was designed to be high enough above the deck to keep water out. Romer gave up this Rube Goldberg contraption when he realized the power of sea swells and the danger of his not staying on watch.

With no sleep even little duties took on the challenge of a trial of strength, but he just didn't have any. Utterly exhausted and suffering from bouts of malaria, he trained himself to catch moments of sleep between waves. He would stay awake while riding up the slope of a wave and on top of it, but as he came down and settled in the trough he would shut his eyes and sleep for perhaps three seconds and then repeat the sequence.

Food was another problem. His little Primus would have been fine on a mountainside or even a larger boat, but on the wet, undulating wooden cross slats of the kayak's frame it was hard to light, let alone adjust. One day the stove caught fire and would have set fire to the boat and the acetylene-filled gas bags if Romer had not instantly thrown it overboard. It was a close call, as well as a costly one—now he had no way to warm his food, which just added to the misery of his soggy confinement. The inevitable consequence of all this was the onset of hallucinations: clouds became islands, wave crests became animals or ships. His mind retreated into a realm of half-truths and half-imaginings.

He didn't imagine, though, the huge shark and her three cubs that invited themselves to lunch one day, circling the boat and then diving under it. The mother came up under the hull and ran her back along the underside. Halfway along she lifted, and the *Deutscher Sport* began to come out of the water. Romer was justifiably alarmed and grabbed the nearest weapon he could find: an American flag on a short pole. The shark had swum off but a few seconds later returned for another rub. This time Romer was ready and slammed the flagstaff squarely on her back as she went under the boat. The monstrous beast appeared off the other beam and leaped into the air angrily, landing with a splash. Romer spun around in the boat looking on all points for her next attack while a minute went by and then a few more. She never returned. If it had not been for the longitudinal flexibility of the kayak, the shark might very well have cracked the boat's back and secured her lunch. Only because the boat wasn't overbuilt or underbuilt did Romer survive that encounter.

On July 18, after six weeks without seeing another boat, he finally spoke with the Yugoslav ship *Epidauro*. The captain kindly gave the

fading Romer five gallons of freshwater, twenty cans of fruit, some bananas, and a little spirit stove. Most helpful, though, was a hat. Romer
now had a fighting chance.

Twelve days later, on July 30, after fifty-eight numbing days at sea,
he arrived at Saint Thomas in the Virgin Islands. He collapsed on getting out of the boat but was cared for by the friendly islanders, who
hailed him as "the new Lindbergh." Just like Lindbergh, who had been
honored with a ticker-tape parade in New York the year before, Romer
received a parade through Saint Thomas when he had recovered suffi-
ciently from his ordeal. The governor of the island, Captain Waldo
Evans, USN, even presented him with a special medal struck just for
the occasion. Considering that the First World War had ended only ten
years earlier, Romer's kind reception in an American territory gov-
erned by a U.S. military officer is all the more remarkable.

If only Romer's voyage had ended there this would be a happy tale,
but it didn't, and his story has a tragic ending. Romer wanted to sail to
New York, so he still had fifteen hundred miles to go. He spent a month
rehabilitating his body and his boat, to which he attached two outboard
engines that had been shipped from Germany, though a shortwave radio he had wanted didn't make it on time. He departed Saint Thomas
on September 8—and sailed right into the jaws of a force 12 hurricane
that was to become known as one of the most destructive in history.
He disappeared, and no trace was ever found of the *Deutscher Sport.*
No search was ever mounted for the missing hero. Was there no one
with Columbus's ability to smell out a hurricane to warn him, or was
he just in a hurry to finish his trip that year instead of waiting for the
next sailing season? Certainly he knew it was well into the "hurricane
season." Was he in a hurry to complete the journey and return home to
Germany to his wife and job? Maritime experts speculated that perhaps
the outboard engines overstressed the hull somehow and caused a structural failure. This is possible, but most accept that the hurricane itself
was enough to do him in. No matter how it happened, the result was
the same—brave Captain Franz Romer was never seen again.

Let the record show that Romer was *not* the first to make an ocean
passage on a kayak. Inuit had done this before, perhaps a millennium

before. Okeley's Mediterranean gambit was also in a fabric-hulled boat. Nor was Romer the first to sail a folding boat across an ocean because William Andrews had done that in the *Sapolio* three decades before. *Nor* was he the first to sail across the ocean in a "bag boat," to use the term favored by today's folding-boat enthusiasts for a boat portable enough to be carried as luggage in a bag before it is erected at a body of water. The *Deutscher Sport* was not a practical folding boat, no matter what Johann Klepper implied with his photos.

What *can* be said for Romer is that he made the first *intentional* ocean crossing in a fabric- or skin-covered boat—the *Sapolio* had a solid deck and hull bottom. Those who claim that Saint Brendan did this have no evidence beyond their wishful thinking. Romer's voyage is completely authenticated. Yet his voyage was not intercontinental; he failed to reach the North American mainland.

One more thing—calling the *Deutscher Sport* a "kayak" is not really accurate. It was never meant to be double paddled and was designed primarily as a sailing craft. "Sailing canoe" is the class of boat that it was most like, and that's the fairest description of what it really was. Romantics will argue this point, but purists won't.

Whatever it's called, or whatever "first" Romer achieved or didn't, the quality of the Klepper design and that of the man who sailed it are indisputable. Franz Romer was a great pioneer who shared the best qualities of Bernard Gilboy—audacity, intelligence, a scientific approach, bravery, and persistence. Fittingly, the main street through Dettingen is today named Kapitän Romer Strasse.

While Romer was in the middle of the Atlantic sweating it out, another German began his attempt to cross the Atlantic. Unlike Romer, he had no money, no factory support, and no lofty ambition to boost struggling German industry. No, his impulse was the oldest of them all—love. Paul Müller felt that if he could cross the Atlantic in a small boat he would become famous like Lindbergh, make a lot of money, and then be able to marry his sweetheart and buy a little farm where they could find happiness forever. Happiness had proven elusive for the shy, bespectacled forty-two-year-old.

Müller's poverty was common for many laborers in Germany in 1928. The war had crippled industry, and the reparations exacted by the victors at the Versailles conference made economic recovery nearly impossible. What was uncommon about Müller's situation was that he had something of a past—a past the normally quiet man didn't like to talk about.

Müller saved his money for two years to pay for the small boat that he was having built in a Hamburg boatyard, the one he proposed to use on his transatlantic voyage. The big day came when the boat was finished, so Müller handed over the final payment and headed down the Elbe River—only to capsize a short while later. Enraged at the boat's lack of stability he flew back into the boatyard like a fox in a henhouse and smashed everything in sight, including the boat's builder. The police were called and Müller hightailed it away, still furious. He ducked into his girlfriend Agathe Gavinski's home and hid there, confessing all. She protected him. Why was true happiness so hard to find? he wondered, wiping the sweat and dust off his spectacles and the blood from his knuckles.

Who needs sailing experience when love is the spur? Not quick-tempered Paul Müller, the failed parachute tester, who somehow coaxed this worn-out fishing boat across the Atlantic in 1928 in an effort to earn enough money to marry his girl.

When the heat died down, he came out of hiding, got his anger under control, and, using the little bit of money he had left over, plus more from Aga, he bought a worn-out fishing lugger eighteen and a half feet long that he found on the Hamburg waterfront. No matter that some of the planks seemed a little springy—it would have to do. He decked her over, built a little cuddy forward, and named her for his *liebchen* Aga. Being a lugger, she had the minimum of lines to play with, and her main and jib could be doused in a hurry. What better boat to sail across the Atlantic for someone who had virtually *no* prior sailing experience, other than his capsizing!

Up the Elbe River he went on July 6, 1928, toward Cuxhaven. Unfamiliar with anchoring or mooring, he drove his boat high up onto a sandbank at high tide and got stuck there. For five days he tried to pull her off, but it wasn't until he begged a favor from a Dutch fisherman that she was freed. The fisherman towed the little boat into his homeport at Schiermonikoog and there the townspeople, hearing Müller's lovelorn story, raised a little money to help him on his way. Müller had foreseen his need to ask for money and so had painted the words "From Hamburg to America" on the side of his boat and on the sail "Home Happiness Sweetheart." This was sure to get conversation going, and conversation would lead to his sob story and that would lead to . . . free goods.

As helpful as the Netherlands was, Belgium was unfriendly. War memories lingered there, and the undocumented German sailor was not welcome. He couldn't afford a passport or proper shipping papers, so he simply did without them. As the Belgian authorities debated whether or not to impound his boat and ship him home, he slipped his moorings and sailed down the North Sea into the Channel. This is easier said than done because the French coast in the Channel is home to numerous sandbars and submerged rocks that make finding passable channels into port difficult. On top of that, the weather was bad, which made the water turbulent. He had no way to heave-to or set a riding sail, having just a single mast, but somehow he managed to stay afloat in the old tub.

At Le Havre a sympathetic compatriot bought him provisions to keep him going. At Cherbourg a like-minded Englishman helped him. In the Channel Islands he found more helpful people. There, they looked at his boat, heard his story, and told him that his boat was unfit for the Bay of Biscay—indeed an understatement! They helped him replace the rotten wood and fix the sail, provisioned him, and taught him some rudimentary sailing techniques.

Somehow little *Aga* conquered the Bay of Biscay and set into Santander, Spain. Müller received aid from the Spanish fishermen, including a set of foul-weather gear. He pushed on to Portugal. By begging at every port he managed to work his way down the coast and then across to Rabat, Morocco. Because it was under French control, he received a hostile reception there, as he had in Belgium. But Providence smiled once more on him when the Dutch consul intervened on his behalf with the local police. Sailors in port pitched in to buy him more provisions, and he was on his way down the coast to bleak Cape Juby, then over to the Canaries. It was winter now on the equator, so it wasn't as hot as when Romer had been there. Müller had different problems, in any case. He still had no money, and his provisions had run out. Following on Romer's heels he made Las Palmas, and for the umpteenth time a kindly person came forward to help him with supplies—Müller must have perfected his hound-dog face, because soon he was provisioned as well as he ever would be and so he set off into the trade winds on (you guessed it) Valentine's Day, 1929.

His goal was the Antilles, but shoddy navigation put him farther north than he intended, which meant more miles to landfall. Out of food, but not out of luck, he arrived in the Bahamas nearly starving on April 22. After a few days' rest he crawled up the back of Cuba, stopping in Havana, where again he received help after running onto a reef. Yet more media attention legitimized and further sentimentalized—if that were possible—his story, so that people were now anxious to meet and help him.

From Cuba he went north to Florida. Coasting along, he fell asleep at the helm one day and wrecked *Aga* near Fernandina. His luck became unbelievable when the Jacksonville German-American Club came forward with a gift of fifty dollars (about a thousand dollars today) to buy a secondhand replacement boat. Instead, Müller got members of the local U.S. Coast Guard station to help him repair *Aga*, which he sailed north, hoping to reach New York. Approaching Charleston, South Carolina, on the night of June 25 he ran into a terrible storm and was thrown onto Kiawah Island, were *Aga* was again wrecked. He didn't know how far he was from civilization or how safe the island would be when the tide turned, so he took what kerosene he had left, doused the little boat that had seen him across the Atlantic, and set it ablaze as a signal for help. This wasn't a romantic gesture reminiscent of a Viking ritual, as others have described it; rather it was a desperate help signal by a man who feared for his life. When no one showed up he swam for Snake Island. From there he spotted a light in a house on John's Island, fully seven miles away—and began to swim there! Fortunately, a local had spotted the burning *Aga* and was rowing down the channel to investigate. He found Müller in the water and pulled the exhausted sailor into his rowboat. Perhaps the German didn't know that alligators inhabited those waters?

How lucky can one man be? As soon as he reported his story the next day to the authorities in Charleston, he was declared a hero by the mayor, who personally arranged for Müller to be put up in the city's best hotel free of charge and given free meals and laundry service. The mayor, Thomas Porcher Stoney, then initiated an appeal to raise money to buy the foreign visitor a brand-new boat! Further, he announced that Aga Gavinski would be brought to Charleston—"America's Most Historic City," he liked to remind the gentlemen of the press—where the two would be reunited and then married in a public ceremony. When Müller announced his intention, in that case, to sail back to Germany with his bride, the mayor gleefully countered that their departure should coincide with the grand opening of the John P. Grace Memorial Bridge, set for early August.

Everything looked bright for a festive occasion just a few weeks away. Money for the new boat came in slowly but steadily. The local newspaper gave almost daily updates on Müller's doings and the search for a suitable boat, and he received offers of a free farm in upstate New York, if he would just clear the land, along with offers from a movie studio and a book publisher.

Then an unexpected snag occurred. Even though a local travel agency had arranged for the North German Lloyd line to provide Aga with free transportation from Germany, she couldn't get an entry permit from the American Embassy in Berlin. Stoney was furious, as this threatened to upset the photo opportunity he had set up for the bridge opening. He telephoned Charleston's Congressman in Washington and demanded that someone rattle the cage over at the State Department. Congressman McMillan contacted Henry Stimson, the Secretary of State, who promised to investigate the matter, but even after another week had gone by, Aga still hadn't got her passport stamped. Why would she, a simple children's governess, not be allowed into the country when all the world loves a lover and a good love story *and* she had the power of a U.S. cabinet official behind her?

Perhaps it had something to do with the fact that the embassy in Germany knew more about the polite, soft-spoken German mariner's past than he had told Charleston's reporters and mayor. It seems that Müller had been arrested before World War I on a felony count serious enough to cost him fourteen years in prison. While locked up during the war he asked to join the air service, but when he was told he was too old, he volunteered to "test" parachutes. Was he sane? Perhaps it was because of some inside knowledge that the German consul at Charleston, Herr von Dohlen, excused himself at the last minute from being Müller's best man at the wedding—how would it look back home for an up-and-coming politician to be seen endorsing the marriage of a simple German girl to a known felon and probable mental case?

This is all speculation, though. Eventually Aga got her passport stamped, the North German Lloyd line got her to New York, and she arrived in Charleston by train August 28. Meanwhile, the new boat had arrived and been modified for the intended voyage, and the bridge had been opened. The mayor missed his photo op at that one but made up for it by arranging the much-publicized wedding of Paul and Aga at the Francis Marion Hotel, where he gave away the twenty-nine-year-old dusty blonde woman of gentle manners and kind ways who spoke no English. During the ceremony she wore a donated wedding dress and received a donated wedding ring and shared with her husband a piece of the donated wedding cake atop which was set a replica of the donated new boat, *Aga II.*

Finally a bit of sanity crept back into the whole affair when Müller announced that he would sail on to New York alone and also make the return Atlantic crossing alone. While he was doing that, Aga would stay in Charleston where she would work as a nanny for the McElwees, a Charleston doctor and his wife.

At 4:00 P.M. on September 2 Müller ended his long, profitable stay in Charleston and cast off for New York in the *Aga II,* which had intentionally been built as a near replica of the original. After all the fuss, furor, and expense the German sailor had caused for the citizens of Charleston and especially for Mayor Stoney, it must have come as a supremely ironic slap in the face when they learned that Müller had wrecked their gift only a short way up the coast on Ocracoke Island, North Carolina, September 14. The boat was a total loss.

That was not the end of the maestro of mooching's sailing days, as will appear later. Müller had one more adventure up his oilskins.

———•◆•———

In faraway Australia love tugged at Pauls Sprogis's heart, too. To understand what Sprogis felt, think of Dustin Hoffman rapping on the church window in *The Graduate*, screaming, "Elaine . . . Elaine . . . !" Elaine was the name of Sprogis's beloved, too, but she did not return his affection. Sprogis was a stranger in a strange land. Born Latvian, he ran away from home so as not to have to fight for the Russians in the 1905 war against Japan. He was now living an impoverished life Down Under. But Elaine was not merciful, and Sprogis suffered.

This was not the first unfulfilled relationship in his life. After skipping out of Latvia he had gone to Germany to resume his college studies, but he soon found the kaiser's regime every bit as authoritarian as the czar's. The police were highly suspicious of a foreign student in Hamburg. Was he a socialist, or nihilist? He didn't have a job and he couldn't get one without papers. To solve that problem he bought false papers from a crook in Hamburg, Germany's capital of crime, and changed the name on the documents from "Fred Kuball" to the poetically appropriate "Fred Rebell." Using these papers he traveled the world as a ship's stoker, easily one of the worst jobs anywhere, until he eventually settled down in western Australia. He earned money as a lumberjack and with it looked for a mail-order bride back home in Latvia. From university intellectual to stoker to lumberjack: he had come down hard to reality, but at least he was trying. Lonie, a farm girl in Latvia, accepted his offer of marriage. He sent her the fare for the steamer and anxiously awaited her arrival. Lonie turned out to have a farmer's appetite ... for men, and when she got on that big ship and met all those officers in their fancy uniforms ...

Sprogis/Rebell married her though she was in the "family way" by the time she got to Australia, but later found that her appetite for male company didn't end with men in officers' uniforms. He played the cuckold for a dozen humiliating years before running away once again.

In Perth he fell in love with the beautiful Elaine, the love that would save him, he thought. He admired "the black of her hair, the luster of her dark, crystal-clear eyes, her nicely arched eyebrows." Yet, older and wiser, he saw her faults, too, "First, she had protruding knee-caps." Rebell knew he couldn't have everything, so he mused philosophically, "But what are protruding knee-caps when a man loves as I loved?" Ah, yes, the more he cried her name, though, the more strongly she rebuffed him. He was knocking on forty-five at this time; she was a mere nineteen. "Elaine ... Elaine ... !" his heart cried, but she would have none of him. Out of habit he ran away yet again, this time across the continent to Sydney. He hit Sydney just as the worldwide economic depression did. Starting on Wall Street, it had spread out to the rest of America and then to all the world, with the result that jobs were scarce, and the new kid in town was at the back of the line.

Rebell led a miserable hand-to-mouth existence on the government dole. Thoughts of suicide entered his head. He climbed to the Gap, the high point at the entrance to Sydney Harbor, and thought about jumping off. Looking down, he had a revelation—perhaps he should emigrate to America? At the American Consulate in Sydney he was told that few people were being admitted into the United States at that time because of the Depression. Rebell boldly told the official that *he* would manage to get in, with or without papers. It wouldn't be the first time he had sidestepped officialdom.

One thing that can be said about Rebell: even in his darkest hour, he *never* quit. Rash, romantic, delusory, socially inept—he was all those, but he marched on when many others would have jumped from the Gap, and many did in those years. Rebell was different, to say the least, but his idiosyncratic thought process whipped up a new plan of attack to save his unhappy life—he would get a little boat and sail it to America! He must have once again mused philosophically: what were a mere *nine thousand ocean miles* to a man running away from a broken heart?

To effect his scheme he needed cash, more than he could save from the pittance he received from the government's handout each week. Since no company would hire him, he became an itinerant handyman, even though what he knew about carpentry was entirely self-taught. He earned one-fifth his pre-Depression weekly wage, but the work led to a real job building seaside cottages, though for greatly reduced wages. Driven to make his latest dream come true, he worked long hours and saved every shilling he could.

With his hard-earned savings he bought for £20 a secondhand eighteen-foot centerboard sloop, an open boat of a class sailed then in amateur races in Sydney Harbor. Even though he had no sailing experience, Rebell realized that since this boat was only a lightweight racer, her hull might not stand the pounding she would receive on the Pacific. Therefore he reinforced her hull by doubling the ribs, and he added an external keel. He couldn't afford to buy enough wood to deck her over, so he settled on improvising a canvas spray hood-cuddy forward using a lightweight frame. This would, in practice, be an open-boat voyage across the Pacific, the first since Gilboy's.

While Rebell prepared his boat, he continued to work by day and studied in the evenings. Because he knew nothing about sailing or navigation, he taught himself both from books at the Sydney public library. From how-to manuals he learned he needed navigation instruments, but these were astronomically expensive, so he set out to make his own. Using scrap-metal pieces, a hacksaw blade, a Boy Scout telescope he bought for a shilling, and a piece of a stainless steel knife blade he sanded flat and polished to a mirror finish—he made his own sextant . . . and it worked! For a taffrail log he twisted some aluminum strips around a piece of broom handle and attached this with a line to an old alarm clock he gutted and reworked so that the minute hand on the face ticked off each mile traveled. It worked! For chronometers he used two cheap watches set in homemade gimbals, each to check the other. Navigation charts also were too expensive, so he copied an old atlas by hand and realized only on the voyage that some of the islands he came upon hadn't been discovered when the atlas was published!

Provisioning posed another problem. He estimated that he needed at least six months' food to begin the trip. He couldn't afford store-bought canned food, so he bought bulk staples like flour, rice, barley, and peas and put them in old kerosene tins with screw-cap tops. Used tins, coated with asphalt on the inside, held thirty gallons of water. Cooking would be handled with the ubiquitous Primus stove that so many adventurers found useful.

Just when Rebell thought he had solved all his problems and could depart on his trip, he received a demand for back taxes. He considered whether to pay or not, but when he looked around and saw all the people who had been on the dole since the economic decline without ever having tried to find work, as he had, he decided it would be immoral to pay his taxes just so the money could be passed on to these "loafers." Not paying his taxes meant, though, that he wouldn't be able to get a passport. A *passport*? Had bureaucratic red tape and the lack of proper documentation ever stopped him? He would make his own later. Now it was time to get going. In a final dramatic flourish of public self-pity he emblazoned on his boat the name *Elaine*. The doleful violin music playing between his ears must have been at full pitch.

On New Year's Eve 1931, a day when most people are toasting their happiness with their loved ones, Rebell set out from Sydney alone. As he passed under the nearly completed bridge, he stood up and waved a pathetic, unanswered adieu to his adopted homeland. This was the end of still another failed relationship. What would he find in America?

Not long out of the harbor he had a brief bout of sea-sickness, but that disappeared after half an hour, never to come back. Day by day he learned the skills needed to balance the boat and soon he was so adept at the

Latvian Pauls Sprogis with the sextant he made from hacksaw blades and a dime-store toy telescope. It got him safely across the Pacific.

art that, he claimed, he usually spent less than an hour a week at the tiller. He needed to adjust the sails only if the wind blew harder or changed direction. At first the large ocean swells scared him, but he got used to them and rejoiced in the buoyancy of his lightly loaded boat. His onboard stock of provisions for a six-month cruise weighed less than half of Romer's for a three-month cruise! Rebell's spirits rose as the miles spilled out behind him. For once in his life he was living a romantic dream and succeeding. The weather was squally and variable, but to him it didn't matter. Out on the sea there were no governments to hassle him, tax collectors to demand money, or women who said "No." He said of this time that "the Viking spirit stirred in my breast."

During the first leg of the voyage only one storm was strong enough to force him to down all sails and lie-to a sea anchor, but he didn't have a sea anchor. As little *Elaine* bobbed and spun in the growing hillocks of green water, he scrambled to tie two oars and a sheet of cloth into something resembling a kite, which he weighted at one end and threw overboard at the end of a long line. It worked and the boat came under control again, but not for long. The drogue line soon wore through where it rubbed on the bobstay. With the "sea anchor" lost, Rebell boldly hoisted the jib and ran with the storm. *Elaine* tore along like a freight train as he manned the helm, soaked by the elements because he did not own a set of oilskins.

Continual gales punished *Elaine*, and eventually a crack developed in one of her forward planks. It was a small opening, but large enough to require Rebell to bail every two hours. He had no foot or brass hand pump—it was bucket-and-chuck-it with an empty tin. At night he rigged a tin so that as the water level rose in the boat, the floating tin would bang on a board, awakening him. He used this "alarm clock" system until it got on his nerves one day, and he dove overboard with a handful of pitch that he mushed into the crack from the outside. It ended the leak for good. Rebell was lucky no sharks were in the vicinity.

He had first planned to stop in New Zealand, but the storms and his shaky navigation caused him to pass to the north of it. Not to worry—he would surely find the Fiji Islands. After five weeks of sailing he found that his watches were not working properly. By luck he had skimmed a book on watch repair back at the Sydney library, so he confidently took the watches apart, reworked the main springs, and soon had them back together and working as good as new.

Rebell's success as a sailor, instrument-maker, watch repairman, and self-reliant human being wasn't enough to satisfy an emptiness that he still felt in his soul, caused by more than just a failure to find a life partner. All his life he had been seeking something more. Now, having sailed for five weeks on the sea, alone with the vastness of the ocean, he felt a greater power enter him. He had grown up an atheist, but now he experienced an epiphany and turned to prayer to ease his burden. "God, Almighty, Who hearest every prayer, please let me see the sun at noon, so that I can take a sight." Moments later, according to Rebell, a double bank of clouds parted and the sun shone forth for the first time in nearly a week. He shot his sight with a new-found religious conviction that turned to absolute fervor in the coming years, but for now, at least he knew where he was. He was only 150 miles from the Fiji chain.

After "forty days and forty nights" Rebell's little ark found solid ground again when he spied an island. Unable to find an entrance into the lagoon, he sailed on for another week until he came to Yanutha, an island south of Vita Levu. He landed, replenished his water supply, and bought some fresh fruit from the locals. The next day he left for the Fijian capital, Suva (where Voss and Luxton had split up) on Viti Levu.

Over the course of the next few months he worked his way northwest, bucking the prevailing winds. Gilboy and Voss had come the other way—the easy way—around, but that was never Rebell's way. When he reached Suva, the British authorities were at first suspicious but finally allowed him to enter. The local newspaper picked up his story and made him an instant celebrity—he was often approached by locals to recite his story. He spent two weeks in Suva resting and re-fitting. His wooden centerboard had rotted away before he reached Yanutha, so he had to replace it. At a picnic he was invited to he fell in love, characteristically, though this time with a seventeen-year-old. It couldn't have been too serious, since the name of his boat didn't change. Kind-hearted islanders donated materials to repair and even improve *Elaine*. They gave him a new sail, fixed the cracked plank, found a compass, barometer, and new charts for him, and even replaced the rusting shrouds and stays. For the first time in his life he felt appreciated.

The refitting accomplished, however, he sailed off to Naitamba, where he fell for nineteen-year-old "gentle Betty," the daughter of the plantation owner whose hospitality he was sharing. With her he enjoyed thrilling afternoons of hiking the island trails and stolen moments picking wildflowers, but, alas, they weren't meant to be, so after nine days he sailed on, once again alone.

In late May he reached the Samoan capital, Apia, where Robert Louis Stevenson and his wife had settled before his early death. Naturally, Rebell made a pilgrimage to the melodramatic scene of love's labors lost and there commiserated with the spirit of the dead author, but dead spirits are not half so entertaining as living girls, and soon he latched onto a lovely sixteen-year-old native, Eda. He later wrote, "We met casually, and I was enslaved before I quite knew what was happening." He suffered his enslavement for five weeks before tearing himself away.

In typically quixotic fashion Sprogis foolishly tried to sue the U.S. Navy when his lightly built *Elaine* was smashed at San Pedro during a storm after his arrival. He was deported to Latvia.

During late July and early August he worked north again and one day ran into a huge school of sharks, so many that he thought there must be hundreds of the vicious brutes around him. Soon they had spotted the *Elaine* and were diving under her and thumping her sides with their tails. Rebell was frantic. He considered driving the boat up onto a nearby reef for protection, but realized that would only make him a castaway. Instead, he reached for a spear and began jabbing the sharks nearest the boat. Still they thronged, like a swarm of maddened bees. He struck at them along their backs so many times that the spear tip bent and then broke off. He lashed a knife to the shaft and attacked them again, but just as quickly as they had arrived, they were gone. He then understood that they had come to his boat only to feed off the dozens of small fish that had been trailing him during the passage. Once the largest of those were consumed they lost interest.

In mid-August he reached Christmas Island, where he was greeted by Paul Rougier, a jovial French planter, who made him welcome. As the two became friends and Rougier learned Rebell's story, he advised him not to take the matter of entering the United States without a passport lightly. Together they worked one up that Rebell then wrote out in his own neat handwriting. Rougier himself signed the "passport," wrote in the dates of Rebell's arrival and departure, and stamped it. Rebell was not a man without a country, he was a citizen of the world!

On Christmas Island, Paul Rougier convinced "Fred Rebell" that he needed a passport, even one of their own devising, before U.S. officials would let him enter the United States.

From Christmas Island it was a straight shot north twelve hundred miles to the U.S. Territory of Hawaii. He was now entering the waters just east of the area where Amelia Earhart and her navigator, Fred Noonan, would vanish less than five years later. No one would send out rescue ships if Rebell were lost. He was completely on his own, and somehow life was better like that.

Nearly ten months after leaving Sydney he arrived at Honolulu. When asked by an immigration official to produce his passport he pulled out his Christmas Island "document." The official stated that it had to be issued by a government, to which Rebell replied, "I am my own government."

God sometimes blesses beasts and children, and sure enough Rebell slipped through the clutches of officialdom and was allowed to stay, though the immigration officer did not stamp his "passport." That would be done later after the Hawaiian press got in on the act and turned him into the hero of the moment, whereupon everybody on Oahu wanted to be his friend, including the mayor of Honolulu who, without any authority to do so, boldly signed and dated his "passport." Life in Hawaii was good for Rebell. During the five weeks he was there he lectured at schools, visited the homes of the powerful, and received food and equipment from the locals. His feat of daring and solitary courage was a break from the gloomy economic news that was the usual media fare.

The longest leg of his journey was now before him, and he couldn't put it off any longer without risking running into winter storms along the way. In fact, he had probably tarried too long in his island idyll. On November 3 he set off on the twenty-two-hundred-mile run east to the California coast.

A month into the trip he was hit by a northeast gale. His sea drogue wouldn't do its job in the strong variable wind that swung around the compass points unpredictably. The boat took a real beating, skidding around the thrashing water. Suddenly it was thrown over on its side, and the rail kissed the water. Rebell thought it was the end. Luckily the boat rolled upright, but the tiller had been broken and the pintles (hinge pins) were mangled from the force of the sea. A more immediate danger was that the boat was flooded, and he had to bail it out quickly. Then he noticed that his sea anchor line had parted. In desperation he yanked up the wooden centerboard and attached it to the anchor line. Over it went and tamed the wild, veering motion somewhat, but not much. The *Elaine* could turn turtle any moment. There was nothing more he could do . . . except pray. So he said a prayer and awaited God's answer.

In the morning, when he awoke, the gale was completely gone and he was alive. He attributed both of these blessings to God. Eleven days later, on December 28, he was put to the test again by another gale that broke his repaired tiller, blew out his best sail, and tore away his improvised sea anchor. He improvised again: he put an anchor in a canvas sack and threw that out to anchor the nose of the boat into the wind, but soon the flukes of the anchor cut the cloth of the bag and he lost both. He fought the gale until sundown and once again survived. On New Year's Eve, one year after setting out, the winds blew up again and by the next day came at him in gale force. It was like this all the way to the California coast, but it was partly his own fault. If he had not lingered in Hawaii playing to the media and his admirers, he would have been ashore before most of these winter gales came along.

On January 7, 1933, he finally moored at San Pedro, just west of Long Beach. His nine-thousand-mile journey was over. His troubles with the Immigration Department weren't, though. Three days later, a severe storm caused several boats at San Pedro to slip their moorings. One, a navy launch, slammed into the little *Elaine*, breaking ribs and springing planks. The sailboat was then blown up on shore, or she would have sunk right there. Rebell retrieved his few belongings from her and was allowed to stay in the pier boathouse—where the Immigration officer found him. He demanded to know Rebell's intentions, and when the Latvian–Australian–Christmas Islander citizen of the world gave him typical Fred Rebell answers, he was thrown in the lockup.

The next day, Harry Pidgeon, the second man to sail alone around the globe, after Joshua Slocum, and whose book about his voyage in his homemade boat *Islander* had inspired Rebell, showed up in person to speak on Rebell's behalf. When that failed, a few days later a press photographer came to take his picture and soon his story was in the national press. Orders came down to release the new media darling immediately.

Rebell then embarked on a lecture tour managed by a professional agent. Hollywood even made some noise, but never a movie about his life, and eventually when the brouhaha died down he was back to being a handyman again. This time he worked at a boatyard for rich swells, who enjoyed the novelty of having a minor nautical celebrity fussing around their expensive boats.

In October 1935, after he had pestered the U.S. government for eighty-five dollars to compensate him for the loss of *Elaine*, the hulk of which he sold for thirty-five dollars to an Australian, a paddy wagon pulled up to his boatyard, and he was arrested. At the end of the month he was shipped to Galveston, Texas, and from there deported to Bremen, Germany. Two days later he arrived back at Riga, Latvia, from where he made his way to his parents' home, which he had left twenty-eight years earlier. There he stayed for many months until he decided to return to Australia in 1937. Whether he entered this time with or without a passport hasn't been determined, but he died there in 1968.

Down the coast from San Pedro, thirty-three-year-old Dana Lamb and his wife Ginger of San Diego were contemplating a small-boat trip that January 1933 when Rebell's arrival hit all the newspapers. Their voyage would not cross oceans, but it would be lengthy. They planned to go down the Pacific coast of Baja California, cross over to the Mexican mainland, and proceed down to Panama. They would make the trip in a canoe-ish, surfboard-ish, sneakbox-ish boat that Dana had dreamed up and that the two of them were building out of cheap lumber and canvas, *Vagabunda*, about seventeen feet long and three and a half feet wide.

Dana, a Dartmouth-Princeton man, and Ginger were bright and breezy sorts who wouldn't let something as distasteful as the Depression put a crimp in their travel plans. No, south they would go no matter what, and deal with any situation as it arose.

Their trip down the Mexican and Central American coasts eventually stretched to thousands of miles and as many adventures. They wrote a light-hearted travelogue of their three-year jaunt, *Enchanted Vagabonds*, which became a best-seller when published in 1938. All the "best people" read it, including Franklin D. Roosevelt, who was so impressed that he appointed the Ivy League explorer and his wife as advisors to the military on jungle survival. Some professionals scratched their heads over this.

Despite the Great Depression, Dana and Ginger Lamb enjoyed an exotic tropical vacation in their homemade boat *Vagabunda*. They began their voyage with $4.00 in their pockets.

A few years later the Lambs made another trip to Mexico and Central America, where they explored Mayan ruins. They wrote another well-received account of it, but it attracted its share of skeptics who wondered just how much of it was true and how much was just well-polished malarkey. After World War II Dana became an investment banker in New York and wrote many books on the joys of fly-fishing.

There was one more intentional small-boat voyage before World War II. With war threatening, 1939 was not the best year to begin a long ocean voyage, but a thirty-seven-year-old iconoclastic Englishman, Harry Young, ex–merchant mariner, put out, anyway. His self-designed and self-built boat was a crude, stubby affair only thirteen feet, nine inches long with a flat deck and no sort of cuddy at all. It sported a length of old steel I beam, about ten feet long and nine inches deep, for a keel. She was rigged as a gaff sloop with a mainsail on a long boom that must have been a bear to handle in a blow. He left Staten Island on June 5, reaching the Azores in thirty-nine days, despite running into severe weather. He spent a month cruising the islands and August 4 embarked on the Portuguese ship *São Miguel* for England. Why end his voyage in the Azores, so close to a complete ocean crossing? Like sailors we've already met, and some we are about to, he had his own reasons, and that is all that mattered to him.

Thus ended the last planned small-boat voyage across an ocean (or nearly so) until after the already brewing war.

Art on facing page: Navy pilot Harold Dixon and crew pose in front of the five-year-old Goodyear raft that saved their lives when their Douglas Devastator torpedo bomber ditched in the Pacific in 1942.

7

BIG FEAT, LITTLE NOTICE

THE 1940S

♦ THREE MEN IN A RUBBER RAFT ♦ NAVY HERO POON LIM: THANKS,
NOW LEAVE ♦ JACK SCHULTZ: LIKE FATHER, LIKE SON ♦ LIKE FATHER,
LIKE DAUGHTER ♦ POSTWAR HOPES: THE *NOVA ESPERO* ♦

THE PROBLEMS OF THREE SMALL PEOPLE DON'T AMOUNT
to a hill of beans in this crazy world," Rick tells Ilsa in *Casablanca*,
Hollywood's greatest film, released at the height of World War II. How
could the world stop to worry about the calamities, dangers, and misadventures of a few when the lives of millions were at stake, as well as

the future of entire nations? Holocausts, apocalypses, and tragedies on an epic scale raged across the face of the earth while individual lives were merged into great swaths of humanity clashing over titanic causes. Individual instances of tragedy or triumph got little notice amidst the universal suffering of those years.

During a conflict such as this war, whose battlefields spread across the entire planet, there was no room for frivolous little boat rides across oceans. Harry Young arrived in the Azores *before* England declared war on Germany in September 1939. The only noted ocean passage by a yachtsman during the war years was Vito Dumas's circumnavigation in the thirty-one-foot *Lehg II.* Dumas was an Argentinean, and since Argentina was a neutral country, he had no iron in the war's fire.

The war itself was the cause of many great episodes in maritime history, though most of them fall outside the scope of this narrative. The two that do are both tales of survivors, men who took to life rafts after the sinking of a ship or downing of an airplane. Thousands of sailors and airmen owed their lives to life rafts and other improvements in lifesaving technology since the nineteenth century. The *Nonpareil* concept of a huge inflatable boat had by the 1940s shrunk down to the size of a small suitcase, practical to place on nearly every warplane. A downed airman needed only open a carbon dioxide bottle to inflate the fabric raft. The Merriman-Boyton suit would evolve into the inflatable life vest by World War II, and into the all-weather floating survival suit after the war, with the advent of advanced synthetic fibers. The survivor of a sinking ship or ditched airplane in the 1940s had an infinitely greater chance of survival and rescue than his predecessor a generation or two before.

Just five weeks after America entered the war, a U.S. Navy Douglas Devastator piloted by Harold Dixon took off on January 16, 1942, from a carrier in the South Pacific on an antisubmarine sortie. His bombardier was Anthony Pastula and rear-seat gunner was Gene Aldrich. After a few hours on patrol they turned back to the carrier, but when they arrived where they thought the flattop should be, it wasn't. Dixon radioed for a fix, but either he wasn't heard or the carrier was maintaining radio silence. A short time later, their fuel almost gone, he told his crew to prepare to ditch.

The Devastator, like most airplanes, could be expected to float for some time after a ditching because it was nothing more than a big, hollow aluminum tube, with both fuselage and wings providing buoyancy. In reality, however, it was unpredictable how long an airplane would float: sometimes they would go right down, and sometimes they would float long enough for a crew to off-load valuable survival gear, including water and food. The great World War I ace Eddie Rickenbacker was flying as a passenger in a B-17 bomber on a secret mission to Douglas MacArthur during World War II when the plane went down in the Pacific. He ordered the young crew to abandon the plane as quickly as possible, and they took three inflatable life rafts but could not take all the food and water on board. The plane floated for a time before sinking, long enough, some of them later thought, that they could have retrieved the supplies and still got out themselves. One of the crew died during their twenty-one-day ordeal before they found land (though, in fairness, his death was likely due to stress from a recent appendectomy). Some of the survivors bitterly criticized Rickenbacker after the war for his order, but their accusations were unjustified.

Dixon and his crew proved that Rickenbacker's fears were warranted when their own plane hit the water. They had barely unstrapped their harnesses and grabbed the life raft when the hefty torpedo bomber plunged to the depths, leaving them floating in their life vests. It happened in an instant. Wet, frightened, with the sun fading fast, they struggled to open the carbon dioxide bottle and inflate the raft. When they did, it was upside down. For twenty awful minutes in the choppy water and gloom they tried to flip it over, but it weighed forty pounds and, because of its shape, they couldn't get a grip properly while hanging in their life vests. Back and forth they pushed it with no success. Dixon ordered them to stop, recompose, and think. Pastula then suggested tying all their shirts together to make a line and using that to wrap the raft and then "unwind" it. All credit goes to the young navy bombardier for this inspiration under difficult circumstances. What he had rediscovered was Alfred Johnson's solution to the same problem sixty-six years earlier—and it still worked.

They clambered into the eight-by-four-foot inflated rubber raft. Like any natural compound, rubber decays over time. This raft, made by Goodyear in 1937, was five years old. Could it still hold air? Had the rubber become brittle? Not only was its age a concern, but so was its size. Its *outside* dimensions were eight by four feet, but the tube walls took two feet off each of those dimensions. In other words, three grown men were confined to a six-by-two-foot well which itself was divided by another tube thwart about one third of the way back from the bow. Where would they put themselves?

It would have to do. They took stock of their equipment: a Colt .45 with two extra clips, a pocketknife, a pair of pliers, a piece of line, a police whistle, a rubber-repair kit, and a small signaling mirror. That was it. No food, no water, no long-distance signaling device like a Gibson Girl or even a simple radar reflector, devices that would come later in the war. If they weren't rescued in a few days, what hope did they have?

They rotated watch the first night and in the morning their hearts leaped when they heard the sound of an airplane. It was American. Frantically they waved, but it just roared high overhead without so much as dipping a wing. Dixon's thoughts after this turned to the drift of the boat. He knew the waters they were in and that the Japanese held some of the islands. He also knew how they treated prisoners. Therefore he began to think of ways to control the drift of the raft to try to steer it away from any island they suspected to be in enemy hands.

The Colt .45 is like a hand cannon, large and loud. Hundreds of birds sailed around the raft, and Dixon aimed the Colt .45, but try as he might, even at a range of only a few yards, he never managed to down a bird. The boat's motion threw off his aim and soon salt water got into the mechanism and froze the action, ruining the pistol. They then took the spring out of one of the ammo clips and tried to fashion it into a fishing hook with the pliers, but that tool was so poorly made that the pivot pin snapped at the first squeeze.

A few days into their odyssey Dixon had another inspiration. He ordered the others to remove the grab line that ran around the outside of the raft. Tying it to one of their deflated life vests and knotting the other end around the carbon dioxide bottle fastened at the bow, he threw the life vest in the water, where it acted as a drogue. Now he could ease the motion of the raft in rough seas or stop it if he thought the wind was blowing them to an unfriendly island. Dixon gave himself a lot of credit for being able to control the boat's direction for the rest of the ordeal, emphatically stating that he and the others didn't "drift"; they went where he wanted them to go. With due respect to his experience and efforts, most knowledgeable mariners would disagree with his assertion.

After five days at sea the men still had not run into a squall. As the sun pounded them unmercifully that afternoon, almost as a joke, they sang the old spiritual "It Ain't Gonna Rain No Mo." In the evening it did rain. Using their life vests and clothes, they soaked up as much water as they could and squeezed it into a canvas sack for later use; by this method they provided water for themselves for the next five weeks.

For food they learned to catch fish by spearing them with the knife. Their technique was to wait for a fish to swim alongside the raft and when it was in range, in one quick sweeping motion of the arm drive the knife down into the water, into the fish, and back up into the air over the raft. The fish would fall off the blade and then be quickly divided. The first fish they caught in this way became their first meal in seven days. Later they would become so adept at this they could catch small sharks. Birds, too, supplemented their meager diet.

With the promise of a reasonable supply of water and food, Dixon ordered the men to paddle south. They used their sole remaining pair of shoes as hand paddles and set to work. It's doubtful such paddling was effective, but Dixon estimated they paddled at least a hundred miles this way. If nothing else, it gave them something to do and the feeling that they controlled their destiny to some extent. Maintaining a healthy mental attitude and the belief that you will survive seems to be the single most important aspect of surviving at sea.

In reality, of course, nature still controlled them. Day by day, little pieces of equipment rusted to powder or were washed overboard by a swamping wave. Their clothes became rags, which further disintegrated and were used as fishing line or water sponges, but even those were washed away as the days wore on and the sea mauled the little raft. Sharks, including evil-looking leopard sharks, scraped alongside. After a month the only thing they had on the raft was the police whistle on a lanyard around Dixon's neck. Wracked by storms or the searing sun, the men endured their torture for thirty-four days, but then began to recite their own eulogies. They began to suspect that their carrier group had given them up for dead weeks earlier.

Later that day Aldrich said he was sure he saw a cornfield. Dixon and Pastula thought he was raving until they crested the next swell and saw for themselves in the distance the green fields of an island. Was it enemy held? After a terrifying passage through the coral reef surrounding the island, they landed, naked, unarmed, and unable to walk. Dixon picked up a piece of driftwood, unbent his wizened body to a nearly upright posture, and said to his crew, "If there are Japs on this island they'll not see an American sailor crawl. We'll stand, and march, and make them shoot us down like men-o'-warsmen."

The Imperial Japanese army was not on the island, however—they encountered only a native village and the commissioner from New Zealand. They had landed on Puka Puka in the Danger Islands after having drifted—"voyaged" if you believe Dixon—more than a thousand miles from their ditch site. The commissioner and his wife cared for them and contacted the navy by radio, and the men were picked up seven days later.

Their rescue caused an abrupt change in U.S. Navy policy. Until that time it was thought that a man could survive on a raft without food or water for only a few days. Thus only token searches had been mounted for survivors. Once their story got out the navy changed to making serious, systematic, prolonged searches for downed airmen and shipwreck survivors. In the end the suffering of Dixon, Aldrich, and Pastula led to the saving of hundreds of other lives, including that of the future forty-first American president, George Herbert Walker Bush, who went down in the Pacific in his torpedo bomber two years later.

Later in 1942, the same year as Dixon's saga, the British merchantman *Benlomond* slipped out of Cape Town bound for Dutch Guiana (now Suriname) on the northeast coast of South America. Crossing the South Atlantic was dangerous, however, because Admiral Dönitz's U-boat wolf packs played a coordinated game of seek and destroy with the German navy's merchant raiders like the infamous *Atlantis*, which was disguised to look like an unarmed neutral cargo ship but had quick-deploying cannons hidden by false panels. Dozens of Allied ships had already gone down along this route thanks to the wiles of the Kriegsmarine.

On November 23, 1942, the *Benlomond* joined them. A U-boat's two-torpedo salvo got her fifteen days out, and she sank fast. On board men scrambled to don life jackets and launch the life rafts, but the ship was ablaze, and seconds later the boilers blew. Out of the wreckage bobbed a few heads, including that of Poon Lim, a twenty-five-year-old seaman from Hainan Island off the coast of China, who was second steward on the ship. Coming to the surface he saw a life raft about a cable's length away with men on it and swam toward it. Just then the U-boat broke surface and took prisoner the men on the raft. Lim called out, "Save me, or I drown!" For a moment the submariners on the conning tower looked at him, but one finally waved and said, "Good-bye." The sub dived, leaving Lim treading water. (Much the same thing had happened to survivors of the *Bismarck* sinking less than a year earlier, when British warships rescued a few but left most to drown despite their pleas. Feelings had hardened on both sides as the war progressed.) The raft the sailors had been on had meantime drifted away. It took Lim an hour to find another one and when he crawled onto it, exhausted, he found himself alone on the wide sea.

The raft Lim was on was nothing but a crude eight-by-ten-foot frame of wooden planks on about six metal drums. (Rafts like this had been built by boys around the world for years from scrounged fifty five-gallon drums and boards. Many a boy sailor had imagined adventures on the local creek or pond on such a raft.) These rafts were stowed on slides built on the sides of ships. With slides instead of davits it was easy to launch each half-ton raft, just by unclasping one pelican hook. Simple rafts like this had already saved hundreds of lives. On his raft Lim

Poon Lim poses in a life raft similar to the one that he rode in for 133 days until rescued. This picture was part of a U.S. Navy re-creation of the Chinese sailor's ordeal for a training film. Lim later had to enlist the aid of President Truman to emigrate to the United States.

found what Dixon and his men would have considered a bountiful larder: six large boxes of hardtack, ten cans of pemmican, a bottle of lime juice, five cans of evaporated milk, ten gallons of water, and for after dinner, two pounds of chocolate!

Lim's first days at sea were anxious, but not altogether frightening. The raft came with balks of timber and a sheet of cloth so a canopy could be erected as shade from the sun's burning rays. His sole occupation now was to keep a weather eye out for ships, and finally at the end of the first week one appeared. He lit a signal flare and sure enough the ship changed course and came his way. Then it changed course again and veered away. He used up the rest of his flares trying to get it to turn back, but it didn't. Perhaps her captain considered him to be yet another Kriegsmarine ruse.

Lim drifted around the equatorial seas unable to control the direction his raft took and with no idea when he would reach a shore, any shore. Rains were frequent and the sun manageable with the canopy, so conditions had been relatively easy compared to other survival horror stories, but when his food ran out on the fiftieth day he had to start working to sustain himself. First he made some fishing gear. He untwisted some strands of rope until he had a length of twine and to this attached a primitive fishing hook made from the battery compression spring of his inoperative flashlight. Using a barnacle for bait, he caught his first fish. Only a few inches long, it nevertheless proved the concept could work.

Excited at the promise of fresh food, he gouged into one of the wooden planks of the raft around the head of a nail until he undermined it. Carefully he levered it out enough so he could finally grasp it with his teeth and get it all the way out—he was so afraid of losing it that this seemed the best way. Using the small fish he caught with his spring hook, he baited the hook he bent from the nail. He pierced a small fish's tail with the hook so that it would be alive and still wiggling when dropped into the water. From then on he caught fish large enough to last several days. He filleted these with a knife he fashioned from one of the pemmican cans. He caught freshwater in the canopy and transferred it to a container. Water wasn't always plentiful, and sometimes he went without, but never to the extent Dixon did.

As the weeks drifted into months, he learned other tricks, for example, to sun-dry his fish before eating it. Better still, for a varied menu, he learned that if he used seaweed to make a little nest on top of his canopy and then put some rotting fish meat into the nest, gulls would land there. While they were distracted eating he snatched them and wrung their necks. Now he had fowl as well as fish. He further discovered that rotting gull meat attracted sharks, and he learned how to wrestle small sharks on board, as Dixon's men had, and dispatch them with a weighty water jug.

On the hundredth day of his ordeal six airplanes flew in formation overhead. One of them actually saw his tiny dot of a raft on the large ocean and flew lower. Lim saw a bomb drop from its wing—a smoke bomb! But the seas were so rough that day the seaplanes could not land. Once again he was alone.

For one more month he survived by his wits until he noticed that the color of the ocean was changing from black to green, and there were more land birds flying around. He must be getting near *somewhere*. On day 133 after the *Benlomond* went down, on April 5, 1943, Lim spotted a sailboat in the distance. He stood up on the plank bench and waved a cloth over his head. The boat changed course toward him.

It was a Brazilian fishing boat crewed by a poor fisherman and his family. They took Lim on board and despite the language barrier understood his plight. His first meal was beans with freshwater. Over the next three days the family continued to fish because they were too poor to return without a catch. During that time the father came to think so highly of Lim that he offered the shipwrecked sailor his daughter's hand in marriage! Very diplomatically Lim declined and was taken to shore anyway.

A British consul in Brazil arranged for Lim to be sent back to Britain. His first stop was Miami, where the American press jumped on his story. His 133-day ordeal was the longest survival in a life raft. When the U.S. Navy heard about him, they arranged for him to reenact his survival techniques for a training film. Absurdly enough, when Lim then asked to join the U.S. Navy, he was turned down for having flat feet!

So back to Britain Lim went. King George personally presented him with the British Empire Medal while his employer, the Ben Line, gave him a gold watch—the gift every employee dreads. Maybe that's what drove him to want to return to America.

When he applied for readmission, his request was denied because the annual quota for Chinese immigration had already been filled. It literally took a presidential order by Harry S. Truman in 1949 to get him in. At the time, Democrat Truman was under a lot of heat from Congressional Republicans who blamed him for being soft on the "Reds" and losing China to Mao's communists. Truman's best political—and humanitarian—move was to grant Lim's request.

The pugnacious little sailor settled in Brooklyn, New York, where he worked in the shipping industry until he retired in 1983. When asked how it felt to hold the record for the longest survival at sea in a life raft, he stated, "I hope that no one will ever have to break that record." So far, no one has.

A few months after Lim's rescue, in the skies over his homeland of China, U.S. Army Air Force Major John G. "Dutch" Schultz was co-pilot of a four-engine B-24 bomber after another long-range mission against Japanese positions at Hong Kong. Schultz was an "old man" at forty-five and should have been back in the States training younger pilots, rather than right-seating a Liberator, but that wasn't his way. Service in the U.S. Army Air Service and Royal Air Force in World War I was followed by pioneering commercial routes for the young Pan American Airways in the Caribbean. During the 1930s he was a reserve pilot for the Marine Corps and wrote short stories for magazines that encouraged young men to earn their wings. Schultz was a leader of men who led from the front.

The B-24 was low on fuel because they had made three passes to pinpoint the target, and now it couldn't make it back to base in Yangkai, China. The pilot ordered the crew to bail out, but in the rush a Chinese observer, along on this run, deployed his parachute inside the plane. The only way to save his life was to belly-land the big plane in one of the rice paddies below. Schultz volunteered to stay aboard and help the pilot make the dangerous landing.

The bomber made a good belly landing, but on the slippery paddy it kept moving as if it were sliding on oil. From inside the cockpit the pilots could see the wall of a dike rushing at them dead ahead. It was unavoidable. When the bomber's nose struck, the front of the plane crumpled as the rear of the fuselage drove into it. The three men were killed instantly.

John E. "Jack" Schultz, son of Dutch, was in high school back in America at the time of the crash. After the war young Schultz went to visit his mother, who had remarried and was living in Ecuador. At the end of his visit the eighteen-year-old decided to see a little of South

America before returning to the States, where he planned to study at the University of Chicago. So on May 11, 1947, as Nathaniel Bishop had done before him, he set out to walk over the Andes Mountains from Quito down into Peru. He took with him a backpack, a double-barreled shotgun, and twenty-one dollars.

A week later he had traversed a 13,000-foot pass and made the Río Napo, a tributary of the Amazon. He bought a sixteen-foot Indian dugout canoe for eleven dollars and continued his journey by river. Along the way he fed himself by fishing and hunting monkeys in the jungle. He preferred monkey to parrot meat. A thousand miles from where he began he arrived at Iquitos, Peru, broke, but happy.

Life was good for the youngster who had so much of his father's adventurous spirit in him. Why quit the voyage now? Why not go on down the Amazon? His twenty-one dollars gone, he worked for several weeks repairing cars and trucks, something few locals knew how to do. With his earnings he bought a larger dugout canoe, a *casco*, more suited to the bigger waters of the Amazon. It differed from his first in that it was a foot longer, seventeen feet, and had a more sophisticated construction. A slit was cut into one edge of the cedar log and then its innards gouged out through this slit. Next it was placed over a fire and very slowly spread open, making what had started as a two-and-a-half-foot log into a four-foot-wide boat. Schultz paid eleven dollars for this native handiwork, and as events turned out he got his money's worth, as he had from his first eleven-dollar canoe.

Paddling the new boat baffled him until a native told him he couldn't paddle a *casco* like an ordinary dugout. He had to paddle from the bow with short inward chops of the paddle. This technique was successful, and soon he was making long daily runs on the twisting, muddy river. Sometimes he would stop at a native hut along the river and stay the night, but usually he rafted up to a floating clump of hyacinths, stretched his mosquito netting over the boat, and slept until morning as he continued to float downstream. His best daily run was 110 miles.

About halfway down the river he wondered why he should stop to fly to America, even though his mother had offered to send him the airfare. The dugout, which he had christened *Sea Fever* in honor of the

John Masefield poem, was proving so reliable on this big river that he thought he could sail her across the Caribbean and right up to the United States. His father had pioneered Caribbean air routes, so why not have an adventure there himself?

At Manaus, where the Amazon is joined by the Río Negro, the river widens enough so that winds can sweep over the water and sailing is possible. Schultz was taken under the wing of the local governor, who was intrigued by the young man's adventure and introduced him to a carpenter who could help improve the boat's seaworthiness. Schultz and the carpenter added internal frames, added plank washboards as Voss had done, fitted a small centerboard and rudder, and finally carved two masts to make a ketch rig. He rigged the boat with a sliding gunter mainsail and a simple leg-o'-mutton mizzen. Awning canvas served for sailcloth.

Schultz had another benefactor, an American expatriate who gave him sailing lessons and books on the subject. Another American gave him navigation tables and a plastic sextant recently developed for use on lifeboats. (A version of that sextant, still available, is the first navigation tool used by many amateur yachtsmen today.)

Thus equipped and full of self-confidence in his new "vessel," Schultz set forth once again, though this time his destination was not just the Amazon delta, but Miami,

Eighteen-year-old John E. "Jack" Schultz, ready to take on the Amazon River in a sixteen-foot Indian dugout canoe. His father would have been proud of his pluck.

Florida, U.S.A. Almost immediately he capsized. Schultz, the sailing novice, had broken one of the cardinal rules of small-boat handling—never cleat the sheets. Both his main and jib sheets were cleated, and over he went in a sudden gust of wind. He was going down, too—the several hundred pounds of scrap iron fastened in the bilge for ballast were pulling *Sea Fever* to the bottom. Schultz unsheathed his knife and slashed at the ropes holding the iron. He didn't get all of it off, but enough so the boat floated back toward the surface, though it refused to come up all the way. A witness to his blunder came out to rescue him in another boat.

Humbled, but wiser, he tried again and learned to sail his boat over the next few weeks. He found the Amazon beautiful and peaceful and the people helpful. Only once did he have a real scare. That was when he ran aground one night, and after he had jumped into the shallow water to push off, a vicious piranha bit him in the lower leg. The little fish took a small souvenir of flesh before Schultz could leap back into his boat.

Starting again on his long voyage, he came first to Macapá on the north shore of the Amazon Delta. Here he wisely upgraded *Sea Fever*—hoping to make it a less wet boat—by building up the washboards, installing canvas decking, increasing the size of the rudder, and finally stowing a donated compass and bilge pump. With ten pounds of crackers, a hundred oranges, ten gallons of water, and a few other rations he was ready to tackle first the Atlantic and then the Caribbean.

Overconfidence once again got the best of him, but he was soon humbled because after he had left the dangerous delta and its awesome estuarial bore—a daily small tidal wave found on many river mouths around the world—he got seasick on the Atlantic. By now it was December 13, 1947, and the affliction was to stay with him for much of the six months of his trip north, but never did he surrender to it. As bad as the nausea was the fact that all his efforts to improve the boat back in Macapá still hadn't stopped the leaking that had plagued the boat since the Amazon. Now the motion of the ocean had made the leaks much worse—endless, in fact. Every half hour he was forced to work the bilge pump. What with the sickness and the war with the bilge pump, when was he ever going to have time to open his books and learn how to navigate?

In order to round up and get on a northerly track, Schultz needed to put sea miles behind him and to get away from the coast and the tidal inrush into the delta. *Sea Fever* didn't show much inclination to sail into the wind, so it took him days to make just the first hundred miles. Navigation was done mostly with aircraft sectional charts and then mostly by dead reckoning after his one and only watch stopped.

Not knowing where he was, a few days later he stumbled sick and worn out into the cove of a little island he later learned was the infamous Devil's Island prison. In 1948 about fifty prisoners were still there, and they tended his saltwater blisters and helped him restock his provisions before he pushed on toward Trinidad. Six days later he fetched that island, but the saltwater sores were back, as well as a fever. He wound up in the hospital for a tedious week, and it took treatment with penicillin to bring him back to health.

While he was in the hospital, the story of his novel adventure got around the island, and he was visited by the American consul, who invited him to his home when he had recovered. Then the consul happened to mention that he was looking for a contractor to remove some piles that the U.S. Navy had sunk off the coast of the island during the war, which by agreement had to be removed after the war. The local contractors, he felt, were all trying to gouge Uncle Sam. Broke again, Schultz offered to undertake the work for about half of what the locals had bid. The doubtful consul gave him the contract with the proviso that he at least have some local help. Eighteen-year-old Schultz rented a diving helmet and air pump, found a book called *How to Use Dynamite*, hired a helper, and proceeded to blow up the pilings at their base. He was flush with cash for the rest of the journey home.

He tried once again to improve the seaworthiness of the boat. This time he increased the weight of the centerboard, reworked the sails, and tried to stop the leaks in the planking and the canvas deck covering. He also added oars and a sea anchor. When this was done he sailed from Trinidad to Grenada in only twenty-four hours. At the entrance to Saint George's harbor, he learned what Fenger had before him: the local tides and currents are wildly confusing for newcomers. Without local knowledge it took Schultz another twenty-four hours to make the last five miles to the harbor.

From Grenada he sailed north and was completely surprised when he ran into Virgin Gorda. He was once again sick and down with a fever, also like Fenger, and had to go to a hospital on Tortola. When he was able to sail again he went on to Puerto Rico and departed there for Miami on June 4. Still weak from sickness and the heat, he didn't see a reef ahead of him and holed his boat. Reacting quickly, he dove over the side, shoved in a wooden bung, and continued on.

He stopped shortly at Great Inagua in the Bahamas and also at a little island off the coast of Cuba, where he stayed with an impoverished fishing family while he patched his boat and caught his breath for the last leg. He reached Miami on June 30, 1948, having traveled some six thousand miles by dugout canoe. It had been a test of man-

Schultz's *Sea Fever* was modified many times on its journey from the Andes down the Amazon, and up the Caribbean to Miami. Its sails were made from canvas awning material.

hood and character that his father would surely have understood and approved.

———————◆·◆·◆———————

The "Reds" that Congress didn't think President Truman was doing enough to stop were successful in Europe, as well as Asia. Stalin had parked the Soviet Red Army in Eastern Europe, with no intention of taking it out. Germany became a divided nation, and trapped in the Soviets' new police state of East Germany were our old friend Paul Müller, his wife Aga, and their children. Müller had mastered the sea before, and to save his family now from the horrors of Stalinism he intended to do so one more time.

The Wannsee is a beautiful lake in the southwest corner of Berlin remembered today mostly for the evil that was planned at a lovely tree-shaded villa on its shores one week in January 1942—Hitler's extermination of the Jews—but most local people thought of it only as a place of recreation, especially pleasure boating. It was here that Müller, for a song, acquired an eighteen-foot rowboat in early 1949.

That spring he added an external hollow wooden keel into which he stuffed nearly a thousand pounds of scrounged scrap metal. Next he added a cuddy, flush decking, and in the stern a little cockpit for the helmsman. In a hurry because each day the Russians were tightening their grip on the people, he gave her a simple sloop rig, with the mainsail laced onto the mast and boom, and a small jib. During rough weather he would deploy a sea anchor over the stern.

Dubbing his craft the *Berlin*, he intended to sail her across the canals that connect Berlin to the Elbe River, then downriver into West Germany, out to the English Channel, and by stages to Argentina. For navigation he had only a compass and the memories of his previous voyage.

It was decided that he and his teenage daughter, also named Aga, should leave first, and when they made it to South America they would earn enough money to buy the freedom of his wife and young son. The two began their hazardous voyage in August and by good fortune eluded the communist guards and informants as they worked their way through the elaborate canal system that connects the Wannsee with the Elbe. Arriving at the river undetected, they went downstream past Hamburg and out to the Frisian Islands. It was now November 1949. The shifting sands of the Frisians, as any reader of Erskine Childers's classic *The Riddle of the Sands* knows, were difficult to navigate, but it seemed better to work coastwise through the sands along the Netherlands than to attempt the North Sea immediately. Finally they made the jump to England, and after weathering several storms during the late fall they managed to reach Ireland. All along the way, kindhearted people helped the pitiful refugees when they landed. To Paul it must have seemed like a second youth, a second 1929.

Time was critical, and they couldn't afford to wait out the winter in harbor. Theirs was a mission of life or death to get Aga and the boy out of East Germany, so Müller boldly resolved to attempt a crossing of the Bay of Biscay in *midwinter*. This would have seemed suicidal in any yacht, let alone an ersatz rowboat, and he was warned against it. Yet, with his faithful daughter helping, he managed to pull off the seemingly impossible—taking the tiny craft across the tempestuous body of water in the worst season of the year. They reached the north coast of Spain on March 22, where they put in for water, shelter, and a well-earned rest from the spring gales. When it looked as though there would be a break in the weather the two were off again, working their way around Finisterre and then down the coast of Portugal. On April 24 the *Berlin* arrived at Las Palmas in the Canaries. The worst was over; now would come the easy run across the Atlantic along the balmy trade route.

Müller did not plan to take the trade route, however. Probably for political reasons he decided to go down to South Africa and from there cross to Argentina. The trade route would have landed him on the coast of Brazil, and as Brazil had been at war with Germany, perhaps Müller doubted he would be warmly received there and feared that he might even be detained. Müller had perfected the art of depending on the kindness of strangers, but did he fear a lack of Brazilian hospitality?

The northern crossing would have been much easier, but he had made his plans and would not change them despite entreaties from concerned yachtsmen in the Canaries. Down the coast of Africa they proceeded until on July 3, 1950, at Bassa, Liberia, Paul Müller died suddenly. At age sixty-three, the strain had finally gotten to the man whose personal motto was "Never back, never back." His loyal eighteen-year-old daughter, who had never known peace in her young life, set off for the capital, Monrovia. Along the way she was robbed of the pittance she had, but eventually she did get home to Europe and for a time lived in Ireland.

The Müllers' odyssey and their suffering were not unique in the annals of refugees escaping from oppressive regimes.

The last small-boat voyage of the 1940s worth mentioning is that of brothers Stanley and Colin Smith, of Yarmouth, England. The two had grown up as wharf rats at their father's Isle of Wight boatyard, with dreams of one day sailing across the Atlantic in a boat of their own design and construction. Postwar rationing and the need to use raw materials for exported products made it difficult for them to find enough wood to build a boat, so they hit upon the idea of going to Nova Scotia, where wood was unrationed and cheap, to build her. They would sail her back home.

In early 1949, while crossing on the Cunard liner *Aquitania*, they designed the simplest strong boat they could conceive. It was a twenty-foot clinker-built dingy with a six-foot-three-inch beam. To save money and construction time, it wouldn't have a proper cabin, but rather an inverted seven-foot dingy sitting astride the gunwales. This alone would provide protection from the waves and sun.

Arriving in Halifax, they soon made friends and were offered the use of the basement of an old chapel for a boat shop. In less than three months their *Nova Espero* (New Hope) was ready to launch. (What a wonderful name for a boat built in the uncertain years following the war.) It was carried out of the basement and then down to the water by truck, where the mast, fittings, and other final details were installed. From there it went to Dartmouth, where the brothers departed on July 5 before a crowd of well-wishers, including the mayor, who gave the young men a letter to present to his counterpart in Dartmouth, England, at the end of the voyage.

The voyage across was wet, rambling, yet wonderful. They encountered a few storms and were often blown off track, but the brothers were young and resilient. It was part of the fun. Along the way, Stanley suffered an inflammation in one of his hands, but that didn't keep him from writing poetry and making drawings, while Colin was once washed overboard and rescued. One day the boat crested a wave and dropped into the trough right onto the back of a much surprised porpoise.

After a forty-four-day jaunt, on August 18 they reached Dartmouth. There the locals laid out a great reception and congratulated the brothers on a bravely performed feat of seamanship. Stanley and the *Nova Espero*, however, were not ready to retire from ocean sailing.

Art on facing page: The GP-A or Seep is remembered today not for its miserable war record but for its improbable round-the-world trip with Ben Carlin behind the wheel.

·8·

GOOFY AND GALLANT

THE 1950s

◆ JEEPS CAN CROSS ANYTHING, INCLUDING OCEANS ◆ ONCE MORE FOR
NOVA ESPERO ◆ SWEET *SOPRANINO* ◆ DR. BOMBARD'S BOMBAST? ◆
ESCAPE FROM THE FOREIGN LEGION BUT NOT THE SHARKS ◆ *TREKKA*:
BOY MAKES GOOD ◆ BY LOG ACROSS THE ATLANTIC ◆ *L'ÉGARÉ* EARNS
ITS MERIT BADGE, SORTA ◆ DR. LINDEMANN CROSSES IN A *REAL* KAYAK
◆ WHAT'S A NICE BALLOON LIKE YOU DOING ON AN OCEAN LIKE THIS? ◆

FOLLOWING THE POIGNANCY OF THE 1940S WITH ALL THE
decade's monumental drama of a world at war, the 1950s may seem by
contrast petty and almost forgettable. The truth is that the 1950s were
every bit as serious as the 1940s. The Cold War had replaced the hot

one, and the struggle for world dominance between the combatants was almost as profound and bloody as the preceding contest. Yet that is not how the decade is often remembered. It is remembered for its great contrasts, such as the important struggle for civil rights in America and the emergence of silly, self-absorbed ennui-ridden suburbia. In Britain prosperity reemerged as industry once again produced world-beating products, yet the "angry young man" brand of art and politics told Britons they were doomed. In Europe the spread of prosocialist ideology in the salons and on campuses blithely ignored the deadly reality of the philosophy just a few kilometers away on the other side of the Iron Curtain. The peoples of the Third World fought just struggles of liberation against colonial powers, only to see their countries taken over by Moscow-backed terror franchises. In America, now the world's strongest force in popular culture, the dichotomy of the sublime and the ridiculous could be seen on television with the dramatic mastery of *Playhouse 90* versus the inanity of *I Love Lucy*; and in engineering with the technical brilliance of American aerospace and architectural design versus the sophomoric faux female anatomical elements on the fronts of American cars like the Cadillac and the Edsel.

On the seas, for small-boat sailors, it was also a decade of stark contrasts and head-shaking bewilderment. There was great nautical achievement and there was absurd stuntsmanship. The voyages made during the decade run the gamut from boldly brave to bizarrely opéra bouffe. It was hardly a forgettable decade on the land or on the water.

The most bizarre of all the small-boat voyagers of the 1950s was Australian mining engineer Ben Carlin. What he did *couldn't* be done— but it was. During the war Carlin's vital role was to supervise the construction of latrines on various military bases across the Near and Far East. He would later claim that those regions had never seen plumbing like what he installed. One day in 1946 he was at an American air base in India where American vehicles were being collected to be turned over to the Indian government when he noticed a boat on the field. On closer inspection he found that it wasn't really a boat; it was more like a jeep, yet not really a jeep. It had a scow-type body, a jeep windshield, and four wheels buried in its hull-body.

The vehicle that Carlin saw, was a U.S. Army GP-A (General Purpose–Amphibious), the American answer to the Wehrmacht's *schwimmwagen*, a little amphibious workhorse based on the Volkswagen. The schwimmwagen and the GP-A, colloquially called the Seep (seagoing jeep), were little scout cars that could quickly ford streams and cross lakes without skipping a beat. Their job was to move a vital piece of information or equipment or a person somewhere else in a hurry. At least that was the idea. Americans thought that if the German army had one, they needed one, too, but in the rush to put a small amphibious vehicle into production in early 1942 they didn't do enough field-testing, so when it finally went overseas the Seep was too heavy at 3,650 pounds, and too slow with only sixty horsepower, and hard to maintain. Interestingly, the fifteen-foot, two-inch hull of this motorized dud was designed by the noted yacht designers Sparkman and Stephens, though the failure of the Seep was not their fault. None of that mattered to Carlin as he looked at the GP-A with a gleam in his eye that day in 1946. What he saw was beautiful; it had potential. He knew then that he had to have one, and that with it he would cross oceans.

After being discharged from the Australian army, he headed straight to Toledo, Ohio, where he tried to talk Willys-Overland, the manufacturer of jeeps, into sponsoring a round-the-world trip. They weren't interested. Neither was Ford, which had built the GP-A. Consumed by his desire to succeed, Carlin decided he would fund the trip on his own earnings, back pay the Indian government owed him, and winnings as a skillful poker player. He then scoured the United States for a GP-A, but discovered that because so many of them had been sent overseas, most to the Soviet Union, few were available. He finally found one he thought was in excellent condition at a government auction in Maryland, but when he bought it (through a mild swindle in league with an American friend), he discovered it needed a lot of work. His GP-A had dead batteries, clogged carburetor, rusty fuel tank, and locked transmission, characteristic of vehicles that have sat, unused, for a long time. At least he had the vehicle, so with a few grumbles he fixed the problems and drove it away.

Carlin's next stop was an Annapolis boatyard, where he set out to modify his GP-A to make it seaworthy. He had two big problems. The first was buoyancy; even empty, the original Seep was barely able to float (in the rush to production its weight had been underestimated by fully thirty percent!). To solve this he built an all-weather cabin of Masonite over the hull to provide shelter and keep the seas from washing in over the low deck. The second problem was harder to solve: fuel capacity. He struggled with several solutions, but finally had an aged tinsmith make a huge 386-gallon belly tank to fit under the hull between the wheels.

Concern for the integrity of the spot-welded hull caused him, as a final safety precaution, to have the whole underneath coated in liquid neoprene by a firm in nearby Wilmington, Delaware. He thought (wrongly) that his "boat" was the first ever to be so treated. German U-boats were coated during the war with a rubber-like substance to absorb sonar pings, and today all submarines are given an "anechoic" skin for the same reason. Many other modifications followed, including installing a heavy radio taken from a Sherman tank and rerigging the original steering mechanism, along with constant battling with leaking "sealed" joints.

It wasn't until the autumn of 1947 that Carlin's GP-A was ready for sea trials on the Chesapeake. Everything went wrong. The steering was vague, the boat continued to leak, the windows fogged up, his seat was too low to see easily outside, and, worst of all, the belly tank, which had cost him so much time and money, when empty exerted too much up-force under the hull and when full caused the craft to wallow.

Despondent, lacking funds, his visa about to expire, he considered giving up. He had already spent six thousand dollars, which in those days was enough to buy a very nice home in one of those new suburbs springing up all over the country. In an effort to increase his pressure on the Indian government, which still owed him back pay, he relocated to New York City to be closer to their consulate. He drove the GP-A to a boatyard in Brooklyn and left it there while he lived on thirty cents a day for meals. When his money came from India, he made final alterations and prepared for sea.

During the war he had met an American Red Cross canteen worker who had looked him up when he was in Annapolis. Now in

New York, she announced that she wanted to marry him and accompany him on his voyage. Elinore Arone was a nice girl from a nice Massachusetts family, but she also had an adventurous streak and was pretty, and Carlin needed help. He took her on as first mate in both senses of the term.

On June 16, 1948, the newlyweds rode the tide down the East River and out into New York Bay bound for the Azores, only two thousand miles away. They didn't get quite that far. Within the first few hours Carlin knew his boat was bad. It yawed constantly, the rudder couldn't hold a course, and it sat so low in the water that it was hazardous just to open the overhead hatch. In the cramped cabin hung engine fumes, which made Elinore so violently ill that a few days later she sank into something like a coma. Carlin, out of concern for her and realizing that the trip was not feasible, swung the bow southwest toward the Jersey shore, where he landed at the Shark River on June 21.

A national magazine heard of their saga and stepped in. They paid Carlin five hundred dollars for the exclusive rights, and with that he made the needed modifications to the GP-A, which by now he had christened *Half-Safe* after hearing the tag line from a deodorant commercial. Another departure was made on August 7 and after some good going the prop shaft thrust bearing cracked. They had no spare and they knew also that, having made only three hundred miles in five days of hard motoring, they hadn't enough fuel to make the Azores. While adrift and awaiting rescue, Carlin realized he would have to scuttle his boat rather than leave it as a hazard to ships. By great luck the passing tanker *New Jersey* picked them up, hoisted *Half-Safe* up into two empty davits, and took them to Montréal, its destination. The rescue by this particularly helpful ship was doubly fortuitous by saving not only the Carlins but *Half-Safe*.

From Montréal they drove east to Halifax to try once again. While Elinore went back to the States to earn cash, Carlin busily made yet more modifications, the most important of which was an increase in the fuel tankage, attempted by rigging up two surplus aircraft drop tanks in a tow-bridle arrangement. It proved impossible to coordinate the tanks so that they wouldn't crash together or cause too much drag or ram the boat. In other words, getting the system to work was maddeningly difficult, and after spending nearly a year on the problem, he ran out of funds. During the winter of 1949–50 he worked as an engineer on a merchant ship and dreamed of ways to make a tow tank feasible. It had been nearly four years since he had first seen a GP-A.

In the spring of 1950 he found the solution: a single custom-made tow tank with a capacity of 336 gallons and with an empty, buoyant conical nose and dead weight aft to keep the rear firmly in the water. Dragging this well-behaved tank behind on a stout nylon, shock-absorbing tow rope had the collateral benefit of damping *Half-Safe*'s fuel-robbing yawing motion. Even better, Carlin finally solved the whole steering problem when he added two plywood skegs on the tail of the body, which further improved directional stability.

When Elinore returned from the States the pair were ready to give it another shot. They departed July 19, 1950, at noon and soon cleared Halifax. Though Elinore was again sick, the much improved motion of the boat allowed her to acclimatize herself, and in a few days she was over the worst of it. She and Carlin split steering duties and now, because she had a hand in the management of the boat, she felt even better.

The Ford engine in the *Half-Safe* was built primarily for street use, not marine use. Under the conditions that Carlin now ran it, long hours without varying the engine speed, carbon deposits began to build up inside the combustion chambers, causing preignition pinging. To scrape off the deposits, a common maintenance job on cars up until the 1970s, Carlin had to whip off the cylinder head, clean it, and then reinstall it. This job took five hours each time, but since the motor was an L-head, was much easier to do than if it had been a modern overhead valve engine.

In heavy seas they tried to lie-to a sea anchor, but it didn't work because of the irregular underwater profile of the hull and the long arm of the towed tank. To prevent broaching, they had to keep the engine at idling speed and use the rudder to keep pointed into the waves. Though this wasted fuel and was wearying, at least it was an easy solution. Carlin had come so far technically with *Half-Safe* from his first trial on the Chesapeake that small problems such as this and the fact that the radio didn't work at sea as it had on land didn't bother him. With one pair of eyes always on watch, the radio failure wasn't as big a loss as Carlin had feared. He later found out that the electrolytic action of the salt water was shorting out the antenna where it attached to the body. It was a simple problem to solve, but neither he nor the technician who installed the radio had foreseen it.

Steady progress was made and, perhaps for the first time in their unconventional marriage, Ben and Elinore seemed to be enjoying themselves. It was not a perfect match, as Elinore was quiet-natured while Ben had a sharp, sarcastic tongue made all the worse by his compulsive, driven personality. He *would* cross the Atlantic in that damned machine if he had to tow it while swimming—something he had once done on the Severn River at Annapolis to save it from sinking when a bad leak developed.

Half-Safe made about three knots through the seas while burning about a gallon of fuel for every two and a half miles. To refuel they had to shut down, pull in the tow tank, and pump from it into an onboard main tank. This operation chewed up three hours about every third day. Even so, on August 4, their seventeenth day at sea, they found themselves more than halfway to their goal, having burned only 360 gallons of their total capacity of 882 gallons. Would they actually get across the Atlantic in a jeep?

A few days later it didn't look like it. On August 10 the Carlins heard a heart-stopping *bam!* under the boat. They couldn't imagine what had gone wrong. Ben immediately dove under to check for damage, and found, to his relief, that the nylon straps holding the belly tank on had worn out on the port side, and the tank had sunk down on that side, making its starboard end whack *Half-Safe*. It was a simple matter to cut the starboard straps and release the now-empty tank to solve the problem. Previously they had pumped the belly tank fuel into the towed tank and refilled it with seawater as ballast.

Nine days later, thirty-two days out of Halifax, they actually arrived at Flores in the Azores. This would be the worst leg of the transatlantic trip. Over the next few months they worked along the Azores, over to Madeira, and then to the Canaries. On Friday, February 23, 1951, they landed at Cape Juby in Morocco, having done the impossible—crossed the Atlantic Ocean in a jeep, of sorts!

That isn't the end of the story. Carlin's goal was to go around the world, and though Elinore had threatened many times—ever since Annapolis—to quit the venture, they continued on together, though not enjoying marital bliss à la the Müllers. From Cape Juby they drove up through Saharan Morocco to the Strait of Gibraltar. Crossing that, they reached Spain and then France. In June 1951 they made a well-publicized victory circuit of the Arc de Triomphe before touring other European capitals. Crossing from Calais to Dover amphibiously, they reached England, where Carlin completely disassembled and rebuilt *Half-Safe* in anticipation of the next legs of the round-the-world journey.

Half-Safe was a hit wherever it went on land or sea, though even the charms of Paris weren't enough to save the Carlin marriage.

It took four years for the couple to start that next leg, and during that time Ben wrote a book about their transatlantic voyage, *"Half-Safe": Across the Atlantic by Jeep*, which sold well internationally, bringing in enough money for the couple to live comfortably and pay for improvements to *Half-Safe*. Many steel parts were replaced with lightweight aluminum and plastic; the cabin was enlarged; the hull was made more rigid and waterproof; onboard tankage was increased; the interior was made more comfortable. When he had finished Carlin had also shaved nearly six hundred pounds from the weight, which would make the boat easier to handle and drive.

On April 22, 1955, they set off to recross the English Channel and work their way by road to India via Iraq, Iran, and Pakistan. In

Calcutta they accepted an offer to go to Australia with *Half-Safe* to promote book sales, so they and the GP-A went there by ship. When the sales tour was over they came back to Calcutta by ship to continue the tour, but it was here that Ben and Elinore mutually agreed that she would return to Europe. She just couldn't face the prospect of more time at sea in *Half-Safe* because of her tendency to seasickness. Also, she had decided to divorce Ben. Adventure was one thing; sado-masochism was something else.

Carlin now recruited a young man from Perth, Barry Hanley, to help him make the sea crossing from India to Burma. He considered the wartime Burma Road to be impassable, though on this point he was wrong. From Rangoon they traveled on to Bangkok, then to Saigon and Da Nang. There they put into the South China Sea and made the crossing over the pirate-infested waters to Hong Kong. From Hong Kong they went to Japan, where Hanley, like Elinore before him, escaped.

In June 1957 Carlin found yet another victim to subject to a long sea passage in enforced confines with him as he planned the dangerous transpacific crossing. This was Boye "Jingo" Lafayette DeMente, a twenty-eight-year-old American journalist living in Japan. DeMente suspected he could get a good story, but he didn't reckon on Carlin's increasing irascibility and vicious sarcasm. They left Wakkanai, Japan, on June 12 on the first leg of an island-hopping Pacific crossing, towing a new fuel canister with a 450-gallon capacity. By the time they chugged up to Anchorage, Alaska, on September 2 it was even money who would kill whom first, DeMente or Carlin. Along the way they endured the unwanted attention of the Soviet navy, terrible storms and even a tidal wave, and run-ins with Japanese fishing trawlers. Carlin suspected that DeMente planned to jump ship the first place they landed, and he was right.

But the abandonment by DeMente wasn't what worried Carlin the most. As he later wrote, for the past seven years he had been consumed by the thought of landing at Anchorage. He knew the final road run from there to Montréal would be all downhill. Yet getting to Anchorage across the Pacific would end the sea challenge of the journey—and in a way end the purpose of his life. What had driven him

all these years—a dozen now since had he first conceived the idea—
would be over.

When Carlin arrived at Montréal, thus achieving his round-the-
world goal, he got some publicity, but never as much as he thought he
deserved. Embittered, he tried to settle in the United States, where he
married again (his third marriage, including one before Elinore). Even
the birth of a daughter, his only child, wasn't enough to level his turbulent personality. He was divorced again and headed back to Australia,
where he found work in a boatyard. He died in 1981 at age sixty-nine, a
cantankerous, lonely man.

Half-Safe was put on display at his boyhood school, Guildford
Grammar School in Western Australia, where it remains today, a testament to the fact that even when dreams come true, happiness and fulfillment don't always result. Like some of our previous adventurers, Carlin had sought to give meaning to his life and cast himself as a great man
through nautical adventure. His voyage was to be a monument to himself. However, like some of the others before him, he found that it was
a fool's quest. He died without having won what might have given him
true happiness—the love of any of his three wives or of his daughter.

Elinore Carlin returned to the United States after her split from
Ben in India. She never remarried and positively refused to speak of her
time with Ben. Instead she carved a career for herself in New York
City as a lawyer recruitment specialist, a tough field that in the 1960s
was the province of men—but who were mere male lawyers to a woman
who had crossed an ocean in a jeep with Ben Carlin?

———◆———

Sanity returned to small-boat voyaging a few months after *Half-Safe* arrived at Cape Juby. The *Half-Safe* adventure had been rather silly, but
the relaunching of the *Nova Espero* was sensible. Stanley Smith and a
new sailing mate, Charles Violet, refurbished and improved the *Nova
Espero* for another transatlantic run. Since her first voyage a proper
cabin had replaced the up-turned dinghy, and the rig had been altered
to a yawl, so in bad weather they could have a mizzen riding sail. The

little twenty-foot gunter-rigged boat had become something of a celebrity in England, so when the men departed they were cheered on by a gaggle of press folks at the South Bank Exhibition in London. This was in early May, during the 1951 Festival of Britain, organized to show the world that Britain was coming out of its postwar slump and that its industry was strong, vigorous, and ready for the future. The crew of *Nova Espero* had on board sample British products to take to New York as symbols of Britain's industrial vitality. The most dramatic proof of this was that they had *no* freshwater on board. Instead, they took with them equipment for a new British chemical desalination process they planned to use for all their freshwater.

Two weeks after their departure Smith and Violet were caught in a nasty blow in the mouth of the English Channel, with Ushant, France, as a menacing lee shore. Hour by hour they lost sea room while riding to a sea anchor and having hoisted the riding sail. When nearly on the rocks they prepared to inflate their life raft. What good that would have done on a rocky lee coast is doubtful, but it was all they had. They were saved when the wind suddenly moderated and they were able to hoist the jib and work off the shore. A few days later they were sliding down the Bay of Biscay toward Spain and the trade-wind route.

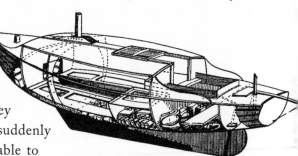

The lovely *Nova Espero* gained a mizzen mast and a proper cabin for its second Atlantic crossing in 1951. Stanley Smith and Charles Violet depended on desalination kits to make potable water en route.

Gales struck again, and while riding to the sea anchor one of their rudder gudgeons came loose, meaning the rudder was held by one hinge only. In this vulnerable position *Nova Espero* was hit by a rogue wave and nearly turned over, saved only by her heavy keel. When the storm abated they rigged a jury steering system and headed for Horta in the Azores to make permanent repairs.

Leaving Horta, they soon discovered that marine growth on the hull was dramatically slowing them down. Because they therefore might not have enough desalination chemicals to last to New York, they wisely chose to make for Nova Scotia, where the little boat had originally been built, because the winds were more favorable to making a fast landfall there. Once arrived, Smith and Violet scraped the hull, repainted it, and proceeded to New York, arriving at City Island on September 11, 110 days after leaving Dartmouth, England.

Another sensible British boat crossed the Atlantic that summer. This was the beautiful little *Sopranino*, designed by the J. Laurent Giles firm for British yachtsman Patrick Ellam. Ellam's prior sailing experience included time on the North Sea and the Bay of Biscay, so he was not a rank amateur. His previous boat had been the sailing canoe *Theta*, on which he had made several crossings of the English Channel—no mean feat. Now he wanted something bigger, dryer, and with more storage because he proposed to cross the Atlantic.

As a young designer for the J. Laurent Giles firm, Colin Mudie penned the lines for the lovely *Sopranino* and accompanied its owner Patrick Ellam on its transatlantic voyage.

The design the Giles firm handed him produced a boat nineteen feet, eight inches long, with a beam of five feet, four inches. She had a little cabin forward with two bunks and a chart table, while amidships there was a steering cockpit. The tall marconi rig was counterbalanced by a large lead slug bolted to the fixed keel. Like the *Nova Espero* before her, the *Sopranino* was nothing more than a big dinghy, though perfectly conceived in every detail and proportion, and by far the prettiest little hull set to water of all our small-boat voyagers so far.

Colin Mudie was the young designer with the Giles firm who had actually designed the boat, and when Ellam offered him the chance to make the transatlantic trip with him he gladly accepted. The pair set out from Falmouth rather late in the season on September 6, 1951. Like Smith and Violet, they soon found themselves in a raging gale off Ushant, but they had fifty miles of sea room, and a better suited boat. Before their departure Mudie had wisely decided to cut down the tall mast and slightly reduce the weight of the keel to improve buoyancy and lower windage. These changes paid off in their first blow. In fact, they were so unconcerned that they simply hove-to and lay down in their bunks. Even beam on to the seas the little *Sopranino* behaved like a champ and merely rocked gently.

Eleven days out they made the Spanish port of La Coruña but were forced to remain there for more than a week while Mudie recovered from food poisoning. After a stop in Lisbon to scrape the hull they pushed on to Cape Saint Vincent and then Casablanca on the coast of Africa. There it was Ellam's turn to hold up progress. Carelessly, he was on a seawall while huge ocean swells were battering it. One of them washed him off and then pummeled him against the stone wall. It was ten days before he recovered from his injuries.

On January 11, 1952, Ellam and Mudie pointed west toward Barbados. Pushed along by the trade winds, they averaged nearly a hundred miles a day, much of that under the control of a self-steering arrangement they had concocted. Self-steering at the time was only beginning to make use of mechanical devices, and balancing the rig in the manner of Slocum or Fenger was still the norm. Self-steering was effective only if the basic boat design was good, and the *Sopranino's* certainly was. On their best day they made an impressive 134 miles.

Reading poetry, fishing, and listening to the radio were the principal pastimes of these very decent chaps on this idyllic ocean ramble. Their cruise was perhaps the first-ever transoceanic voyage in a small yacht that wasn't full of the storm and stress we've come to expect our adventurers to suffer. These were two competent sailors, though not professionals. They had a well-designed and well-built boat, and they had brought along provisions that were more than ample for the voyage. The predictability and comfort of the trip set the example for thousands of yachtsmen in fiberglass boats in later years. The easy grace and polite behavior of Ellam and Mudie also set a standard for those who followed. How very different from the howling rants of Carlin and his desperate attempt to prove something to the world. The best leaders lead by example, and that is what the voyage of Ellam and Mudie in the *Sopranino* did: they led yachting into a new era.

On February 9, 1952, they made Bridgetown, Barbados. Later still, they completed their voyage in New York, after having put ten thousand miles under the keel.

Another voyage that seems so peculiarly 1950s-ish was the scientific expedition of the young French doctor Alain Bombard across the Atlantic on an inflatable boat. In 1951 Bombard was so much disturbed by the twenty-one lives lost in a trawler sinking on the north coast of France near Boulogne that he began to brood about the whole problem of shipwrecks and their survivors. He pondered the dying shipwreck survivors in Théodore Géricault's famous painting, *The Raft of the "Medusa,"* and wondered why people died so quickly after sinkings when it seemed that there were enough natural resources available for sustenance.

From his ruminations he came up with a theory that survivors could last indefinitely on fish and other marine life even if they had no freshwater. This bold proposal was scoffed at by some, but Bombard's force of personality and his evident intelligence and background caused others, including prominent scientists, to think that the theory was worth investigating. This was the early 1950s when virtually everyone who traveled in those days still did so by ocean liner, not airliner. If Bombard's theories were correct, many lives might be saved.

With a research grant to study at the famed Museum of Oceanography in Monaco, he went there and converted theory into numbers and charts. Most of his work involved detailed chemical analyses of fish and plankton, to find out how much of the various types of salt each species contained, what natural sugars were available in each, and what was the water percentage per type of flesh. He came to the conclusion that if a castaway were to squeeze six to seven pounds of fish flesh per day and mix the liquid with a small quantity of seawater, that person would meet his or her water needs and still avoid nephritis, inflammation of the kidneys due to excessive salt intake. He posited, too, that castaways had to supplement this diet with plankton, because only in plankton could various necessary vitamins be found at sea.

Until Bombard's work it was thought that the average survivor on the seas could last for thirty days without food and ten days without water. Bombard's diet, if correct, could sustain a castaway indefinitely or until his will to live ran out; Bombard's studies had shown that most died from despair rather than physical privation.

Moreover, to prove his theory Bombard was prepared to put his life on the line. He proposed a transatlantic voyage by inflatable *without food or water* on board. This was a doubly risky venture. It would be the first transoceanic voyage for an inflatable boat (in the modern sense of the term—not like the raft *Nonpareil*), and it would be all the more hazardous because of the total absence of supplies.

Members of the scientific community, as well as Bombard's friends, were divided over his prospects for success. His first child had recently been born, and this seemed a foolish and grandiose project by a young man eager to make his name. Bombard would not be dissuaded, however, and so with the backing of a Dutch businessman he planned his voyage, bought the equipment, and on October 19, 1952, set out from Las Palmas in the Canaries. An Englishman who had earlier signed on for the voyage disappeared at the last minute. Bombard was alone.

He named his inflatable *L'Hérétique* in defiance of his critics. It was fifteen feet long and six feet wide, equipped with a smallish gunter sail and leeboards. The drifting voyage down the trades to the West Indies would be long. On board Bombard had only a fishing skein, one long and one short fishing spear and some fishhooks and line, plus a few books. Since he had originally planned it to be a two-man voyage, the boat was commodious for him alone—though there wouldn't be a dry moment the whole trip because of the low freeboard. Also, he had no chance of catching rain in the floor of the inflatable because it would be too full of salt crust. He would have to catch it in the sail or in clothes spread open, as some of the earlier voyagers had.

His first night out proved to be nearly his last. Leaving his sail up he settled down for a good sleep, expecting the weather to hold until morning. But during the night the wind increased, and so did the swells, until one wave, probably not very big, broke over his wood transom and pooped *L'Hérétique*. In a panic Bombard woke up, thinking the boat had sunk under him. When he realized the boat was full of water, he bailed out, but from then on he knew that he was no longer in the

Fifty years after the event the debate continues over how much, if any, freshwater Dr. Alain Bombard took aboard his inflatable during his controversial voyage.

scholarly confines of the museum library in Monaco. He was exactly where he had told everyone he wanted to be, so he'd have to live with it—or die with it.

Four days into the voyage there was another calamity when his own carelessness caused his best sail to be washed overboard. His second-best sail, the only one remaining, had a tear in it, so he spent the better part of a day sewing it. Not a week into the voyage and things were looking dark. And they got worse. Even though it should have been raining with some regularity, he claimed that it was three weeks before he saw his first squall. He had been successful catching fish and pressing water from their flesh, but even so, his strength was decreasing. He knew he would become weaker, but he was tortured by saltwater sores and diarrhea from the poor diet.

Bombard depended on an air cushion to keep him out of the inflatable's wet floor, but one day when it went overboard he imprudently decided to swim after it. Before he dove over he tossed out his sea anchor, believing it could hold *L'Hérétique* while he retrieved the cushion. Once he was in the water and swimming toward the cushion he realized that the anchor had not gone into the water as it should have, but rather had been caught by a puff of air and was now acting as a parachute sail, pulling the boat steadily *away* from him. Anyone who has ever been tossed out of even a small sailboat knows how hard it is to swim after a runaway boat. Bombard saved himself only because he was a highly trained swimmer who had previously swum the English Channel competitively. He had to swim hard for an hour before the sea anchor finally settled into the water and the boat stopped drifting.

Fifty-three days into the voyage the British steamer *Arakaka* came abreast of him and stopped. He accepted an invitation to come aboard, thinking it would be a good time to wire his wife and let her know that he was well. The British crew offered him a hot meal, which he at first refused, but after getting a whiff from the galley he allowed himself to eat a fried egg, a small piece of liver, and a little fruit. Later he was to regret this for two reasons: it gave his critics an excuse to condemn him; and—a more immediate reason—after he reboarded his boat he suddenly had awful stomach cramps. His system just couldn't handle the fruit fibers and grease of the eggs.

Back in his inflatable he writhed in pain and felt all the worse for having learned while on board that his navigation had been way off. He was ten degrees farther east than he had hoped and still had six hundred miles to go. It was a bitter blow, especially since the meal aboard *Arakaka* had restored his normal appetite, and now he could think of nothing but three-course table meals.

Twelve more days of suffering followed until December 23, when he arrived at Barbados, sixty-five days after leaving Las Palmas. The British governor of the island, a former prisoner of the Japanese, knew something about physical privation and lavished every courtesy on the doctor.

The world was not so kind. Though many accepted Bombard's tale of voluntary privation completely, others doubted his story and said that it was impossible to go without water to the extent he claimed. Perhaps the air chambers had freshwater in them, perhaps a few gallons of water were suspended under the boat when he set out? Some members of the yacht club in Las Palmas reported that Bombard had aboard twenty-five gallons of water and enough food for three months. His claim that he received help only from one passing ship is challenged by photos purportedly showing him receiving aid from the Dutch ship *Bennekom.*

It is possible, but not likely, that Bombard did what he claimed he had done. Whether or not he left the Canaries without freshwater is almost irrelevant. The one glaring fact often overlooked is that he was sailing in a region and at a time of year where squalls were routine. The surface area of his boat was large enough to allow him to stretch out his sail as a big rain catcher. If he didn't pass through a squall during those first three weeks, as he claimed, then he still had an ample supply of fish because they are abundant in the area. Maybe it would be correct to say that Bombard's theory was, to a degree, found valid during those first few weeks, though even this is a stretch. Would his experiment have worked in other parts of the world, and under less-than-ideal circumstances? Certainly not.

None of this really matters much. The reason for his "scientific expedition," done fairly or not, was largely obviated within a few years by the advent of routine transatlantic passenger jet flights. Britain's De-Havilland Comet and America's 707 killed passenger ships, as roll-on roll-off cargo containers killed thousands of tramp freighters and banana boats. The "golden" era of shipwreck sagas was coming to an end. Bombard would be remembered mostly for the line of inflatables that bear his name.

Two other young men who could have used Bombard's luck on their life raft journey were Fred Ericsson and Ensio Tiira. They were two ex-sailors who, running away from troubles in Ericsson's native Sweden and Tiira's Finland, had decided on a whim to join the French Foreign

Legion. This was not the brightest move, as many could have told them, but they had led impulsive lives and they saw it as a chance for a fresh start. After training in Algeria they were put on a troopship bound for the French colony of Indochina. The year was 1953, and Ho Chi Minh's Viet Minh communists needed some attention in the north.

The "fresh start" they were seeking now looked more like a quick end; realizing the magnitude of what they were headed into, the two decided to jump ship. It wasn't so easy to do, however. First, they were in the Indian Ocean, the most treacherous in the world and practically devoid of island refuges. Second, native French officers and tough ex-SS sergeants kept the ship under tight control, so even getting to the railing was difficult when near a harbor. Their break came because the troopship they were on was Norwegian and had only been chartered by the French government. The mostly Norwegian crew felt sympathetic toward the Scandinavian duo and agreed to help them slip overboard. The plan was that once they entered the Strait of Malacca between Sumatra and Malaysia, they would release a four-by-four-foot aluminum tube life raft, jump in after it, and then paddle to shore. It might take them hours of paddling, but surely they would make the town of Kutaradja on the northwestern tip of Sumatra.

With only a few pieces of bread, a hunk of sausage, and some cheese, along with wine in a rubber hot-water bottle, the two made ready for their escape. They stole civilian clothes from some sailors and waited for the night when the steamer entered the Strait. True to their word, their Norwegian supporters helped them elude the patrolling deck guard, release the small raft, and jump over the side. In a moment they were paddling away in the direction of the shore as fast as they could. Time was of the essence because when the tide changed, the current through the Strait would be westerly, taking them back into the large Indian Ocean.

Suddenly alarms blared on the ship. With legendary efficiency, the ex-SS guards had noticed almost immediately that the raft was missing. To the horror of Ericsson and Tiira, the ship slowly swung around and came back toward them, its huge searchlight sweeping the sea like the tongue of a giant anteater. The two escapees quickly changed direction to avoid the light and get out of the path of the searching steamer. Fortunately, their boat was so low in the water they were often hidden behind ocean swells. After what seemed like hours, the light was switched off and the steamer resumed its course toward Saigon. The two had succeeded in escaping, but as dawn broke they saw no land and hadn't a clue where they were.

This morning of February 23, 1953, was the beginning of a horrible ordeal. On a raft half the size of a sheet of plywood, the two men were exceedingly cramped, crowded together on a cloth-webbing "floor." Paddling was difficult because the raft's square shape made it want to spin rather than go straight, but on and on they paddled, hoping to see a line of green on the horizon. They saw nothing that first day. Eventually they realized they were out of the channel and back in the Indian Ocean. Fighting waves of fear, they tried to paddle against the current and regain the channel, but after a few days of exhausting effort they gave up. The meager supplies they had brought, thinking they had only one night's paddling and a day or two's walk ahead, were quickly consumed. They prayed for rain and looked for fish; they did manage several times to catch and eat small crabs they found crawling on clumps of seaweed or pieces of floating branches.

Giving up on getting to Sumatra, they used a paddle for a mast and a shirt for a sail and tried to bear off to the northwest for India. It was a long shot but the only one they had. Day by day they found themselves alone on the ocean because, surprisingly, no ships came into view. Were they that far out of the shipping lane they wondered?

Then the sharks came. Their only defense was their paddles, but they beat off attack after attack by the marauding monsters, who slashed not only the perimeter of the raft but right up through the center, through the cloth webbing. The paddles won the day, but with the web deck in tatters they had nowhere to huddle away from the next onslaught.

After two weeks of this horror they finally caught some rain on the side of the rubber hot-water bottle. By now they were so weak it hardly had any effect; they needed much more water and more food. Their attempts to catch fish failed, and there weren't enough crabs.

Then a turtle swam by. They quickly wrestled it on board, and Tiira, who alone had sufficient remaining strength, managed to kill it with a piece of broken mirror glass. He and Ericsson drank the blood, but it wasn't enough. Ericsson died on the eighteenth day.

Holding to a promise they had made to each other, Tiira did not shove his dead friend's body overboard. He had used a length of line to reweave a platform for the raft, and he now tied the corpse to it. This act of loyalty nearly cost him his life.

Four days later, Ericsson's distended and decomposing body attracted more sharks. They lunged up onto the platform again and again, ripping off pieces of the dead man's flesh and trying also to pull Tiira into the water. He fought wildly to fend them off and maintain his balance but realized that the only way to get rid of them was to surrender Ericsson's corpse. He slipped the knots and let the body slide overboard. It was an awful feeling to break his promise, but, worse, he was now completely alone on the wide, inhospitable ocean. Even the corpse had been a kind of company.

Every day was now a lonely struggle to accumulate enough rainwater on the side of the rubber bottle to survive. The turtle meat had been supplemented by some other thin picking, but it wasn't enough. Tiira realized too that he was never going to make India because he was heading west toward Ceylon instead of northwest. He had been on the raft a month, and he knew he was dying.

On the thirty-second night he opened his dull eyes and thought he saw a ship. It was

Legionnaire Ensio Tiira jumped ship to avoid battling the communist Viet Minh forces in Indochina. He wound up fighting sharks in the Indian Ocean instead.

quite nearby, or was it a hallucination? No, Tiira could see men on deck—why didn't they look his way? He had no flares, and his flashlight batteries had long since died. He was too weak to shout. The ship would be past him in a few seconds. Somehow he managed to do the only thing that could have saved his life—he rapped the dead flashlight on the aluminum side of the raft. The hollow ping drew the attention of the men on board, and he was rescued by the British freighter *Alendi Hill*. He had drifted six hundred miles and weighed now only fifty-six pounds but was lucky to be alive.

A Frenchman who had not joined the Foreign Legion was Jean Lacombe, a New York–based photographer. On April 19, 1955, he left the Mediterranean port of Toulon in his small, but sensible, eighteen-foot cutter *Hippocampe*. He then worked his way west to Barcelona and through the Strait of Gibraltar to Las Palmas, and from there made a trade-winds crossing to Puerto Rico, from which it was an easy sail north to Atlantic City and then New York, where he arrived on July 20.

Ten days earlier, another sensible boat had begun an even longer voyage, skippered by a young man who defied the stereotypical view of Western youth in the 1950s as seen in the movie released that year, *Rebel without a Cause*. John Guzzwell, a Briton living in Canada, wasn't full of anxiety, or sociopathic tendencies; he just wanted to sail—and sail and sail and sail. Inspired by Ellam and Mudie's voyage in the *Sopranino*, he asked the J. Laurent Giles firm for a design based on the Ellam boat. He stipulated, though, that it be capable of an around-the-world voyage.

The Giles firm's solution to the problem was a boat much like the *Sopranino*, but two feet longer, or almost twenty-two feet long. The ten percent increase in length allowed a huge increase in interior capacity and a larger keel. Thicker planking was also specified because Guzzwell and Giles both knew that ocean debris, like logs, was more likely to be encountered in the Pacific and Indian Oceans than in the Atlantic, where the *Sopranino* had made its crossing.

Guzzwell rented space beside a fish-and-chip shop in Victoria, British Columbia, and began constructing the boat. He had learned the rudiments of boatbuilding from his father back on the Channel Island of Jersey but had never before built one from scratch himself. On the few afternoons when he took a break from building, he would go to the maritime museum in Victoria to gaze on Voss's restored *Tilikum* for inspiration. He taught himself lofting, steam bending, carvel planking, and so on, and in only nine months had created in red cedar and oak what Giles had conceived on paper. Photos taken during construction show what a masterful job he did. The boat, which he named *Trekka* (from the South African *trek*, to make a journey), was a thing of beauty built by a true artist.

After completing and launching the boat at Victoria he headed down the west coast of North America, but off Cape Flattery, Washington, he was hit by a gale. South of Cape Mendocino, California, he again lay-to in a gale, then when the wind speed dropped, he got under way. The wind increased to seventy miles an hour. He ran before it under storm jib and streaming warps. After a day he pulled the jib down and again lay ahull.

John Guzzwell's woodworking artistry as applied to the hull of his *Trekka*.

He stopped in San Francisco, one of the world's most beautiful ports, and while there met a family who would play a large part in his coming adventures: the Smeetons, a retired couple then sailing their forty-six-foot teak double-ender *Tzu Hang* around the world. Miles Smeeton, a former brigadier in the British Army, and his wife, Beryl, had no sailing experience when they bought their yacht, but they were game for adventure and prepared to try anything before the rot set in. Guzzwell was just a younger version of the pair, and soon a friendship developed. They all agreed that in tandem they would make the voyage to Hawaii.

Guzzwell had perfected the technique of twin headsail self-steering, a practice then being popularized by the writings of the French maritime adventurer Marin-Marie, and to everyone's surprise he reached Oahu before the much larger *Tzu Hang*. They continued to sail together south to Fanning Island, then Samoa, Tonga, and New Zealand. *Trekka* was hoisted out of the water in New Zealand, and Guzzwell joined the Smeetons as crew to help them make the difficult run to and around Cape Horn. The voyage became an epic struggle between humanity and nature when the *Tzu Hang*—all forty-six feet of her—pitchpoled down a huge wave and hit the water upside down. Beryl Smeeton broke her collarbone and twisted her ankle, and the yacht lost her masts. When the boat righted the situation looked bleak for the trio until Guzzwell used his carpentry skills to construct a jury rig that saw them safely to port at Coronel, Chile.

From Chile Guzzwell flew to South Africa to help his mother pack her belongings and move back to the island of Jersey. That done, he flew back to New Zealand, blew the dust off *Trekka*, added a fiberglass bottom layer to the hull, and returned to sea. He had been separated sixteen months from his beautiful boat, with which he felt a spiritual bond, and it was now time to complete the circumnavigation he had started almost three years earlier.

He left the North Island April 21, 1958, and crossed the Tasman Sea to the Great Barrier Reef. Skirting the reef, as Bligh had done, he made the Torres Strait. He was lucky that the weather was cooperative during this stretch, yet it also attests to the quality of his boat and his abilities as a skipper that the voyage was remarkably uneventful. In a smaller boat he would have been knocked about more, and supplies would have been marginal, but *Trekka*'s almost twenty-two feet made her roomy enough for one man and enough food to last each leg.

Just as spring began in the Southern Hemisphere Guzzwell reached the Indian Ocean. He left the Coco Islands in early October and arrived at Durban, South Africa, at the beginning of December. On one noon-to-noon run he made an impressive 155 miles even though he was sailing alone. He spent a month in South Africa before heading northwest to Saint Helena, Ascension Island, and then Barbados. He had now crossed three of the world's great oceans in his little home-made boat, mostly without fuss since the great blow off the Pacific coast of California.

After traversing the Panama Canal for the princely sum of $2.16 in fees, he made for the Galápagos Islands and after that Hawaii. When he arrived there on July 29, 1959, he had technically completed his round-the-world voyage. Even so, his goal was to get back to Victoria, and he reached there on September 12, four years and two months after his departure. Years later his pride and joy *Trekka*, joined the *Tilikum*, her predecessor and inspiration, in Victoria's maritime museum, where they no doubt inspire future generations of voyagers.

◆ ◆ ◆

Tilikum wasn't the only dugout to make an ocean crossing. Hannes Lindemann, a German doctor working for the American tire company Firestone in Liberia, had met Dr. Alain Bombard on a trip to Morocco and was intrigued by the Frenchman's theories, though highly skeptical. He decided to test them himself and because he was living in a country where dugouts were common, he set about to build one for a run across the Atlantic.

The canoe he created from a mahogany log was twenty-three and a half feet long and thirty inches wide. Under it he attached a laminated wood keel weighted with 250 pounds of lead. It was decked over with plywood, had corkwood sponsons on either side, and was covered in fiberglass for strength and resistance to teredo worms. She was rigged as a gaff-rigged sloop, with an aft cockpit. Lindemann's design had been influenced by reading Voss's account of his circumnavigation in *Tilikum*.

After his first stab at dugout construction went up in flames, Lindemann built *Liberia II*, which proved unstable on his first attempt at the crossing. It was too tender laterally, and the rudder was too weak. After seventeen days at sea he returned to the African coast and shipped the boat back to Germany. He deepened and added weight to the keel, upgraded the rudder, and made a few other modifications.

Then he conducted sea trials off the coast of Portugal, but these went poorly, so he made more modifications.

Finally, on October 25, 1955, Lindemann set out from Las Palmas, the jumping-off point in the Canaries for so many of these voyages. The *Liberia II* was now a much better behaved craft. Though Lindemann was anxious much of the trip, fearing of ocean predators and speeding cargo ships, he was never attacked or rammed. His biggest problems at first were storms and saltwater sores, but then the loss of his rudder drove him to the edge psychologically, even though compared to most people he had an iron will and was rigidly self-disciplined. The rigors of the trip nevertheless caused him at one point to think he ought to abandon it and accept rescue from the next ship he met. He resisted this easy way out, however, and proceeded on.

Light winds were a mixed blessing when they followed a storm because on the one hand they gave him a respite from the heavy seas, yet on the other they lengthened the trip which prolonged his physical agony. During this time when he needed even larger supplies of food and water he found himself jettisoning cans and boxes. He would realize later that the drugs he had been taking to stay awake were making him delusional, and it was during these times of semi-insensibility that he made astounding mistakes like dumping provisions.

Oddly enough, though his voyage started out as an investigation of the viability of the Bombard hypothesis, he never put it to the test, which is a shame because with Lindemann's medical education and personal integrity he certainly could have provided reliable insight about its practicality. Yet all along the way he ate fruit and drank canned milk and freshwater. His doubts about Bombard had blossomed before he left.

The *Liberia II* arrived at the harbor of Christiansted, Saint Croix, on December 29, 1955. He had been at sea sixty-five days.

———◆◆———

Alain Bombard gets the credit, or blame, for launching another raft of dreamers. The group were Canadians under the leadership of Henri Beaudout, who had organized an explorer's club for Canadian youth.

He wanted to demonstrate that Bombard's theories were correct and also set a good example for the club's members by making a pioneer voyage across the Atlantic by wooden raft. (Thor Heyerdahl's *Kon Tiki* adventure in 1947 had inspired a host of copycat rafters, including sixty-one-year-old William Willis and his rather large *Seven Little Sisters*, which made a journey from Peru to Samoa in 115 days in 1954. The remarkable Willis will appear in detail in the next chapter.)

Beaudout's group of Québecois enthusiasts built their raft, about seventeen by thirteen feet, of nine trunks of red cedar bound with hemp rope. A platform was built on the raft with a little cabin in its center. A pre-Roman style bipod mast supported a large square sail, and along the sides of the raft there were sweeps. Beaudout's craft, *L'Égaré* (Stray Ones), was a giant leap backward in technology. The *Nonpareil* of 1867 was considerably more advanced!

On June 11, 1955, the pile of logs shoved off from Montréal for the trip down the Saint Lawrence. Sixty-six days later *L'Égaré* was blown ashore on the coast of Newfoundland by Hurricane Connie, which came early in the season. The fact that Connie was early doesn't excuse Beaudout for heading out to sea so late in the season. His passage down the Saint Lawrence had been so miserably slow that he should have abandoned the voyage and waited until the next season before departing. Most late-season departures wind up in unhappiness, and *L'Égaré*'s experience was no different.

Beaudout and his gang built another raft the next year, predictably called *L'Égaré II*. It had a radio and a few supplies, but not much more. Being French-Canadians, their loyalties remained strong to the old country, and they were hoping to add credence to Frenchman Bombard's theory.

Having learned from the previous year's mistake, this time they left almost a month earlier, on May 24, 1956, and not from Montréal, but from Nova Scotia. For crew Beaudout had with him Jose Martinez, Marc Modena, and Gaston Vanackère, as well as two cats. Their days were occupied trying to maintain a course, navigating with a sextant, and fishing. According to Bombard's recommendation, they caught and pressed fish and netted plankton. A month into the voyage, perhaps because of the diet, Martinez became very ill and had to be taken off by a passing fishing boat.

The others soldiered on and managed to reach the English Channel and by August 20 they were only twenty miles from the Lizard. At this point they launched flares and were then towed into Falmouth, having survived eighty-nine days at sea. Their voyage proved nothing as far as Bombard's theories went. It was just one more bizarre addition to a zany decade of voyaging.

Hannes Lindemann, in the meantime, had returned to Las Palmas, intending to make another crossing. This time he would do what Romer had mistakenly been given credit for doing—cross the Atlantic in a kayak. Lindemann's kayak was a real kayak, not a large sailing canoe. It was an off-the-shelf Klepper Aerius two-seater; the only modification was the application of an extra spray cover sewn onto the decking from the stern to the mast socket forward of the coaming. The frame and hull were standard offerings from the Rosenheim factory. Lindemann, though by this time a minor nautical celebrity in Germany, insisted on paying for the boat himself even though in postwar Germany money was hard to come by for anyone, including doctors.

To the boat he added an outrigger for balance and for propulsion a mainmast on which he could hoist either a gaff or a square sail, and behind him he mounted half a kayak paddle as a mizzenmast, from which he could hoist a small square sail. He had completely discarded all belief in Bombard's theories except for the notion that despair among castaways is more dangerous than physical privation. This he totally accepted and reinforced by studying the works of the German psychiatrist Johannes Schultz, who propounded *autogenics*, a type of self-hypnosis in which one can gain control over a difficult situation by mentally removing oneself from it. (Henri Charrière, the prisoner on Devil's Island who wrote *Papillon*, claimed that self-hypnosis during his years of solitary confinement saved his life.) To help him achieve mental harmony Lindemann took along a copy of the ancient Hindu devotional text *Bhagavad Gita*.

Under the deck of the kayak he stuffed four hundred pounds of food, camera equipment, navigation tools, and spare parts. Nonkayakers are always surprised at how much can be stored aboard one of these little boats, but, up to a point, more equipment meant more ballast and a more stable motion. Lindemann later pointed out that the Klepper's motion was much more gentle than the *Liberia II*'s, even though the latter had a lead-ballasted keel.

Consciously following in the footsteps of his fellow countryman Franz Romer, Lindemann glided his seventeen-foot *Liberia III* out of Las Palmas on October 20, 1956, bound for the Antilles. On the very first day of the voyage things began to go wrong. His outrigger became loose, his boat sat too low in the water, and his doubled spray skirt around the cockpit didn't keep out water. Also, the chemicals that he had used to waterproof the spray skirt affected his skin, so he began itching. Scratching in a salty environment only aggravates the skin, so Lindemann knew then this would be a tough journey. Mentally he was prepared, or so he thought. He knew this time not to take drugs that would affect his mental judgment. He also knew that he must rest more and force himself to sleep even if conditions were dangerous. Lack of sleep was a greater danger. Before leaving he had adopted the mantra, "I shall succeed, I shall make it." He repeated that to himself now as he dealt with the loose outrigger. The next day his leeboard floated away, but he tried to accept this philosophically. If he let little disasters eat at him, he could never handle the bigger ones. Mental control would make or break this voyage. He must remain optimistic.

It was a difficult journey over the next few months. He began to hallucinate. Talking waves and talking spray skirts asked him questions and made demands. Ships appeared that weren't really there, and sometimes he had the sensation of going backward. A month out, when the ship *Blitar* stopped to offer him food, he forcefully declined their help, much to the crew's surprise. Lindemann had determined that one of the psychological boosts he needed was to feel complete independence from outside help. To accept help meant he was weak. He had to convince himself that he wasn't, and therefore no help could be accepted. He repeated his mantra, "I shall succeed, I shall make it."

On December 15, during a storm, a swell flipped the boat over and Lindemann found himself, semidelirious, in the water with the boat moving away from him. He came to and swam for the upturned hull, but algae growth made it slippery to hold onto. Being over six feet tall, his arm reach was long enough that he could hold the boat in a giant bear hug. Hour after hour he rode out the storm in this position. Fatigue had caused the inattention that probably led to the boat turning turtle in the first place, and now he couldn't resist it any longer. He fell asleep on the overturned hull.

When he awoke he found he had spent nine hours clinging to the slippery fabric hull. He had to get it righted and get back in. He used the classic Johnson maneuver—tying a line to the opposite side and pulling it over. It worked on the first try. Back in the boat, it took him an hour to bail, but he left in about twelve gallons of seawater as additional ballast. When this was done he took stock of the damage. His camera was gone, as was a compass; a flashlight had fallen out, but he had a spare; his anchor had plunged to the bottom, too, along with a hundred other little things—but where were his food tins? They were gone, too, all of them except for some cans of evaporated milk. Fortunately he still had his speargun, so, after repeating his mantra, he shot a fish and enjoyed a good meal. He *would* make it, he told himself again.

Two days later he capsized again, this time losing the invaluable speargun. He righted the boat easily, got back in, bailed as before, and chanted his mantra. By now he knew he must be close to some islands, but where were they?

After two more days of hope and cautious optimism, his rudder partly came off because one aluminum pintle had corroded away in the salt water. Without the rudder he was at the mercy of the seas because he also had no sea anchor. The wind would spin the boat beam on to the waves at any moment and it would capsize again. Now, though, he had mentally tuned himself to automatically respond to setbacks by thinking positively. He quickly devised a way to fix the rudder with a loop of wire and jumped into the water to make the repair. It worked, and he was out of immediate danger. Next he set out to sew a new sea anchor. He would do whatever it took to succeed.

A few days later, Christmas Eve, the rudder pedals went limp under his feet. Looking aft he saw that the rudder had completely fallen away. Had he not sewn the replacement sea anchor after the last rudder failure he would have been lost in the next storm, but now the weather had eased and he could still sail on by using a paddle held astern for steering.

Hannes Lindemann stands by *Liberia III,* the first real kayak to cross an ocean in modern times. It was no coincidence he followed Romer's route.

Bad weather and hallucinations plagued him the final two weeks of the voyage, yet he persevered. On the seventy-second day he rolled up on the beach at Saint Martin, triumphant. There he rested a few days, had his rudder permanently repaired by a local mechanic, and then continued on to his ultimate goal, which he reached on his seventy-sixth day out. It was Saint Thomas, Romer's original landing point. Hannes Lindemann was actually the first man in history to cross an ocean intentionally in a true kayak.

———•◦•———

Colin Mudie had become involved in what turned out to be another small-boat venture at this time. It all started one dreary day in 1956 while he was sitting in his London flat with his wife Rosemary and a few sailing mates. Kicking back and forth some "what ifs," the group developed the notion that it might be possible not just to sail a boat across the Atlantic on the trade-winds route from the Canaries to the West Indies, as the little *Sopranino* designed by Mudie had, but to fly a balloon across. If that could be done it would be the first transoceanic flight in history by a balloon. For a hundred years aeronauts had been trying to do that, beginning with the America showman John Wise. He, and many others, had failed. Why not see if they could be the first?

For the next two years the Mudies and their friend Arnold "Bushy" Eiloart, along with his son Tim, made a career of seeing their dream turned into reality. Because of Mudie's growing reputation as a serious designer of small boats and Eiloart's connections as a successful small businessman, the team were able to get the early support of key figures in British industry and government. As their plans crystallized, no less a figure than Prince Philip offered them royal patronage and from that moment their logistical success was assured. That didn't mean their operational success was, though.

All along the team members knew there was a good chance that the balloon would have to ditch at sea, as so many had before them. In case of this, Mudie designed a brilliantly conceived tunnel-hulled gondola made with the then-advanced process of foam-cored construction. He

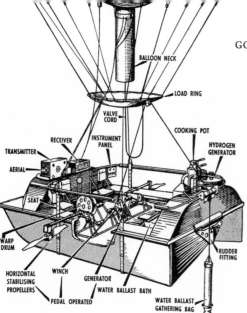

included a mast with twin headsails to be mounted in the front of the gondola if the balloon went down. When the balloon was aloft, the mast would be towed in the water as part of the guide rope weight. A guide rope trails behind a balloon along the water or ground; if the balloon rises, it has to carry more of the rope's weight and is therefore brought back down; if the balloon sinks, it carries less

The feature-packed gondola of the *Small World* balloon. Quirky Rube Goldberg–type accessories sat atop a sensible Colin Mudie hull.

of the rope's weight and consequently rises. In effect, the guide rope is an automatic compensator. All balloons lose some gas because of small leaks and the normal expansion of gas during the warmer daylight hours, followed by contraction at night. This variable expansion and loss make them gain or lose altitude, both of which have to be compensated for. A guide rope can do this, but so can simple ballast like sand that can be jettisoned. The Mudie-Eiloart team would use both forms of ballast, plus two horizontally placed propellers powered by pedals to provide lift. Propellers had been tried earlier in the century with unsatisfactory results, and the team would have the same experience.

The *Small World*, as the balloon was called, on December 11, 1958, was inflated with hydrogen on Tenerife. The crew of four—Colin and Rosemary, and Bushy and Tim Eiloart—cast off that evening and soon were wafting westward on the trade winds, as had been planned. If the gas held out they would make the West Indies in a week.

Flying in a balloon is a somewhat surreal experience: crew members see the ground move below but don't feel movement at all. The balloon in effect becomes a giant air molecule moving with other air molecules. Only when there are competing up or down drafts does the equilibrium become disturbed, and four days into the trip that's exactly what happened. The *Small World* entered a storm, the gondola was knocked around, and Mudie broke his ankle in one of the lurches when he got it caught under a piece of equipment and the other crew members couldn't tame the wild lifts and plunges of the balloon. They had to valve out gas before the balloon rose too high and the bag burst, but the balloon then lost too much lift and began dropping into the turbulent sea.

A rapid descent in a balloon usually causes the underbelly of the balloon to push up into the bag to form a "parachute." In fact, in the nineteenth century some balloonists purposely rigged their balloons to dump gas so they could parachute to the ground in front of awed, and paying, audiences at county fairs. The parachute effect slowed the *Small World* enough so that when it hit the water the impact was less severe than it might have been. Eiloart separated the gondola from the bag on the moment of impact, and the unburdened bag instantly shot skyward into the darkness of the storm and disappeared above the clouds, leaving the fifteen-foot gondola bobbing on the water fourteen hundred miles from Tenerife and seventeen hundred from the West Indies. Now would come the real test of Mudie's experimental design.

They hunkered down in the gondola that first night and just let the seas rock them along. Their guide rope acted as a trailing sea anchor and quelled the worst of the motion. At dawn the injured Mudie, who all had agreed would be in command if the balloon had to ditch, ordered the others to erect the mast and ship the rudder. Both of these tasks proved difficult on the pitching small boat, but Mudie's calm manner and voice of experience gave the others the confidence to keep trying despite repeated false starts. It took

The *Small World* crew made more water miles than air miles. The gondola-turned-sailboat saved four souls.

nearly two hours to do both jobs, but when the twin headsails were un-furled, the boat started forward with a satisfying tug. Tim Eiloart rigged a taffrail log and estimated their speed at just under four knots, which was quite good for a hull shaped as oddly as that on the *Small World*.

The boat, when it wasn't raining, remained almost completely dry. The high sides gave them ample freeboard and allowed them to stretch a tarpaulin over the top that kept them dry and also shaded them from the sun. Water supplies were minimal, six gallons fresh and four more available by using the Permutit chemical treatment Stanley Smith and Charles Violet had used aboard the *Nova Espero* a few years before. Mudie told the others that because of the uncertainty of making land-fall on Barbados, their target, they must conserve water and ration it to half a pint per day each.

Of all the castaways encountered so far, these four had the easiest time of it. Mudie suffered the most because of his broken ankle, while lack of water gave Tim Eiloart severe abdominal pain. Even so, daily runs of seventy-five miles or more buoyed their spirits. Mudie skippered, navigated, and even took his turn at the helm despite his broken ankle.

Two days before Christmas their hopes were greatly raised when they saw a submarine over the stern. It followed them briefly, but when they signaled for assistance it dived. Later they learned it was a Soviet boat on a secret patrol near the American coast. It obviously didn't re-port their position.

For a Christmas present the sea snapped off the rudder, but they reattached it with some strapping, and the boat moved on. Rainwater somewhat supplemented their supply of water and though they had a reasonable stock of provisions on board, they ate little because of their thirst. The water made by the Permutit chemical desalinator tasted foul, so only Tim Eiloart drank it because of his terrible thirst.

On December 30 a freighter passed within a few hundred yards of them but failed to see them. They didn't mind this so much because they knew each day they were getting closer to Barbados. In the early morning of January 5, 1959, they finally made out the green trees and sandy beach of the island. They landed that afternoon, thus closing out a decade of very odd small-boat crossings.

9

DOING YOUR OWN THING

THE 1960s

♦ THE *CRAIG* AND THE RIVER GODDESS ♦ KENICHI HORIE BRINGS SHAME AND GLORY
TO HIS FAMILY ♦ YOUNG JOHN RIDING VS. THE OSTAR GEEZERS ♦ ROBERT MANRY
FIGHTS SUBURBIA ON THE ATLANTIC ♦ THE WEST WIGHT POTTER STORY ♦ THE BIRTH
OF THE "CAPSULE" BOAT ♦ THE FIRST GREAT ROWING RACE ♦ FRANCIS BRENTON:
TRANSOCEANIC ON THE CHEAP ♦ WILLIAM WILLIS: HAVE HERNIA, WILL TRAVEL
♦ JET JOCKEY MAKES AN *APRIL FOOL* OF HIMSELF ♦ THE SHAGADELIC ROWER ♦

IN THE BEGINNING OF THE 1960s MOST YOUNG DREAMERS
didn't think of crossing oceans in little boats, nor even in airplanes, as
Charles Lindbergh had inspired their fathers' generation to do. Kids
in those first few years of the decade wanted to be spacemen, "the fastest

guy alive," according to the theme song from the kids' TV show *Fireball XL-5*. The Russians had put up *Sputnik I* in late 1957 and then the first cosmonaut, Yuri Gagarin. America responded with *Explorer 1* and then astronaut Alan Shepard. The cosmos itself was the great ocean for dreamers, not the Atlantic, Pacific, or Indian.

The sailors who took up the ocean challenge during these years usually did not expect to receive acclaim. They knew the world's attention was above the clouds now. These were sailors who for the most part dared the far waters for the same reason that Gilboy probably did—a calculated risk, pitting one's own abilities against the ocean. It was not a prize to be won but a puzzle to be solved. There was a rich crop of would-be small-boat navigators during these years, but surprisingly few of them left great memoirs, as their predecessors had. The relative lack of literary chest-beating reinforces the theory that these were mostly quests for personal fulfillment rather than glory. If that is the case, then these journeys brought a refreshing change from some of the brash stunts of the 1950s.

Two of the earliest recorded voyages from this time barely drew a ripple of response from the media, though they were worthy efforts. American merchant mariner Dayton J. Lalonde sailed his twenty-foot *Craig* from Los Angeles on June 4, 1959, to Sydney, Australia, where he arrived on May 27, 1960, after having survived a hurricane off Mexico and two cyclones. The next year British soldiers John Alexander, Hugh Burt, and Adrian Corkill completed a nine-thousand-mile passage from Hong Kong to Falmouth, England, aboard the twenty-foot all-steel *Ganga Devi*, a boat named after a Hindu river goddess. Seeing the voyage as a test of courage, the men departed in December 1960 and arrived July 9, 1961.

<hr />

The world took little notice again of a small-boat sailor until 1962. It was Kenichi Horie who broke all expectations of who and what young

Art on facing page: Kenichi Horie sails *Mermaid (Kodoku)* into San Francisco Bay, putting immigration officials on both sides of the Pacific into a tizzy.

Japanese were by defying his own staid conformist culture and breaking the mold.

Horie learned to sail as a member of his high school sailing club. Club rules were rigorous in the extreme—it was run almost as a military organization, and the numbers of dropouts and washouts were quite high. Horie loved the sport and survived in the club. During the summers he typically spent thirteen-hour days on required club duties, often doing heavy lifting for the more senior boys. On completing school he went to work at his father's auto parts business in Osaka and saved his money with the then-secret dream of one day sailing across the Pacific. The Pacific was the only large body of water available to Japanese sailors then, and now, because of the military and political tensions of the region. In the early 1960s Horie had had enough of hearing his country's few yachtsmen talk about proposed transpacific trips. Most of them said they would do it "one day," but that day had never come for any of them. Horie quietly saved his money and practiced sailing in anticipation of making "one day" a reality.

In September 1961 he visited Akira Yokoyama, one of Japan's few small-boat designers. Yokoyama had introduced a new design that year for a light-displacement nineteen-foot sloop with a cabin and built in plywood. Horie bought a set of plans from him and had the boat built at a boatyard near his home in Osaka. To economize because he was paying his own way entirely, he specified inferior grades of wood for some parts and the use of old-fashioned glues instead of modern formulations. Through a friend he was able to get a sail donated by a fabric manufacturer. Could he really cross the tempestuous Pacific on a boat made of second-rate materials?

As the boat came together, when Horie cautiously revealed his plans to some of his friends, they were unanimously concerned about the boldness of the trip and warned him about the unrelenting hazards of the Pacific Ocean, especially since he would be trying to cross by the northern route directly to San Francisco. But he insisted on going and began to provision the boat for a voyage of 120 days. His greatest fear in provisioning was to not overload the boat, though he later realized he should have taken more with him. He believed in Alain Bombard's theories and almost incredibly shipped only eighteen gallons of water! He thought that beer, wine, and rainwater, plus liquid from his canned food, would be enough supplements. His last logistical concern was not having a passport, but at the time passports were not routinely issued in Japan, and to obtain one he would have to announce his intention to leave Japanese waters by small boat—a plan he knew would cause the government to stop him. Having been previously denied exit papers, he chose to forgo the paperwork and sneak out instead.

He set Saturday, May 12, 1962, as his departure date because he knew that day many small sailboats would be in Nishinomiya harbor between Osaka and Kobe participating in weekend races. He would mix in with them and work his way out to the Kii Strait, leading to the Pacific. Light winds hampered his initial progress, but eventually he made it out past the strait, only to run into a strong gale. His boat, named *Kodoku* (Mermaid) after the manufacturer of the sailcloth, was blown around unmercifully. Horie hadn't expected the boat to be so tender with a 650-pound fin keel, and had kept his provisions to a minimum. Even the angular chines of this plywood craft didn't ease the rolling, and he got seasick, an affliction that would sour the first half of the voyage for him.

The upside to this first storm was that the coast guard patrol boat he had feared was nowhere to be seen. The weather was so bad they had no reason to think that any small craft would be out. This freedom helped Horie put some miles under the keel, so he accepted the storm philosophically. The stormy weather stayed with him for three weeks, with few breaks between big blows. He was so miserable and sick that he cried. When his crying failed to ease the wretchedness he decided to get drunk and just sleep through the rough weather. This wasn't a wise thing to do, but he got away with it and *Kodoku* sailed on. He wound up having to fight his way through four howling storms in three weeks. If they had come later in the voyage he might have been ready for them, but this early he was frightened and unsure of his craft.

At the end of May he encountered waves twice the height of his mast. One had only to curl over on him to smash the marginally constructed boat. A huge swell that pounded into the boat smashed in the starboard aft porthole and flooded the interior of the boat. As an economy measure, Horie had used only plate glass in this one porthole instead of safety glass, as in the others. It was a penny-wise, pound-foolish decision, but now it was too late to do anything except nail a patch over it. He had more drastic things to worry about. For example, a radio report told him that a loose World War II mine was bobbing around near his location, and the navy was out looking for it.

Wet, cold, unable to hold down solid food, Horie endured a lot the first month at sea. Even with his doubts and fear he never once thought of turning back. It was hell, but heaven was on the other side of the Pacific, and he wanted to be the first Japanese to sail that way alone in a small boat.

When the weather moderated he found that the *Kodoku* could sail quite well. Often he could sail under twin staysails, but when the wind was too much abeam he would set the main and genoa. He later gave up on the genny, complaining that it was too tiresome to bend on and take off as the wind changed. He believed that any small boat needed only a normal jib on an ocean passage if it had twin staysails.

With any combination of sails, he learned to balance the boat by adjusting his own position, since he was really "live ballast" and his weight placement was critical. He learned that at some points of sailing it was best if he lay crossways in the boat on a board that spanned bunk to bunk. The *Kodoku* also had a little trimming rudder aft of the main rudder to fine-tune the balance.

Once he became acclimated to the boat's motion, always more than, say, *Sopranino*'s or *Trekka*'s, which had much fuller keels, he began to enjoy his trip. The light winds that punctuated the gales were depressing, but they gave him time to enjoy his surroundings. One day a U.S. Air Force Albatross seaplane flew around him for a while, trying to ascertain whether or not he was shipwrecked. About halfway through the passage he saw a bright flash in the southern skies and later learned that it was caused by a nuclear bomb test detonation near Johnston Island, southwest of Hawaii. He also witnessed a frenzied shark attack on the school of fish following the boat, as Fred Rebell had reported thirty years earlier.

On July 24 he met the American steamer *Pioneer Minx*, which offered to assist him, thinking at first that he was lying dead on the deck.
He declined the food and water they offered, but asked if they would
send a message home to let his parents know he was safe. They did.

On August 12 Horie felt a surge of emotion as he passed under the
Golden Gate Bridge, entering San Francisco Bay. Gliding past Alcatraz
Island, he wondered if he wouldn't wind up in that prison himself, entering the country illegally, without a passport or visa. Unknown to
Horie, after his departure from Japan his friends had leaked the story of
his daring voyage. So, when he landed near Fisherman's Wharf, the
waiting assemblage of press and well-wishers was an indication that he
needn't fear American bureaucracy. The mayor presented him with a
key to the city, and he was hailed as a great symbol of America and
Japan's newly found friendship. Back home in Japan some stiff-necked
bureaucrats wanted to deal with him harshly for not following the rules,
but they were shouted down by his fellow countrymen who appreciated the fact that one of their own had showed the country that conformity isn't the only way to happiness.

———————

In 1964 another Pacific Ocean tale unfolded when Damanihi Tepa barely
survived for 155 days in a twelve-foot motorboat. He and Natua Faloho
had left Maupiti in French Polynesia, bound for Bora-Bora only twenty-
seven miles away, but when their engine failed they began to drift. Faloho
died after 141 days, but Tepa arrived alive on Tau Island on July 6—fourteen hundred miles later. He fed himself during the ordeal by spearing
fish with a scissor blade lashed to a piece of the boat's planking.

Also that year, when twenty-five-year-old Englishman John Riding was shut out of the Observer Singlehanded Transatlantic Race, the
OSTAR, for not having the requisite safety equipment (radio transmitter, inflatable life raft, and life jacket) aboard his self-designed cold-
molded twelve-foot *Sjö Äg* (Norwegian for *Sea Egg*), he departed Plymouth anyway, intending to set the record for the smallest transatlantic
passage. He got to the Azores and then made a tough sixty-seven-day

passage to Bermuda, arriving early in 1965 after surviving several knock-downs in the twin-bilge-keel boat. From there he crossed to Newport, Rhode Island, and in that sacred preserve of the megayacht caused a sensation in his diminutive cockleshell. He would later sail down the East Coast to the Panama Canal and through it to San Diego. Once he arrived there the vast Pacific lay before him, a mystery too large not to examine one day in the little *Sjö Äg*.

The most influential small-boat voyager after Alfred Johnson was un-questionably Robert Manry, whose transatlantic crossing in thirteen-and-a-half-foot *Tinkerbelle* inspired dozens of other small-boat voyages and also inspired many less adventurous people to become simply week-end boaters.

Manry, a copy editor for the newspaper *Cleveland Plain Dealer*, led a typical suburban life in postwar America. He owned a house in Wil-lowick, Ohio, and there lived with his family, his wife, two children, and a dog. A station wagon in the driveway completed the picture of bour-geois bliss. Something was missing, of course—life wasn't bliss but bourgeois boredom for him. Manry, like Ishmael, felt that "drizzly No-vember" in his soul. He was middle-aged, mortgaged, and moody. Day by day as he toiled to edit newspaper articles dealing with other people's exciting lives, he heard the clock on the office wall ticking away the mo-ments of his own life. Not that he shared his dread with his family or friends, but of course it was there, simmering.

One day he spotted an ad in the paper for a used boat for sale "cheap," an Old Town lapstrake dinghy. Soon the Manrys were enjoy-ing family weekends on the local small lake. As they gained confidence in the boat they even went out onto Lake Erie to test their skills. Some-where along the way it occurred to Manry that if he could handle the dinghy on Lake Erie, and if the boat were just a little better equipped . . . he could take on the *Atlantic*!

When he announced his revelation to his wife, Virginia, this un-derstanding and wise woman endorsed his plan. That alone is remarkable; few of the adventurers we have chronicled led routine married lives. Most of them were bachelors, heading that way, or somehow desperate. Manry was the very model of a middle-class man, and his wife absolutely understood his deeper needs. She was an astute pscholgist and spouse who deserves much of the credit for Manry's eventual success.

Manry later wrote that the idea of making the trip in the *Tinkerbelle*, named after Tinker Bell, the fairy character in *Peter Pan*, came to him only *after* he had upgraded her, but this seems unlikely. One has only to look at the boat where it is today in the Western Reserve Historical Society museum in Cleveland to know that the dinghy was rebuilt with serious blue-water sailing in mind. Probably this fabrication was for his employers, from whom he asked a summer's leave of absence, saying that he

Postwar boredom translated into nautical notoriety: Ohioan Robert Manry in his evocative little *Tinkerbelle*. In the middle of the 1960s Space Race, the accomplishment of a modest man inspired the world.

would sail the Atlantic on a friend's twenty-five-foot yacht. He was, rightly, concerned about their reaction if he told them his true plans. Eventually, though, he did reveal his real intentions to his employers and asked the *Plain Dealer* to sponsor him, offering the paper his story. What a journalistic coup if he succeeded! They turned him down. Later, once he began his voyage, they took him off the payroll.

In upgrading the dinghy he first decked it over in plywood. Aft he left a foot well and forward built a little cabin where he could store supplies and even duck into in a gale. His meticulous construction of this cabin—tapered slats of wood that were carefully glued and screwed in place—shows that he knew all along the boat would take a beating. For a simple daysailing boat he would have used only flat, simple shapes of plywood and would have built the cabin much lower. As constructed, it sat tall over the deck. Many other improvements were made, including heftier running rigging, better sails, an extended daggerboard in steel instead of wood, and a stronger rudder, including a spare. He greatly increased the integrity of the hull by laying on a veneer of fiberglass, another job he did neatly, especially considering the difficulty in covering a lapstrake hull.

He wisely tested the improved sloop-rigged boat on Lake Erie and found that it suited his needs. Then he left home in the family station wagon, with the dinghy on a trailer, heading for Falmouth, Massachusetts. From there he departed June 1, 1965, bound for its sister city of the same name in England.

Manry's journey across the Atlantic demonstrates how much things had changed—yet stayed the same—since the days of Johnson, Andrews, and Blackburn. Those nineteenth-century navigators had one huge advantage over Manry—they could count on encountering ships at regular intervals along the way. Most of the early voyagers in fact relied on finding their positions from passing ships. If they ran out of food or water, it would be only a few days before a ship passed by and supplied or rescued them.

Manry couldn't count on that. Ships by the 1960s were very large, and there were far fewer of them plying the North Atlantic routes. Without sails they required minuscule crews. Almost all operations at sea, including navigation, were performed from the bridge, so there weren't as many "eyes" on deck as there had been. The only advantage Manry had that the earlier transatlantic voyagers hadn't had was a Gibson Girl emergency radio. He had bought a surplus model. How useful it would have been had *Tinkerbelle* foundered is questionable. In any case, other than the radio, he probably was in a more perilous situation than all his predecessors.

His route lay somewhat to the south of the normal route that skirts the Grand Banks, and a storm he met the second day blew him even farther south. Early on, psychological pressures from fear of the sea, fatigue from strain of preparing for the voyage, and exhaustion from the actual moment-to-moment sailing of the boat, built to a point where he began to hallucinate. He imagined there was an assassin on board, he saw strange lights, he visited a place of sea mountains, dogs barked, some young boys came on board to give *Tinkerbelle* the once-over. He was close to losing control. He needed to sleep, and to do that in the small boat he would unship his rudder, throw out a sea anchor, and, to ease the motion further, set a riding sail on the backstay. All this done, he would curl up in his cabin and sleep on top of his supplies.

Not far out into international waters he spotted a Russian fishing trawler. Russian trawlers were known to be often blinds for Soviet electronic spying missions, and not surprisingly he soon saw an American submarine. The Cold War was silently being fought in front of him in the very waters where Johnson and Blackburn had waged war against halibut with their trawls.

On June 13 sharp winds and steep waves skewed the little boat around dangerously. He stopped sailing and deployed the sea anchor and just as he was feeling satisfied with his work a curling wave struck *Tinkerbelle*, tossing him into the ocean. Connected to the boat by a lifeline, when he resurfaced he found the boat had righted itself—almost to his surprise. The fact that the sail had been furled, and the buoyancy provided by the tall cabin combined to get the boat upright quickly. He crawled back in, soaked but safe.

Manry began to hallucinate again because of lack of sleep. He had unwisely taken dexedrine pills, an amphetamine, and was on an artificial high. Lindemann had learned the dangers of these, and now it was Manry's turn to medicate himself into danger. Three more times that day he was knocked down; each time he managed to pull himself back in. A few days later he was knocked down a fifth time, and this time his spare rudder was broken, his first one having broken after an encounter with a shark the previous week.

He repaired one of the rudders and sailed on. The favorable winds were nothing like what Horie endured in the Pacific. On good days Manry could set twin staysails, using oars as staysail booms. With this setup and a following wind, the boat was self-steering, so Manry could leisurely sit with his back to the hatch and read. He clocked off good runs of about fifty miles per day. At night he simply downed sails and deployed the sea anchor and drifted a few miles eastward.

Unknown to him, back home he had become a celebrity. Word had leaked about his voyage, and the few ships he spoke with along the way reported his positions to an eager public. The *Plain Dealer*'s biggest rival, the *Cleveland Press*, helped whip up Manry fever in the Buckeye state, and when each new front-page gushing story appeared in the *Cleveland Press*, the *Plain Dealer* was made to face its own stinginess, lack of imagination, and disloyalty to one of its employees.

That was the very year, too, that satellite television had been developed, and Winston Churchill's funeral in January was the first program simultaneously seen on both sides of the Atlantic. Now Manry's "little guy against the Atlantic" story presented another opportunity for transatlantic news. Newspaper reporters and television crews from the United States rushed to England and hired boats to look for Manry. The Royal Air Force and Royal Navy also got in on the hunt. When Manry was still a week away from landing, American television reporter Bill Jorgensen found him, jumped out of his boat, and swam over for an interview. In Falmouth, England, the rest of the Manry clan had been gathered so the media could record the teary reunion, and the whole voyage slipped out of Robert Manry's hands and into those of the international press. Being the focus of the international media was not what Manry had planned, but, being a newspaperman, he knew it could help his family financially, and it did. Trying to horn in on the glory at the last moment, the *Plain Dealer* people dropped from an airplane a T-shirt with their name emblazoned on the front and a note asking Manry to wear it. They had already put him back on the payroll. Manry tossed the note away and refused to don the shirt.

The mild-mannered suburbanite landed at Falmouth on August 17 to a positively stupendous welcome. It was probably the largest welcoming committee and ceremony held for any small-boat voyager ever, before or since. Exclusive literary contracts with newspapers and book publishers, interviews on television, and appearances on both sides of the Atlantic stocked the suburban family's financial larder and made Manry the best-known figure in American yachting circles since Joshua Slocum. The success and attendant publicity about Manry's voyage would lead in very short order to a whole fleet of little boats being launched and would-be Robert Manrys risking life and limb for a piece of the publicity pie.

Manry himself returned to Cleveland a local superstar. He bought a twenty-seven-foot yacht and took his family on a cruise down the Mississippi, around the Caribbean, and back up the East Coast—repeating Bishop's and Blackburn's voyages. Tragically, Virginia Manry died in 1969, the victim of an automobile accident. Robert Manry remarried, and died of a heart attack in 1971, all too young, while driving in a car with his new wife—but at least he had tasted victory once before he departed.

Hardly noticed during Manry's triumph in 1965 were the fine voyages being made by engineering prodigy John Letcher Jr. He had sailed from Los Angeles to Hawaii in 1963 aboard his twenty-year-old *Island Girl*, a slab-sided, twenty-foot, three-inch plywood cutter. In 1965 Letcher made the passage between America's newest states, Hawaii and Alaska, in only forty-four days, experimenting along the way with self-steering techniques. (His *Self-Steering for Sailing Craft*, published in 1974, remains the definitive book on the subject.)

Stanley Smith, the designer and builder of *Nova Espero*, meanwhile had established himself as a boatbuilder on the Isle of Wight in southern England and there was producing a wonderful little fourteen-foot plywood sailing dinghy, the West Wight Potter. (In the United Kingdom, "to potter" means the same as "to putter" in the United States.) When a customer in Sweden ordered one, Smith decided to deliver it personally. Normally, this would not have been much of a feat because he could have skirted the coast to Dover, crossed the Channel to Calais, coasted the Low Countries to the Elbe River, traversed northern Germany via the Kiel Canal, and crossed the Baltic to Sweden—but that's not what he did. He decided to go offshore, instead: directly from the Isle of Wight up the Channel into the North Sea, around the Skaw in northern Denmark to Sweden.

Smith left the Isle of Wight late in the season on October 12, 1965, and beat his way up the English Channel. It was tough going against the westward Channel current, occasional force 7 winds, and the fog, but he eventually made Dover. East winds kept him at his mooring until October 22, when he turned the corner and made for the North Sea. For five days he remained at the tiller of the little boat almost constantly because he was sailing northeast along the swell of enormous seas. The brave little Potter rose and fell to each challenge, and on October 26 Smith was rewarded with a respite from the fray—he was able to sleep for five straight hours.

WEST WIGHT POTTER

300
00E

THE HISTORY MAKING, ONLY 14 FT. SAILBOAT KNOWN THAT SLEEPS 2 ADULTS IN 6'3" BERTHS.
COMBINES AMAZING COMFORTS, STABILITY, AND HANDLING...AND BOASTS
AN INCREDIBLE HERITAGE OF SEAWORTHY ACCOMPLISHMENTS.

Perhaps the most beloved commercially produced small boat on the market, the *West Wight Potter 14/15* is still built today. This 1960s ad shows the early gunter-rigged version.

He awoke to a helpful following wind, but it later veered to the west and rose to force 7. On the wide and wild North Sea he had no choice but to put out his sea anchor—an old tire in the middle of a line that led out from and back to the boat—and bend his little jigger on the mizzen. His cleverly designed storm rig saved the boat, even though his radio told him that the winds had risen to force 9. Like other sailors before him in bad blows, he decided that he had done all he could, so he retired to the Potter's little cabin to get more sleep.

When he awoke and faced the weather he found that he was being blown toward the west coast of Denmark at the rate of 1 knot. The blow lasted for several days, and all the while he was helpless to fight it and could only ride it out. He would be smashed in the surf of the sand bars in fifteen hours if something didn't change. Time ticked away like a death sentence. When he finally made out the Danish shore through the gray, driving mist of the storm, he shot off distress flares. No one saw them. There was no doubt now that he and the plywood Potter would face the unknown shore alone. As best he could he prepared his boat for the worst. He inflated some buoyancy bags, checked the sea anchor line, and once more made sure his own safety tether was secure.

Then he saw a fishing boat coming toward him, barely able to fight the maelstrom itself but soldiering on nevertheless. Smith threw it a tow line, but it was too late to help the little Potter. The boat was already in the pounding surf, and breaker after breaker slammed into it and its sole crewman. Smith had to abandon his boat and try to save himself, so he cut his tether and started to swim to shore. Immediately he was caught in the fierce suction of the undertow and pulled under. Again and again he struggled to the surface but was pulled under again. The last time he came up and gulped air he found himself in the arms of men on shore who had been alerted by a radio message from the fishing boat. Smith was saved.

The tough little Potter was washed ashore near the village of Hvide Sande on the west coast of Jylland (Jutland) and suffered only minor damage. After a brief hospitalization for exposure and exhaustion, Smith stayed at the home of Peder Sorensen, the fisherman. Together the men planned Smith's next move, and a week after his crash landing at Hvide Sande, Smith put into action their plan. He would skirt the Skaw entirely, and the Potter was trucked the forty-odd miles to the village of Struer, where it put into the inland waters of the Limfjord. Navigating around the islands in the fjord, Smith reached Aalborg, where he took aboard his Swedish customer for the last stretch. Fortified with a more powerful motor, the little Potter continued out the Limfjord and across the Kattegat to the west coast of Sweden, reaching the village of Kloster on November 17 after 780 miles of harrowing adventures.

Four decades later, thousands of sailors around the world enjoy both wooden and fiberglass versions of the strong little Potter 14 that Smith so thoroughly tested that fall. This type of boat would make even more dramatic ocean voyages later.

———◆———

The *annus gloriosus* for small-boat sailing was 1966. A hundred years had gone by since the publication of John MacGregor's seminal book *A Thousand Miles in the "Rob Roy" Canoe on the Rivers and Lakes of Europe*, which virtually began the sport of pleasure sailing in small boats. During spring and summer, less than a year after Manry's wake-up call in *Tinkerbelle*, boats built all over the world that winter were putting to sea for hoped-for conquests of the oceans.

Kenneth Weis's *Thumbelina* at twenty feet was hardly tiny, as the name implied, at least not by the standard Manry set. Weis nevertheless had to employ all his sailing abilities when he guided his homemade boat from Vancouver to Auckland, New Zealand, following in the wake of his fellow countryman John Guzzwell.

Bill Verity's *Nonoalca*, also homemade, was much more in line with the trend of the time toward miniaturization at a tiny twelve feet. This boat had a displacement hull of edge-glued mahogany strips covered with fiberglass. Topsides, Verity had installed a roller-reefing Bermuda sail, roller-furling jib, Hasler-type self-steering, and a "driver's cabin." The *Nonoalca*, named for a Mexican mythic figure, was therefore the first of what we will now call "capsule" boats—small boats whose hulls are carefully integrated with the cabin so the skipper can control the boat from within the dry cabin. The steering cabin not only offers comfort but, more important, protection from the elements; it also removes the risk of being washed or thrown overboard. The capsule boat is such an obvious benefit to the small-boat sailor that one wonders why it hadn't appeared long before; structurally it isn't difficult to build, even from timbers or plywood. From the cozy cabin of the pioneer *Nonoalca*, therefore, Verity helmed her while sitting in a lawn chair and peering through portholes. In just sixty-five days he rode the Gulf Stream from Port Everglades, Florida, to Tralee, Ireland, arriving in July, while staying dry encased in his well-designed minicruiser. It was the driest crossing since Brude's *Uræd* sixty years earlier, though much speedier.

Down in the jungles of Colombia that spring, Francis Brenton, a British world traveler and adventurer who wandered from country to country working only long enough to get cash to continue, bought two dugout canoes from the Cuna Indians. He had a deal with the Field Museum in

Long Islander Bill Verity, a turret gunner in Navy carrier planes in World War II, continued to seek adventure after the war with a series of ocean crossings, including a recreation of the Saint Brendan voyage and one in his capsule boat *Nonoalca*.

Chicago to sell one canoe to them for their ethnology exhibits. Brenton thought it would be a grand experience to deliver the canoe in person by sailing it across the Caribbean to the Mississippi, up that river to the Illinois River, and so to Chicago. He lashed the two canoes together, named the resulting craft *Sierra Sagrada*, and set out in early May 1966. What started as a lark wound up becoming the greatest boating adventure of the 1960s, if not indeed the century. But before that story played out, other adventurers would make the headlines.

David Johnstone was sitting on a stool at a pub in Farnham, England, watching television the day Robert Manry landed at Falmouth. Johnstone, a giant of a man, was something of an unsettled square peg who at thirty-five hadn't found a square hole yet. He could do many artistic, musical, and mechanical things, but what he couldn't do was be happy anywhere. His employment record was several pages long, with many jobs lasting just weeks, days, or less. Mostly he stayed at home with his widowed mother.

Watching Manry receive the accolades from the large crowd made Johnstone envious. He wanted applause, too. Why hadn't the world appreciated his many talents? A sudden brain wave swept over him. Hadn't he recently read something about those two Norwegians who rowed across the Atlantic in the last century? Anyone could *sail* a small boat—he could—but how many could *row* across? Why didn't he establish a record for rowing the smallest boat across the Atlantic? That would let the world know what a great man he was. That very day he wrote an ad and placed it in a national newspaper, seeking men willing to go with him. Having made up his mind, he would not be dissuaded from this transatlantic attempt, even if it killed him—and those who went with him.

Johnstone's ad elicited a number of responses, but only two seemed like real possibilities. One was from an ex-paratrooper, John Hoare, now journalist for a county newspaper. Hoare was twenty-nine, a keen swimmer, sports car driver, and enthusiast for true adventure stories. His personal hero was Albert Ball, the quiet, sensitive Royal Flying Corps ace from World War I.

Johnstone recognized Hoare's intelligence and physical stamina but also appreciated the fact that Hoare wasn't the type to want to take over the project. He was acutely aware of that potential problem with his other applicant, Captain John Ridgway, a serving officer in the Parachute Regiment and a born leader. Ridgway was every bit as tough as Hoare, though a little older, yet he had more maturity and could even bring money to the project. Nevertheless, Johnstone rejected him out of hand at their first meeting, and though Ridgway tried to phone him many times over the next few weeks, Johnstone ignored him. Not to be denied, Ridgway announced that he would mount his own transatlantic rowing expedition and race Johnstone and Hoare across.

Johnstone was in shock. The newspapers had already found out his plans, and his picture and story had been featured in the national press. This was *his* idea, his chance for glory, and now this upstart army captain was horning in. He had to work faster.

His first move was to visit Colin Mudie, who had left the J. Laurent Giles firm and established his own design office in London, and ask for a custom-designed rowboat. Mudie dove right into the problem and came up with an improved surf boat, not completely unlike the Harbo-Samuelsen boat, but intentionally shorter at fifteen and a half feet and cold molded instead of clinker built. It was a first-class design with an enclosed hatch aft, a sheltered foredeck, plenty of hand grips on top and under the hull for emergencies, a trimming rudder aft, and a radar reflector at the bow. Johnstone raised the money to pay for the boat through a literary agent he retained to sell his story to newspapers and book publishers. While the boat, to be called *Puffin*, was being built, he and Hoare raced to research what provisions they would need, where to launch from in the United States, and all the other details that went into planning such a voyage. All the while they kept a weather eye out for Ridgway and his unwelcome activities.

Ridgway sent conflicting signals. Sometimes he was going ahead with the voyage and other times he wasn't. Johnstone thought these signals were tricks, but in fact they weren't. Ridgway simply couldn't, on short notice, raise the funds that Johnstone and Hoare had, and he also had trou-

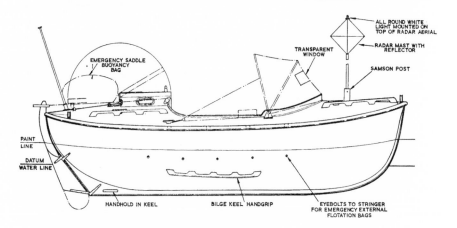

Colin Mudie designed the *Puffin* rowboat.

ble finding a suitable rowing partner. Those two problems solved themselves almost magically. First, a friend told him about a simple dory-type
boat built by a company in north England. Phoning the firm, he learned
they had one in stock that they could ship to him immediately at a price
of only £185, which Ridgway was able to pay by check. It was a great stroke
of luck. Next, a sergeant in Ridgway's own paratroop regiment walked
into his office and announced that he would like to be his partner. Chay
Blyth was a gregarious, physically fit Scotsman with whom Ridgway a
few years before had won a minor canoeing competition. He hadn't
previously asked the younger man because Blyth was married. After
speaking persuasively to Blyth's wife, Ridgway accepted him as partner.

More good luck befell the new partnership when the British Army
announced that it would support their effort by allowing them leaves
of absence and by helping with transportation arrangements. It was a
real race now, though Johnstone and Hoare were several weeks ahead in
their planning. Johnstone told the press that he intended to start from
Boston, but this was a diversion because in fact he intended to leave
from Virginia Beach, five hundred miles to the south. He felt that the
sooner they made the Gulf Stream the sooner they would get a free
boost toward England. Hoare dissented from this view, preferring the
northern departure point, but Johnstone's fragile ego would countenance no second-guessing, and he barked his partner into submission.
It was to be a costly display of hubris.

Johnstone and Hoare arrived in the United States on May 1, 1966,
and established a base in Norfolk, Virginia. For the next few weeks they
purchased supplies, studied navigation, and answered questions from
reporters, who had followed them. Almost every day they got news
about Ridgway and Blyth, but these reports were often mistaken about
when the pair would leave England or where their dory *English Rose
III* was—still in England or already shipped to Boston. The uncertainty
played on Johnstone's tightly stretched nerves.

Then they learned the paratroopers had landed in Boston on May
18. Johnstone and Hoare quickly finalized their preparations and departed on May 21 after being towed from Norfolk around Cape Henry
to Virginia Beach. They managed to get a twelve-day jump on the *En-*

John Ridgway and Chay Blyth proved that simple is good. Their *English Rose III* was nothing more than an old-fashioned dory powered by old-fashioned sweat.

glish Rose III, but Ridgway and Blyth, meanwhile, were making good use of their time ashore.

The Cape Cod fishermen they met on their arrival in Orleans, Massachusetts, were only too eager to give them counsel once they saw that the men intended to use a dory. Many of their fathers and grandfathers had been dorymen, and there was no shortage of advice on improving the boat and making it more seaworthy. The freeboard was built up nine inches, some short decks and covered dry areas were fashioned, and, perhaps most useful of all, the old hands prevented the installation of a keel. They said that the secret to the success of a dory was that with its flat bottom it could slide down a wave front, rather than tripping over a keel as it went. Buoyed by the enthusiasm and warm wishes of the local fishermen Ridgway and Blyth optimistically set off on June 4. They felt confident they would catch up to the *Puffin*.

Johnstone and Hoare's first eleven days at sea were dreadful. Instead of smartly striding out and catching the Gulf Stream as they had planned, they staggered between Cape Henry and Cape Charles the first week, all the time within sight of land. Another week found them *south* of their starting position and only about fifty miles out to sea. Whatever advantage they had over *English Rose* was squandered. Their poor showing was caused partly by their inadequate rowing regimen, but also by the appalling easterlies that resisted their efforts. Up north, the *English Rose* had to contend with the same unusual easterlies, though their progression was more orderly and on track.

Back in the western Caribbean, Francis Brenton's canoe-raft, the *Sierra Sagrada*, was pushing northward under schooner rig and side-by-side jibs. Because of the split style of the rig, Brenton could balance the boat well enough that it would self-steer. Tuning the sails to balance the boat allowed Brenton to get maximum speed out of an admittedly poor hydrodynamic shape because he didn't need to drag a rudder. Navigation was rudimentary—he had no proper nautical charts, and his only instruments were several toy compasses that he hoped would last the voyage before rusting out.

One of the truly greats: Francis Brenton capped his legendary career with a round-trip tour of the Atlantic aboard a dugout canoe.

The first week in June, as he approached the western tip of Cuba, the wind suddenly died and there was an eerie calm. Brenton landed on Cuba's Island of Pines to await a change in the weather, but smugglers on the island and unlit planes passing overhead at night caused him to think that whatever was brewing weather-wise would be easier dealt with than Castro's security forces, even with his British passport. He reluctantly headed *Sierra Sagrada* out to sea and a day later was hit by a string of squalls. These squalls soon merged into one continuous storm, which the weather reports from Miami told him was the precursor to an early-season hurricane, Alma. He couldn't turn back, yet he was three hundred miles from the nearest friendly port, facing a coming hurricane on a raft held together by jungle vines.

———◆◆◆———

Out on the Atlantic, nearly nine hundred miles from the American coast, Johnstone and Hoare were also feeling the effects of Hurricane Alma. It kicked up a strong force 9 gale, which they couldn't fight against, so they lay-to the sea anchor for three days and rode it out. Johnstone calmly spent the time trying to teach himself the finer points of celestial navigation.

Ridgway and Blyth were closer to the continent by the time Alma cut its destructive pathway north to New England. When word came over the radio that it was heading their way, chills ran down their backs. There wasn't much they could do to get ready but check the lashings on all their supplies and deploy the sea anchor. Blyth asked Ridgway if he realized that within a few hours they might both be dead. The tough parachute officer maintained a stiff upper lip and said nothing.

———◆◆◆———

Brenton at first tried to ride out the tempest under bare poles, but the strain on his raft seemed greater that way, especially with waves crashing into his stern. He hoisted the jib, hoping to calm the motion, and found that the boat took off like a champ across the waves. When he had the sail and rudder trimmed, he lashed the tiller in place and retired to the tiny cabin to get out of the weather. In that manner he rode out the worst of Alma and sped toward his destination, making a good three hundred miles before the worst of the winds finally ebbed. The raft's flexible construction saved it from destruction, making this a rare instance of running before a hurricane successfully.

In mid-June he reached New Orleans, bought a twenty-horsepower engine, and motored his way up to Chicago. The white-shirted, dark-tied officials of the Field Museum didn't quite know how to respond to the novel way Brenton had delivered their canoe specimen.

Brenton lashed together two dugout canoes to make the *Sierra Sagrada*. He found the vine binding recommended by the Cuna Indians was better than modern synthetic rope.

All the rowers also survived Alma, though Ridgway and Blyth had the worst of it. When the weather system settled down again, unfavorable winds continued to hamper both efforts, and progress for Johnstone and Hoare was barely perceptible some days. Both teams now knew they hadn't brought enough food or water to last the trip, and each intended to beg water and food from passing freighters.

William Willis, the rafter who sailed *Seven Little Sisters* to Samoa in 1954, achieved another raft journey in 1963–64 at the age of seventy on a tri-hulled craft, *Age Unlimited*, made from steel pipes; this trip was from Peru to Australia. Now in the summer of 1966, inspired by Manry, he abandoned rafting and took to small-boat voyaging. On June 22 he departed New York aboard the eleven-and-a-half-foot *Little One*, a dinghy with a hundred-square-foot sail. He hoped to reach Plymouth, England.

That same day, Johnstone noted in his log that during the previous five days *Puffin* had made only sixty-five miles—or just *thirteen* miles a day! Hoare joked that they wouldn't get to England until 1968. They continued to worry about their dwindling food supply and tried to supplement it by catching fish, without much success. Even so, they had no plans to give up.

Up north on the same day Ridgway was about to jump into the water to cool off from the searing sun and stale, post-hurricane heavy air when Blyth, larking about, happened to knock him back into the boat. Just as Ridgway got up on his elbows, a large scimitar-shaped fin sliced through the water near the gunwale—he had missed becoming shark food by the merest fluke of luck. Both men where badly shaken by the near brush with calamity, but when they calmed down they sorted through their food stock and found that some had been spoiled by salt water during the battle with the hurricane. Getting help from a passing ship was now urgent. They also realized that they must redouble their efforts to put miles under the keel. They too had been making entirely too little progress, though not as little as their competitors.

<hr />

Willis had unwisely set out in *Little One* not wanting to believe that a hernia he had suffered on the *Sisters* raft would affect his ability to skipper the dinghy. He was the type of man who in his mind never grows old and refuses to believe that his own body could let him down. In his youth Willis had left his home in Hamburg, Germany, to earn money to support his impoverished mother and siblings. His voyages took him all over the world and around the Horn, but just before World War I he jumped ship in Galveston, Texas. Loading heavy bales of cotton there hardened an already robust and well-developed physique, and soon he built a reputation as a great amateur wrestler, something he would be proud of all his life. With his earnings he built his own ranch in Texas, but restlessness drove him around North America as he tried his hand

Wrestler, wrangler, rafter, and writer William Willis finally met his fate aboard *Little One*.

variously as a logger, longshoreman, construction worker, and many other things. He was a two-fisted guy who fought with hoboes on trains and with the law when he got to a town. Hard, physically active by choice, he nevertheless harbored dreams of becoming a cartoonist or a writer. He spent some time writing poetry on the Monterey peninsula in California before that area evolved into the artist colony it is today.

Around the time of World War II, now middle-aged, Willis married a New York theatrical agent he had met on a ship and tried to settle down in the wilds of Manhattan. He held menial jobs, worked out at a gym that had been bought by Richard Fox of the *Police Gazette* years before as a gift to a friend, and wondered what his next adventure would be. Thanks to his wife's earnings he had been able to indulge his rafting dreams and now *Little One*.

Hurricane Celia arose in the Leeward Islands the second week of July and a week later was beating itself out on the shores of Newfoundland. *Little One* got hit by its fierce winds, and Willis had to nail down the kayak-style spray skirt that fit over the gunwales. While he was struggling to maintain an even keel his hernia flared up, causing an agonizing pain in his abdomen. At age seventy-three he lay doubled over in the Atlantic during a hurricane trying to work the splayed muscles back in with his fingers. The dinghy rolled excessively despite two hundred pounds of lead ballast. Willis wondered how, in his condition, he would be able to jettison the lead in an emergency. Outside, the screeching wind made the rigging hum a frightening tune, and thunderous waves smashed down onto the canvas spray skirt, finally ripping it out of its fastenings. Crippled Willis was deluged with water. In this darkest of hours, after he had gotten his hernia under control, he lay under the loose spray skirt and composed a poem to his wife.

He survived the storm, but a few days later realized he must have help. He scanned the horizon for a ship and though he saw several over the following days and weeks none was ever close enough to rescue him. It was nearly a month before an American freighter bound for Rotterdam stopped to offer assistance. Willis refused to be taken on board, probably because he wanted to have medical attention in America, where his wife could visit him. The captain therefore radioed the

U.S. Coast Guard, which dispatched a rescue vessel. He and *Little One* were picked up late in the evening of August 20.

———◆–◆–◆———

The rowers in *English Rose III* had also, by late August, met some ships, which helpfully reprovisioned them and gave them accurate positions. Ridgway and Blyth, who sometimes spoke of defeat, managed each day to progress, and by now they felt they would make it. On August 27 they spoke with the ship *Finnalpino*, which gave them a position of only 250 miles from the coast of Ireland.

The *Puffin*'s crew weren't even close to home. Since their start they had developed a better rowing regimen, but the damnable east winds hindered their progress nearly every day. Johnstone's log is a continuous report of east winds and days spent lying to a sea anchor because rowing would have been futile.

A week after meeting the *Finnalpino*, Ridgway and Blyth reached Irish waters and rounded Aran Island. A lifesaving boat came out to offer assistance and towed them into harbor at Kilronan, thus ending their ninety-three-day, thirty-five-hundred-mile row across the Atlantic, the first in seven decades.

In the absolutely saddest and cruelest irony imaginable, the very day that Ridgway and Blyth stepped ashore to savor their triumph, September 3, David Johnstone made the last entry in his logbook. Two weeks earlier Hurricane Faith had arisen in the Caribbean and begun its long and winding route northward. Faith went on to establish one of the longest hurricane tracks ever recorded as it went diagonally over the Atlantic and eventually reached the Faeroe Islands and then Scandinavia. The storm was a freak of nature in a summer that witnessed many unusual climatic conditions. It was horrible bad luck that the little rowboat *Puffin* was directly under its track as it spun its deadly winds toward Europe. Johnstone could be criticized for starting out from Virginia, against the advice of others, including his partner, but the storms that summer were so unusual that neither he nor anyone else could reasonably have foreseen them.

The last known photograph taken of John Hoare and David Johnstone. Even John-stone's overbearing personality couldn't stand up to a hurricane.

A final deadly calamity happened aboard the *Puffin*. Five weeks after the last logbook entry, the upturned barnacle-encrusted hull was spotted eight hundred miles south of Newfoundland by the Canadian warship *Chaudière*. Its bow was submerged and there was a small hole in the side. A shackle that should have been connected to a lifeline was found flopping empty in its eyebolt. The sea anchor's line was torn off near its cleat. John Hoare had joined his hero Albert Ball, who had also disappeared while engaged with the enemy. And for David John-stone his sad, prolonged quest for acceptance was finally over.

The *Puffin*'s hull hadn't yet been found in the fall of 1966 when John Fairfax, a Briton who had lived overseas his whole life, arrived in London from Argentina. London in the mid-1960s was his kind of place, a "happening" town. What better place to be than the West End with all the pretty "mod birds" in miniskirts, craps tables in the casinos, and free-flowing booze at all the parties? Fairfax took it all in—in a double shot. Life was great, but after he blew the last of his cash at a casino, he had to get down to the really serious purpose that had brought him to England. He had evolved a plan to outdo both of the teams that were rowing the Atlantic that year. If he could get the necessary backing, five thousand pounds, he estimated, he would row the bloody thing alone from the Canaries to Florida. He just had to find the right geezer to advance him the cash.

In Homestead, Florida, Delta Airlines copilot Hugo Vihlen was finalizing his sailing plans at the beginning of the new year, 1967. Using money from his ample salary, he had ordered the construction of a six-foot, fully enclosed capsule boat that a professional naval architect had designed for him, shaped like a stubby coast guard lifeboat. Vihlen wanted the world's record for smallest boat to cross the Atlantic, a goal that had crystallized after he read Kenichi Horie's and Robert Manry's accounts of their voyages.

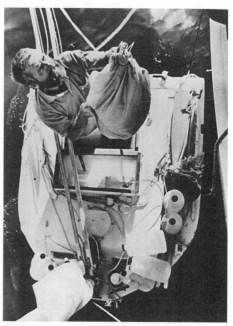

Vihlen had the funds and the connections to bring his plans to bear quickly. By late March his little boat *April Fool* was shipped to Morocco, and he was ready to sail it back to Florida. Local bureaucracy delayed him for a week until April 5, when he finally put out from Agadir. Maddening contrary winds frustrated the little boat's attempt to get away from shore. *April Fool* was a poor sailor with

Six feet of transatlantic chutzpah, Hugo Vihlen's *April Fool*.

little directional control and no ability to sail against the wind. Two days later it was blown back onto the Moroccan shore, where Vihlen emerged angry, but determined. Some sailors at the local yacht club told him his twin staysail ljungström (lapwing) rig might work once he was out in the trades, but here he needed to tack offshore, so they recommended he try an easy-to-make lateen rig and increase the rudder size.

Within days, by the magic of his American Express card, he was able to get all of this done, and on April 15 he set out once again. The lateen sail wasn't much of an improvement over the previous rig, but this time he had a sea anchor which prevented him from losing ground when the wind blew against him. On his fourth day, however, he had made just thirty-four miles. It was useless to go on in a boat that didn't sail well, so he turned back to the coast and landed there on April 22.

In the United States two other voyagers were embarking on their adventures. Ikuo Kashima, a photographer from Japan, left Long Beach, California, near where Fred Rebell had landed, on his way to a 101-day crossing to Yokohama aboard his little sixteen-and-a-half-foot *Korassa II*. He had previously crossed the Atlantic from Genoa, Italy, to New York in 1964–65 in his nineteen-foot *Korassa* (a Japanese rallying cry). This time his crewmate was a hamster.

* ◆ *

Francis Brenton of the *Sierra Sagrada* left Chicago June 6, 1967, the beginning of one of the most audacious and ingenious small-boat voyages ever, bar none. He evidently had been inspired by Mudie's *Small World* attempt nine years earlier, because now he set out to make the same trade-winds voyage across the Atlantic by balloon. Like all his adventures, this attempt was to be mostly self-funded, and since he had trouble even paying his apartment rent from his earnings at a photo-finishing laboratory, it would have to be a very economical operation.

Brenton found out that the cheapest way to make a balloon float was to fill it with hydrogen and that the cheapest way to generate hydrogen was to use calcium hydride, which at the time was $2.60 a pound, with six hundred pounds needed to float the balloon he was building. It was to be a very unusual cube-shaped design with fifty-foot sides; squares were cheaper than spheres to construct—though much less strong. The balloon fabric was to be cheap, ordinary plastic sheeting that could be glued together with minimal fuss. It was needed for only one flight, so why not?

Transporting the balloon and the eighteen drums of calcium hydride to the coast of Africa was his next worry. He could barely afford airfare for himself, let alone all his gear, so he chose the only option open to him—go by canoe. Since the Field Museum had bought only one of the canoes that made up the *Sierra Sagrada*, he still had the other, the longer one. The original twenty-six-foot raft had survived a roaring hurricane in the Caribbean—certainly, he figured, it could survive the Atlantic.

To replace the canoe that had gone to the museum he built a hollow, carvel-planked canoe. His first plan was to load the drums of calcium hydride into the new canoe, but after he fiberglassed their steel shells to protect them from corrosion, they wouldn't fit into the tight space, so he transferred them to the original canoe.

One of the few items donated to Brenton was an Evinrude engine by the company itself. Using it and, when the wind was fair, his sails, he traversed the length of Lake Michigan to Sault Sainte Marie and east through the other Great Lakes up the Saint Lawrence Seaway to the mighty Atlantic. Some people just can't be stopped! In Newfoundland he went ashore at several points to check his gear and buy last-minute provisions. One final purchase was a red fiberglass kayak to be used as a tender, but also possibly as a balloon gondola, a much less sophisticated version of what Mudie had designed for the *Small World*!

Hitting the open ocean on August 15 was a relief to Brenton. Onshore life was a scramble to satisfy others and perform the complicated necessary tasks that modern society extorts from a person. Here he was free. He had made all the decisions that got him here, and as he surveyed his decks he was filled with satisfaction that his little empire of two canoes had been earned by his own labor and was his to dispose of as he saw fit all the way to Africa, if things went according to plan. On his second day out a Russian trawler ran up to him, and the crew passed down supplies and a good-luck note. They had heard about his voyage on the radio.

His main bill of fare was canned beans or canned spaghetti. For energy he had chocolate bars and dates. In Newfoundland he had bought a couple of cases of sardines for only six cents a can, so initially he was well fed, and at a price he could afford.

The trip across the Atlantic was a frenzied sequence of storms, calms, equipment failures (including loss of his rudder), spontaneous and ingenious repairs, bouts of thirst, rainwater collection, near misses with ships, and so on. The biggest difference between Brenton's crossing and those that preceded it was that Brenton was in effect piloting a catamaran. If the boat was tossed over by a wave, there was virtually no way to right it. It would then become a life raft—with all his supplies lashed *below* the waterline.

As the weeks went by, Brenton's watch and other implements of navigation failed. On September 28 he flagged down the German cargo ship *Hornsee*, which gave him his position as only about seven hundred miles from France. He was too far north, but most of the way across. For two more months he inched southward, but the winds were against him almost every day. The *Sierra Sagrada* became so encrusted with speed-robbing barnacles that he had to cut them off with a handsaw while leaning over the side. In the middle of November his jib blew out and with it any possibility of southing against the wind. So after 106 days on the Atlantic he accepted an offer from a Russian ship to take him and his boat to Agadir.

Arriving in Morocco he connected with a ship that offered to transfer him and his boat to Dakar, Senegal, for free. Departing from Senegal would save him a thousand air miles, so he accepted. However, once he got there other logistical problems presented themselves, so he pulled stakes and hitched another free ride, to the Canaries. His luck remained good when a Spanish air force colonel there offered him any assistance he needed to prepare the balloon.

To convert the calcium hydrite into hydrogen, Brenton had only to pour ordinary water on it. The oxygen atom of the water is immediately absorbed into the chemical, and two atoms of hydrogen are freed. The process happens so fast, however, that heat is given off, and that heat can cause a spark, and the spark can blow up both the hydrogen and the balloon (as happened to the *Hindenburg*). Brenton laid out his balloon and tried to get the process to work safely, but after two small explosions and the burning of a major part of the balloon, he was forced to give up—it was too dangerous. Defeated, he began to pack his equipment.

Just then someone told him about a chemical plant on the island that produced hydrogen gas as a major by-product. They had read about Brenton's proposed voyage and were willing to fill up his balloon for free. The only problem was he no longer had a usable balloon. That difficulty was overcome when a plastics company on the island offered to make him a new gas bag, again for free, a job they completed in only ten days. It was a significant improvement over his first one.

On April 3, 1968, hundreds of locals came out to help launch the balloon. Mostly they hindered the operation, and at the critical moment of launching, one assistant failed to cut a restraining line. The balloon leaped over onto one side and dragged on the ground, with Brenton in the basket. The air force officer who had been so helpful earlier was hit by the basket and knocked into the ocean; he wound up in the hospital. Brenton fell out of the basket just as the balloon rose majestically out to sea. It was the end of the dream. Later the Spanish air force dispatched planes to shoot it down before it became a hazard to air traffic.

The bloom was finally off Brenton's rose on the Canaries, and after thanking everyone, he boarded the *Sierra Sagrada* and sailed it back down to Dakar to visit friends. Later still he made a forty-seven-day passage back across the Atlantic. Arriving on the eastern seaboard, he went up the Intracoastal Waterway, back to the Great Lakes, and finally to Chicago—all in a dugout canoe. Yes, this really happened!

———◆———

Hugo Vihlen was back in Africa to try again with *April Fool* in the spring of 1968. He had lightened his stock of provisions, but his total weight had increased because now the boat sported a gasoline outboard engine to use in case of contrary winds. More important, he switched his launch point from Agadir to Casablanca, which stood at the edge of the sea where a current drifted westward.

Not wanting to waste a week with paperwork, as had happened the year before, Vihlen had the boat brought to the water by crane on March 30, got in, fired up the three-horsepower Johnson and headed out. As soon as he got past the seawall, however, and met real ocean waves, his motor drowned out. He was in a dangerous position because the fishing fleet was returning and he was in their way with no engine and all his sails still in their bags. He quickly bent on the sails and headed away from the harbor, but in the wrong direction, north. Once again his boat would not sail well against the wind.

As the boat drifted north he worked on the engine to remove the moisture. Later that night he got it to start, and so turned south against the wind and headed toward his goal, the Canary Islands. There he would surely find his longed-for trade winds. He arrived there sixteen days later, picked up his coveted trades, and scooted off westward for sixty-nine days, finally arriving in Florida on June 21 after 4,480 miles. Vihlen's careful planning, determination, and guts had finally won for him the prize he worked so hard for—he held the record for crossing the Atlantic in the smallest boat ever, just under six feet. Manry and Riding in the summer of 1965 had wrested it away from William Andrews, who had held it since 1892 with his voyage in *Sapolio*. Now only three years later Vihlen had it. This tough, ex–Korean War jet jock would later have to fight to keep it, though.

Vihlen had more trouble with bureaucrats on both sides of the Atlantic than he did with nature during his 1968 crossing.

Seventy-five-year-old William Willis was at it again that summer, too. In 1967 he had tried for the second time in *Little One* and come within four hundred miles of Britain before being clobbered by Hurricane Chloe. After he lost his sails and most of his food, he had to be rescued by a Polish trawler. Now in the summer of 1968 he would make his third attempt. Which old axiom would hold true for him: "Third time lucky" or "Never three on a match"? He left Montauk, Long Island, on May 1 to find out. He was never seen again. When *Little One* was later found, rudderless and with a broken mast, Willis's logbook, still inside, showed a last entry date of July 17. The Atlantic had finally pinned the old wrestler.

Swinging John Fairfax had spent his time in England making connections, finding the right people, and doggedly sticking to his goal of making the first single-handed attempt to row the Atlantic. His first big break came when he met the legendary boat designer Uffa Fox at the Earl's Court Boat Show. Fox at first wasn't interested in the project, but there was something about Fairfax's body language and determined speech that won over the famous yacht designer. Perhaps Fox saw in the bold, outrageous Fairfax a youthful version of himself. Whatever it was, a few months after their meeting the young man had plans from Fox and thus, more important, the imprimatur of the grand old man himself to wave under the noses of possible backers. It opened many doors.

On January 20, 1969, Fairfax was ready to shove off from Las Palmas. The Fox-designed rowboat, the *Britannia*, was a major step forward in the art of ocean rowing. It was twenty-five feet long with a self-bailing cockpit. The bow and stern were each fitted with canopied covers made from thick, shaped pieces of foam. Should the boat go over, the canopies would provide righting moment. In fact, tests showed it would self-right in just two seconds. Under the deck were watertight compartments for stowage. A multiposition daggerboard could be used to trim the boat. However, the key to the whole design was a sliding seat like the ones found on sculling shells. Fairfax would be the first

Shagadelic hipster John Fairfax aboard *Britannia* pulling westward. This flamboyant rower later invited his girlfriend to join him on a Pacific crossing.

transoceanic rower to put his arms *and* legs into the effort, and this is the feature that would make his voyage a success.

At launch the *Britannia* was loaded down with all the luxuries of the day for such a voyage. He carried spear guns for fishing, which he used effectively the whole time, and even a portable generator to run his radio and other electrical appliances. With a large stock of food and water aboard, he could survive for a very long voyage. It wasn't expected that this voyage would be all that long, as he was taking the trade-wind route, but the supplies were there if he needed them.

He did need them. Even with the fine qualities of the boat and the helpful trade winds, the *Britannia* made a lethargic crossing of 180 days—half a year! Fairfax worked hard at the oars, but winds, the sea, and the heat worked against him. He found, too, that the boat didn't behave well when the wind was astern. It would yaw and require corrective strokes, which made maintaining a rowing rhythm difficult. Even with this one flaw, Fairfax would not have made it across if he had had a lesser boat.

When the *Britannia* touched the beach at Miami on July 19, not that many people around the world cared. Most people were glued to their televisions watching *Apollo 11*'s flight as the lunar module prepared to land on the surface of the moon the next day.

———◆——

In the final months of the decade, the twenty-foot *Nimbus* made a west–east Atlantic crossing with George Cadwalader and Duncan Spencer aboard, while John Riding finally began his attempt to cross the Pacific in his tiny *Sjö Äg*, departing from San Diego.

· IO ·

THE PURSUIT OF HAPPINESS

THE 1970s

◆ BY LUGGER TO AUSTRALIA ◆ AOKI AND VAN RUTH ◆ DAVID BLAGDEN
TAMES A *WILLING GRIFFIN* ◆ THERE'S NO PLACE LIKE HOME,
THANKFULLY: SHANE'S *SHRIMPY* ◆ BAS'S BOAT ◆ WEBB CHILES IN AN OPEN BOAT
◆ MEXICAN MINIMALIST MARINER CARLOS ARAGÓN ◆ SPIESS GIRL ◆

SMALL-BOAT SAILORS OF THE 1970S REFLECTED THE PRE-
vailing culture of the time: most of them went not only for adventure
but also for spiritual self-fulfillment. This was the decade when new-
age philosophies and practices such as Zen, est, transcendental medi-
tation, gestalt, and a host of others became part of mainstream culture.
"Get in touch with your feelings" was the mantra of the times.

Like most people through the centuries who have embarked on voyages away from kith and kin to "find themselves," most of our sailors eventually wound up at home having learned what Ulysses had learned when he finally returned to Ithaca or Dorothy when she got back to Kansas. Yet, like all travelers, our sailors were happier, more content, and wiser for having made the journey.

———◆———

The first long small-boat voyage of the 1970s was something of a misfire, though it had lasting ramifications. English schoolteacher David Pyle set off in April 1969 with a companion, David Carrick, to sail from England to Australia in an open boat. Pyle's boat *Hermes* was a plywood Drascombe Lugger, a type designed by English boatbuilder John Watkinson to be a spacious, dry, daysailer for families who wanted to spend a Saturday on the water. It was eighteen feet, nine inches long, with at first two lug sails, though later these were changed to gunter and leg-o'-mutton. Pyle, and others, soon saw the potential of the design for greater things, and he decided to prove its seaworthiness.

Pyle fitted his boat with some nonstandard equipment. These included inflatable sponsons twelve feet long by nine inches wide along the gunwales for added stability during bad weather (much the same as the ones Romer had used on the *Deutscher Sport*), a built-up foredeck, and two watertight bulkheads. He also carried a radar reflector, signal flares, an emergency radio, and a large inflatable life raft. The raft is perhaps a strange addition, considering that some foam blocks would have made the *Hermes* self-rescuing. Deploying and boarding a separate rescue craft are often more dangerous than simply remaining in the original boat, if it can still float.

Their track took them across the Channel, down the canals of France to Marseilles, and from there a 150-mile crossing of the Gulf of

Genoa to Italy. Around the boot of Italy they went to Greece, but on their way to Turkey their rudder came unhinged, which forced them to land on the island of Kalimnos for repairs. Pyle and Carrick arrived in Turkey on July 28. Next they shipped the boat by truck and rail to Mosul near the navigable head of the Tigris River. In Iraq the boat was hit by a ferry and its planks sprung, so they sent it by steamer to Bahrain, where the men repaired it at a local yacht club. When it was seaworthy again they skirted the coast for nine hundred miles to India, but with the onset of the monsoon season they decided to ship the boat through to Malaysia, rather than be caught in the Bay of Bengal.

Now, in the first month of the new decade, they left Singapore bound for Djakarta, Indonesia, which they reached on February 2. They sailed through the Indonesian archipelago, then crossed the Timor Sea, arriving on April 2, 1970, at Darwin, Australia.

The voyage was only a qualified success because Pyle had to ship *Hermes* by road, rail, and steamer along the way. Yet there were several thousand blue-water miles under the Lugger's keel, and this was enough to ensure that Watkinson back in England had more orders for Luggers than he could handle. He subcontracted with another firm to build the boat in fiberglass, and in one of these Webb Chiles later in the decade would begin the most audacious open-boat voyage yet.

At twenty feet, nine inches, Hiroshi Aoki's plywood *Ahodori II* was just a shade shorter than John Guzzwell's *Trekka*. In this homebuilt plywood Bermuda yawl, Aoki crossed from Osaka to San Francisco in 1971. He went south to the Galápagos next, then Easter Island, around Cape Horn, and up to Buenos Aires. He tied the knot of his eastabout "hard way" circumnavigation on January 12, 1973, back in Japan.

In 1972 American John Van Ruth decided that Stanley Smith's little West Wight Potter 14 was big enough to make a real ocean passage. Two years earlier he had bought one of the gunter-rigged boats from a manufacturer in California who was making the hulls in fiberglass instead of the original plywood. Van Ruth planned to sail to

Panama, so after cramming food, wine, tequila, beer, his pet cat Yelapa, and a pistol into the dinghy-sized boat, off he went toward the "ditch" (the canal). Cruising along down the coast of Mexico, he reconsidered his plans. Maybe Hawaii would be more fun? He swung the helm over and headed west toward the setting sun.

En route to Hawaii he suffered a number of misadventures. He had navigation problems, a pesky shark had to be shot, and somehow he lost his cat overboard. After eighty days and a final struggle with the lee shore of Cape Kumakahi, he took a tow into Hilo Bay. There, surely, he got out one of his bottles of brew and no doubt toasted Stanley Smith and eulogized Yelapa.

———————

That same year, David Blagden, an American actor who emigrated to England after an adventurous youth working now and then on cargo ships, began to dream of and doodle small boats. Acting as a career, he found, was an unreliable profession with sometimes long breaks between parts, and it was during one of these breaks that he conceived the idea of competing in "Blondie" Hasler's Observer Singlehanded Transatlantic Race, the OSTAR, in a small boat—the only problem was he couldn't afford one.

By hard work and persistence he got the Essex Boat Company (now Hunter Boats Ltd.) to build for him a slightly modified version of their nineteen-foot Hunter, after working out an installment plan to pay for it. Though he now had a boat, he still didn't have permission to enter the OSTAR because boats less than twenty feet long were not allowed, and all competitors had to prove that they had undertaken a single-handed voyage of at least five hundred miles.

To overcome the first hurdle Blagden approached Blondie Hasler directly. The rugged ex-commando—who had led the "cockleshell" kayak raid against German shipping at Bordeaux in occupied France—respected young, determined men like Blagden. Hasler had spent a life in small boats breaking the rules, as when he entered his modified Folkboat *Jester* in the first OSTAR. He had converted it to a Chinese junk rig with an unstayed hollow mast and had eliminated the cockpit in favor of a single opening hatch forward of the cabin. *Jester* wasn't the kind of boat that came to mind as a "yacht," at least as Sir Thomas Lipton and Sir Tommy Sopwith thought of yachts.

Seeing a kindred spirit in Blagden, Hasler suggested that the race committee relax the rules. They did. Blagden then made a qualifying solo voyage out into the Atlantic and back during which his boat, *Willing Griffin*, was knocked down in force 7 winds, but the boat popped upright immediately, and though seasick for a time, he came back to port with infinitely more confidence in his and the boat's sailing abilities. He was in the 1972 OSTAR.

Contestants in the race that year included boating and aviation legend Sir Francis Chichester in his 57-foot ketch *Gipsy Moth V*, Martin Minter-Kemp in the sleek 65-foot *Strongbow*, and Frenchman Jean-Yves Terlain in the monstrous 128-foot schooner *Vendredi Trieze* (Friday the 13th)—remember, this was a *single-handed* race! Blagden had no chance of winning against these fearsome entrants, but it was the gallant attempt that mattered.

The race began on June 17 at Plymouth, to end at Newport, Rhode Island. In one photograph of the start, *Willing Griffin* can be seen actually leading *Vendredi Trieze* by a nose. It didn't turn out to be a photo finish, however. Blagden took a somewhat southerly route to avoid the Gulf Stream, but the larger boats, relatively less affected by it, took the more direct route. Not long into the race Blagden found that his water supply in tanks had been contaminated, so he put in at the Azores for replenishment. It seems to be a mistake to carry all one's water in a couple of tanks or a few plastic sacks; there is less chance of contamination when water is in several dozen smaller plastic bottles with screw-top lids. Manry had done this seven years earlier in a much smaller boat.

Once back at sea, Blagden muddled onward against storms, doldrums, knockdowns, and the knowledge that Alain Colas had already won the race in the seventy-foot trimaran *Pen Duick IV* after only twenty days and thirteen hours. It would take *Willing Griffin* all that and another month before she made the finish line at Newport on August 8. On a handicapped rating, however, Blagden managed to place a very respectable tenth out of fifty-nine competitors. His voyage opened the door for many other single-handers in small boats—eventually they had a race of their own, the Mini-Transat. Sadly, Blagden would lose his life several years later in a boating accident at sea.

The second Briton to head to sea in defiance of land-bound critics was twenty-two-year-old Shane Acton of Cambridge. After schooling he had joined the exceptionally rigorous Royal Marine Commandos, but though a capable soldier he found the life too regimented. He wanted adventure, but he also wanted space. When his hitch was up he returned to Cambridge and worked menial jobs until he had saved four hundred pounds, which he used to buy a secondhand eighteen-foot Caprice bilge-keel cruiser similar to that owned by the German yachtsman Rollo Gebhard, who had crossed the Atlantic in one a few years earlier. This boat had been designed for jaunts along the River Cam or maybe coasting along East Anglia, but Acton had larger plans for it. First, he renamed it *Super Shrimp*, though he and his friends would always refer to it as just *Shrimpy*.

He had never been on a sailboat before, but he headed down the Cam and out into the Wash. His destination was Falmouth, and port by port he worked his way there, learning how to sail as he went. In Falmouth he ran the boat up on an out-of-the-way mudflat to sit out the winter while he earned cruising money doing construction work. He taught himself navigation with a cheap plastic sextant, had twin headsails made to allow self-steering downwind, provisioned the boat with 120 cans of food and thirty gallons of water, and added foam flotation.

On June 3, 1973, Acton put out from Falmouth, announcing that his next stop would be somewhere on Cape Finisterre in Spain, not an inconsiderable goal for someone who had never sailed on the ocean or navigated with a sextant. But he had £20 in his pocket and a lot of brass, so off he went. Ten days later he made the cape and two days later was safely in port at Viana do Castelo, Portugal. Fully confident now that he could sail anywhere his wanderlust-struck heart desired, he worked his way to Las Palmas by July. He lingered there for a few months and when funds ran low hired himself out as a navigator for a Danish sailor who wanted to go to Gibraltar. This cycle of sailing, soaking up the local scenery and culture, and then working tricky boating jobs for pay would be Acton's modus operandi over the next seven years. It set him apart from many other sailors who are only "port" oriented—get somewhere, resupply, and then move on. Acton followed his own way and enjoyed the process.

He reached Barbados January 3, 1974, after a speedy thirty-nine-day passage. During this time he perfected his use of the twin headsails and, like John Letcher Jr. and others, could take long breaks from the tiller to read, sleep, or cook. He lingered in the Antilles for six months and then set off for the San Blas Islands along the northern coast of Panama. At a local harbor he met some free-spirited young people who were hitching rides aboard yachts to take them no place in particular. One of these vagabonds was Iris Derungs, a Swiss woman who had once walked across the Sudan, living on whatever the Massai tribesmen offered her. She was young, beautiful, and adventurous. Soon she and Acton became friends, and she signed on to see the rest of the world with him. Together they transited the Panama Canal, and there before them lay the wide Pacific—and years more of adventures.

Another Drascombe open boat similar to Pyle's made an Atlantic crossing the same year that Acton started out. This was a twenty-one-foot, nine-inch Longboat sailed by Geoffrey Stewart from Gibraltar to Saint Vincent in 59 days.

However, 1973 ended on a sad note for small-boat sailors. John Riding had managed to span the Pacific from his starting point in San Diego in his twelve-foot *Sjö Äg*, but that summer had disappeared somewhere in the Tasman Sea on a passage between Auckland and Sydney. As the year ended, hope of finding the thirty-three-year-old alive died, too.

Another death two years later was less surprising. Bas Jan Ader was a professor of art at the University of California, Irvine. He had been born in the Netherlands but had emigrated to America at twenty-one. Ader's métier was performance art, usually captured on film. Colleagues and art connoisseurs cite the highlights of his contribution to the 1970s art scene as photographs showing him riding a bicycle into a canal in Amsterdam and others showing him jumping off a house roof in California. Especially admired is the performance piece in which he cried real tears while being filmed.

To add to this impressive oeuvre of performance art, Ader declared he would make a transatlantic crossing in a thirteen-foot Guppy sailboat he had acquired from Melen Marine in California. The Guppy was a tiny sloop with a fixed keel, not at all a bad boat for normal sailing. He added lifelines strung all around the stays, a hefty hand-operated bilge pump, and a windvane-type self-steerer on the transom.

A self-steering vane dominates the transom of trendy California artist Bas Jan Ader's Guppy 13 as he prepares to cross the Atlantic as a "performance piece" of art in 1975. It was his last show.

Ader entitled his voyage—er, new performance piece—"In Search of the Miraculous." With it he wanted to express the themes of social alienation and nomadism, he said. After sending farewell postcards to his many admirers he departed Cape Cod on July 9, 1975, bound for Cornwall, England. His half-submerged boat was discovered off the Irish coast in January of the next year, empty. The world of 1970s modern art had lost a master.

Super Shrimp set sail from the Galápagos Islands for the Marquesas in French Polynesia January 4, 1975, and forty-five days later anchored there at Nuku Hiva. For three more years Shane Acton and Iris Derungs meandered about the Pacific, touching down anywhere their fancy brought them. Tahiti they found an overdeveloped bore—it was now full of boutiques and had lost its natural charm. In Australia they received a magnificent welcome, and their boat was even inspected by Prince Philip, a keen yachtsman who was then visiting that country. In

Shane Acton aboard *Super Shrimp* with his mate, Iris Derungs. With no prior sailing experience he circumnavigated the Caprice sloop and then wrote one of nautical literature's classic books, *"Shrimpy": A Record Round-the-World Voyage in an Eighteen Foot Yacht.*

Brisbane they met C. E. "Nobby" Clark, the man who had built their Caprice boat in his boatyard on the Isle of Wight about a dozen years earlier (he had since emigrated).

In Bali, Derungs temporarily left Acton to fly home to see her mother in her native Switzerland. Acton traversed the Indian Ocean during the first three months of 1979, a good time for such a small boat, but when he tried to go north up the Red Sea he ran into many delays from the suspicious Saudi Arabian coast guardsmen and port officials. At least his boat was not impounded, as would happen to an American small-boat sailor a few years later.

This American was Webb Chiles, a skilled yachtsman who made his living going on great sailing adventures and then writing books about them. A philosophy and literature major in college, he wrote poetic passages about his maritime mishaps and personal anxieties that caught the mood of the reading public somewhat as Bernard Moitessier's writings had.

Having read of the impressive adventures in Drascombe boats he purchased a Lugger, gave it the abstruse name *Chidiock Tichborne* (after an English traitor), and with it proposed to make the world's first circumnavigation in an open boat. It was an audacious plan, even for a man with two circumnavigations under his belt, including rounding the Horn in a boat with a cracked hull.

He departed San Diego on November 12, 1978, hoping to beat the worst of the weather, but he ran into some unexpectedly fierce storms, as Rebell had forty years earlier, and was knocked down. The boat's seaworthy design and his great ability as a seaman saved the situation, though he lost various possessions with the dousing. Losing things out of an open boat would be a problem for years to come as he worked westward.

He fetched Nuku Hiva five weeks later and Tahiti on January 16, 1979. After spending the summer months of the south-

Webb Chiles during his attempt to be the first to circumnavigate in an open sailboat.

ern hemisphere there, he continued westward through the Pacific to Suva, Fiji, where he wisely sat out the cyclone season. As the 1970s came to a close, he had overcome many obstacles and made the longest voyage by far in an open boat, exceeding even Captain Bligh's. It was a wonderful accomplishment, but he had the rest of the Pacific to cross, as well as two more oceans.

In 1977 Carlos Aragón attempted something amazing—to cross from Acapulco, Mexico, to the Marquesas on, not in, a fourteen-foot, nine-inch Finn-class dinghy, nothing more than a shallow dinghy. He had tried once before, in 1975, but abandoned the venture when caught by a fierce storm near the equator. This time he practiced extensively off the Mexican coast in all types of weather so that when he departed on April 28 he felt completely prepared for what he anticipated would be a four-month ordeal. His boat, the *Golondrina*, was rigged with a homemade self-steering gear. But the built-in water tanks developed leaks and gave the water a polyester flavor, so Aragón resorted to catching rainwater in a bucket for his freshwater. In addition to food he took along special preparations of vitamins mixed with antibiotics, which he injected himself with on a regular schedule. The self-steering gear wasn't as effective as simply balancing the tiller with a bungee cord, so he used only that low-tech system.

Twenty days into the voyage another equatorial storm thundered in on him, and his fight for survival was on. Two years earlier he had tried to run from a storm but found himself only deeper in it. This time he hove-to, trying to maintain his position to the south as much as possible. For seven harrowing days the storm battered him as he clung to the tiny hull ensconced in his dry suit, which was no longer dry because it had torn. After a hellish week the storm gave up, and Aragón emerged the victor.

Pride goeth before a capsizing, and sure enough on June 30 a freak wave struck his boat on the beam—or at least what little beam the *Golondrina* presented to the sea—and Aragón was thrown into the water. To right the boat he had to unship the mast and use the boom as a lever on the upturned centerboard. Climbing out on the boom, he finally managed to plop the sloop to an even keel, and then he could begin the wearying task of bailing her out and getting her going again. A few days later he hit on the notion of using a plastic sheet as a spinnaker, and when he had rigged it, this sail pulled the boat toward Polynesia like a horse heading home.

After five thousand miles and 107 days at sea, he arrived in the harbor at Nuku Hiva on August 9, a justifiably proud young Mexican sailor.

The Atlantic Ocean was challenged by another small-boat sailor in the summer of 1979. Gerry Spiess, a teacher from Minnesota, longed for real adventures away from his "blackboard jungle." A few years earlier Spiess had designed a ten-foot stubby craft. When he tried to build it in his garage, he found he couldn't bend critical timbers without breaking them. Finally, though, he learned how to make glued laminations, and from that point on his boat, *Yankee Girl*, went together smoothly. *Yankee Girl* was an interesting design for reasons other than her diminutive size—we've already seen smaller (Vihlen's six-foot *April Fool*). Taking a cue from the *Jester*, Blondie Hasler's Folkboat, Spiess had just one hatch in the top aft section of the "cabin." There was no cockpit to worry about flooding, and underneath there was only the slimmest of keels, more of a skeg. For stability he counted on a deep V-shaped hull ballasted with food, water, and other heavy objects. Spiess must have learned from Hugo Vihlen about being stuck in adverse winds in a close-coupled boat, so he too shipped an outboard, a four-horsepower Evinrude, and no less than *sixty* gallons of premixed fuel!

Unlike many of our adventurers, Spiess was a meticulously careful planner, continuously poring over the details of

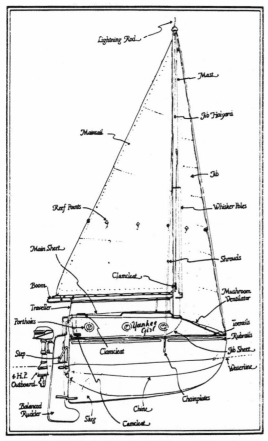

Gerry Spiess's ten-foot *Yankee Girl* was a minimalist semi-capsule boat that bested the Atlantic and the Pacific.

the proposed voyage, trying to prepare for all eventualities. (In fact, of all the people interviewed for this book, Spiess stands out as the most thoughtful. His list of supplies, provisions, and tools taken on the voyage, reprinted in his book, *Alone Against the Atlantic*, is a veritable primer in long-distance small-boat cruise planning and should be studied by anyone who plans such a voyage.)

Spiess employed Bill Verity's concept of the totally enclosed capsule boat: lines and tiller can be handled from the safety and comfort of the cabin. However, Spiess added a very sensible twist to the design—the sliding hatch slid far enough forward so Spiess could sit on a little seat attached to the transom. In effect, he could steer the boat from either inside or out, depending on weather conditions and his need for a clear line of sight. This was yet another case of careful planning and attention to detail; it was also a wonderful example of ingenuity. Continuing his preparations, Spiess made a dramatic test of the boat on White Bear Lake, Minnesota, in a storm so fierce the weather service issued tornado warnings. The boat heeled over to the rail with the sail fully up as the winds bore down on it, but it was controllable. Spiess could now trust *Yankee Girl* to the open Atlantic.

Yankee Girl was hardly high-tech, she was just very well thought out. Spiess built her with simple tools at home.

On June 1, 1979, he set out from Norfolk, Virginia, on the voyage that had consumed his thoughts for so many years. It wasn't easy going because the wind and the current were often against him. When he didn't have the wind from the sky he flipped on the "iron wind" of the Evinrude and kept working eastward. He purposefully limited himself to sixteen hours a day sailing and eight hours resting. On an earlier sailing voyage he had nearly come to catastrophe when he tried to press on after staying awake more than thirty-three hours. He mustn't make the same mistake this time. He prudently chose not to take amphetamines, either. Nevertheless, after only a few days he began to hear voices, and they stayed with him most of the way.

Nine days into the voyage he was averaging only a little over thirty miles per day. He had hoped to find the Gulf Stream about sixty miles offshore, as the locals in Norfolk had told him he would. Finally, on June 10 *Yankee Girl*'s hull kissed the warm, green northeastern-bound current, and prospects looked good for the impatient mariner.

Reality was not so good, though. The Atlantic churned itself into a fit as near-hurricane winds from the east fought against the Gulf Stream. Spiess found his sea anchor ineffectual, so he either hove-to, which *Yankee Girl* did fairly well, or lay ahull. The pounding of the fifteen-foot seas on the hull was intense, but the plywood boat was well built and stood it well. The captain was not standing it as well, though—he had to endure the beating huddled in the overpacked boat while he tried to calculate how many days he could make his provisions last. It seemed now it would take him at least a hundred days to make England. Suddenly the boat lurched over, and the mast smacked the water, lying there in spite of the half ton of ballast in the lower part of the hull trying to pull the mast back up. Spiess frantically pushed and leaned all his weight on the opposite side of the hull, now the cabin roof, and the boat suddenly righted. Looking out a port window he could see that the lashing holding his extra gas tanks, which he had counted on for emergency flotation, had been torn off, and the tanks were gone.

Spiess couldn't relax until the severe gale subsided on June 15. He had triumphed over a solid week of horrendous weather, lost some equipment, and suffered an inrush of water through a mistakenly open hatch, but he had learned the hard way. If the weather would only moderate, he felt the voyage could still succeed. In a moment of uncharacteristic carelessness he climbed on the deck in the still-high seas to unlash the jib. Just then a huge wave slammed into the stern of the boat and threw it sideways. Spiess went into the water but fortunately was wearing his safety harness and tether. If he hadn't been, he would never have regained the boat in those seas.

With reasonable weather again he resumed sailing. With the jib sheet connected to the tiller on one side and surgical tubing stretched to the tiller on the other side, the boat would self-steer. John Letcher Jr. had illustrated this technique in his book eight years earlier, and by now many yachtsmen had adopted it. On June 23 Spiess was pleasantly surprised to find he had made good twelve hundred miles—a third of the way there.

He had favorable conditions about a third of the time. When winds were slack or unfavorable he would motor or do chores. Day by day the miles began to reel away. His emergency fallback plan had always been to cut the trip short at the Azores, but as he entered July he gave up on that and headed straight for Falmouth. He arrived there July 24 after only fifty-three days and five hours and 3,780 statute miles.

***

Shane Acton finally negotiated his way through the political red tape and got *Shrimpy* out of the Red Sea and on its way up the Suez Canal. In July Iris Derungs rejoined him in Greece, and together they spent the summer slowly working across the Mediterranean. In France they cut across the Canal du Midi to the Gironde and then the Bay of Biscay.

It took them six months into the next year to finally reach Cambridge, but when they did, the university town erupted in admiration for its black-sheep sailor lad who had left all those years before. Now he was a conquering hero having made a thirty-thousand-mile circumnavigation in a £400 boat, unquestionably the greatest small-boat feat of the 1970s. The mayor led the reception committee and Prince Philip sent a congratulatory telegram. As Acton basked in the accolades, he thought to himself even then that he wouldn't be home for long.

Art on facing page: No one has ever paddled more miles than Canadian legend Don Starkell, here with his son Dana as they savor the success of their 12,000-mile paddle to the Amazon.

THE GOLDEN DECADE

THE 1980s

◆ NEW TECHNOLOGY   ◆   DON'T FORGET THE CATAMARANS: THE *RAG TAG FLEET*   ◆
STARKELL AND SONS: EPIC CANOEISTS   ◆   SVEN THE SWEDE: THE EDISON
OF SMALL-BOAT BUILDERS   ◆   THREE MEN DUKE IT OUT FOR WHO'S
SMALLEST   ◆   THE FIVE HUNDRED DAYS OF SERGE TESTA   ◆   ED GILLET
KAYAKS AND KITES TO HAWAII   ◆   FRENCH IMPRESSIONS   ◆

A CAREFUL EXAMINATION OF THE 1970S TALLY OF SMALL
boat voyages shows that there were surprisingly few. Those that were
made, like the round-the-world attempts by Aoki, Acton, Chiles, and
Riding, were impressive efforts, but considering the pioneering ventures
in the 1960s by Horie, Manry, Vihlen, and the rowers, one would think

that many more microboat sailors would have launched in the 1970s. What happened?

There were three factors that conspired to keep the number of small-boat voyages in that decade relatively small. The first is that at any one time only a very small fraction of the population is willing to risk their lives to achieve a goal that will have no financial benefit or add to personal freedom. A small-boat voyage is undertaken against all *practical* considerations. This fact will always ensure that there are never many such voyages.

The second factor is that the 1970s were a time of tremendous political upheaval. Wars in Southeast Asia, the Middle East, Central and South America, and all over Africa may have caused some otherwise adventurous spirits to stay at their moorings for fear of imprisonment, vessel confiscation, or worse.

The final factor that may have adversely affected small-boat voyaging in the 1970s was the generally bad fiscal climate of the decade. Oil shortages, exorbitant interest rates, deficit spending, inflation, and the shift to postindustrial economies in the West didn't leave would-be small-boat sailors much room to indulge a passion. Many of our voyagers lived on the economic fringe of society, anyway, so an economic crunch impacted them to a greater extent than those with larger boats.

In the 1980s, however, things were different. A bumper crop of mariners attempted daring voyages in small boats and other odd craft. It was almost as if a dam burst and all those who had postponed trips in the 1970s now came rushing toward the surf. The two factors responsible for the renaissance of small-boat voyaging were a better economy and new technology.

There was a return to free-market values in Western nations and the imminent collapse of the Soviet bloc and all the proxy wars it had promulgated. The world saw a "go-go" economy unlike any it had seen since the middle 1960s. "Trickle-down economics" was the buzz phrase from Washington to Wall Street to London. With spare cash lying around, available at low interest rates, more people could put little boats in the water without ruining themselves financially.

Another factor that helped spark the resurgence was the advancement of technology on two fronts, electronics and materials. What had started as high-tech navigation and communication systems for the military in the 1960s and 1970s now trickled down to the yachtsman. The average boater could buy small waterproof radios that could operate over long distances on twelve volts or even internal batteries. Pricier, but not totally out of reach, were miniaturized loran units, and late in the decade the miraculous GPS (global positioning system), which ended the servitude of mariners to the sextant the way Marin-Marie and John Letcher Jr.'s innovations in self-steering had freed them from the tiller. Kenichi Horie had used a battery-operated direction finder on his transpacific crossing, but it was useful only close to the coast. With a GPS anyone could know where they were in the world within a hundred feet at any time, even in midocean.

Gerry Spiess had a portable EPIRB (emergency position-indicating radio beacon) on *Yankee Girl* that he could switch on to call for rescue at sea. Such a unit sends a signal that is detected by a satellite and relayed to receiving stations back on earth, alerting the authorities to an emergency and its location. Spiess never used his, but the peace of mind it gave him helped him decide to proceed with the voyage. Now in the 1980s the price and size of EPIRBs, like all the rest of boating electronics, were shrinking. Their quality, reliability, and features were steadily increasing, too.

In boatyards builders no longer thought of wood as the only material for boats, even one-offs. Fiberglass had grown in popularity since the 1950s, but even aluminum could be used now that the price of TIG (tungsten inert gas) welding had come down. Any tinkerer could weld steel or stainless steel in his home workshop using a very low-cost MIG (metal inert gas) welder. The use of stainless steel on yachts rose dramatically during these years. Easy to form, ABS (acrylonitrile-butadiene-styrene) and acrylic plastics became common materials for making boat parts, as did exotic composite materials like carbon fiber and Kevlar. These modern materials freed boaters from the age-old, dangerous problems caused by springing planks or leaking caulked joints.

The sailors of the 1980s had at their disposal the materials to make boats stronger, lighter, and simpler and also the electronics to make voyaging in them safer. The combined trickle-down effects of a roaring economy and brave new high-tech world produced the largest and most unique flotilla of small boats to sally forth since the 1860s and the best competition among small-boat sailors since the *Puffin* versus *English Rose III* duel of 1966. Some old friends would return to the hunt, too.

Douglas Hill and Michael Cullinane, twenty-four-year-old Californians, made a noteworthy journey in the spring of 1980 when they took an airplane down to Trinidad with an eighteen-foot Prindle catamaran, *Rag Tag Fleet,* in the cargo hold. After they had waded through the morass of customs they went to the beach, assembled the boat, and set sail north, following Frederic Fenger's 1911 route up the Leeward and Windward Islands. Hill was a highly experienced boater, and though Cullinane was less so, he had backwoods skills that were useful as they made camp each night on island beaches. The boat was mostly stock except for its port hull, fitted with a watertight compartment for their emergency supplies, and the trampoline, which had additional strapdown points to tie on their other gear.

As the summer progressed they worked their way up to Miami, arriving there on July 29, having suffered only two capsizings the entire transcaribbean voyage, which speaks well of their sailing ability aboard a cat in those tricky waters.

Canadian Don Starkell and his two sons, Dana, age nineteen, and Jeff, eighteen, were heading south that same summer of 1980 in what would become the greatest canoe voyage ever made. Their aim was to paddle from Canada to the mouth of the Amazon River, a voyage of twelve thousand miles or nearly halfway around the world. One of Don's goals was to earn the title for the longest canoe voyage ever, and another—to have a bonding experience with his sons.

They left Winnipeg, Manitoba, June 1 in their red twenty-one-foot fiberglass canoe *Orellana* and paddled south along the Red River until they reached the Continental Divide. By muscle first and then by truck they portaged the boat across the Divide and put in on the Minnesota River. Down this they went to the Mississippi and down that to New Orleans. Along the way they were broiled by the merciless summer heat and humidity, while Dana suffered even more because he was asthmatic.

Don Starkell had been a national long-distance canoeing champion before the trip started and knew something of what to expect from the daily grind, although he hadn't been used to the heat they now encountered. His sons were less well prepared, especially Dana with his poor health, but Jeff was the one who was to give up on the trip. After leaving Louisiana they paddled west and then south along the Gulf Intracoastal Waterway to the Mexican border. Here they fought a constant battle against the formidable beam seas of the Gulf of Mexico. Their long boat wasn't built for this type of pounding along the surf line, and even though all three worked mightily to prevent it, the *Orellana* capsized, on September 23, spilling many of their supplies and making it tough to reach their next goal, Laguna Madre. That winter Don and Dana recuperated in Veracruz, Mexico, while Jeff returned to Canada to resume his study of electronics. He had enough of the brutal demands of ocean paddling in a canoe.

Starkell was a stern taskmaster who was sure this voyage would improve Dana's health. He thought his son had become addicted to asthma medicines and that a vigorous life might cure the affliction, even though the young man was inclined to less strenuous pursuits such as guitar playing, at which he was something of a prodigy.

In the spring of 1981 they rounded the Yucatán Peninsula but were greatly concerned about what lay before them. The small nations of Central America were, with the exception of Belize, involved in wars, with various guerilla factions backed by Washington, Moscow, or Havana. In addition to the geopolitical machinations, the countries were beset by drug traffickers and their minions, corrupt local officials. It was impossible to know who was loyal to whom and who was working in an official capacity—very few—or who was freelancing—very many.

The two Starkells entered these dangerous political shoals intending to cross them as quickly and invisibly as possible, but their hopes were thwarted nearly the first day. On May 10, while attempting a dangerous open-water passage across the Gulf of Honduras from Belize directly to Honduras, to bypass Guatemala, they spotted a Guatemalan patrol boat coming after them. They tried to reach shallow water so the motorboat couldn't follow them, but its speed enabled it to cut them off. Jeering soldiers interrogated the Starkells at gunpoint for several hours and searched *Orellana*. Eventually the father, son, and canoe were released, but by then it was late in the day, and so they were forced to camp on Guatemalan soil that night, something they had hoped to avoid. Off at sunrise the next morning, they hadn't quite reached the Honduran border when two armed men in another canoe tried to rob them. Just then the patrol boat from the previous day hove into view and the bandits fled.

Honduras turned out to be no safer than Guatemala. Late in May while camped on the shore they were taken prisoner by men claiming to be militiamen on the lookout for communist Sandinista agents from Nicaragua. They were then force-marched seven miles into the jungle while their captors taunted them by pricking their backs and necks with knives. Locked up in a filthy jail overnight, they were released the next day only through the intervention of a local influential English-speaking businessman. When they got back to the canoe they found that much of their gear had been pilfered.

As they left Honduras, a shadowy American of unknown background warned them about Nicaragua, telling them they would be mistaken for American agents by the Sandinistas and arrested. Starkell decided to confront the possibility head-on by landing at the first Nicaraguan town he came to and asking for a pass through the country. What he got instead was what the mysterious American had predicted—they were arrested. The Sandinista interrogator accused the two of being spies and of having arrived from a mother ship stationed somewhere offshore. Starkell denied all, and two days later they were released, though even more of their equipment was now gone.

When they weren't in trouble with their fellowman, nature stepped in to make their voyage traumatic. High seas, inquisitive sharks, exhaustion, and lack of food and water turned what had been planned as a "bonding experience" between father and son into a test of individual character. The fiberglass *Orellana* cracked frequently and leaked in many places as they paddled along the Panamanian and then Colombian shores. Fortunately they were able to buy polyester resin and glass cloth along the way to make repairs.

The fiberglass canoe *Orellana* was designed for three paddlers, though only two would complete the voyage 21 million paddle strokes later.

During the early winter of 1981 they regrouped on the island of Trinidad, and after New Year's crossed to Venezuela, where they entered the Orinoco River. Three months later, when they reached the end of the river, they had paddled ten thousand miles, but still had another two thousand to go. They completed their amazing odyssey on May 1 when they reached Belém, Brazil, after paddling to it from the Amazon River's confluence with the Río Negro. Their canoe, like their clothes, was held together by patches, but it had made it, barely. Don had achieved his goals of making the world's longest ever canoe trip and bonding with his sons, but, best of all—Dana's asthma was completely cured.

The ever-inquisitive and experiment-loving Swedish boatbuilder Sven Lundin had become interested in metal boat construction in the late 1970s. He wheedled a donation of quarter-inch sheet aluminum from a

In *Bris,* Swedish amateur boat designer Sven Lundin began to show the flare for innovation that became his hallmark.

Swedish mill in return for what they hoped would be some good publicity; they also provided a workshop and welding tools, and throughout 1976–78 he fused together his newest creation, the *Aluminium-Bris* (*Bris* is Swedish for "breeze"; Lundin's first *Bris* boat was wooden). The nineteen-footer had a conventional beamy hull with a deep keel, and topsides it was much like some of the larger European-style cruising yachts, with a series of windows below its gunwales which carried around

Designing radical boats and living a radical life keeps the smile on Sven Lundin's face. He is to boat design what Ed "Big Daddy" Roth was to hot rods or Burt Rutan to experimental aircraft.

aft to the transom. On deck was a cabin with a 360-degree view. A diesel engine was installed on the port side ahead of the geographic center of the boat and canted inward toward the centerline. Uncharacteristically, Lundin, usually an unconventional freethinker, even installed a flush toilet, perhaps as a concession to the many women crewmates he seemed to find and sign on along the way on his adventures.

Late in 1979 he sailed *Aluminium-Bris* from Brännö (at Göteborg, Sweden) to Argentina via Madeira, intending to then sail around the Horn, but a hernia forced him to land. In typical Lundin fashion he was able to cajole the Argentineans into performing the necessary surgery free and giving him a place to recuperate for the same price.

By May 1980 he was healed and ready to go, but it was then late autumn in the Southern Hemisphere, and conditions at Cape Horn were horrendous. Undeterred, the jovial navigator left in mid-May from Mar del Plata, Argentina, and sailed south for several weeks. It wasn't until June 16, just a week before the beginning of winter, that Lundin crossed the longitude of Cape Horn. He couldn't be elated at having finally achieved his goal, however, because when he looked down at his aluminum hull he wondered if it was about to dissolve under him. Ever since leaving the hospital at Mar del Plata he had noticed corrosion on the plating, and in some places already fifty percent of its thickness had dissolved away. The wide Pacific lay ahead, but at the rate he was shedding skin he would never make it across. Therefore he turned back and made for the Falkland Islands. In doing so he had rounded the Horn in a homemade small boat—a golden star in any sailor's logbook—twice.

———— ◆◆◆ ————

Gerry Spiess was out in *Yankee Girl* again during the summer and fall of 1981. He departed Long Beach, California, on June 1, bound for Australia in his old boat that had been upgraded for the longer Pacific crossing. This time he had on board a four-and-a-half-horsepower electric generator, an Autohelm electronic tiller, and satellite navigation equipment. He also brought along much more confidence, having already worked out the bugs on the Atlantic voyage.

His departure from Long Beach was a media circus, so he put into Catalina Island for two days of rest to get his head straight for the long voyage ahead. At sea again, he found his satellite navigation system wouldn't work, so he used a cheap plastic sextant instead.

In one interesting encounter, he met people in Hawaii who had known Fred Rebell back in the 1930s. A very different meeting, between Hawaii and Fanning Island, was with an aggressive marlin, which he had to fight off with an M-1 carbine. The big fish with a beak tried to attack his boat, but he as raised the gun to sight on it, it disappeared, so he was not holed as Gilboy had been.

Breezing along under twin jibs or when there was no wind using his outboard motor, he made Fanning Island, Samoa, Fiji, New Caledonia, and finally Sydney on October 1, 1981. For his 7,800-mile voyage in a homemade boat he won that year's Slocum Award. Ironically, he gave up long-distance boating shortly thereafter, having gotten bored with it. Instead he became a long-distance motorcycle traveler. During one trip he rode his motorcycle from his Minnesota home to the southern tip of South America and back.

Webb Chiles's attempt to circumnavigate in the open boat *Chidiock Tichborne* resumed in May 1980. Having sat out the cyclone season, he left Suva, Fiji, on May 7 bound for Port Moresby, New Guinea. Three days later, in a moderate breeze and sea, while Chiles was asleep, the *Tichborne* pitchpoled down the front of a wave, apparently having tripped on its centerboard over a large fish, perhaps a shark. Chiles woke up to find himself airborne and the mizzenmast above him coming down at him like a spear. Man and boat hit the water separately and far enough apart so that Chiles wasn't skewered, but he lost most of his belongings, including most of his food and water. The nearest land was three hundred miles away.

He spent two miserable weeks adrift in the swamped boat being blown west. At last as he approached a small island he saw it was surrounded by a reef that he knew *Tichborne*, even with its centerboard up, could never cross. Therefore he got into his inflatable life raft and drifted over the reef, abandoning *Tichborne* to the mighty Pacific. It looked as if his open-boat voyage was over. People on the island, Emae, nursed him back to health. His second day on the island he was stunned to find that the *Tichborne* had not drifted westward over the ocean, but had been blown south and then back onto the island, where it was found upside down in the surf, damaged but repairable.

Five months later, Chiles finished the repairs. Reprovisioned, he set off to continue his voyage. In late April 1981 he made Cairns, Australia, and during the following months worked north to Indonesia and Singapore. Early in 1982 he crossed from Singapore to Aden (Yemen) nonstop, thus setting the record at 4,058 miles for the longest passage in an open boat—and he did it alone, in forty-seven days.

Sailing up the Red Sea he ran into hurricane-force winds, but even they could not do what the Saudi Arabians did when he stopped at Rabigh to change his rudder after damaging his original one on a coral head. They stopped him, confiscated his boat, and then threw him into prison for spying. They claimed he was transporting a bomb into the country. Nine days of futile protests ensued, but ultimately Chiles was deported and his boat held as evidence. Legal wrangling for nearly a year did nothing to move the Saudis, so Honnor Marine in England, the builders of the boat, offered Chiles another one. His voyage, which had

Honnor Marine generously donated a new boat to Webb Chiles after the Saudi government confiscated *Chidiock Tichborne*. *Chidiock Tichborne II* sank in the Canaries shortly thereafter, thus ending Chiles's quest.

been followed closely in many nautical publications around the world, had done much to help their bottom line, so it seemed only fair.

The builders shipped the *Chidiock Tichborne II* to Chiles in Egypt, and there he recommenced his voyage in May 1983. Things went well through the Mediterranean but fell apart completely in the Canaries. The boat was harbored at Las Palmas in November while Chiles went to visit a friend on Tenerife. In his absence a storm blew through the island, and his boat was sunk at its mooring, taking down with it all his possessions. It was the last straw. After a nearly five-year voyage Chiles lost interest in continuing in an open boat and opted for a more traditional yacht as his next vessel. As he had never failed to report in his many magazine articles written during the trip, he had suffered greatly. Enough was enough. It would be left to someone else in the next decade to make the first complete circumnavigation in an open boat.

———— ◦ ⟩ ◦ ⟨ ————

In 1982 and 1983 there was a great three-way battle for the record for the smallest boat to make the west–east Atlantic crossing. None of the three competitors were originally aware of the others, but each one believed that if he succeeded in crossing the "pond," no one would ever beat him. They were all wrong, but they made for an exciting two years.

The first man to go was Tom McClean, the ex-paratrooper turned Atlantic solo rower. He now re-emerged as a sailor and made a respectable fifty-two-day west–east crossing in a nine-foot, nine-inch boat, *Giltspur*. He left Saint John's, Newfoundland, in June 1982, aboard his slab-sided sloop with virtually no interior room because it was crammed with provisions and electronic gear. To power the electronics McClean used a wind-driven generator, the first on a record-setting small capsule boat. So tight was the

Competition from other small boaters delayed the retirement of Tom McClean, here shown aboard *Giltspur*.

space that he had to eat his meals standing up, shoulders poking up through the hatch. Along the way a well-intentioned cargo ship approached, assuming he was a castaway, and nearly caused a disaster when little *Giltspur* was drawn dangerously close to her massive propellers.

After his arrival at Falmouth on August 12, feeling that he had secured for a long time the record for the smallest boat ever to cross west to east, he announced that he looked forward to a relatively normal future with his family. But the best-laid plans of sailormen and mice "gang aft agley"—two weeks later an American truck driver broke his record by a mere nine inches of length.

Competitor number two was Bill Dunlop, a laconic, forty-year-old down-home down-easter who set out from Portland, Maine, on June 13, also bound for Falmouth, England. His nine-foot *Wind's Will* was a cus-

Trucker turned solo-sailor Bill Dunlop. For light reading on his voyages he brought World War II histories.

tom-made fiberglass capsule boat with a deep keel and a *half ton* of ballast! Topsides he had a pup-tent-shaped cabin with clamshell hatches. With these opened he could sit with his back toward the bow and row the boat.

Dunlop was no sloppy amateur. He had one transatlantic crossing in a large yacht under his belt, and when it came time to design *Wind's Will* he engaged a professional boatbuilder, though he was heavily involved. He taught himself celestial navigation by reading and rereading a textbook "at least seventy-five times," he claimed. He freely admitted he wasn't a genius, but he was careful and determined.

Dunlop's goal was to take the record from Gary Spiess's ten-foot *Yankee Girl*. He had no idea what Tom McClean was up to, and was surprised seventy-eight days later when he arrived in Plymouth to find that he had taken the record away from the Briton, who had taken it from Spiess only sixteen days earlier. Dunlop's voyage from Maine was a thousand miles longer than McClean's and more fraught with misadventure. As his food stocks began to dwindle, Dunlop pressed ahead under full canvas even in bad weather. Several times his boat spun through a series of rapid 360s with its mast lying parallel to the water, and once it even turned turtle—all this *with a half ton of ballast*! His radio got soaked and broke down three days into the voyage, and that left him out of contact with his family and supporters for two months, causing them to fear he was lost. Only when he was two hundred miles from the Channel was he spotted and reported safe. To while away the long hours at sea he took two books to read—Adolf Hitler's *Mein Kampf* and William L. Shirer's *The Rise and Fall of the Third Reich*. Like the radio, these weighty tomes were soaked three days into the trip, and so presumably Dunlop had to wait until he got to England to find out how they ended.

The third man trying for the record that year was Wayne Dickinson, a thirty-eight-year-old computer specialist from Florida who had shipped his teardrop-shaped eight-foot, eleven-inch *God's Tear* up to Quincy, Massachusetts, for launching. The most sophisticated capsule boat designed thus far among the small boats, *God's Tear* consisted of a

Wayne Dickinson's beautifully crafted *God's Tear*. Falling asleep near a lee shore of Ireland led to an unholy experience.

fiberglass hull, multiple Plexiglas ports for excellent visibility—though high in sunlight and heat entry—and a unique "sprung mast" —resembling half a drawn bow—that supported a roller-reefing headsail. All lines led into the cockpit.

Dickinson made a mistaken late-season departure in October, but only two days later was towed back into harbor by the coast guard when he failed to make any real progress. Surprisingly, he decided not to wait until the normal sailing season the following spring, but pushed ahead a few weeks later. He left Port Allerton, Massachusetts, on November 4 with enough food and water for a hundred days. He was seen again eighty days later, on January 25, when he fired a flare to get the attention of the freighter *Brookness*. He asked the ship for his position and to report him as well. What had been planned as a fifty-day trip now looked as if it would easily double that.

It more than doubled in length; in fact, it nearly *tripled*, lasting 142 days in his tiny cocoon. Dickinson made yet another bad mistake when, having endured four and a half months at sea, he fell asleep just as he was about to make landfall. He knew he had missed the Channel and his destination port of Falmouth, but as he dozed off he didn't realize that staring him straight in the face was the unforgiving rocky west coast of Ireland.

He awoke as the hull of *God's Tear* was thrown up and smashed against the rocks. Again and again the hull was battered, and it cracked apart like an egg. All traces sank to the bottom. Dickinson was lucky to tumble out alive, but he was in shock from the cold winter weather and the suddenness of his calamitous arrival. He thought he was ship-wrecked on a deserted island in the Hebrides. God must have been smiling on the lucky Floridian, because he had actually been cast onto Aranmore Island, and the lighthouse keeper there found him. Dickinson was unable to move, so the keeper had to enlist the help of local fishermen to carry him to the keeper's home.

The result of Dickinson's ordeal was that he now took the record from Dunlop for the smallest boat to make the west–east crossing—eight feet, eleven inches. A record won by one inch! As Dickinson lay in the lighthouse keeper's cottage recuperating, Tom McClean was sawing wood and making new plans.

McClean's plan was to saw two feet off the stern of *Giltspur* and make another record attempt that summer. He ended his early retirement and once again took the now seven-foot, nine-inch boat to Newfoundland. He landed in Oporto, Portugal, having reclaimed the record sixty-two days after he left. He would hold the record for ten more years, but then lose it to Tom McNally, the itinerant small-boat sailor from Liverpool who just wouldn't give up. McNally was a contender in the beautiful cold-molded six-foot, ten-inch *Big C* that summer of 1983, but his effort failed when the boat was sliced open by the propeller of a Russian trawler that had come to his assistance. The voyage had taken all the money McNally had, and now his boat was ruined. Indefatigable, he shook it off and made plans to try again even as the Russian vessel brought him home.

Nor was Bill Dunlop giving up. He no longer set his sights on the west–east Atlantic record. Now he simply wanted to sail around the world in his tiny

Liverpudlian Tom McNally in combat trim, trying to wrest the title for smallest transatlantic crossing. His arch-competitor Hugo Vihlen later became a good friend.

ship *Wind's Will*. He departed from Maine on July 31, 1983, passed through the Panama Canal, and reached Hawaii. Island-hopping across the Marquesas and points west, he was bound for Australia. On June 23, 1984, he left the Cook Islands confident that it was downhill to the southern continent. He was never seen again. *Wind's Will* and its humble, heroic skipper were gone without a trace—that is, until a plastic food container was found on a Queensland beach. In it was a note dated October 16 saying that Dunlop had wrecked on an unknown island without food. A search of the islets of the Great Barrier Reef proved fruitless, and neither boat nor body was found.

By 1984 Shane Acton had had enough of cold and damp England. He put *Super Shrimp (Shrimpy)* back in the water and headed south to France, without Iris, who had moved back to Switzerland. He motored through the canal system to the Mediterranean, passed Gibraltar, and once again made a transatlantic passage. He intended this time to explore the Amazon River. After cruising through much of the Caribbean and sailing up and down the Intracoastal Waterway on the east coast of Florida, he headed west to Central America. He settled in Costa Rica and lived for part of each year there on a tiny uninhabited island just offshore.

Super Shrimp was later destroyed by a hurricane, and sadly, Acton, a heavy smoker, contracted lung cancer. He reluctantly returned to Cambridge for treatment but died at age fifty-five in early 2002, bereft of possessions but forever rich with experience.

◆ ◆ ◆

Another circumnavigator was Australian boatbuilder Serge Testa. He had heard of Acton's and Dunlop's voyages, but wanted for himself the crown for smallest boat to circumnavigate. To start his quest, he had five hundred pounds of marine-grade one-eighth-inch aluminum sheeting delivered to his shop and *without boat plans* started cutting and welding. Within a few months his fertile mind and deft hands had created the eleven-foot, ten-inch *Acrohc Australis* (*acrohc* is colloquial Italian for "thing"), an ingeniously designed sloop, a capsule boat that featured a rather large, open interior. Even though the boat was built for speed, there was enough room inside to sleep lying flat and move about somewhat. There were also six watertight stowage compartments arranged so that the boat had, in effect, a partial double hull. *Acrohc*'s deep, nearly full keel also had a 260-pound bulb at its end, so even under full sail Testa could sit topsides at the tiller and steer without upsetting the stability. This feature demonstrated Testa's understanding of the human dimensions of long-distance cruising. He didn't intend to martyr himself for 142 days as Dickinson had.

After hanging a four-horsepower outboard on the stern, Testa departed Brisbane on June 11, 1984, intending to do a west-about, which is normally considered the "easy" way, though in a twelve-foot boat nothing would be easy. Initial sea trials showed that the boat had a dangerous neutral balance—in other words, the center of effort and the center of lateral resistance were aligned vertically, making the boat zigzag continuously on a run before the wind. To get rid of the yaw Testa added a split bowsprit and moved the headsail out. Now the boat balanced well enough to sail safely.

Serge Testa's mighty twelve-footer, *Acrohc Australis,* in which he gained the record for smallest circumnavigaton. He built the boat without paper plans.

For the next few months he sailed up and around the northern coast of Australia until he arrived at Darwin. On New Year's Eve he set out for the Cocos Islands despite being warned about the cyclone season. He felt his homemade boat was up to any strain, and the worst that could happen was that he would be dismasted. In that case he would drift to Africa, which didn't worry him because he had enough provisions to last. Sure enough, just a few days out he was struck by a cyclone with winds so high the waves were blown flat. Testa toughed it out for several days until the wind died and then he proceeded as normal. His boat *was* well designed.

From the Cocos he aimed to South Africa instead of the Red Sea and the Suez Canal. He had read of Webb Chiles's difficulties and of the generally bad political climate in the area and wanted none of it. After a short stay on Réunion Island he caused his own "climate" problems on *Acrohc* when he carelessly set his alcohol stove on fire. It needed refilling while he was cooking pancakes, but instead of turning it off completely, he foolishly tried to refill it while it was still lit. It blew up in his face. Instantly he dived overboard, but as he hit the water he was already turning around to reach back for the gunwale. In a flash he was back on board, the fire in his beard extinguished but not the one on board. He was down in the cabin again in an instant, reaching for the fire extinguisher. He won the battle, though barely. Salt air on burned flesh drives home a lesson permanently.

After stopping at Cape Town he worked his way across the Atlantic via Saint Helena and Ascension. He finished the transatlantic crossing at Natal, Brazil, but because he didn't have the correct visa he was forced to move on after only three days. In Venezuela he put aside his sextant and bought a satnav, a small satellite navigation unit then coming on the market. He liked it for the obvious advantages that he no longer depended on the sun and it was more accurate than sun shots, but even more so for the fact that he no longer had to open his hatch in heavy seas to shoot a sight.

Even though he now had satnav, it wasn't hooked up to an electronic tiller. Testa steered by hand from inside or outside the cabin, though often he just set his homemade self-steering vane instead. The vane too could be adjusted via a cable drum and endless line while he was inside the dry cabin. His best single-day run on the trip was 120 miles—a creditable distance for a boat with such a short waterline length.

Testa completed his voyage on May 18, 1987, when he returned to Brisbane. During the three years of the voyage he had spent more than five hundred days at sea, sailed through four cyclones, grounded several times without serious damage, and been hit by a whale. *Acrohc Australis*, the boat that was built not by paper plans but by eye, now held the record for the smallest boat solo circumnavigation.

Ed Gillet launched a mostly stock twenty-foot double Necky Tofino kayak into the surf at Monterey, California, in the summer of 1987, beginning what he thought would be a forty-day run to Hawaii. The Tofino's few nonstandard features were a raised wooden floor so he wouldn't have to sit in saltwater all the time and two inflatable sponsons along the side of the hull, like Romer's. He knew he couldn't really paddle twenty-two hundred miles over the ocean and climb the great Pacific swells by muscle power alone, so he added a Jalbert J-15 parafoil kite to the gear list. The lightweight, easy-to-launch kite made the voyage possible, though only just.

Ed Gillet at the start of his kite-powered kayak voyage to Hawaii.

It took only a couple of days for Gillet to realize that his raised wooden floor wasn't high enough and that there was no position he could wiggle into that would ease the pain of the saltwater sores on his derriere. Also, his hands erupted with great open sores only made worse by contact with the seawater as he paddled. He found too that he had brought too few clothes for the cold Pacific waters off northern California.

Only a week had gone by, but already the voyage was torture. Surely he only had five more weeks to go, he thought. He checked his progress when possible with a sextant and one of the new pocket navigational calculators that was preprogrammed to prompt the user for required sight data. To his utter frustration he learned he wasn't making progress as quickly as he had thought he would. A calm now plagued him, leaving him motionless a thousand miles off the U.S. coast. Day after day he was forced to paddle the boat forward, knowing that if he did not he would risk disaster because it was beginning to look like a race between the wind and his food supply. Would the one come back before the other ran out?

Finally, after two weeks, the trade winds came and he could relaunch the kite. The boat sliced through the water like a determined porpoise, heading steadily toward the islands. A few days of good going suddenly turned into another possible disaster when the winds veered to the southeast and he began sailing north at an alarming rate. If the northern drift kept up, he would miss Hawaii and make landfall in Japan, or at least his corpse would.

Two months into the passage his food ran out. No fish bit the lures he trailed, so he ate his toothpaste and fantasized about gourmet dishes. His only hope seemed to be to reach the shipping lanes and light flares at night. On day sixty-three at sea he tried to take a sight but found his view obscured by a mountain. He cursed the inconsiderate rock and put down his sextant. Then it struck him—Hawaii at last! He landed the next day.

Sven Lundin, by now rather irascible, had in the meantime shipped his deteriorating *Aluminium-Bris* back to Sweden, complaining that the mill that provided the aluminum had given him the wrong alloy, while they countered that his construction techniques were flawed. The result was that Lundin gave up on metal-boat construction and turned to new technology.

By the late 1980s Ludin had some thirty years of boatbuilding experience and experimentation behind him, and the lessons learned, combined with an absolutely original mind and perhaps even a spark of genius, now brought him to full stride as a designer. Lundin had become to small boats what France's Henri Mignet was to small aircraft in the 1930s when he designed the radical HM-14 tandem wing *Pou du Ciel* or what "Smokey" Yunick was to automobile racing in the 1960s and 1970s. Like these men, Lundin was a self-taught visionary who, perhaps *because* of a lack of formal education, could see the essence of the art, unlike formally trained engineers whose sense of imagination had been dulled by too much time at university studying numbers, problems, and accepted solutions, rather than *feeling* the problem and *feeling* toward a solution. To pass classes engineers have to learn to solve problems their professor's way, and that conformity often numbs the imagination. The Mignets, Yunicks, and Lundins had never had to conform to the stultifying yoke of academic approval and, like the Impressionist painters, were therefore free to create something new and exciting.

For the past twenty years Lundin's projects had been evolving in complexity in the areas of structures, interior layout, and sail plan, but always they retained that touch of Lundin-esque design boldness and humor. Now he was to make a quantum leap forward. The design that became the *Bris VI* was his magnum opus of small boats. It was idiosyncratic, of course, but also a brilliant expression of Lundin's theories on what a safe long-distance small boat should be. The little fifteen-foot capsule boat he created would inspire many imitators.

The *Bris VI* was built in an attic between 1986 and 1988. Lundin stuck to a simple Masonite mold sheets of two-inch-thick Divinycell, a rigid PVC (polyvinyl chloride) foam that he had cajoled its Swedish manufacturer, DIAB International, into donating to him. On the out-side of the foam he applied nine layers of polyester fabric, using a spe-cial epoxy that retained some flexibility after curing, and on the inside went two layers of fiberglass. The sandwiched hull was both very light and extremely strong, but also flexible enough to bounce back from cer-tain collisions at sea, such as running over logs or whales or perhaps even hitting a floating cargo container. Willow trees survive hurricanes because they flex, whereas oaks usually don't, even though their wood is stronger—their weakness is in their rigidity. Lundin applied those principles to the *Bris VI* and in so doing advanced the art of composite construction. Sandwich-core construction had been used for decades, but not the specific combination Lundin pioneered, and this evolution was part of his great achievement. He chose a polyester (Dacron or Terylene) outer skin as opposed to fiberglass because his research had shown that poly-ester had better abrasion-resistant properties, and since the boat was de-signed with a flat bot-tom so that it was beachable even on shin-gle, abrasion resistance was important.

Bris VI's innovative sail plan is designed for maximum simplicity. The top mast is demountable, and the jib tack pivots from the mast.

Originally the boat was to have been ketch rigged, but as he built it, the sail plan evolved into a single mast forward, only ten feet tall, to which a topsail on its own spar could be added in light airs. This kept the moment arm above the cen-ter of gravity shorter and therefore allowed a more shallow keel. Lundin's keel was a four-by-four-inch T-shaped bronze bar that weighed 350 pounds. Though lightly ballasted for a fifteen-foot boat with a five-foot beam, Lundin felt that the boat's strength would allow the boat to sur-vive even if it pitchpoled or turtled. These possibilities were "part of the fun" of sailing small boats, he said with his usual humor.

German and Swedish homemade boats built to Lundin's design principles: simplicity and resiliency.

Other novel features included a centerboard trunk that wasn't in the center of the hull, but right forward at the bow. The combined effect of the board forward and the rudder aft effectively located the center of lateral resistance near midships, and enhanced the tracking of the boat because of the long separation between the underwater blades. In other words, by using two small, widely spaced blades (centerboard and rudder), Lundin had achieved the type of yaw-dampening stability usually found in a full-keeled design. Such tracking would aid, too, in self-steering.

The *Bris VI* did not have an engine but could be propelled by two very Lundian adaptations. The first was a yuloh, a long Chinese-type sweep that pivoted in a transom-mounted bracket. He claimed he could muscle his way into harbor against a force 8 wind with this. The other means of propulsion, for use on land, was a unicycle-like attachment that fit into the rudder pintles, allowing Lundin to pedal the boat from place to place like an old-fashioned ice cream vendor. An axle bar had to be installed first under the center of gravity while the boat was still in the water; it was fitted over the bronze shoe and held in place by rope guys that went up to the gunwales. Moving the fifteen-hundred-pound fully loaded boat in this way could only be done on very flat terrain, such as paved marina lots. Even going downhill was a danger because there was no effective braking.

Just before launching the boat in France in the summer of 1988 for his proposed trip to the United States and Canada, Lundin received a phone call from a woman who wanted to meet him, having heard of his sailing adventures. Lundin met Olga, an artist (a good one, too, though Bas Ader's admirers might not have thought so), and very soon they were married. They made a honeymoon voyage the next summer, sailing from Baltimore in southern Ireland to Saint John's, Newfoundland. Olga had no previous sailing experience, so Sven taught her along the way, and she became a competent sailor in her own right. The remarkable little *Bris VI* battled storms, westerly winds, and a contrary current to make an impressive forty-seven-day passage. During the entire trip the newlywed Lundins stayed snug, dry, and happy in the spacious cabin. If only honeymooning William and Mary Andrews had been so lucky back in 1901.

The final word on the 1980s must be French—*formidable!* In this incredible decade of small-boat sailing, no smaller, odder, or more unlikely sailing craft made ocean voyages than the ones Frenchmen launched on the waves. France, as a nation, has great sailors to boast of—Tabarly, Gerbault, Colas, Moitessier, and others. These men had undertaken important long-distance voyages and had won transoceanic races against first-class international competition, yet for some reason, during this decade, French sailors developed a taste for microvoyaging—voyaging in small craft that were not necessarily boats.

Some of the claims for transatlantic crossings are somewhat specious or at least a matter of semantics. Newspapers and popular magazines of the day rushed to give each quirky adventurer full, undisputed credit for having achieved whatever remarkable ocean voyage he claimed to have made, while boating journals often looked on these "feats" with a more skeptical eye. Here, the facts as they are known are given; the reader can judge the merit of each venture.

◆ In early 1983 Christian Marty became the first person to cross the Atlantic Ocean on a sailboard when he made a thirty-seven-day passage from Dakar to Guyana. A support vessel accompanied him, but he steadfastly refused to allow it to make headway at night while he slept aboard. Every mile was thus made while standing on his board. Marty, a bold yet self-effacing adventurer, was also a competitive skier and hang-glider pilot. A career pilot with Air France, he was the pilot-in-command of the Concorde airliner that tragically crashed in Paris in 2000 when a piece of runway debris was sucked into one of its engines.

◆ Baron Arnaud de Rosnay disappeared in November 1984 while attempting to pilot his sailboard between Quanzhou, China, and Taichung, Taiwan, two countries officially still at war. De Rosnay had previously tried unsuccessfully to windsurf from the Marquesas to Hawaii, but he had succeeded in crossing the English Channel to Dover and back to France in 1981. A few months before the Taiwan Strait attempt he had successfully crossed from Cuba to Miami.

◆ In November 1986 Laurent Bourgnon and Fred Giraldi sailed a mostly stock Hobie 18 from Puerto Rico, Gran Canaria, to Guadeloupe in twenty-one days. For meals they ate precooked emergency rations.

◆ Stéphane Peyron became the first person to cross the Atlantic on a sailboard *unassisted* when he arrived on July 28, 1987, at La Rochelle, having left New York forty-six days earlier. The filmmaker's twenty-five-foot carbon-Kevlar-epoxy sailboard had a "sneak-box"-type hull into which Peyron crammed his supplies, and himself in rough weather. The next year he attempted to reach the magnetic North Pole; after he left Resolute, Northwest Territories, he spent the next twenty-three days picking his way through ice floes. He reached Crescent Island on August 23, but ice stopped him there, only sixty miles from his goal.

◆ On April 2, 1988, Rémy Bricka, a professional one-man band who plied his trade on the European version of the Borscht Belt, set out from Tenerife to *walk* across the Atlantic. This had been tried before in 1899 when a certain Professor Miller left Atlantic City in canoe-like shoes, sponsored by Captain Young of Young's Pier. Miller turned back after going only a mile. Bricka didn't turn back. Shod with thirteen-foot, nine-inch canoe-like skis, or shoes, he evidently trudged along using a very long double-bladed paddle for propulsion and balance. He also had a kite to fly in the trade winds, which helped pull him along. He towed a catamaran-type support raft carrying his food and gear—including a flute to soothe his nerves during storms. At night he slept on the raft. After 3,502 miles, he arrived in Trinidad on May 31. Had he "walked" in the strictest sense of the word, or had he really drifted across on the catamaran? That was open to debate. Despite the questions, Bricka enjoyed the notoriety the "feat" had given him back home and his one-man band routine became more popular than ever. A couple years later he would don his water shoes again for an encore.

⇒ 12 ⇐

RECORDS
AND REDUX

THE 1990s

◆ STEPHEN LADD *SQUEAK*S THROUGH A WAR ZONE ◆ "ANT" STEWARD
DOES IT IN THE OPEN ◆ WE'RE GREAT, BUT DON'T TELL ANYONE ◆
FRIENDS AND FOES: VIHLEN VS. MCNALLY ◆ DELAGING THE QUESTION
◆ GVODEV AND GLASNOST ◆ LECOMTE SWIMS FOR LOVE ◆

IT SEEMED AS IF MOST OF THE GREAT FEATS IN SMALL
boats had been accomplished by the end of the 1980s. Serge Testa's brilliant circumnavigation in his aluminum *Acrohc Australis* appeared to be the last chapter in a fascinating subsection of maritime history. What was left to do in small boats that hadn't already been done?

The 1990s turned out to be a time of polishing the art, rather than pioneering it, with a few exceptions. Hugo Vihlen came out of a long retirement to vie again for his title, the French continued to do mystifying Gallic things on and in the water, and for the first time since Fred Rebell, an Eastern European made waves in a small boat.

•◆•

The early 1990s were a boom time in Seattle. The misty velveteen mountains of the Pacific Northwest rang with "high-tech" this, "dot com" that. Microsoft, Boeing, Starbucks, stock options, video conferencing, skyrocketing real estate prices—hold on for the ride. As the tide of economic prosperity flooded in, everyone's boat floated higher. What a great time to be up there in the cool rains of that deep green and wet blue corner of America.

Not for Stephen Ladd, though. Ladd was an urban planner in his late thirties whose career brought him into direct contact with the explosive growth of the region and the hordes of newcomers moving there from California and points east. Ladd was single, nonmaterialistic, and for the past fifteen or so years had repressed the wanderlust that had spurred him as a teenager to tramp around the globe and sniff out its darker, more redolent corners. Coming home in his twenties and playing office clerk all those years hadn't been easy. Sooner or later he knew the dam would burst.

It finally did in 1990, so to satisfy his urge to move on, he quit his job and built a nifty little twelve-footer to his own design. The boat, named *Squeak*, after a dead pet cat, was a cold-molded double-ended rowboat that also sported two spritsails in a cat yawl arrangement. Ladd cleverly thought of using the rowing seat as a split bulkhead, creating a totally enclosed sleeping cabin in which he could stretch out to his full height; also, closing a deck hatch made the cabin waterproof. The bow of the boat was fitted with a storage compartment hatch and another bulkhead. The hull weighed a mere 250 pounds, even with a single layer of fiberglass glued to it for strength and abrasion resistance. In this

Art on facing page: Stephen Ladd fights to regain his twelve-foot *Squeak* during his odyssey through Central and South America.

boat he intended to make a long cruise down the rivers of North America to South America and back.

Ladd took *Squeak* to the Milk River in Montana in the back of a van and put it in on August 11. A cloudy meandering stream that starts in the United States, the Milk veers north into Alberta and then returns to the States, where it eventually joins the Missouri River. It was tough, slow going the first few weeks, with Ladd continually fending off from rocky canyon walls and scouting for eddies that indicated hidden rocks. In early September he reached the Missouri, and his daily runs picked up speed. Late in October he finally entered the Mississippi and was on his way to New Orleans.

The captain of a Norwegian freighter berthed in Mobile, Alabama, offered to transport Ladd's boat to the Panama Canal in exchange for doing light ship's chores, an arrangement he gladly accepted. Just as winter began to set in, his boat was hoisted on deck, and down toward the Canal Zone they steamed. Along the way one of the ship's officers regaled him with tales of the dangers of sailing along the Central American coast, including shoal waters and strong tides, to which the stoic captain standing nearby quietly added that he calculated Ladd to have a ninety percent chance of being robbed, and a fifty percent chance of being killed.

When he arrived at Colón, Panama, Ladd learned that the captain knew what he was talking about. The city was full of thieves, prostitutes, and other leeches all looking for a sliver of opportunity to take his money or his boat. While trying to get his boat cleared through formalities, he took to running through the streets from office to office so as not to be accosted. If it was this bad in the city, what would the coastal jungles be like?

Squeak was transported to the Pacific side of the Canal on the deck of a large yacht and relaunched. For the next six months Ladd sailed and rowed south along the mountain jungle coastlines of Panama and Colombia. He stayed for a while on a small island with an old German named Dieter who had been in the Hitler Youth and remembered with affection his wartime exploits—shooting American tanks with *panzerfausten* (bazookas) and later escaping from a Red Army POW camp.

Landing at Buenaventura, Colombia, after a near-disastrous cap-sizing, Ladd managed to bum a series of truck rides for his boat over the Andes to the upper Meta River, which joined the Orinoco, but not until after passing through a remote region that was the home base for antigovernment Communist rebels. Ladd rowed hurriedly downriver, often at night with the help of two flashlights mounted in his bow. Several times he was stopped by armed men who demanded to know his business, but each time he was let go when he proved he wasn't a guerilla.

From the Meta he passed to the Orinoco and after that into the Caribbean. Like Fritz Fenger and John Schultz before him, he followed the Antilles north. Along the way he capsized again, met smugglers, and nearly melted in the tropical heat. He was arrested briefly in Haiti but then boldly sailed along Cuba's northern coast—a no-no for Americans, but he did it anyway. His three-year, fifteen-thousand-mile voyage ended in May 1993 when he landed in Miami. In many ways it was a tougher and gutsier voyage than some of the transoceanic voyages already described.

Another gutsy sailor was Anthony "Ant" Steward, a South African, who set out in 1991 to do what Webb Chiles didn't do—sail alone around the world in an open boat. Chiles said at the time that the only reason he didn't "tie the knot" and complete his voyage was that only the "easy" part remained—a trade-wind crossing of the Atlantic. Some found that a rather churlish assertion. Anyway, for twenty-seven-year-old Steward, a big man with a big heart of determination, words didn't matter—deeds did. He intended to tie the knot and take home the honor for himself.

Steward's initial problem was cash. He didn't have much and couldn't afford to have a new boat built. Shocking his friends, he bought the plug (the inner male mold for a fiberglass hull) for a nineteen-foot racing boat and turned it into his boat. The price was right, but the plug was very lightly built, intended to receive layers of fiberglass matting, not the pounding of great oceans around the world. Steward was confident it could take it.

He was not a desperate amateur, however, but a champion dinghy sailor who had many miles and hours aboard wet boats, sailing at competitive speeds. Seeing potential in the "hull," he outfitted it with a mast and sails, doing most of the work himself. The mast had double spreaders and twin headstays, was tall for such a small boat and consequently

The boat plug that became the *NCS Challenger* was never meant to see water, but low-budget necessity breeds invention.

risky, but Steward had no intention of "hangin' about" waiting for winds. He intended to storm around the world, not cruise, and the big rig would give him power in light airs. To keep the boat level he added a large bulb keel that gave her a ponderous six-foot, six-inch draft.

He left Cape Town accompanied only by a blue teddy bear to the cheers of friends and the jeers of those who considered him crazy. Maybe the latter group were right. Five days out Steward capsized his boat, now named *NCS Challenger*, and was thrown into the water. The boat popped up again and began sailing on, with him still treading water. Fortunately, he was tethered to the boat and made it back on board. Many times later in the trip when he suffered a knockdown he *wasn't* tethered.

Racing across the Atlantic turned into a struggle for survival when he was nearly run down by a ship, suffered food poisoning, broke his sextant, and then lost his navigation papers during a capsizing. He had to follow gannets to make land at Ascension. Worse than his own problems were those caused by others. After he arrived without food or water at Barbados, government officials made him wait for two days at anchor before giving him permission to land. The government of the mostly black island objected to his South African nationality.

Steward traversed the Panama Canal, then made Galápagos and the Marquesas. Equipment failures in the Pacific slowed him down, and he narrowly averted disaster when he ran into a log that knocked his keel loose but fortunately not off. A dismasting before Samoa threatened to delay his trip into the hurricane season, but he daringly spliced his spinnaker pole to his boom and stepped those as a mast for a gaff mainsail that he cut from his genoa. Rube Goldberg would have loved the man because under this jury rig he still made a good ninety miles per day and outraced an inbound hurricane to New Caledonia east of Australia.

From Brisbane he sailed north and then west to Darwin. On July 13, 1992, he capsized. He had suffered so many capsizings that by now he had lost count, but this time it was bad—very bad. The boat turned turtle during a raging storm and his deck fittings were broken away. Steward had to slice through his shrouds and stays to unship the mast so the boat would right. When it did he was at the mercy of a strong storm that blew him several hundred miles downwind over the next four days. He then found himself heading straight for the reef around Cerf Island off the southernmost tip of the Seychelles, but with no way to bear off because he could set no sails. The *NCS Challenger* struck the reef hard, broke off the keel, and rolled over. Steward was thrown onto the reef, and the only way to make it ashore was to battle his way through a gang of sharks that circled menacingly inside the lagoon. The half mile to shore was a fight between the brutes and the blade of Steward's sheath knife.

South African Anthony "Ant" Steward stands aboard the wreckage of his *NCS Challenger* that started out as a boat mold. He rebuilt her and completed history's first open-boat circumnavigation.

Islanders came to Steward's rescue, and he was sent to a local hospital. They later collected what they could find of his boat and arranged to have it shipped to South Africa. After he had recovered Steward flew there, supervised the repairs, and then shipped it back to Cerf Island, where he resumed his voyage. On his way to Cape Town he nearly died of angioedema, a hereditary blood disease, because he forgot to take his medication. This necessitated another trip to the hospital, but still he wouldn't give up.

Months later he finally arrived at Cape Town and thus became the first ever to circumnavigate in an open boat. He had learned that no part was the "easy" part, no matter what Chiles said.

———◆———

As brash and extroverted as Steward was, Englishmen Chris and Stuart

Newman were reclusive. The two brothers worked on North Sea oil rigs for a living, but they would take long breaks from that lucrative work to go on adventures together. They probably sailed a plywood catamaran across the Atlantic one time and another time crossed in an inflatable with a sail. Since they both absolutely eschewed publicity and financed their own adventures, there is very little documentation or pictorial evidence of their feats.

What is certain is that during the summer and fall of 1992 they built, with the help of the British kayak manufacturer Chris Hare Marine, a custom-made twenty-foot sailing canoe. The hull itself was really two undecked Kevlar canoes mounted atop each other gunwale to gunwale with a long opening cut out for the helmsman. The forward portion of the hull was closed off to create a dry sleeping cabin, while aft there was a similar, though smaller, storage area. A forty-four-square-foot sail provided propulsion, a small fixed keel prevented leeway, and a five-foot outrigger added balance.

The boat, christened *Spirit of Cleveland*, presumably for the brothers' home county in northern England, was shipped to Portugal. They departed Lisbon November 3, bound first for the Canaries, and from there they would cross to Miami. By Christmas Day they had already made Martinique after sailing thirty-six hundred miles in only forty-four days.

Their hope of reaching Miami was thwarted when sharks attacked, trying to get a fish the men had landed. The attack was so brutal it overturned the boat, spilling the brothers out. They spent that night straddling the upturned hull in shark-infested waters, but in daylight the next morning they were able to right the boat—no small accomplishment with an outrigger. When it was righted they found the mast destroyed and much of their gear missing. Now it was a matter of survival, so they broke out their paddles and made for Jamaica, which they reached January 10, 1993, following a fifty-mile pull.

After this great feat of British seamanship the Newmans disappeared back to their cherished anonymity and left it for others to proclaim their heroics.

Of the hundred or so sailors so far, none measures up to Tom McNally for sheer perseverance. The man just wouldn't quit. By 1992 McNally had been at the small-boat game for twenty years. He wanted the record for the smallest boat ever to cross the Atlantic, west–east, or east–west, one, the other, or both, and as long as he breathed air he devoted his energies to achieving that goal.

McNally's evil genius over the years had been Hugo Vihlen, who held the record for smallest boat for many years, the six-foot *April Fool* until Eric Peters's five-foot, ten-and-a-half-inch *Toniky Nou* took it in 1983. McNally suspected that Vihlen would fight to protect his record, so he set about to build a boat small enough that no one would ever challenge it. It would be shorter than he was tall—only five feet, four and a half inches.

As usual, McNally had to rely on the kindness of strangers and sponsors to finance the construction of the boat and the expenses of the voyage. He had become Liverpool's most famous "yachtsman," year after year asking for donations and scrounging parts for his boats. In fact, he made a career of hustling for sponsors to keep him on the water.

Vihlen hadn't been idle, though. In 1992, he too prepared for another transatlantic run. He spent sixty thousand dollars of his own money building and equipping a high-tech composite capsule boat, *Father's Day*, made from a sandwich of fiberglass and Airex foam. Not knowing about McNally's intentions or the size of his latest boat, Vihlen made his five feet, six inches long. He thought that this size would help him *hold* the record because at the time, for some reason, he was not aware of Peters's achievement. He didn't know he had lost his title in 1983.

Vihlen wanted to launch his boat from Nags Head on the Outer Banks of North Carolina because that was only about a fifteen-hour drive from his home, and from there it was just a short hop to the Gulf Stream. As word leaked out about the voyage, the U.S. Coast Guard heard of it and swung into action to stop it. Vihlen had spent twenty-five years regretting and resenting the fact that the coast guard had forced him out of the water just a few miles from the shoreline in Florida on his first crossing, back in 1968. Now here they were again, intruding where he felt they had no business. He received a letter from the Fifth U.S. Coast Guard District prohibiting the attempt and a phone call in which he was told the service considered his boat "manifestly unsafe." He resented the government's presumption that its role was to save citizens from themselves.

If U.S. waters were un-available to him, he would just have to drive to Canada and launch from there. It would be a shorter sail, any-way. But after launching in Nova Scotia he found that contrary winds wouldn't al-low him to get out to sea. He hired a crane to lift the boat back onto its trailer and set off for Newfoundland to try from there.

In one of those great mo-ments of historical seren-dipity, one of the first people Vihlen met on the Saint John's waterfront was Tom McNally. The two men knew of each other and their goals but had never met before. The Briton spotted the bright red *Father's Day* and immediately knew his com-

Retired airline pilot Hugo Vihlen stands triumphant atop his five-foot, four-inch *Father's Day* after re-capturing the record for the ocean crossing aboard the smallest boat.

petitor had taken the field. He approached Vihlen, who didn't know who he was, and asked him what the "S" in Vihlen's middle name stood for. Vihlen, taken aback by the question from a total stranger, slowly replied "Sigfried." At that moment McNally extended his hand and introduced himself to Vihlen as if they were old colleagues who had found each other after a long separation. Both men were at first cordial, then friendly, and then mutual admirers.

They made an odd couple. Vihlen was well groomed, wore new clothes, drove a late-model tow vehicle, and had all the advantages money—all from his own labor—could buy. McNally was a little shabbier in appearance and dress. He had no support staff or tow rig. He couldn't solve problems with a credit card as the American could. McNally had drifted early in his life and never really established a career—other than building and sailing impractically small boats. Vihlen had worked hard, invested wisely, and got all he owned in the way Horatio Alger had prescribed. He had been fortunate financially; McNally, a sometime artist, sometime poet, had not. Yet each man saw in the other the beauty of their shared dream, and all differences faded in the warmth of that mutual understanding.

McNally offered to show Vihlen his latest boat, the *Vera Hugh I, Pride of Merseyside*, already afloat at the pier just a hundred yards from *Father's Day*. When he saw it, Vihlen's heart sank. It was an inch and a half shorter than his own boat.

A few days after the meeting and after several dinners together, Vihlen decided to proceed with his attempt anyway. He thought the *Vera Hugh* wasn't well made and that McNally's provisions and equipment weren't up to a successful Atlantic crossing. McNally had no sea anchor and scanty food rations and for power used a cheap car battery that vented explosive fumes. Even so, he refused to give up his habit of smoking while at sea. Vihlen hoped the man, for his own good, as well as for competitive reasons, wouldn't launch.

Vihlen launched on June 30, but the very next day he was windbound against the coast again. This was not only a repeat of what had happened in Nova Scotia but also what had happened in North Africa in 1967. He knew he had to abort his start. He accepted a tow back to harbor.

Vihlen decided that when he was home he would add an outboard motor to the stern of the boat and cut two inches off the bow. No matter what McNally did, he would be back next year with a smaller boat. Before he left Saint John's he made a magnificent sportsmanlike gesture: he donated to his rival all his own provisions so that McNally would at least have a decent chance to survive at sea. Vihlen also kindly donated better charts to McNally after he returned home to Florida and could mail them.

—◆—

McNally now had the field to himself, but he was windbound also. Giving up on Canada, he begged a lift for his boat back to Europe, and in December he launched his little capsule boat *Vera Hugh I, Pride of Merseyside* from Portugal. He spent 134 days drifting in the trades the fifty-five hundred miles to San Juan, Puerto Rico, which he reached in May 1993, having nearly died of food poisoning and the lack of freshwater. After recovering in a hospital he sailed the final thousand miles and landed at Fort Lauderdale, Florida, which by coincidence was not far from Vihlen's home in Homestead. Finally, at age fifty, he had the record for the smallest-boat Atlantic crossing.

—◆—

The duel was on. Vihlen modified his boat as planned and returned to the contest, but still his biggest obstacle was the U.S. Coast Guard. He went so far as to hire expensive legal counsel to fight the ruling, and when that failed, mounted a minor publicity campaign to shame them into letting him go. A pretty much one-sided compromise was reached when the coast guard told him that if he could get *one* professional naval architect to state on paper that *Father's Day* was a serviceable boat, they would let him sail. He knew that no naval architect would stake his reputation on a boat like his and resented being played with by a governmental agency whose bills had been paid by his taxes. He would have to work around them.

Secretly, he and his launch crew drove to New England and prepared to launch from Cape Cod. On June 1, 1993, he got a tow offshore and settled in for the long two-month slog across. But just as night fell an airplane began circling overhead. He popped out of his cabin and looked up—the coast guard had come to get him. Soon a patrol boat hove into view and against his will towed him back to port.

On land, Vihlen swallowed his anger and calmly announced that he was heading south, home to Florida, to continue the legal fight. But as soon as he was out of the coast guard's clutches, he loaded *Father's Day* and headed *north* to Newfoundland. On June 14 his launch crew sent him off early in the morning, but almost immediately there was an equipment failure when an accidental jibe tore out the "boom box" that attached the twin booms of the Ljungström rig to the mast. The voyage was over before it had started.

Furious, disappointed, angry, upset—Vihlen was all of these at once. Four attempts in two years to launch had been thwarted. He simply had to go that day—it was already late in the season. His son Dana, leader of the launch team, headed out in a motorboat to tow him in. Within minutes they were knocking on doors in town buying parts and stainless steel fasteners to make a quick repair. A machine shop rushed to fabricate a new box. Remarkably, they had everything needed built and installed by the end of that same afternoon. For the fifth time *Father's Day* was launched, and this time was the charm. Later that night Vihlen reached the waters of the Grand Banks and began the journey to reclaim his crown.

He had planned on a sixty-two-day crossing, but close encounters with whales, terrible storms, a near collision with a trawler, the failure of his radios—in other words, all the typical mishaps small-boat voyagers have had to deal with since Alfred Johnson—slowed his progress, and the sixty-one-year-old sailor remained at sea for a shocking 105 days aboard the tiny capsule boat. On his last day, having gained the English Channel and thus officially considered to have made the crossing, he asked to be plucked from the sea by a trawler that then steamed toward Falmouth. He relaunched a mile from shore and motored in. Hugo Vihlen again owned the title for the smallest-boat crossing of the Atlantic Ocean in either direction.

Tom McNally made plans to fight back with a minuscule three-foot, eleven-inch boat, and when Vihlen later heard about that he announced his intention to build a three-foot, *eight*-inch aluminum boat. The battle would continue between these two friends and rivals.

The French continued to do weird things on the water. In February 1995 Guy Delage arrived in Barbados claiming to have *swum* across the Atlantic. No one disputes that the forty-two-year-old Delage left the Cape Verde Islands in mid-December 1994, and some generously allow that Delage may actually have been in the water all the time, except while sleeping or waiting out storms. Others, taking note of the support catamaran Delage "towed" behind him, say that it is more likely he rode or was pulled by the boat most of the way. The twin-hulled vessel had a sleeping compartment, room for provisions, and, more interestingly, a spray dodger that could act as a drift sail in the trade winds, and also, suspiciously, a daggerboard. It is doubtful that Delage could have outswum the craft, let alone kept even with it. Furthermore, what about sharks? A swimmer cannot see his surroundings very well, and there would have been no effective way for Delage to know whether or not a shark was coming at him. There have been too many cases already of voyagers, such as Romer, being pestered by curious sharks to believe that Delage wouldn't have had to spend much of his time atop the drifting support vessel.

Delage's claim is reported as a matter of record, but he should not be considered to have actually swum across. However, his catamaran was only thirteen feet long, so, in that sense, his was a transoceanic small-boat journey.

The collapse of the Soviet Union in the early 1990s finally opened the gates of that imprisoned nation for people to come and go freely. Though many foreigners went there to visit the former "workers' paradise," few Russians could leave because they simply couldn't afford to travel or pay foreign prices. One such impoverished Russian decided to see the world before he died, anyway, even though he had only the equivalent of five dollars in rubles when he started out. That was Eugeny Gvodev, a retired marine engineer.

Gvodev's story is typically Russian. Having worked hard his whole life for the state, he had to endure years of being ignored and then arrogance from his own government while he tried to get a passport. After five years some invisible bureaucrat finally stamped the right document, and he had his passport. During this time Gvodev acquired an eighteen-foot fiberglass trailer-sailer he named *Lena*, but provisioning it was nearly impossible because of food shortages. What food was available had to be bought on the black market, costing a fortune. Yet he endured. For navigation he couldn't hope to buy a handheld GPS, so he would use an old sextant and a cheap Soviet-era radio for time checks. It would work, and he would endure. When sailing down the Caspian Sea in winter he was denied permission to buy bottled gas for his stove in Odessa because of a local political imbroglio. Consequently, his precious canned food froze and burst the tins. In Albania he was robbed by greedy bureaucrats. Yet he endured.

Russian Eugeny Gvodev was the first Eastern European since Pauls Sprogis to venture freely in a small boat. He circumnavigated this eighteen-footer on a microscopic budget.

Only through the kindness of fellow boatmen he met along the way was he able to pass through the Dardanelles, traverse the Mediterranean, and reach the Canaries. Even so, because of poor diet and stress, he lost several teeth and his fingernails began to drop off. Yet he endured.

By the middle of 1996 the unstoppable Russian had reached the Indian Ocean, where he met Serge Testa at the Cocos Islands. Testa and other yachtsmen championed his cause, helping with donations of food, water, and sailing equipment. Eventually Gvodev returned via the Red Sea to his home waters in the Caspian Sea. His voyage, the first great small-boat cruise by an Eastern European since Fred Rebell, was a tribute to the man and to all the former Soviet people who had learned how to endure during their years of living in a centrally planned police state. This humble sailor showed his country the value of the lone individual versus the moribund narrow-mindedness of an all-powerful government.

Happily, Gvodev returned to a hero's welcome and was able to secure the funds to build a little twelve-footer for his next voyage. He set out in this boat on another circumnavigation in May 1999.

———— ·•·• ————

True to his word and his ambition, Tom McNally built his tiny three-foot, eleven-inch boat in which he hoped to wrest the title from Hugo Vihlen once and for all. He called the little capsule boat *Vera Hugh II* and with it intended to make an east–west Atlantic crossing in small stages. This boat was technically the best one McNally ever used. Relying on his usual friendliness, force of character, and sheer determination, he had gotten donations of material and labor from people and industries in England who wanted a Briton to hold the sailing record for smallest boat across. Even though McNally had little money to contribute, the boat, a high-tech Kevlar and carbon-fiber hull crammed with very sophisticated navigation and communication gear, was worth around £55,000—even more than his main competitor's self-financed boat *Father's Day*. McNally was *serious* this time. His amateurish efforts were a thing of the past.

On March 4, 1998, he launched from Cape Espartel, Tangier, bound for Las Palmas but ran into bad weather. Sitting in enforced confinement during the storm must have been hell for the Liverpudlian, but he had chosen this life and it had become his *raison d'être*. He lived for this, and he almost died for it.

Off the coast of Morocco *Vera Hugh II* was caught in steel fishing nets laid by local fishermen. As the little boat bobbed up and down on the swells, the netting tore at the hull fittings and threatened to rip off the keel. McNally had no choice but to dive into the cold water and work through the night cutting away the quarter-inch netting with a *hacksaw*. This must have been incredibly difficult, as anyone who has cut cable with a hacksaw even in a home workshop can attest. McNally, driven by desperation to save his boat, attacked the net for twelve hours, most of that time underwater. Hundreds of times he dove down, grasped the cable, found his mark, and sawed. After a few strokes it was back up for air and then down again into the darkness to find his last cut and repeat the process.

In the morning the boat was freed and, exhausted, McNally climbed back into *Vera Hugh II*. Now his real problems began. Just as he finished, the Moroccan fishermen showed up. Furious at finding their nets mutilated, they de-

Tom McNally's *Vera Hugh II*, in which he hopes to wrest the title away from Hugo Vihlen for the smallest boat to make an ocean crossing. This three-foot, eleven-inch boat is worth an estimated $80,000!

manded compensation from the Briton. He refused—what money did he ever have?—and slammed down his Plexiglas hatch cover. Immediately he fired up his expensive radio gear and called the British Embassy in Tangier. The Embassy called the Moroccan government, which posthaste dispatched an armed patrol boat to rescue McNally. Fortunately, one was in the area and in a short time it had chased away the fishermen and provided escort for the *Vera Hugh II* until it was out of the area.

After a mere twenty-day passage McNally made Las Palmas, but on pulling the boat from the water found that the hull had been badly damaged by the netting. It would require extensive repairs, so he postponed the Atlantic crossing until the work could be done. Would this sailor ever be allowed by Fate to make a simple cruise?

———————

A claim much more credible than Guy Delage's that he had swum the Atlantic was made by Frenchman Ben Lecomte in 1998. Motivated to undertake the journey to raise money for research in cancer—the disease that had killed his father—he started out from Cape Cod on July 16 with a support boat, a much larger one than Delage's (and he wasn't attached to it). Before he left Massachusetts he asked his girlfriend in France to marry him, but she demurred and invited him to ask *after* the crossing. With that dream deferred, yet undaunted, the would-be lover swam each day while his friends in the support boat watched for sharks and provided updates to the media back in France. The support boat was equipped with a special antishark electromagnetic field that in theory repelled the animals from a twenty-five-foot radius, though the watchful eyes of his companions were more trustworthy.

After swimming each day Lecomte would collapse exhausted on board the boat, then after a rest begin a four-hour, nine-thousand-calorie meal to restoke his boiler, as it were, for the next day's effort. This went on for more than a month, until he could no longer take it. He reached his physical limit and had to put in to the Azores for a week's rest. During this stop, he telephoned his girlfriend and again asked her to marry him. She gave him the same reply—wait.

It took Lecomte seventy-three days of swimming, but finally he landed at Quiberon in northwest France on September 25, having swum 3,716 miles. It is fair to declare this the first authenticated swim across the Atlantic. But the larger question remained: would his girlfriend marry him? On the beach at Quiberon Lacomte sank to his knees and asked her a third time. Her answer: "Oui."

13

NEW FACES
AND OLD

THE NEW MILLENNIUM

◆ IT'S A GIRL! ◆ ELVIS HAS LEFT THE MARINA ◆
THE HUMPBACK KAYAK ◆
THE GLORY OF SPAIN ON A SEA-DOO ◆

HAPPILY, AS WE APPROACH THE END OF THE STORY OF small-boat voyaging thus far in the annals of boating, we finally come to the tale of a lone woman voyager.

Joanna Crapo was the first woman to sail across the Atlantic in a small boat, way back in 1877, but she did that with her domineering husband, who allowed her hardly any responsibilities other than preparing food. Naive, young, impetuous Mary Andrews died with her aging, vainglorious husband on their ill-advised fall departure from Atlantic City in 1901. There were notable single-handed voyages by women in the last half of the twentieth century, including Ann Davison's Atlantic crossing in her twenty-three-foot *Felicity Ann* in 1952 and the circumnavigations by Naomi James in 1977 and the lone voyage (all but eighty miles) of Tania Aebi that ended in 1987, but these were large boats, volumetrically at least, and, not surprisingly, capable of ocean passages.

At the beginning of the new millennium a new face appeared on the small-boat scene and made a worthy voyage, hopefully the first of many by women small-boat skippers. This was Raphaëla le Gouvello, a French veterinarian. She wanted to cross the Atlantic on a sailboard and while carefully researching the idea contacted Stéphane Peyron, who himself had crossed in 1987 (see page 304). Peyron gallantly offered her the use of his old boat and helped her with logistical planning. Le Gouvello undertook a strict regimen of physical conditioning to prepare for the ordeal and in the spring of 2000 was ready to go. She departed from Senegal, West Africa, on February 25 aboard the twenty-five-foot sailboard, something like a long, thin sneak-box made of carbon, Kevlar, and epoxy.

As meticulous as her planning and training had been, even le Gouvello could not have foreseen a very rare instance of two and a half weeks of windless weather in the trades during March. Without wind she drifted south with the current, but while she was making no forward progress she still had to eat, and she soon realized that her remaining supplies wouldn't last to the West Indies. A French patrol boat, *La Fougueuse*, came to her rescue and replenished her stores.

When the winds returned she worked north and then west and typically could reel off seventy miles per day. On her fifty-ninth day she landed on the Rock of Diamond in Martinique, having crossed 2,750 miles of open ocean alone. She immediately made plans to sailboard across the Pacific Ocean, but again it would only be after carefully assessing all the variables, including weather. Having learned from the mental torture of

Art on facing page: Raphaëla le Gouvello crossing the Atlantic on her borrowed, highly specialized sailboard.

drifting becalmed for two and a half weeks, she wanted to make sure that during the summer months of her crossing an El Niño–type condition wouldn't kill the Pacific trades and leave her in irons.

———— ◆ ————

Earlier, in the spring of 2000, le Gouvello's compatriot Rémy Bricka also had Pacific plans. With the backing of an Alsatian sauerkraut company, he stepped into his fiberglass canoe shoes once again, strapped on the tether to his support float, and in March 2000 strode off into the Pacific Ocean from near Marina Del Rey in Los Angeles. To be technically accurate, it seems obvious that Bricka wasn't really "walking" across the whole ocean any more than Delage had really "swum" the Atlantic a few years earlier. However Bricka's feat was so whimsical in nature that you can't help but like the guy and admire his brass for undertaking it. You *want* to give him credit for it. A pho-

When not walking on water across oceans, Frenchman Rémy Bricka is a professional "one-man band."

tograph showing Bricka performing in his one-man getup perfectly captures the personality of the man and the spirit of his ocean walks. The picture shows him in a gaudy white Elvis-type leisure suit, wearing a rhinestone-encrusted fedora, strumming a guitar-lute instrument, with fiery sparklers whirling around on his back, while a pure white dove sits serenely atop the headstock of the guitar. It is high-energy, lowbrow entertainment where the only important thing is that the audience smiles and has a good laugh. Bricka looks as if he's having a great time, and maybe that was the reason he did his ocean walks—to keep 'em smilin'.

An early spell of bad weather drove Bricka back after the initial departure, and so he tried again in April. Incredibly, the clown prince of micromariners hoofed it—or floated—two thousand miles over the next five months before he called it quits south of Hawaii and was rescued. Maritime history's loss was French music's gain.

Welshman Peter Bray became the first person in modern times to kayak across the North Atlantic unsupported. During his first attempt in the summer of 2000 his custom-built twenty-one-foot boat sprang a leak and flooded. He was forced into an inflatable life raft, but the bottom

Welshman Peter Bray paddled his humpbacked kayak *Newt* from Newfoundland to Ireland in 75 days.

was torn when he smacked into the kayak. Consequently, he spent thirty-two hours sitting in freezing water before he was rescued. Fortunately, he was wearing survival gear.

On June 23, 2001, Bray departed again from Saint John's, Newfoundland, in another boat built from the molds of the first one but with improvements to increase survivability. Like his first boat, this one was equipped with satellite navigation and communications and an aft "camel-back" cabin he could duck into in bad weather or at night. Power for his electronics came from solar panels.

Bray managed to get a commendable three knots or so from the boat, though the paddling was of course tiring and lonely. Several small but crucial equipment failures slowed him down—the rudder controls broke twice, and the camel-back hatch hinge failed, nearly causing another flooding (like the one the year before). He made emergency repairs as each piece failed, but because he didn't have proper repair parts and had to fabricate makeshift pieces out of anything he could find, he lost time.

While making one repair he cut his finger, and the few drops of blood that fell into the water soon attracted a shark. By paddling steadily Bray convinced it he was a machine, not food. A killer whale also came calling and try as he might he couldn't shake it, even though he changed course several times. Finally he told it in a loud voice to leave, and it did!

Bray arrived at Beldereg, County Mayo, Ireland, seventy-six days after leaving Canada, completing a voyage that was all the more laudable because it helped raise £100,000 for a children's charity.

———◆———

One common news feature that faded late in the twentieth century was the aristocratic adventurer. Newspapers used to be full of wealthy noblemen setting aviation records in biplanes, racing cars at Brooklands in England, scaling some mountain, or finding lost treasure in Egypt. It was the classic fodder of "ripping yarns." With the new century it seemed as if those days of bold blue bloods were over.

What a treat to find that one such adventurous aristo still remains. He is Count Álvaro de Marichalar y Sáenz de Tejada of Spain, brother-in-law of Princess Elena. On February 23, 2002, Count Marichalar set out from Rome on the Tiber River aboard a personal watercraft, his destination Miami. For twelve hours a day he zoomed along on the nine-foot Bombardier Sea-Doo west toward Gibraltar and then into

Spanish aristocrat Álvaro de Marichalar y Sáenz de Tejada astride his Atlantic-conquering Sea-Doo in the summer of 2002.

the open Atlantic. A support boat that he slept aboard carried six crew, food, fuel, and spare parts.

Making an ocean passage on a personal watercraft is physically demanding. The hull slams into oncoming wave crests continuously, and each time the seat smacks the rider in the crotch. To avoid this in even a moderate chop the rider has to stand upright on the foot rests. The count spent nearly his entire voyage standing, and at one point he kept at it for thirty-one hours straight. Along the way he was thrown a few times, once in shark-infested waters. He also battled huge waves, which were tricky to negotiate because if he crested them at speed he ran the danger of pitchpoling, a terrifying, life-ending experience on a personal watercraft.

After four months, fifty-two hundred miles, and three hundred gallons of fuel, Marichalar landed at a Miami marina on June 22. When he had rested for a few days, he announced to the press his desire to cross the Pacific the same way someday.

CONCLUSION

TO SEA, OR NOT TO SEA: THAT IS THE QUESTION

A FINAL WARNING BEFORE YOU GO

AS WE APPROACH THE SAFE HARBOR OF OUR CONCLUSION, I hope you have enjoyed this book and were as glad to learn about these incredible stories of small-boat voyages as I was to tell them. These sagas are wonderful because they are *not* stories about great naval battles with a cast of thousands or the yachts of megarich industrialists with bank vaults of millions; rather, they are about "normal" men and women who with modest means accomplished great things. Some undertook journeys to escape a bad situation, others to find adventure, others to make a profit, and yet others to test themselves. Many of these boats were homemade, and often the skills to sail them were self-taught. This is high adventure and high achievement on a human scale.

The danger of reading a book like this is that a reader may suppose that since so many of these waterborne feats of derring-do had happy endings, the danger isn't all that great, and anyone who goes to sea in a small boat has a good chance of finishing a voyage across an ocean. Wrong. What have not been reported here are all the voyages that ended in turning the boat around and going home or that even ended in death on the high seas. These voyages haven't been reported for two reasons. First, unsuccessful voyages aren't very interesting, and therefore writers and reporters don't cover them much. It is hard for the historian to find any information on them. Also, when a voyage ended prematurely, there is no logbook or memoir of the voyage because few of us write publicly about our failures, and corpses can't. Publishers don't like "downer" stories because readers normally won't buy them. Many would-be small-boat voyagers are therefore lost to history. (See Other Notable Voyages in the appendix.)

The great keeper of small-boat records, Englishman D. H. Clarke, reckoned that transoceanic small-boat sailors had only a seventy percent chance of success. He made that estimate twenty years ago, but not all that much has changed since then. Even with the advent of miniaturized electronics, including small radar sets and CARD (collision avoidance radar detector), small boats continue to be lost at sea because of collisions with whales or cargo containers, negligence by the sailor in not tethering himself into the boat at all times, or catastrophic structural failure. Even the most cautious skipper cannot eliminate chance from the equation. Shipwrecks happen—sometimes with deadly results.

With the advances in satellite navigation, EPIRB, and CARD (eminently suitable for even the smallest boats), boaters do stand a somewhat better chance than when Clarke issued his warning. Things have improved to perhaps an eighty-three percent chance. In other words, a sailor has as good a chance succeeding single-handing a very small boat across an ocean as he would have playing Russian roulette with a six-shot Colt Model 1861 navy revolver.

If you are "dead set" on attempting a small-boat voyage, consider the following. First, read, read, read! The literature of small-boat voyaging is extensive and gives the best preparatory lessons available other than actually sailing a boat. Learn from others' mistakes, learn what made them successful, and carefully think about the writer's motivation for voyaging and whether or not you have that same need. Remember, too, that what looks easy in a book usually isn't in the real world. If Leonardo da Vinci had written a book on painting and you read it, do you think you could whip out a *Mona Lisa*?

The two most beautifully written books on pleasure boat sailing that I know are Richard Maury's *The Saga of "Cimba"* and Frederic Fenger's *Alone in the Caribbean*. Whereas Maury's book has little on small-boat handling, Fenger's is a veritable textbook on the subject. Joshua Slocum's *Sailing Alone Around the World* is another masterpiece, but Slocum's boat *Spray* was not small by our standards, nor was the *Cimba*. Slocum's *Voyage of the "Liberdade"* is more germane to our subject. In this book he tells of building a part dory, part sampan in 1888, ten years before the *Spray* voyage, to evacuate his family from South America after his cargo ship was wrecked.

I consider these the ten essential reads (see full information in the bibliography):

1. *Alone in the Caribbean*, Frederic Fenger
2. *The Venturesome Voyages of Captain Voss*, John Voss
3. *Tinkerbelle*, Robert Manry
4. *Shrimpy*, Shane Acton
5. *The Mutiny On Board H.M.S. "Bounty,"* William Bligh
6. *Shackleton's Boat Journey*, F. A. (Frank) Worsley
7. *A Voyage of Pleasure*, Bernard Gilboy
8. *Escape to the Sea*, Fred Rebell
9. *Alone Against the Atlantic*, Gerry Spiess
10. *A Thousand Miles in the "Rob Roy" Canoe on the Rivers and Lakes of Europe*, John MacGregor

Second, try entering an organized event such as one of Chay Blyth's challenges (www.challengebusiness.com). Blyth and his organization will help you purchase or rent a suitable boat, work with you on acquiring the necessary skills, deal with the documents and legalities, and then support you during the event. This is probably the safest way to go.

Last, if you are going to "go it alone," do it in a proven design. Some of the boats I've described in the book are still available to amateur builders in plan form.

14-foot Sloop *Happy* from
Benford Design Group
605 South Talbot St., Suite 1
Saint Michaels MD 21663
410-745-3235

TLC 19 from
Dudley Dix Yacht Design
24 Saint Anthony's Rd.
Box 26524
Hout Bay 7872
South Africa
27-21-790-2838

Sopranino and *Trekka* from
Laurent Giles Naval Architects Ltd.
P.O. Box 130
Lymington, SO41 9FA
United Kingdom
44-1590-673255

Many custom designs from
Colin Mudie
Bywater Lodge,
Pierside
Lymington, SO41 5SB
United Kingdom
44-1590-672047

Roberts 19 from
**Bruce Roberts Inter
national Yacht Design**
P.O. Box 1086
Severna Park
MD 21146
410-349-2743

The great *Bris VI* by Sven
Lundin, who changed his name
to Sven Yrvind, is available in
plan form, but the mercurial
Yrvind is difficult to locate. I
recommend an Internet search
for "Sven Yrvind."

The next generation: Bill Teplow aboard his
Potter 19 Chubby in which he sailed from San
Francisco to Hawaii in the summer of 2002.
Teplow's voyage in a well-built production
boat shows what can be accomplished by an
experienced amateur sailor with ample provisions and modern electronics. Though depending on passing ships for aid, shooting
noon sights, and looking out for sprung
planks are worries of the past, even modern
would-be Alfred Johnsons and Bernard Gilboys
must be prudent, resourceful, and brave.
Crossing an ocean in a small boat will always
be thrilling—and dangerous. Even a thousand
years after the first Inuit did it, men and
women will continue to challenge the enormity
of the ocean in small boats that are no more
than a speck on the sea.

ROWERS AND OTHER STRANGERS

THE 1960S ROWING VOYAGES OF JOHNSTONE AND HOARE, Ridgway and Blyth, Fairfax, and McClean opened the floodgates for many others to begin long-distance rowing voyages. In fact, more people attempted transoceanic rowing voyages over the past forty years than made small-boat journeys across oceans under sail. Rowing is a feat of athleticism as much as seamanship. Many are attracted to its relative simplicity versus sail-handling. Additionally, most of the rowboats are really survival pods with oarlocks, so there may be a sense that rowing is a safer means of crossing an ocean. Statistics show that ocean rowing is still a dangerous sport and can be deadly. It shouldn't be attempted by the unwary in substandard craft. The utter brutality of the sea has turned even "survival pods" into coffins.

Listed below are the many rowers who have succeeded in crossing the Arctic, Atlantic, Indian, and Pacific Oceans since the 1960s. In addition to rowers, also given are some long-distance peddlers—people who "row" with their feet.

NAME	YEAR	BOAT
ARCTIC OCEAN CROSSING NORTH TO SOUTH		
Alexander and Eugene Smurgis	1993	*Max-4*
ATLANTIC CROSSING WEST TO EAST		
Gérard d'Aboville	1980	*Capitaine Cook*
Tom McClean	1987	*Skoll 1080*
Don Allum	1987	*QE3*
Sean Crowley	1988	*Finn Again*
Joseph Le Guen	1995	*Pour les Sauveteurs en Mer*

NAME	YEAR	BOAT
ATLANTIC CROSSING EAST TO WEST		
Sidney Genders	1970	*Khaggavisana*
Don and Geoff Allum	1971	*QE3*
Peter Bird and Derek King	1974	*Britannia II*
Curtis and Kathleen Saville	1981	*Excalibur*
Hugh King-Fretts	1984	*Hulu*
Amyr Khan Klink	1984	*Paraty*
Sean Crowley and Mike Nestor	1986	*Finnegan's Wake*
Andrew Halsey	1997	*Brittany Rose*
Rob Hamill and Phil Stubbs (winners)	1997	*Kiwi Challenge*
Pascal Blond and Joseph Le Guen	1997	*Atlantik Challenge*
David and Naida Rice	1997	*Hannah Snell*
Ian Blandin and Robert Cassin	1997	*Spirit of Jersey*
Eamonn and Peter Kavanagh	1997	*Christina*
Steve Issacs and Mark Stubbs	1997	*Toc H Phoenix*
Peter Hogden and Neil Hitt	1997	*Hospiscare*
John Searson and C. Clinton (medevacked)	1997	*Commodore Shipping*
Wayne Callahan and Tim Welford	1997	*Team Ryvita*
Steven Lee and John Bryant	1997	*Kielder Atlantic Warrior*
Danniel Innes and Pete Lowe	1997	*Golden Fleece*
Graham Walters and Keith Mason-Moore	1997	*The George Geary*
Duncan Nicoll and Jock Wishart	1997	*Mount Gay Rum Runner*
Andrew Watson and Russel Reid	1997	*Bitzer*
Simon Chalk and George Rock	1997	*Cellnet Atlantic Challenge*
John Van Katwyck and Geoff Gavey	1997	*Endeavour*
Jim Shekhdar and David Jackson	1997	*Boatcom Waverider*
Michael Elliot and Louis Hunkin	1997	*The Cornish Challenger*
Charles Street and Roger Gould	1997	*Sam Deacon*
David Immelman and		
D. Mossman (medevacked)	1997	*Key Challenger*
Stein Hoff and Arvid Bentsen	1997	*STAR Atlantic*
Martin Bellamy and Mark Mortimer	1997	*Salamanca*
Isabel Fraser and Richard Duckworth	1998	*Stylus Misteral Endeavour*

NAME	YEAR	BOAT
Jan Meek and Daniel Byles	1998	*Carpe Diem*
Tori Murden (1st woman, 2nd attempt)	1999	*American Pearl*
Diana Hoff	2000	*Star Atlantic II*
Peggy Bouchet	2000	*SFR*
Patrick Lihurt	2000	*Lune de Mer*
Richard Jones	2000	*Brother of Jared*
Emmanuel Coindre	2001	*Ville de Dinard*
Theodore Rezvoy	2001	*Odessa*
Debra Veal	2002	*Troika Transatlantic*

INDIAN OCEAN CROSSING EAST TO WEST

Anders Svedlund	1971	*Roslagen*

PACIFIC CROSSING WEST TO EAST

Gérard d'Aboville	1991	*Sector*

PACIFIC CROSSING EAST TO WEST

John Fairfax and Sylvia Cook	1972	*Britannia II*
Peter Bird	1983	*Hele-on-Britannia*
Curtis and Kathleen Saville	1985	*Excalibur Pacific*
Mick Bird	1999	*Reach*
Jim Shekhdar	2001	*Le Shark*

PEDAL-POWERED OCEAN CROSSING

Jason Lewis and Steve Smith, transatlantic	1995	*Moksha*
Jason Lewis, San Francisco to Hawaii	1998	*Moksha*

LOST WHILE ROWING

At least six ocean rowers of modern times have been lost at sea, including Briton Peter Bird and Russian Eugene Smurgis, both of whom had previously made successful ocean crossings. Probably hundreds of Inuit kayakers and even thousands of Polynesian long-distance canoeists have been lost over the centuries.

OTHER NOTABLE VOYAGES

THE 1920–1930s

IRA SPARKS SNEAKED ABOARD A SHIP IN SAN FRANCISCO AND reached Hawaii. There he acquired a metal lifeboat, which he intended to sail across the Pacific and Indian Oceans, hoping to reach Mecca! This boat proved so riddled with rust holes that he commissioned a Japanese carpenter to build him a twenty-foot hard-chined sampan, which he dubbed *Dauntless*. He set out in this sloop January 9, 1924, and reached the Philippine island of Mindinao in only seventy-three days. He skirted the coast for a while but finally disappeared.

Pless Schmidt, a Dane, left the Faeroe Islands bound for Bergen, Norway, June 30, 1929, in a kayak-type fully enclosed boat powered by two outboard engines positioned on either side of the hull. He hoped this craft would be adopted by airship operators as a lifeboat. Along the way on what was to be a test run for a transatlantic crossing, he was jostled by an eight-ton whale that knocked off one of his engines. He had to be rescued by fishermen after drifting for three days.

In 1931 Captain Fritz Engler, from the Baltic port of Rügenwaldermünde, Germany, also a ship's officer for HAPAG, set out from Lisbon to cross the Atlantic in a Klepper similar to Romer's. He made the Canaries after a difficult crossing that included crashing into the coast of Africa, where he had to repair the boat. On November 16, 1931, he left Las Palmas, was spotted by the British steamer *Alameda Star* four days later and after that never seen again.

THE 1960s

Englishman Thomas Kehoe departed the Canaries in his seventeen-foot canoe *Saucy Jack* January 11, 1962. Fate unknown.

Sixty-one-year-old Felix Noble, along with a teenage boy, left San Diego November 1, 1963, bound for Hawaii aboard a raft. On November 18 the teenager asked to be taken off when they spoke to a Japanese fishing vessel. Noble carried on alone. On January 15, 1964, as he approached Kawaihae, he accepted a tow into harbor from the U.S. Navy.

Englishman Frank Dye battled force 7 gales in an open fifteen-foot, ten-inch Wayfarer dingy on a seven-hundred-mile journey from Scotland to Iceland in 1963, accompanied by Russel Brockbank. Dye returned to England where he married a woman he met at a boat show, and together he and his wife Margaret continued to make noteworthy long-distance voyages in their utilitarian dinghy. They sailed from Scotland to Norway, above the Arctic Circle, throughout Britain, and many places in Europe, and became the foremost authorities on dinghy cruising. Eventually over ten thousand Wayfarers were built. Their owners are fiercely loyal to the Ian Proctor design and many have emulated the Dyes's pioneering voyages

German Rollo Gebhard made a convoluted voyage to New York in late 1963 to early 1964 aboard his eighteen-and-a-half-foot Caprice class *Solveig*. Departing from the Riviera, he cut west across the Mediterranean, stopped in the Canaries, made a southern trades crossing to Trinidad, and came north via Saint Thomas and Bermuda. Between there and New York he was knocked down by a whale; the impact also caused a crack in the hull, which leaked the rest of the way. Before this transatlantic voyage Gebhard undertook a shakedown cruise through the eastern Mediterranean. During this *Solveig* was shot at by Greek military forces, and Gebhard was arrested in Yugoslavia and later again in the Red Sea.

German Peter Newe made a forty-six-day crossing between the Canaries and English Harbor, Antigua, in a fifteen-foot lateen-rigged boat during the summer of 1966. He later became a ship captain on Caribbean cruise ships.

Bill Verity, a boatbuilder from Long Island, New York, in a precursor to Tom Severin's more famous voyage, built a twenty-foot conjectural replica of a Saint Brendan-era boat and sailed it from Fenit, Ireland, to San Salvador in the Bahamas during the summer of 1969. The *Noamh Breandan* featured a square sail and steering sweep.

Irishman Tom McClean made a seventy-one-day passage in the twenty-foot rowboat *Super Silver* from Saint John's to Blacksod Bay, Ireland, in 1969. It was the first west–east solo row.

THE 1970s

Irishman Enda O'Coineen of Galway failed in his attempt to motor and sail the seventeen-foot Zodiac inflatable *Kilcullen* across the Atlantic. He left Nova Scotia August 2, 1977, and by mid-September had closed to within 350 miles of Ireland when his boat was capsized in a gale and lost its sea anchor. He was lucky to be rescued by a warship that happened to be participating in a NATO exercise nearby.

THE 1980s

In 1980 Verlen Kruger and Steve Landick began a twenty-eight-thousand-mile canoe odyssey in which they paddled down the Missouri River, up the Illinois to the Great Lakes, up the Saint Lawrence and out to the Atlantic. Coming down the east coast they passed the Florida Keys, continued west and entered the Mississippi. Up that they went back to the Missouri. They portaged and paddled to the Arctic Ocean, cut through Alaska, and hit the Pacific. Down the Inside Passage they went and kept going until they reached the southernmost tip of Baja California. They paddled north to the mouth of the Colorado River and then paddled and portaged much of it. Their three-year journey ended in December 1983.

Neither rain nor snow nor threat of old age could stop Verlen Kruger from making astoundingly long canoe and kayak voyages.

New Zealand mining geologist Paul Caffyn enhanced an already impressive paddling resume in 1980 when he and Englishman Nigel Dennis completed the first circumnavigation of Europe by kayak. In eighty-five days they paddled 2,200 miles. The next year Caffyn crowned his career when headed out from Queenscliff, Australia, in an attempt to make a 9,420-mile kayak circumnavigation of that continent. After encounters with storms, sea snakes, tiger sharks, and even crocodiles, he completed his truly epic journey 360 days later.

Eric Peters in the five-foot, ten-and-a-half-inch barrel-shaped *Toniky Nou* left Hierro in the Canaries on Christmas Eve, 1982, and made a forty-six-day passage to Guadeloupe. Peters's boat was, according to maritime historian D. H. Clarke, 1⅜ inch shorter than Vihlen's *April Fool*, and so earned the title for the smallest boat ever to make the east–west crossing.

Howard Wayne Smith aboard *Happy*, a fourteen-foot Jay Benford custom-designed cold-molded minicruiser, sailed from Miami through the Panama Canal to the Pacific on a proposed circumnavigation. In November 1982 the Canadian struck a reef at Noumea, and the homebuilt boat was destroyed. He then built the nine-foot *Happy II* capsule boat from aluminum, but ended his voyage in Australia.

During the summer of 1983, Sven Lundin sailed his twenty-foot cold-molded *Bris* (the first *Bris*) from Sweden to Rhode Island via the Azores to deliver the boat to the Museum of Yachting in Newport.

In 1984, Claude and Geneviève Desjardins, in their eighteen-foot cold-molded, homebuilt *Père Peinard*, designed by Bruce Roberts, sailed from Montréal to Panama, through the canal, to the Galápagos, Marquesas, and ultimately to Brisbane, Australia. The Desjardins began building the boat while still college students and completed it two years later.

Enda O'Coineen, who had failed seven years earlier, made a quick transatlantic crossing in 1985 from July 17 to August 21 in a seventeen-foot Humber inflatable. It had a sail and a fifty-five-horsepower outboard. Along the way the Irishman had to endure the aftereffects of Hurricane Hannah.

Sir Henry Pigott completed a circumnavigation in 1985 aboard his junk-
rigged, homebuilt nineteen-foot,
eight-inch *Glory*. Englishman Pigott
briefly held the record for the smallest
boat to *solo* circumnavigate, but would
lose it quickly to Serge Testa.

In 1986 Verlen Kruger and his wife Va-
lerie Fons paddled two canoes from the
Beaufort Sea north of Alaska all the
way down to Cape Horn via a complicated route that included the Intracoastal Waterway, the Orinoco River,
and the Paraguay River. They then
rounded the Horn in the canoes.

Sir Henry Pigott's small junk, *Glory,* in
which he sailed around the world.

Kenichi Horie sailed from San Francisco back to Japan in his nine-foot,
six-inch *Mermaid* in 1989. This may be considered the world's record for
the smallest-boat transpacific voyage, though some would credit that
to Bill Dunlop on the strength of the message in the plastic container,
which seems to prove he made a landfall.

THE 1990s

Argentinean Alberto Torroba, without navigation instruments, sailed a
dugout canoe he built himself from Panama to Mindanao in the Philip-
pines in 1991. He started the voyage with a compass but lost it four
days out from the Galápagos Islands. He learned to find islands by
guesstimating the angle of stars and comparing what he saw with an
island's known latitude.

Rebecca Ridgway, daughter of Atlantic rower John Ridgway, in January 1992 became the first woman to kayak around Cape Horn.

In 1996 Sebastian Näslund sailed a fourteen-foot lifeboat he had converted from the Canaries to Barbados. He had begun the journey the

previous year in Sweden. Näslund's *Arrandir* was built up on the sides and decked over, using polyester cloth and epoxy, on the advice of fellow Swede Sven Lundin, and had a small cabin. The sail plan was sprit rig main with jib and a small riding sail on a mizzen mast. Näslund's previous building experience had been to assemble a prefabricated bookshelf for his mother.

In June 1997 Kevin Hollander set out on a Yamaha WaveRunner personal watercraft to ride ten thousand miles from New York to Los Angeles. His intended route was up the Hudson to the Erie Canal, across the Great Lakes to the Mississippi, across the Caribbean and through the Panama Canal, and then up the Pacific coast. As it turned out, the two partners who began with him dropped out because of rough water on the Great Lakes. Continuing alone, he was robbed and nearly killed by bandits when he landed on the coast of Mexico. There officials added to his trials when they refused to help him solve paperwork problems that would enable him to get to Panama. After he left them he was struck by a wave that resulted in two of his teeth being cracked. Hollander wisely decided to forgo further travel in Central America and instead turned north back to Texas. He retraced his route to New Orleans, but then kept going and finally arrived in Miami in September. His sixty-five-hundred-mile run set a world's record for travel by personal watercraft.

Thirteen windsurfers crossed the Atlantic with the assistance of the leased support vessel *Kapitan Khalebnikov* in 1998. The huge Russian icebreaker departed Saint John's, Newfoundland, September 14. Each day the windsurfers flew along behind the big ship in competitive miniraces for about four hours. After each run they were brought back on board, even though the ship kept moving eastward. Because of this it cannot be said that they in fact crossed the ocean on windsurfers, but it was an interesting undertaking. The *Khalebnikov* reached Weymouth, Dorset, in England September 21.

NOTES

CHAPTER 1. THE FOGBOUND PAST: 63 AD–16TH CENTURY

9 **landed in Germany in 63 AD.** Pliny the Elder, *Natural History: Book II*, 171.

> *Nepos also records as to the northern circuit that Quintus Metellus*
> *Celer, colleague of Africanus in the consulship, but at the time pro-*
> *consul of Gaul, received from the King of the Swabians a present of*
> *some Indians [Indos], who on a trade voyage, had been carried off*
> *their course by storms to Germany. Thus there are seas encircling the*
> *globe on every side and dividing it in two, so robbing us of half the*
> *world, since there is no region affording a passage from there to here*
> *or from here to there.*

Note the use of the term *Indos* to describe these shipwreck victims, who almost certainly were Inuit. This also may be the first use of the term *Indians* to
describe incorrectly those people of North America and Greenland whose ances-
tors crossed the land bridge from Siberia to Alaska. In other words, Columbus and
the Spanish weren't the first to make the mistake of thinking these people were
from the Asian subcontinent of India.

Pliny (Gaius Plinius Secundus) himself suffered a misadventure by boat. In
August 79 AD he was the admiral of the fleet stationed in the Bay of Naples
charged with anti-pirate interdiction. When Vesuvius began to rumble just before it blew its top and buried Pompeii and Herculaneum, this soldier-lawyer-
historian's curiosity got the best of him and he ordered a ship to take him to view
the area. Despite the hot falling ash and the steady barrage of large chunks of
burning rock raining down before the main eruption, he told his ship's captain to
take him closer to the coast. When he heard of the distress of the local citizens
he ordered that his ship land and the crew rescue those who wanted to be evacu-
ated. The ship's captain demurred, which caused Pliny to gallantly exclaim, "Fortune favors the brave." They landed at Pompeii's port, Stabiae, and offered passage to those who wanted it, but before they could depart the next day, Vesuvius
spewed forth a great cloud of poisonous sulfur gas, and Pliny was overcome. He
was fifty-six years old.

17 **in 1576 and 1577.** Martin Frobisher's treatment and "kidnapping" of Inuit is really a
complicated issue that deserves closer examination. First, it is not fair, nor does it
promote historical understanding, to judge the actions of a sixteenth-century sea
captain with purely twenty-first-century sensibilities. Surviving documents clearly
show that Frobisher was a bête noire, even in the context of his own times. Though
ostensibly a privateer, or a mercenary sea captain fighting for his own country
against the Catholic nations of Spain and France, he was hauled before various
courts and naval review boards on charges of piracy, theft, and even treason. He

served time in jail when convicted, but always received only short sentences. It seems that he was the type of two-fisted adventurer who specialized in stretching the limits a little too far but never far enough to bring down the total wrath of his superiors, in this case Queen Elizabeth and her advisers. The queen needed brave and capable fighting men—even if they were not always gentlemen.

Frobisher's early life may have marked out his future course. Orphaned at age thirteen, then sent to live with perhaps disinterested relatives, he went to sea at seventeen in 1553. On this very first voyage the ship he was on made an illegal foray into Portuguese territory in West Africa, where those aboard traded for gold, ivory, and pepper with a local Portuguese chieftain. The next year he made another voyage to Africa and was sent ashore as a hostage to guarantee the safety of one of the local people who had come aboard the ship. At the end of the trading, when the local man had been returned to land, an argument broke out and the English ship was fired on. She weighed anchor quickly and put out to sea leaving young Frobisher behind to what would certainly be enslavement or death.

By strength of character and good luck, the young sailor survived his captivity and with the aid of the Portuguese was repatriated about four years later to England. He was no longer a boy, though. Within a few years the toughened young man had his own ship and set out on a lifetime of trying to claw his own way up the ladder to material wealth and respectability. There were a lot of bumpy spots along the way.

In 1576 Frobisher raised the funds for a three-ship expedition to search for the Northwest Passage. Off Baffin Island in August of that year he and his crew met Inuit with whom they attempted to promote cordial relations by trading trinkets for food and information. Things went smoothly, and soon enough trust had been established that Frobisher sent five of his men to a nearby Inuit encampment in his ship's only boat. The men disappeared around a headland despite having been told to stay in sight of the ship and were not heard from again. Frobisher spent several days trying to locate the men but was unsuccessful. Frustrated and feeling that his men had fallen into a trap, when a lone Inuit approached his ship in a kayak, Frobisher himself leaned over the rail and with his powerful arms plucked the startled paddler out of his boat and onto the deck of the ship. He tried to use his prisoner to force an exchange for his men, but when that failed he then gave orders to cast off, and his small ship headed east back to England, taking with it their terrified prisoner.

Was this "kidnapping," revenge, or hostage taking? Exchanging hostages in those days was a common and perfectly acceptable practice as shown by Frobisher's experience as a teenager. It was the standard business procedure for two parties who didn't yet trust each other to ensure the safety of their emissaries. Perhaps Frobisher meant to use the man the next summer on his return journey to try to get his crewmen back? Or maybe he was just displaying a bit of the explosive, sudden temper for which he was known. Whatever his true motivations, it did not matter, because sometime after arriving back in England with his prize "specimen," the Inuit died.

The next summer Frobisher did return to the waters around Baffin and looked for his crew. They weren't to be found. Angry, Frobisher tried to capture another Inuit, but this time the wary natives fought back, and Frobisher was wounded by an arrow. There was no longer any chance for peace between the natives and the Europeans.

18 **home ports and the law.** Feest, Christian F., ed. *Indians and Europe: An Interdisciplinary Collection of Essays.* Lincoln: University of Nebraska Press, 1999.

CHAPTER 2. TWO DESPERATE ESCAPES: THE 17TH AND 18TH CENTURIES

30 **once told him to leave.** Though Okeley didn't make it to the New World, the folding boat did. When Captains Meriwether Lewis and William Clark were provisioning their famous Corps of Discovery for its transcontinental trek in the spring of 1803, they directed the government armory at Harpers Ferry build them a lightweight thirty-six-foot collapsible iron boat, which they named *Experiment.* The 176-pound frame of this wonderfully innovative boat was covered in carefully sewn animal skins and could carry four tons.

In June 1805, at the Great Falls of the Missouri River they reskinned the boat with buffalo and elk hides they shot and tanned onsite. Unable to find pine trees from which to make pitch, they sealed the seams with a caulk made of charcoal, beeswax, and buffalo tallow. This failed to staunch the leaks, and to their great regret *Experiment* had to be abandoned.

36 **bread per meal per man.** In the summer of 2002 the actual pistol ball, as well as a few others of Bligh's personal relics from the small-boat voyage, were auctioned by Christie's on behalf of their owners, an elderly couple from New Zealand who were descendants of Bligh's.

CHAPTER 3. VICTORIAN VENTURERS: 1865–1876

44 **skin hunting kayaks.** Kayaks would be called *canoes* by Britons and Europeans for the next century and a quarter. What Americans call *canoes* the British and Continentals called *Canadian canoes.*

53 **when supplies ran low.** Some sources give Mullene's name as Jerry Mallene or Jeremy Lane. A Life Saving Raft Company promotional broadside printed in America names the three men and "Mullene." Mullene was a last-minute replacement for Henry Lawson who as late as June 2, 1867, two days before sailing, was named as the third crew member. Why Mullene wasn't with Mikes and Miller upon their return to New York is unknown, but likely he was a professional seaman who signed on to another ship when Mikes ran short of funds in Europe. Mikes stated upon his return he would soon issue a book recounting the story of his voyage, but there is no evidence that such a book was ever published.

57 **voyage of discovery in 1492!** According to my Croatian sources this is the Croatian story: In 1870 a Croatian calling himself "Nikole Primorca" lived in Liverpool,

where he owned a tobacco shop on Duke Street. However, that year a whiff of salt air overcame his better sense, and he made a bet for £1,000 that he could sail a twenty-foot lifeboat across the Atlantic and back. To make the voyage, Primorca (Di Costa) bought a lifeboat on the Isle of Man that had gained some local fame when it was used to rescue fourteen souls from the ship *Breeze*, which sank in the Irish Sea. Along with the boat came the services of John Buckley, the mate of the *Breeze*, who had skippered the lifeboat to safety. Buckley would take the helm for Primorca.

(A search through *Gore's Directory* for Liverpool for 1867–72 shows no tobacco shop on Duke Street, nor do the census rolls of 1871 list any resident of the street as Di Costa or any variant of Primorac. *The Illustrated London News* says that Di Costa had given up his former profession as a ship's captain after the deaths of his wife and child some years earlier when his ship was wrecked on the Goodwin Sands off Kent.)

58 **windmill on his mizzen mast.** Many windmills were in use in Liverpool in the 1870s, and these may have provided the inspiration for the device. No matter where it came from, it was a bold innovation and speaks highly of the two men's daring. Most mariners are known for their extreme conservatism.

59 **forced them into port at Cork.** This brings up another curious point: Why was Buckley in command of the boat if Primoraz was also a sea captain, as was claimed by *The Illustrated London News* and Croatian maritime historians, and had funded the voyage? In some contemporary newspaper accounts he is also listed as a "captain." Admittedly, the term "captain" in those days was often freely, and not precisely, used. This situation supports the report that Primoraz/Di Costa had lost a ship on the Goodwin Sands and consequently lost his captain's certificate after facing a maritime review board. Perhaps only Buckley was legally able to file the required port clearance papers, which he did at the Custom House, Liverpool, on June 1, 1870; he is listed on the document as "master." Further adding to the mystery is the fact that Buckley himself sent two letters to two newspapers on June 1 thanking various local businesses for their donations of supplies for the voyage. These letters are subscribed "John Charles Buckley, Knt." and do not mention Primoraz or Di Costa. Even if it could be argued that Primoraz's limited English prevented him from writing a letter, this at the very least seems impolite if Primoraz was the main sponsor and Buckley's mate. Was Buckley the main drive behind the whole enterprise, and did Primoraz join him just for the adventure of it? If this is the case, why did Buckley leave the boat after arriving in Boston, and Primoraz continue on the return voyage?

One more conundrum is the fact that all the local papers list the *City of Ragusa* leaving port June 2, though Buckley, who kept the ship's log, cites it as June 3.

61 **which accepted it again.** The 1872 *Gore's Directory* for Liverpool shows that a John Buckley, *mariner*, lived at 87 *Titchfield* Street, and that a John De Costa, *shipping agent*, lived at Waterloo Road and that a Mary De Costa, *licensed broker*, lived at 50 *Titchfield* Street! The 1868 edition shows an *Imanuel* De Costa, also a licensed broker, living at 50 Titchfield Street. There were at least seven *John Buckley*s living

in Liverpool at this time, though only one was listed as a mariner. Who were these people, and what was their relationship to one another?

The *City of Ragusa* is one of the most significant small boats in history because of the technical innovation of its original windmill rig and the fact that it made the first round-trip voyage by a small boat across an ocean. Historians in Liverpool, Birkenhead, and Croatia owe it to their cities to sift through the records to answer the many mysteries that still shroud the Primoraz/Di Costa–Buckley story. It is a disservice to the memory of these two mariners, along with Hayter, that the story can be told with no more precision than it is told here. Photographs of this boat must surely exist, but I have not been able to locate any despite an extensive search. The Boston publisher J. E. Tilton displayed a large photograph of the boat at their offices in 1870. A photograph of Primoraz with either Buckley or Hayter exists in Croatia.

65 **inspired by Boyton's exploits.** Boyton met Verne at the great writer's estate during a cruise down the Loire River in his rubber suit.

65 **the Atacama Desert.** While in Peru, Boyton also searched for Inca treasure by dynamiting pits where mummies were known to be buried.

CHAPTER 4. THE PATHS OF GLORY: 1876–1900

81 **to eke out a living.** Much of the information for the Crapo story comes from my copy of Joanna Crapo's reissue of *Strange, But True*, autographed by her in 1908.

82 **and past Cape May.** Sadly, in some areas the Delaware and Raritan Canal has been filled in and is no longer complete. Just east of Trenton it is now cut off before it reaches the Delaware River, just a short distance away. It would be marvelous if the canal were reopened in its entirety.

95 **its sword and holed it!** Swordfish, in attack mode, can swim in a short burst at nearly *seventy miles an hour*! Their "swords" are part of their upper jaws and flare out gently toward their base to distribute the load. There is no doubt that a swordfish could easily have holed the *Pacific*, just as Gilboy claimed.

98 **making the theater circuit.** I searched through several thousand plays written during the nineteenth century, looking for the script to *Dark Secret*, but was unsuccessful. If any reader knows more about this play, I would be glad to receive the information.

103 **during World War II.** H. G. "Blondie" Hasler was a twenty-eight-year-old Major in the Royal Marines when he led Operation Frankton, a raid on German shipping in harbor at Bordeaux, France, in December 1942. It was Hasler's inspiration to launch five kayaks from a Royal Navy submarine, paddle up the Gironde and Garonne Rivers at night, and attack. Of the ten members of the Royal Marines Boom Patrol Detachment who attempted the raid, only Hasler and his co-paddler Marine William Sparks survived. After attaching their timed limpet mines to German cargo ships, the two made their getaway on foot through France, helped by resistance units who eventually smuggled them into Spain.

After the war, Hasler continued his interest in nautical innovation and developed the world's first commercial self-steering gear. He also helped found, along with the *Observer* newspaper, the OSTAR (Observer Singlehanded Transatlantic Race) in 1960. He competed several times in this race from England to America in his own highly unusual junk-rigged Folkboat, *Jester*.

120 **"honeymoon cruise" on August 28.** Various sources state that Mary South was at one time Andrews's "nurse." I can find no substantiation of this and don't believe it true. The exact character of their marriage is also questionable. Was it ever consummated, or was Mary a willing "actress" in a Young-Andrews scheme? Perhaps they prearranged to annul their marriage after their arrival in Spain or, more likely, after a hoped-for triumphant return to America and subsequent profitable tour. Whatever the real terms of the arrangement were, Captains Young and Andrews and Mayor Stoy were all guilty of perpetrating a slimy stunt that led to the death of an unfortunate, misguided, lonely girl. Duping the unwise for profit seems to be a local specialty in Atlantic City.

120 **the *Dark Secret*, was built.** Though it had the same name as the 1888 boat, *Dark Secret* was an entirely new craft personally built by Andrews in only about ten days' work.

121 **honeymoon cruise was over.** Captain Young went on to build his "million-dollar" pier at Atlantic City, the foundations of which remain to this day. The last vestige of his empire, though, is a seafood restaurant still on the pier bearing his name.

CHAPTER 5. A WORLD TO CONQUER: 1900–1920

124 **fifty years earlier.** Voss's account says that the Indian was a man, Luxton's says it was a woman. Voss includes the story of the alcohol, a substance prohibited to the Indians at the time; Luxton's does not, nor does he mention the skull. Voss, like many mariners, knew how to embellish a good tale. Luxton, by the time he got around to recording his version, had become enamored of Indian culture and wrote with a perhaps too sympathetic pen. Whose version is correct is impossible to say.

125 **Luxton's version of events.** The *Pelican* was evidently the object of a search by the USS *Grant*, a revenue cutter. The *Grant* struck a reef while on patrol for Voss's boat and had to put into Victoria for repairs. That it was combing the area lends credence to Luxton's version of their departure and Voss's alleged criminal past.

125 **pistol just in case.** Ironically, *Tilikum* means "friend" in Chinook.

127 **primer on small-boat handling.** Also known as *The Venturesome Voyages of Captain Voss*.

130 **monocoque are not true.** *Monocoque*, meaning "single shell" in French, is a term used to describe a structure whose strength is derived from the shape of its compound curved skin, rather than an internal skeleton or "space-frame" design. Monocoques are stronger and lighter than space frames and have an unobstructed interior. The secret of the strength of an eggshell is that it is an "arch" in three dimensions—the classic monocoque.

140 **was in for a time of it.** Forty-six years earlier, another small boat made a similar attempt to find help for a shipwrecked crew. When the sidewheeler USS *Sagi-*

naw wrecked on lonely Ocean Island in the North Pacific in 1870, the ninety-three castaways knew they had little chance of rescue because few ships ever sailed in those waters. Ironically, *Saginaw*'s Lieutenant Commander Montgomery Sicard had ordered the boat to visit the island only as an act of mercy in case any souls were stranded there. As a last resort, the ship's twenty-two-foot gig was decked over and rigged as a miniature schooner. Lieutenant J. G. Talbot led four other volunteers in a seventeen-hundred-mile bid to reach help in Hawaii. Unfortunately, shortly after their voyage began on November 18 food poisoning struck most of the crew, including Talbot. Only one sailor, coxswain William Halford, was not afflicted. Even though largely disabled by dysentery, Talbot managed to navigate the boat for thirty days toward Hawaii and they reached Kauai on the evening of December 19. Attempting to land the next morning through turbulent rollers the boat capsized and Halford alone was able to reach shore alive. His report led to the rescue of his crewmates on Ocean Island. The gig is preserved in the historical museum in Saginaw, Michigan.

CHAPTER 6. LOVERS AND OTHER LOSERS: 1920–1930s

148 **between Hamburg and New York.** The information about Romer's proposed flight is based on an interview he gave to a correspondent for the *New York Times* when in Saint Thomas.

148 **too inexperienced a pilot.** The first nonstop flight between the United States and Germany was made by Americans Clarence D. Chamberlin and Charles A. Levine June 4, 1927, a few days after Lindbergh's record flight, in a Bellanca W.B. 2, the *Columbia*, which had been built originally to compete for the Orteig Prize that Lindbergh won. Though their goal had been to fly from New York to Berlin, through a navigational error, common enough in those days, they actually passed the capital and landed in Eisleben.

A Junkers all-metal Ju W-33 aircraft did complete the first east–west airplane flight over the Atlantic April 12–13, 1928. Named the *Bremen*, it was a monoplane leased from Junkers by Baron Günther von Hünefeld, who flew in the airplane along with his two hired pilots, Hermann Köhl, also a German, and James Fitzmaurice, an Irishman. The trio was dubbed "the Three Musketeers of the Air." The *Bremen* took off from Ireland and, off course, made a tricky emergency landing on a small island off the coast of Labrador. Romer may have been a talented amateur flier, but Junkers was correct in assessing his flying skills as insufficient for this flight. Fitzmaurice was a pilot in the Irish air force, and Köhl flew for the nascent Lufthansa.

148 **making folding kayaks today.** All the Klepper historical archives were lost in a fire at the Rosenheim factory in 1995; therefore, the proposal by Klepper cannot be verified. The fact was that mounting such a voyage, including building a custom boat, getting it to Portugal, and provisioning it, and all the other hundreds of large and small expenses associated with the trip would have been beyond Romer's income as a third officer for HAPAG, newly married, during the lean

economic times of the Weimar years in Germany. This lends credence to the reporter's statement that Klepper approached Romer. Even the name of the boat seems a little commercially oriented, rather than personal—*Deutscher Sport*. Why not *Spirit of Dettingen*, or *Maria*? Klepper probably funded the entire trip, including the later purchase of two expensive outboard engines. They hoped the success of this trip would vault the company ahead of its many competitors, which is what seems to have happened.

148 **just east of Munich.** Folding fabric-covered boats go as far back as, of course, Okeley, though perhaps some coracles may have been built that way, too, even earlier. In 1851 an English cleric, the Reverend E. Berthon, devised and marketed a collapsible dinghy. It looked very much like a coracle when erected, but when folded was very flat. In 1883 an English sailor named Terry built a remarkable portable boat that could be transformed from a rowboat into a tricycle! The wheels could be broken down into halves so their semicircles could be used as ribs; the longitudinal frame members of the pedaled trike became the gunwales and keel. On July 25, 1883, he set out from London for Dover, pedaling his strange machine, named, of course, *Amphibious*. He arrived in Dover the next day, transformed his tricycle into a rowboat, and after twenty hours of rowing arrived in France. The trike was remade, and off he pedaled to Paris in triumph.

148 **aft of the cockpit.** This type of diagonal bracing is rare in naval design, but was used in the USS *Constitution* in 1797.

148 **uneven loading in choppy water.** Hogging occurs when the bow and stern of a ship simultaneously bend up or down, thus putting enormous load on the center section of the hull.

148 **Romer** *alone* **designed the hull.** Willi Münch-Khe, *Kapitän Romer bezwingt den Atlantik. Ein Tatsachenbericht* (Potsdam: Ludwig Poggenreiter, 1939).

153 **the most destructive in history.** Known as the San Felipe–Okeechobee Hurricane, this cataclysmic storm killed more than three thousand people and left hundreds of thousands homeless throughout the Caribbean and Florida. It began to build near the Cape Verde Islands, where the SS *Commack* at 17° N, 48° W sent out a radio report of its existence. This was the earliest warning ever given for the birth of a hurricane up until that time, so it is all the more curious that Romer put to sea. It might be that he never heard the report, because even in Florida people were caught by surprise when it struck Palm Beach on September 16 after having crossed *directly* over Romer's intended track. At Lake Okeechobee the huge winds caused a storm surge of up to nine feet that flushed the lake dry and swept away thousands of poor farmers along the lake's southern rim, washing them into the dangerous morass of the Everglades. With fifteen hundred lives lost just from the lake flooding, homes ruined, and local emergencies to deal with, it is no wonder that Romer was never searched for.

159 **fourteen years in prison.** My German source could not find the official record of the crime but suspects that because of the length of the sentence it was robbery. Perhaps robbery with assault is a more accurate assumption, judging by Müller's attack on the boatbuilder.

159 **Was he sane?** A psychologist I consulted about Müller's mental condition theorized that he might have fallen into the Cluster B diagnostic category consisting of individuals who are often antisocial and narcissistic. Additionally, he may have suffered from Histrionic Personality Disorder, a condition where the person exhibits immaturity, excitability, emotional instability, and a craving for excitement and self-dramatization.

CHAPTER 7. BIG FEAT, LITTLE NOTICE: THE 1940s

176 **would come later in the war.** The "Gibson Girl" was an emergency transmitter with a built-in hand generator issued to the U.S. Army Air Corps and Navy for use in life rafts. It tapped out an emergency SOS signal automatically as the operator cranked the handle. Built primarily by the Bendix company in the U.S., it was based on a design originated by the Germans, and improved upon by the British. The figure-eight shape of the case was intended to make it easier for the operator to brace between his legs while seated in the raft. That shape earned it the affectionate name Gibson Girl because of its similarity to the narrow-waisted women in the 1890s pictures of artist Charles Gibson.

179 **and said, "Good-bye."** Lim later said he saw a tricolor flag painted on the conning tower and distinctly remembered two of the colors as white and green. He therefore felt the *Benlomond* had been sunk by an Italian submarine. No Italian sub claimed credit for sinking a ship in that area on that date, though Italian subs were very active off the coast of Brazil.

CHAPTER 8. GOOFY AND GALLANT: THE 1950s

210 **the Dutch ship *Bennekom*.** According to Hannes Lindemann, who was skeptical about most of the Bombard experiment.

216 **food to last each leg.** In later years owners of the wonderful Pacific Seacraft Flickas would enjoy the same advantages. The twenty-foot Bruce Bingham–designed Flicka (Swedish for *vivacious*) is one of the all-time classic small-boat cruiser designs. Its hefty six-thousand-pound displacement hull is made of thick, no-maintenance fiberglass, even though the boat is molded to look like a traditional wooden boat. Upstairs it flies 250 square feet of sail while downstairs nearly a ton of ballast keeps everything upright. A well-proportioned cabin allows for standing headroom, a galley, and even a flushing head. This is the most bluewater-ready production twenty-foot boat ever built. Pacific Seacraft of Santa Ana, California, cast most of the hulls, though some were kit built. After being out of production for some years, the Flicka is back on the market.

CHAPTER 9. DOING YOUR OWN THING: THE 1960s

230 **political tensions of the region.** The Japanese government carefully monitors its territorial waters because of Japan's close proximity to Mainland China and

the Korean peninsula—politically sensitive areas. This wariness about unofficial boats in these waters was especially acute when Horie made his voyage. The two Koreas were, and still are, officially at war, and China had recently been shelling the Taiwanese islands of Quemoy and Matsu across the Strait of Formosa.

232 **to fine-tune the balance.** The little trimming rudder behind the main rudder on the *Kodoku* could be set easily so that the force on the tiller was minimized. The off-set arrangement of this little blade, however, may have allowed sloppy sail trimming habits to develop as it would have been easier for a tired helmsman to adjust the trim rudder than take in or let out sail. If the trim rudder "fought" the main rudder, undue drag would be induced and slow the boat. A trim tab mounted directly to the main rudder would have been a better device.

CHAPTER 10. THE PURSUIT OF HAPPINESS: THE 1970s

266 **instead of the original plywood.** The boats are still being made in California, though now with a marconi rig.

269 **the Mini-Transat.** The Mini-Transat is for singlehanded monohulls of 6.5 meters (21 feet). Created by Briton Bob Salmon, who was concerned that the spiraling costs of racing yachts was keeping good sailors out of ocean competition, it was held for the first time in 1977. Now organized in France, the rules state that the skipper must cross the Atlantic without help of any kind. Only radio receivers are permitted.

273 **circumnavigation in an open boat.** Born about 1558, Chidiock Tichborne became involved in a plot by fellow English Catholics to assassinate Protestant Queen Elizabeth in 1586. When the plot was exposed, most of his fellows got away, but a leg injury prevented him from doing so. He was sentenced to be publicly disemboweled.

CHAPTER 11. THE GOLDEN DECADE: THE 1980s

289 **offered Chiles another one.** The original *Chidiock Tichborne* was finally released by the Saudis, and Chiles's agent sold it to an Egyptian doctor.

BIBLIOGRAPHY

CHAPTER 1. THE FOGBOUND PAST: 63 AD–16TH CENTURY

Carse, Robert. *The Seafarers: A History of Maritime America, 1620–1820.* New York: Harper & Row, 1964.

David, Richard, ed. *Hakluyt's Voyages.* Boston: Houghton Mifflin; London: Chatto & Windus, 1981.

Feest, Christian F., ed. *Indians and Europe: An Interdisciplinary Collection of Essays.* Lincoln: University of Nebraska Press, 1999.

Fuson, Robert H., translator. *The Log of Christopher Columbus.* Camden ME: International Marine, 1987.

McGhee, Robert. *The Arctic Voyages of Martin Frobisher: An Elizabethan Adventure.* Seattle: University of Washington Press, 2001.

Pliny, *Natural History: Books 1–2.* Translated by H. Rackham. Cambridge: Harvard University Press, 1992.

Roberts, Kenneth G., and Philip Shackleton. *The Canoe: A History of the Craft from Panama to the Arctic.* Camden ME: International Marine; Toronto: Macmillan, 1983.

Severin, Tim. *The Brendan Voyage.* New York: Modern Library, 2000; London: Arena, 1983.

Tomlinson, H. M., ed. *Great Sea Stories of All Nations.* London: Spring Books, 1967.

PERIODICALS
Canoe & Kayak
National Geographic
Sea Kayaker

CHAPTER 2. TWO DESPERATE ESCAPES: THE 17TH AND 18TH CENTURIES

Anthony, Irvin, ed. *The Saga of the "Bounty."* New York: Dell, 1961.

Bligh, William. *The Mutiny On Board H.M.S. "Bounty."* Adapted by Deborah Kestel. Edina MN: ABDO Pub., 2002.

Miller, Helen Hill. *Captains from Devon: The Great Elizabethan Seafarers Who Won the Oceans.* Chapel Hill NC: Algonquin Books, 1985.

Okeley, William. *Ebenezer; Or a small monument of great Mercy appearing in the miraculous deliverance of William Okeley.* London: n.p., 1764.

CHAPTER 3. VICTORIAN VENTURERS: 1865–1876

Barton, Humphrey. *Atlantic Adventurers: Voyages in Small Craft.* 2nd ed. Southhampton UK: Adlard Coles, 1962.

Bull, John. *Sail Your Canoe.* Leicester UK: Cordee, 1989.

Davis, Charles G. *American Sailing Ships: Their Plans and History.* New York: Dover, 1984.

Devine, Eric. *Midget Magellans: Great Cruises in Small Ships.* London: John Lane, 1936; New York: H. Smith & R. Haas, 1935.

Harland, John. *Seamanship in the Age of Sail: An Account of the Shiphandling of the Sailing Man-of-War, 1600–1860, Based on Contemporary Sources.* Annapolis: Naval Institute Press; London, Conway Maritime, 1984.

Hodder, Edwin. *John MacGregor: "Rob Roy," Etc.* London: Hodder Brothers, 1894.

MacGregor, John. *The "Rob Roy" on the Baltic: A Canoe Cruise.* London: Sampson Low, 1896; Boston: Roberts Brothers, 1872.

———. *The "Rob Roy" on the Jordan.* London: John Murray, 1904; New York, Harper and Brothers, 1875.

———. *A Thousand Miles in the "Rob Roy" Canoe on the Rivers and Lakes of Europe.* Murray UT: Dixon-Price, 2000; London: British Canoe Union, 1963.

———. *The Voyage Alone in the Yawl "Rob Roy."* Arthur Ransome, ed. Mineola NY: Dover Publications, 2001; London: Grafton, 1987.

A Night with Paul Boyton, and Other Stories. New York: Werner, 1899.

The Story of Paul Boyton: Voyages on All the Great Rivers of the World. London: G. Routledge & Sons, 1893; Milwaukee: Riverside, 1892.

The Thrilling Log; With incidents, hair-breadth escapes, etc. etc., of the little boat "City of Ragusa." Boston: Pilot Press, 1870.

PERIODICALS

Boston Morning Journal
Boston Post
Frank Leslie's Lady's Journal
The Graphic
Harper's Weekly
The Illustrated London News
The Liverpool Daily Post
The Liverpool Echo
The Liverpool Porcupine
The Liverpool Weekly Mercury
Lloyd's List
The New York Times
The Pilot
Sea Breezes
Slobodna Dalmacija (Split, Croatia)
The Sun (Baltimore)
The Times (London)

CHAPTER 4. THE PATHS OF GLORY: 1876–1900

Barton, Humphrey. *Atlantic Adventurers: Voyages in Small Craft.* 2nd ed. Southhampton UK: Adlard Coles, 1962.

Bishop, Nathaniel H. *Four Months in a Sneak-Box: A Boat Voyage of 2,600 Miles Down the Ohio and Mississippi Rivers, and Along the Gulf of Mexico.* Detroit: Gale Research Corp., 1975.

———. *Voyage of the Paper Canoe.* Wilmington NC: Coastal Carolina Press, 2000.

Bull, John. *Sail Your Canoe.* Leicester UK: Cordee, 1989.

Crapo, Thomas. *Strange, But True: Life and Adventures of Captain Thomas Crapo and Wife.* William J. Cowin, ed. New Bedford MA: T. Crapo, 1893.

de Wogan, Tanneguy. *Voyages du canot en papier le "Qui Vive?" et aventures de son capitaine.* Paris: Hachette, 1887.

Garland, Joseph E. *Lone Voyager: The Extraordinary Adventures of Howard Blackburn, Hero Fisherman of Gloucester.* New York: Simon & Schuster; London: Touchstone, 2000.

Gilboy, Bernard. *A Voyage of Pleasure: The Log of Bernard Gilboy's Trans-Pacific Cruise in the Boat "Pacific," 1882–1883.* John Barr Tompkins, ed. Cambridge MD: Cornell Maritime Press, 1956.

Henderson, Richard, comp. *Dangerous Voyages of Captain William Andrews.* New York: Abercrombie & Fitch, 1966.

Manley, Atwood, with Paul F. Jamieson. *Rushton and His Times in American Canoeing.* Syracuse: Syracuse University Press, 1968.

Merrien, Jean. *Madmen of the Atlantic.* Translated by Oliver Coburn. New York: Pitman, 1962; London: Phoenix House, 1961.

Nansen, Fridtjof. *Farthest North.* London: Duckworth, 2000; New York: Modern Library, 1999.

Phillips, C. E. Lucas. *Cockleshell Heroes.* London: Pan, 2000.

Shaw, David W. *Daring the Sea: The True Story of the First Men to Row Across the Atlantic Ocean.* Secaucus NJ: Carol, 1998.

Slocum, Joshua. *Sailing Alone Around the World.* London: Phoenix Press, 2000; New York: Penguin, 1999.

———. *Voyage of the "Liberdade."* Mineola NY: Dover; London: Constable, 1998.

Sparks, William, with Michael Munn. *The Last of the Cockleshell Heroes: A World War Two Memoir.* 3rd ed., rev. London: Leo Cooper, 1995.

PERIODICALS

Atlantic City Daily True American
Daily True American (Trenton, New Jersey)
Frank Leslie's Lady's Journal
The Graphic
Harper's Weekly
The Illustrated London News
L'Illustration
National Police Gazette
The New York Herald
The New York Times
The Spray
The Times (London)

CHAPTER 5. A WORLD TO CONQUER: 1900–1920

Barton, Humphrey. *Atlantic Adventurers: Voyages in Small Craft.* 2nd ed. Southampton UK: Adlard Coles, 1962.

Clarke, D. H. *An Evolution of Singlehanders.* New York: David McKay; London: Stanford Maritime, 1976.

Fenger, Frederic Abildgaard. *Alone in the Caribbean.* Belmont MA: Wellington Books, 1958; London: Hodder & Stoughton, 1919.

————. *The Cruise of "Diablesse."* New York: Yachting, 1926.

Lamb, Dana, and Ginger Lamb. *Enchanted Vagabonds.* New York: Harper & Brothers, 1938.

Luxton, Norman Kenny. *"Tilikum": Luxton's Pacific Crossing, Being the Journal of Norman Kenny Luxton, Mate of the "Tilikum," May 20, 1901, Victoria, B.C. to October 18, 1901, Suva, Fiji.* Eleanor Georgina Luxton, ed. Sidney BC: Gray's, 1971.

Speed, Harry Fiennes. *Cruises in Small Yachts.* 2nd ed. London: Imray, Laurie, Norie & Wilson, 1926.

Voss, John Claus. *The Venturesome Voyages of Captain Voss.* Sidney BC: Gray's, 1976; reprinted as *40,000 Miles in a Canoe and "Sea Queen."* Camden ME: International Marine, 2001.

Worsley, F. A. *Shackleton's Boat Journey.* Doughcloyne UK: Collins Press, 2002; New York: Norton, 1977.

PERIODICALS
The Illustrated London News
National Geographic
Rudder
Sail
The Times (London)

CHAPTER 6. LOVERS AND OTHER LOSERS: 1920–1930s

Doherty, John Stephen. *The Boats They Sailed In.* New York, London: Norton, 1985.

Klein, David, and Mary Louise Johnson. *They Took to the Sea: Including Personal Accounts of the Voyages of Joshua Slocum, Jack London, Rockwell Kent and Other Small-Boat Voyagers.* New Brunswick: Rutgers University Press, 1948.

Maury, Richard. *The Saga of "Cimba."* Camden ME: International Marine, 2001; London: G. G. Harrap, 1939.

Pidgeon, Harry. *Around the World Single-Handed: The Cruise of the "Islander."* New York: Dover; London: Constable: 1989.

Rebell, Fred [Paul Henri Sproge]. *Escape to the Sea.* London: Brown, Watson, 1961; New York: Dodd, Mead, 1939.

PERIODICALS
Charleston News and Courier
The Florida Times-Union
The New York Times
Popular Mechanics
Rudder
The Times (London)
The Yachting Monthly

CHAPTER 7. BIG FEAT, LITTLE NOTICE: THE 1940s

Great Voyages in Small Boats: Solo Circumnavigations. Clinton Corners NY: J. de Graff, 1976.

Merrien, Jean [René Marie de la Poix de Fréminville]. *Lonely Voyagers.* Translated by J. H. Watkins. New York: Putnam; London: Hutchinson, 1954.

Trumbull, Robert. *The Raft.* Annapolis MD: Naval Institute Press, 1992; London: G. G. Harrap, 1942.

Whittaker, James. *We Thought We Heard the Angels Sing: The Complete Epic Story of the Ordeal and Rescue of Those Who Were with Eddie Rickenbacker on the Plane Lost in the Pacific.* Richmond Hill ON: Simon & Schuster of Canada, 1970.

PERIODICALS

The Limerick Leader
National Geographic
The New York Times
The Times (London)
Yacht and Boat Owner
Yachting
The Yachting Monthly

CHAPTER 8. GOOFY AND GALLANT: THE 1950s

Barton, Humphrey. *Atlantic Adventurers: Voyages in Small Craft.* 2nd ed. Southhampton UK: Adlard Coles, 1962.

Bombard, Alain. *The Voyage of the "Hérétique": The Story of Dr. Bombard's 65-Day Solitary Atlantic Crossing in a Collapsible Life Raft.* Translated by Brian Connell. New York: Simon & Schuster, 1954.

Carlin, Benjamin. *"Half-Safe": Across the Atlantic by Jeep.* London: Deutsch, 1955. Published in New York by Morrow as *"Half-Safe": Across the Atlantic in an Amphibious Jeep* (1955).

———. *"Half-Safe" Around the World: By Amphibious Jeep From Montreal Across the Atlantic, Europe, Asia, Australia, Japan and the Pacific to Canada and Back to Montreal.* Thornhill UK: Tynron Press, 1990.

———. *The Other Half of "Half-Safe": Around the World By Amphibious Jeep: From Montreal Across the Atlantic, Europe, Asia, Australia, Japan and the Pacific to Canada and Back to Montreal.* Guildford Western Australia: Guildford Grammar School Foundation, 1989.

Eiloart, Arnold, and Peter Elstob. *The Flight of the "Small World."* New York: Norton; London: Hodder & Stoughton, 1959.

Ellam, Patrick, and Colin Mudie. *Sopranino.* London: Grafton, 1986; Fair Lawn NJ: Essential Books, 1958.

Ellam, Patrick, and June Ellam. *Wind Song: Our Ten Years in the Yacht Delivery Business.* Camden ME: International Marine, 1976.

Great Voyages in Small Boats: Solo Circumnavigations. Clinton Corners NY: J. de Graff, 1976.

Heyerdahl, Thor. *Kon-Tiki: Across the Pacific by Raft.* North Salem NY: Adventure Library, 1997.

Lindemann, Dr. Hannes. *Alone at Sea.* Oberschleißheim, Germany: Pollner Verlag, 1993.

Tiira, Ensio. *Raft of Despair.* New York: Dutton, 1955; London: Hutchinson, 1954.

PERIODICALS

Life
The New York Times

The Times (London)
The Yachting Monthly

CHAPTER 9. **DOING YOUR OWN THING:** THE 1960s

Brenton, Francis. *The Voyage of the "Sierra Sagrada": Across the Atlantic in a Canoe.*
  Chicago: Regnery, 1969.
Clarke, D. H. *An Evolution of Singlehanders.* New York: D. McKay; London: Stanford
  Maritime, 1976.
Fairfax, John. *"Britannia": Rowing Alone Across the Atlantic: The Record of an Adventure.*
  Norwalk CT: Easton Press, 1988; London: Kimber, 1972.
Fairfax, John, and Sylvia Cook. *Oars Across the Pacific.* New York: Norton, 1973;
  London, Kimber, 1972.
Horie, Kenichi. *"Kodoku": Sailing Alone Across the Pacific.* Translated by Takuichi Ito
  and Kaoru Ogimi. London: Collins, 1965; Rutland VT: Charles E. Tuttle, 1964.
Letcher, John S. Jr. *Self-Steering for Sailing Craft.* Camden ME: International Marine,
  1974.
Manry, Robert. *Tinkerbelle.* London: Collins, 1967; New York: Harper & Row, 1966.
Morris, Roger. *Atlantic Seafaring: Ten Centuries of Exploration and Trade in the North
  Atlantic.* Camden ME: International Marine, 1992.
Naydler, Merton. *The Penance Way: The Mystery of "Puffin"'s Atlantic Voyage.* New
  York: W. Morrow, 1969; London: Hutchinson, 1968.
Ridgway, John, and Chay Blyth. *A Fighting Chance.* Philadelphia: Lippincott;
  London: Paul Hamlyn, 1967.
Riding, John. *The Voyage of the "Sea Egg."* London: Pelham, 1968.
Vihlen, Hugo, with Joanne Kimberlin. *The Stormy Voyage of "Father's Day."* St. Paul
  MN: Marlor Press, 1997.
Willis, William. *The Epic Voyage of the "Seven Little Sisters": A 6,700 Mile Voyage Alone
  Across the Pacific.* London: Hutchinson, 1956.
———. *The Hundred Lives of an Ancient Mariner: An Autobiography.* London:
  Hutchinson, 1967.

PERIODICALS
The Daily Telegraph
The New York Times
The Spray
The Times (London)
Yachting

CHAPTER 10. **THE PURSUIT OF HAPPINESS:** THE 1970s

Acton, Shane. *"Shrimpy": A Record Round-the-World Voyage in an Eighteen Foot Yacht.*
  Sparkford UK: P. Stephens, 1993.
Blagden, David. *Very "Willing Griffin": The Story of the Smallest Boat Ever to Compete in
  the Singlehanded Transatlantic Race.* New York: Norton, 1974; London: P. Davies,
  1973.
Chiles, Webb. *Storm Passage: Alone Around Cape Horn.* New York: Times Books, 1977.

————. *A Single Wave: Stories of Storms and Survival.* Dobbs Ferry NY: Sheridan House, 1999.

Henderson, Richard. *Singlehanded Sailing: The Experiences and Techniques of the Lone Voyagers.* 2nd ed. Camden ME: International Marine, 1988.

James, Naomi. *Alone Around the World.* New York: Coward, McCann & Geoghegan, 1979.

Moitessier, Bernard. *The First Voyage of the "Joshua."* Translated by Inge Moore. New York: Morrow, 1973.

Spiess, Gerry, with Marlin Bree. *Alone Against the Atlantic.* London: Souvenir, 1982; Minneapolis MN: Control Data Pub., 1981.

PERIODICALS
Cruising World
MotorBoating
The New York Times
Sail
The Times (London)
Yachting
The Yachting Monthly

CHAPTER 11. **THE GOLDEN DECADE:** THE 1980s

Acton, Shane. *"Shrimpy": A Record Round-the-World Voyage in an Eighteen Foot Yacht.* Sparkford UK: P. Stephens, 1993.

————. *"Shrimpy" Sails Again: From Cambridge to the Caribbean in an Eighteen Foot Yacht.* Wellingborough UK: Stephens, 1989.

Chiles, Webb. *A Single Wave: Stories of Storms and Survival.* Dobbs Ferry NY: Sheridan House, 1999.

Lundin, Sven. *Bris.* Göteborg: Bokförlaget Korpen, 1990.

Lundin, Sven, and Anders Öhman. *Med Bris mot Kap Horn: En Långfärdsseglares Liv och Seglatser.* Stockholm: Rabén & Sjögren, 1985.

Starkell, Don. *Paddle to the Amazon.* Charles Wilkins, ed. Rocklin CA: Prima; London: Futura, 1989.

Testa, Serge. *Five Hundred Days: Around the World on a Twelve Foot Yacht.* Aspley Queensland: S. Testa, 1988.

PERIODICALS
Cruising World
The New York Times
Sail
The Spray
The Times (London)
Yachting
The Yachting Montly

CHAPTER 12. **RECORDS AND REDUX:** THE 1990s

Ladd, Stephen G. *Three Years in a Twelve-Foot Boat.* Seattle: Seekers Press, 2000.

Vihlen, Hugo, with Joanne Kimberlin. *The Stormy Voyage of "Father's Day."* St. Paul MN: Marlor Press, 1997.

PERIODICALS
Canoë-Kayak
Canoe & Kayak
Canoeist
Cruising World
Kanu
Messing About in Boats
MotorBoating
The New York Times
Paddler
Practical Boat Owner
Sail
Sailing
The Spray
The Times (London)
Yachting
The Yachting Monthly

APPENDIX. **ROWERS AND OTHER STRANGERS**

d'Aboville, Gérard. *Alone.* Translated by Richard Seaver. New York: Arcade, 1993.
Fairfax, John, and Sylvia Cook. *Oars Across the Pacific.* New York: Norton, 1973; London: Kimber, 1972.
Ridgway, Rebecca. *À l'école de l'aventure: Le Cap Horn en kayak.* Paris: Arthaud, 1994.

PERIODICALS
Cruising World
The New York Times
Practical Boat Owner
Sail
Sailing
The Times (London)
Winston-Salem Journal
The Yachting Monthly

ACKNOWLEDGMENTS

I HAVE ONLY BEEN THE HELMSMAN ON A SHIP WHOSE CREW has done a magnificent job bringing into port the cargo of precious information that this book is. I am embarrassed that I can only pay off my fine crew with a hearty verbal handshake. I hope they know how much I appreciate the great lengths they went to in revealing an often neglected, but important, aspect of maritime history—small-boat voyaging.

I first want to express my thanks to my eminent predecessors in chronicling small-boat history, Frenchman Jean Merrien and Britons Humphrey Barton and D. H. Clarke. Their work has inspired and been quoted by dozens of other writers over the years, but they did all the original pioneering groundwork. I am glad to have their experience and works to guide me, and it is with humility that I in several instances correct mistakes or misstatements that they reported years ago and which have taken on the mantle of "truth" for writers who followed. I was lucky to have many more resources available to me than they had, most importantly the Internet. With it, I was able to search library databases around the world and find information that was out of their reach when they wrote their seminal histories. I also have the advantage of writing in a post–Cold War world, so that correspondents in former Soviet-bloc nations were now free to provide information that before might have been kept secret.

The Internet also provided a host of qualified research assistants in the form of the International Marine History Information Exchange Group (MarHst-L). This wonderful group was founded by Walter Lewis and Maurice Smith of the Marine Museum of the Great Lakes at Kingston, Canada. They are a fountain of information, and I drank profitably from their waters many times.

I was also lucky in having several great translators who did their work quickly and well despite the sometimes tricky jargon-ridden nature of the original works. They are: Tony Ford, Julia Hemsing, and Jan

Huerkamp of Germany, Gjøran Larssen of Norway, Chrisoffer Ellert of Sweden, and John Predovan and Kristen Kristich (who taught herself Croatian!) of the United States.

My job was made infinitely easier thanks to the professionalism and courtesy of the staffs of the following libraries: the Atlantic City Free Public Library; the W. C. Jackson Library, UNC-Greensboro; the Z. Smith Reynolds Library, Wake Forest University; the Winston-Salem/Forsyth County Public Library; the Herbert H. Bateman Maritime Research Center at the Mariners' Museum, Newport News; the Caird Library of the National Maritime Museum, Greenwich (U.K.); the British Library, and most especially the Library of Congress in Washington. The LoC went above and beyond the call of duty in helping me locate material quickly and efficiently. Its staff was universally polite and helpful, making those thirteen-hour days go by like so many happy moments.

Also helpful were: Andris Cekuls and Klara Radzina of the Museum of History of Riga, Latvia; Damjana Franèiæ of the University Library of Pula, Croatia; Arthur Credland of the Hull Maritime Museum, England; Neil Curtis of the Marischal Museum, University of Aberdeen, Scotland; Anne Gleave of the Merseyside Maritime Museum Archives, England; Roger Hull of the Liverpool Records Office, England; Ernie Ruffler of the Wirral Museum, England; Ivar G. Braaten of the Ålesunds Museum, Norway; Rune Flåten of the Ski Museum, Norway; Marina Mollenhauer and the Mayor's offices of Dettingen and Konstanz, Germany; Klaus Fuest, Staatsarchiv, Hamburg, Germany; Don Conlin of the Maritime Museum of the Atlantic, Nova Scotia; Stephen Nash of the Field Museum, Chicago; Michael Maione of the Ford's Theater National Historical Site, Washington, D.C.; and James Cheevers of the U.S. Naval Academy Museum, Annapolis.

I am indebted to the following historical societies: Archives and Collections Society, Boston Society, Devon History Society, Joshua Slocum Society, and the Royal Humane Society, and most especially to the Archives of the Catholic Archdiocese of Boston.

Psychologist Brian Hawkins provided a profile of Paul Müller, and for that I am grateful.

I also received great help from these kind people:

Paul Adamthwaite, Stephen Alsford, David Asprey, Bob Baird, Len Barnett, Marc Bartolomeo, Bill Bedford, Roland Bepler, Bruce Blackistone, David Bolduc and Mindy Bolduc, Marty Bollinger, Tom Brady, John Bull, Bill Bunting, Matthias Busch, Ian Buxton, Diana Coke, James Comer, Ralph Díaz, Joan Druett, Michael Dun, Patrick Ellam, Don Elliot, Kevin Foster, Angelika Gebhard, Ray Girvan, Harvey Golden, Arno Gropp, John Harland, Jim Hopwood, Ted Jones, Martin Käser, Trevor J. Kenchington, Elaine Killam, Edwin King, Raphaëla le Gouvello, Michel Lopez, Andreas von Mach, Sandy McClearn, Ian Mitchell, Colin Mudie, David Mullington, Bernard de Neumann, Tony Niilus, Richard Pelvin, Gilbert Porter, Suzanne Richardson, Barbara Romer, Patti Satalia, John Schultz, Barry Sheppard, Henning Sietz, Bob Smart, Lin Snow, Gerry Spiess, John D. Stevenson, Anthony Steward, Thomas Theisinger, William Ullman, Hugo Vihlen, Norbert Weismann, Matthias Wenigwieser, and Sven (Lundin) Yrvind.

And these companies: Dudley Dix, Chris Hare Marine, Honnor Marine, Humber Marine, and Bruce Robertson International Yacht Design.

Most especially I want to thank D. H. "Nobby" Clarke—sailor, fighter pilot, and historian extraordinaire—for his generous support and aid. He is one of the last of that generation of men and women who with great quiet bravery and personal sacrifice, yet public cheer and good humor, delivered to the next generation a freer world. They asked nothing in return. We all owe them much.

ART SOURCES

page v: 1890s photo from *A Daring Voyage Across the Atlantic by Two Americans, the Brothers Andrews* (Dutton, 1880); page 4: from Tanneguy de Wogan, *Voyages du canot en papier le "Qui vive?"* (Paris: Hachette, 1887); page 7: *The First Lesson in Canoeing* by Danish artist J. E. C. Rasmussen, reproduced in the *Illustrated London News* (1876); page 11: 14th century illuminated manuscript, Heidelberg University; page 13: Turin map, 1523, in Harrisse, 1892; page 16: Benzoni, 1581; page 18: British Museum, London; page 19: author's collection, print from 1732, artist unknown; page 21: from a 17th century map, courtesy Library of Congress; page 23: from the 17th century, courtesy James Ford Bell Library, University of Minnesota; page 29: 17th century print, from Stephen Clissold, *The Barbary Slaves* (Totowa, NJ: Rowman and Littlefield, 1977); page 31: National Maritime Museum; page 33: National Maritime Museum; page 42: from Edwin Hodder, *John MacGregor ("Rob Roy")* (London: Hodder Brothers, 1894); page 47: from Edwin Hodder, *John MacGregor ("Rob Roy")* (London: Hodder Brothers, 1894); page 48: from Edwin Hodder, *John MacGregor ("Rob Roy")* (London: Hodder Brothers, 1894); page 49: courtesy of the U.S. Naval Academy Museum; page 52: from *Harper's Weekly* (31 August 1867); page 53: from *Harper's Weekly* (9 July 1864); page 55: The Maryland Historical Society, Baltimore, Maryland; page 60: from *Illustrated London News* (1860s); page 64: from *Illustrated London News* (13 March 1875); page 67: from Larry Brown, *Frugal Yachting, Family Adventuring in Small Sailboats* (Camden, Maine: International Marine, 1994); page 72: from Larry Brown, *Frugal Yachting, Family Adventuring in Small Sailboats* (Camden, Maine: International Marine, 1994); page 78: from Capt'n Crapo and Thomas Crapo, *Strange, But True, Life and Adventures of Captain Thomas Crapo and Wife* (1893); page 83: from Nathaniel Bishop, *The Paper Canoe* (1878); page 84: from Tanneguy de Wogan, *Voyages du canot en papier le "Qui vive?"* (Paris: Hachette, 1887); page 85: from *A Daring Voyage Across the Atlantic by Two Americans, the Brothers Andrews* (Dutton, 1880); page 87: from *A Daring Voyage Across the Atlantic by Two Americans, the Brothers Andrews* (Dutton, 1880); page 90: Mrs. Thomas W. Gilboy; page 96: Mrs. Thomas W. Gilboy; page 103: from Artemas Ward, ed., *Columbus Outdone: An Exact Narrative of the Voyage of The Yankee Skipper Capt. Wm. A. Andrews in the boat "Sapolio"* (New York, 1893); page 106: from F. Nansen, *Farthest North*, vol. 2 (New York: Harper & Bros, 1897); page 108: courtesy Long Branch Ice Boat and Yacht Club, New Jersey; page 113: Gloucester Master Mariners' Association; page 115: from Joseph E. Garland, *Lone Voyager* (Boston: Little, Brown & Company, 1963); page 117: Sandy Bay Historical Society; page 121: circa 1900, Atlantic City Historical Society; page 122: Maritime Musuem of British Columbia; page 128: ALB Gjortz; page 132: courtesy Ålesund Museum; page 133: from Frederic Fenger, *Alone in the Caribbean* (New York: George H. Doran Co., 1917); page 139: Frank Hurley/Royal Geographical Society; page 142: Drawn from material supplied by the boat party, from Ernest Shackleton, *South*

(New York: MacMillan, 1920); page 146: courtesy Ortsverwaltung Dettingen, Ortsvorsteher Albert Griesmeier; page 149: courtesy Ortsverwaltung Dettingen, Ortsvorsteher Albert Griesmeier; page 150: courtesy Ortsverwaltung Dettingen, Ortsvorsteher Albert Griesmeier; page 155: *Yachting Magazine* (August 1929); page 163: from *Escape to the Sea, the Adventures of Fred Rebell who sailed single-handed in an open boat 9,000 miles across the Pacific in search of Happiness, with an Introduction by Richard Hughes* (London: Travel Book Club, 1952); page 166: from John Stephen Doherty, *The Boats They Sailed In* (New York: W. W. Norton & Co., 1985); page 167: from John Stephen Doherty, *The Boats They Sailed In* (New York: W. W. Norton & Co., 1985); page 171: from Dana Lamb, *Enchanted Vagabonds* (New York: Harper & Brothers, 1938); page 173: U.S. Navy; page 180: U.S. Navy; page 185: courtesy Jack Schultz; page 188: courtesy Jack Schultz; page 193: U.S. Army; page 200: courtesy Guildford Grammar School; page 203: sketch by Stanley Smith, from John Stephen Doherty, *The Boats They Sailed In* (New York: W. W. Norton & Co., 1985); page 204: courtesy Colin Mudie; page 208: from Dr. Alain Bombard, *The Bombard Story* (London: Readers Union, Andres Deutsch, 1955); page 213: Straits Times, from Ensio Tiira, *Raft of Despair* (New York: E. P. Dutton & Co., 1953); page 215: John Guzzwell, from John Stephen Doherty, *The Boats They Sailed In* (New York: W. W. Norton & Co., 1985); page 223: Peter Stackpole/Time Life Pictures/Getty Images; page 225: courtesy Colin Mudie; page 228: courtesy Colin Mudie; page 228: Harry Jacobs, from Kenichi Horie, *Kodoku, Sailing Alone Across the Pacific* (Rutland, Vermont: Charles E. Tuttle Company, 1964); page 235: Case-Western Reserve Museum, photographer unknown; page 240: author's collection; page 243: courtesy David and Mindy Balduc; page 245: courtesy Colin Mudie; page 247: Mirrorpix.com; page 248: from Francis Brenton, *The Voyage of the "Sierra Sagrada": Across the Atlantic in a Canoe* (Chicago: Henry Regnery Company, 1969); page 250: from Francis Brenton, *The Voyage of the "Sierra Sagrada": Across the Atlantic in a Canoe* (Chicago: Henry Regnery Company, 1969); page 251: courtesy Dave and Mindy Balduc; page 254: Canadian Navy Photo from U.S.C.G. *Duane*, Daily Express, from Merton Naydler, *The Penance Way* (London: Hutchinson of London, 1968); page 255: courtesy Hugo Vihlen; page 260: courtesy Hugo Vihlen; page 262: John Fairfax; page 264: courtesy Hunter Marine; page 271: estate Bas Jan Ader; page 272: Shane Acton, *"Shrimpy": A Record Round-the-World Voyage in an Eighteen Foot Yacht* (Patrick Stephens Ltd., Haynes Publishing Group, 1993); page 273: courtesy Webb Chiles; page 275: courtesy Gerry Spiess; page 276: courtesy Gerry Spiess; page 279: courtesy Don Starkell; page 285: courtesy Don Starkell; page 286: courtesy Olga Lundin (two photos); page 289: courtesy Webb Chiles; page 290: Ajax News Service; page 291: Ajax News Service; page 292: Michael O'Hearn; page 294: Ajax News Service; page 296: courtesy Serge Testa; page 298: courtesy Ed Gillet; page 301: courtesy Sven Lundin; page 302: courtesy Sven Lundin; page 306: courtesy Don Elliot; page 310: courtesy Dudley Dix/Anthony Steward; page 312: courtesy Dudley Dix/Anthony Steward; page 315: courtesy Hugo Vihlen; page 320: courtesy Serge Testa; page 322: David Clapham, NGP Productions; page 324: courtesy Raphaëla le Gouvello; page 326: Corbis Sygma; page 327: Peter Bray; page 329: courtesy Bombardier; page 333: courtesy Bill Teplow; page 339: Verlen Kruger; page 341: Robin Testa.

INDEX

Numbers in **bold** refer to pages with photos or illustrations.

Acrohc Australis (Serge Testa's boat), 295–98, **296**
Acton, Shane
quest for purpose as motivation, 6
"Shrimpy": A Record Round-the-World Voyage in an Eighteen Foot Yacht, 272, 332
Super Shrimp, 269–70, 271–**72**, 278, 294–95
Ader, Bas Jan (Guppy 13), 270–**71**
Adler (minesweeper), 147
adventures. *See* sailing adventures
Aebi, Tania, 325
Aerolite, 56
Aga (Paul Müller's boat), **155**–58
Aga II (Paul Müller's boat), 159–60
Age Unlimited (William Willis's raft), 250
Ahodori II (Hiroshi Aoki's boat), 266
Aldrich, Gene, in life raft, 172, **173**, 174–78
Alendi Hill (British freighter), 214
Alexander, John (*Ganga Devi*), 229
Alfredon (brig), 74
Alfred Vittery (schooner), 97
Alger, Horatio, Jr., 104
Algiers, 20, **21**, 22–28
Alone Against the Atlantic (Spiess), 276, 332
Alone in the Caribbean (Fenger), 135, 331, 332
Aluminium-Bris (Sven Lundin's boat), 286–87, 300
America (Howard Blackburn's dory), 118
Amphritite (German bark), 79
Andrews, Asa Walter (brother of William Andrews), on *Nautilus*, **85**–88

Andrews, Mary C. (wife of William Andrews), on *Dark Secret* (13 feet), 120–21
Andrews, William, 84–**85**, 99, 117
Dark Secret (13 feet), 120–21
Dark Secret (14 feet), 97–99
Doree, 112–13
marriage and honeymoon cruise, 119–21
Mermaid, 100–102
money as motivation, 2
Nautilus, 85–88, **87**
Phantom Ship, 112
Sapolio, 102–**3**
Aoki, Hiroshi (*Ahodori II*), 266
April Fool (Hugo Vihlen's capsule boat), **255**–56, 259–**60**, 314
Aragón, Carlos (*Golondrina*), 273–74
Arakaka (British steamer), 209
Armstrong (mate, *John T. Ford*), 54–56
Arone, Elinore. *See* Carlin, Elinore (wife of Ben Carlin)
Astronom (German bark), 80
A. T. Stewart (pilot boat), 49

Batavia (Cunard liner), 79
Beaudout, Henri, 218–19
L'Égaré, 219
L'Égaré II, 219–20
Begent, Walter "Louis" (shipmate, *Tilikum*), 125–26
Benford Design Group, 332
Benlomond (British merchantman), 179
Bennekom (Dutch ship), 210
Berlin (Paul Müller's boat), 189–91
Bethia, 31
Big C (Tom McNally's capsule boat), **294**
Bishop, Nathaniel
Four Months in a Sneak Box (book), 83
Maria Theresa, 82–**83**
The Voyage of the Paper Canoe (book), 83

Blackburn, Howard, **113**
America, 118
Grace L. Fears doryman, 113–**15**
Great Republic, **117**–18
Great Western, 116–17
Hattie I. Phillips, 116
Blackburn Expedition, 116
Blagden, David (*Willing Griffin*), **264**, 265, 267–69
Bligh, William, **31**
Bounty mutiny, 31–**33**, 40
The Mutiny on Board H.M.S. "Bounty," 332
return to England, 40–41
on Tofua, 34–35
voyage on *Bounty*, 30–**33**
voyage to East Timor, 35–40
Blyth, Chay (*English Rose III*), 246–48, **247**, 249, 250, 251, 253
Chay Blyth's Challenge Business, 332
boatbuilding materials, 281–82
boat design recommendations, 332–33
boat/craft types
balloon-boat, 224–27, **225**, **226**
brigantine rig, **53**
canoe, fiberglass, **279**, 283–85
canoe, wood and canvas, 170–**71**
canoe-like skis, 305, **326**–27
canoes, dugout, 15, **122**–28, 184–**88**, 217–18, 243, 248–**50**
canoes, paper, 82–**83**, **84**
canoes, sailing, 132–35, **133**, 204, 313
Caprice Cruiser, 269–70, 271–**72**, 278, 294–95
capsule boats, 242–**43**, **255**–56, 259–**60**, **290**–**94**, 295–98, **296**, 314–18, **315**, 321–23, **322**
catamarans, 282, 319
catboat, **47**
clinker-built wooden craft, **11**
collapsible hull, 102–**3**

curraghs (skin-covered boats), 10, 11
cutters, 88–89, 214, 239
dories, 68, 69–74, **72**, 89– 90, 113–**15**, 118, 246–48, **247**, 249, 250, 251, 253
Drascombe Longboat, 270
Drascombe Lugger, 265–66, **273**
Finn-class dinghy, 273–74
folding, 102–**3**, 112, 120–21
gaff cutter, 116–18, **117**
gunter-gaff rig, 100–102, **103**
Guppy 13, **271**
inflatables, 51–53, **52**, 172, **173**, 174–78, 207–10, **208**
kayak, Franz Romer's folding, 103, 148–54, **149**, **150**
kayak, Hannes Lindemann's Aerius, 220–24, **223**
kayak, Necky Tofino, **298**–99
kayak, Peter Bray's, **327**–28
kayaks, Fridjtof Nansen's, 105–**6**
kayaks, of Inuit, 6, **7**, 17–20, **19**
kayaks, John MacGregor's, **42**, 44–46
ketch, 54–57, **55**
lateen rig, 85–88, **87**, 98–99
lifeboats, 48–51, **49**, 58–61, **60**, 100, 128–**32**
life rafts, 51–53, **52**, 172, **173**, 174–78, 179–83, **180**, 207–14, **208**
lobster-boat style rig, 100–101
Merriman suit, 62–66, **64**, 174
monocoque, 128–**32**
open, 265–66, **273**, 288–90, **289**, 309–**12**
Potter 19 Chubby, **333**
rafts, 219–20, 250, **251**–53, 261
rowboat, folding, 26–30, **29**
rowboats, 246–48, **247**, 249, 250, 251, 253, 261–63, **262**, **306**, 307–9
sailboards, 304, **324**, 325–26
schooner rig, 91–97, **96**
schooners, 81, 97, 116, 143, 268
Sea-Doo, 328–**29**
Seep (seagoing jeep), 192, **193**, 194–202, **200**
semicapsule boat, **275**–78, 281, 287–88

skin-covered boats, 10, 11–12
sloop, 162–70, **166**, **228**, 230–33
sloop-rigged dinghy, 234–39, **235**
surf boats, 107–11, **108**, **245**–48, 249, 250, 253–**54**
umiak (Inuit boat), 8–9
West Wight Potter sailing dinghies, 239–42, **240**, 266–67
whaleboats, 75–81, **78**
windmill/water propeller, 58–59, **60**
yawl, **47**
Bodfish, David (crew for Nathaniel Bishop), 82
Bombard, Alain
  L'Hérétique, 207–10, **208**
  survival theories, 206–7
book recommendations, 331–32
Bounty (HM Armed Vessel), 30–**33**, 40
Bourgnon, Laurent, 304
Boyton, Paul, 61–62
  Coney Island, 66
  Merriman suit, 62–66, **64**
  Paul Boyton's Water Chutes, 66
  Roughing It in Rubber, 65
  Sea Lion Park, 66
Bradley, Mr. and Mrs. (*Jane Crooker*), 144–45
Bragg, Capt. (*Queen*), 63
Bray, Peter (*Newt*), **327**–28
Brendan, Saint, and curraghs, 9–12, **11**
The Brendan Voyage (Severin), 12
Brenton, Francis
  quest for purpose as motivation, 6
  Sierra Sagrada, 243, **248**–50
  Sierra Sagrada, with balloon, 256–59
Bricka, Rémy (canoe-like skis), 304–5, **326**–27
brigantine-rig boat, **53**
Bris (Sven Lundin's boat), **286**
Bris VI (Sven Lundin's boat), 300–303, **301**
Britannia (John Fairfax's rowboat), 261–63, **262**
Bruce Roberts International Yacht Design, 333
Brude, Ole (*Uræd*), 128–32

Buckley, John Charles (*City of Ragusa*), 57–61
Burt, Hugh (*Ganga Devi*), 229

Cadwalader, George (*Nimbus*), 263
Caird, Sir James (industrialist), 136
Cambria, 44
Camden and Atlantic Railroad Co., 62
Canada (steamship), 81
Canoe Club, 46
canoe-like skis, 305, **326**–27
canoes
  Chris and Stuart Newman's sailing, 313
  Dana and Ginger Lamb's wood and canvas, 170–**71**
  Diego Méndez's dugout, 15
  Don Starkell's fiberglass, **279**, 283–**85**
  Francis Brenton's dugout, 243, 248–**50**
  Fritz Fenger's sailing, 132–35, **133**
  Hannes Lindemann's dugout, 217–18
  John E. Schultz's dugout, 184–**88**
  John Voss's dugout, **122**–28
  Nathaniel Bishop's paper, 82–**83**
  Patrick Ellam's sailing, 204
  Tanneguy de Wogan's paper, **84**
Capitana (Christopher Columbus's boat), 15
Caprice Cruiser, 269–70, 271–**72**, 278, 294–95
capsule boats. *See also* semicapsule boat
  Bill Dunlop's, **291**–92, 294
  Bill Verity's, 242–**43**
  Hugo Vihlen's, **255**–56, 259–**60**, 314–18, **315**
  Serge Testa's, 295–98, **296**
  Tom McLean's, **290**–91, 293–94
  Tom McNally's, **294**, 314, 315–18, 321–23, **322**
  Wayne Dickinson's, **292**–93
Carlin, Ben
  Half-Safe, 194–202, **200**
  "Half-Safe": Across the Atlantic by Jeep (book), 200
  technical challenge as motivation, 4

Carlin, Elinore (wife of Ben Carlin), on *Half-Safe*, 197–201, **200**, 202

Carrick, David (*Hermes*), 265–66

casco (dugout canoe), 184–**88**

catamarans, 282, 319

catboat, **47**

Centennial (Alfred Johnson's dory), 69–74, **72**

Centennial Exhibition, 68, 74

Chaudière (Canadian warship), 254

Chichester, Sir Francis (*Gipsy Moth V*), 268

Chidiock Tichborne (Webb Chiles's open boat), **273**, 288–89

Chidiock Tichborne II (Webb Chiles's open boat), **289**–90

Childs, Kennedy (mate, *William Tapscott*), 50–51

Chiles, Webb, 272–73
    Chidiock Tichborne, **273**, 288–89
    Chidiock Tichborne II, **289**–90
    quest for purpose as motivation, 6

Chris Hare Marine, 313

Christian, Fletcher (acting lieutenant, *Bounty*), 31–**33**, 41

Christopher Columbus (Josiah Lawlor's boat), 102, 103

circumnavigations. *See under* sailing routes

Cito (Norwegian bark), 111

City of Bath (John Traynor's dory), 89–90

City of Ragusa (Nicolas Primoraz's lifeboat), 58–61, **60**

Clark, C. E. "Nobby" (boatbuilder), 272

Clarke, D. H., 144–45, 331

Cleveland Plain Dealer (newspaper), 234, 235, 238

Cleveland Press (newspaper), 238

clinker-built wooden craft, **11**

club-footed sail, **87**

Colas, Alain (*Pen Duick IV*), 268

collapsible hull, 102–**3**

Columbia (Ludwig Eisenbraun's boat), 118

Columbus, Bartholomew, 15

Columbus, Christopher
    Capitana, 15
    curiosity as motivation, 2
    first voyage to the New World, 17
    fourth journey to the New World, 12–16, **13**
    Gallega, 15
    in Ireland, 9
    Santiago de Palos, 15
    Vizcaina, 15, 16

composite construction techniques, 300–301

Coney Island, 66

Corkill, Adrian (*Ganga Devi*), 229

Craig (Dayton Lalonde's boat), 229

Crapo, Joanna (wife of Thomas Crapo)
    New Bedford, 75–81, **78**
    Strange, But True (book), 79, 81

Crapo, Thomas, 74–75
    James Parker, 81
    Manson, 81
    New Bedford, 75–81, **78**
    Strange, But True (book), 79, 81
    Volunteer, 81

Cullinane, Michael (*Rag Tag Fleet*), 282

curiosity, as motivation for sailing adventures, 2

curraghs (skin-covered boats), 10, 11

dangers of sailing adventures, 330–31

Dark Secret (13 feet) (William Andrews's folding boat), 120–21

Dark Secret (14 feet) (William Andrews's boat), 97–99

Davison, Ann (*Felicity Ann*), 325

Delage, Guy (purported transatlantic swimmer), 319

DeMente, Boye "Jingo" Lafayette (crew, *Half-Safe*), 201

Denmark (steamer), 80

De Rosnay, Baron Arnaud (sailboard), 304

Derungs, Iris (companion of Shane Acton), 270, 271–**72**, 278

Deutscher Sport (Franz Romer's folding kayak), 103, 148–54, **149**, **150**

de Wogan, Tanneguy, **4**, 83–84
    Qui Vive?, **84**
    Voyages du Canot en Papier (book), 84

Dickinson, Wayne (*God's Tear*), **292**–93

Di Costa, Pietro. *See* Primoraz, Nicolas (*City of Ragusa*)

Dixon, Harold, in life raft, 172, **173**, 174–78

Donovan, J. C. (*Vision*), 53

Donvig, Capt. (Norwegian boat designer), 130

Doree (William Andrews's folding boat), 112–13

dories, 68
    Alfred Johnson's, 69–74, **72**
    Howard Blackburn's, 113–**15**, 118
    John Ridgway and Chay Blyth's, 246–48, **247**, 249, 250, 251, 253
    John Traynor's, 89–90

dory compass, 69

Drascombe Longboat, 270

Drascombe Lugger, 265–66, **273**

Dudley Dix Yacht Design, 332

dugout canoes, 15, **122**–28, 217–18, 243, 248–**50**

Dumas, Vito (*Lehg II*), 174

Dunlop, Bill (*Wind's Will*), **291**–92, 294

Durango, 121

Ebrus (steamer), 102

Eiloart, Arnold "Bushy" (crew, *Small World*), 224–27

Eiloart, Tim (son of Arnold Eiloart), on *Small World*, 224–27

Eisenbraun, Ludwig (*Columbia*), 118

Elaine (Fred Rebell's sloop), 162–70, **166**

Ellam, Patrick
    Sopranino, **204**–6
    Theta, 204

Emma (schooner), 143

Enchanted Vagabonds (Lamb and Lamb), 171

Endurance (Ernest Shackleton's boat), 136–39, 142

English Rose III (John Ridgway's rowboat), 246–48, **247**, 249, 250, 251, 253
Epidauro (Yugoslav ship), 152–53
Ericsson, Fred, in life raft, 210–13
Escape to the Sea (Rebell), 332
Essex Boat Co., 267
Evolution of Singlehanders (Clarke), 144

Fairfax, John (*Britannia*), 254–55, 261–63, **262**
fame, as motivation for sailing adventures, 2–3
Fanny (dog, *Red, White & Blue*), 49
Father's Day (Hugo Vihlen's capsule boat), 314–18, **315**
Felicity Ann (Ann Davison's boat), 325
Fenger, Frederic "Fritz"
  Alone in the Caribbean (book), 135, 331, 332
  daggerboard design, 133
  Yakaboo, 132–35, **133**
  fiberglass canoe, **279**, 283–**85**
Fieschi, Bartolomeo (*Vizcaina*), 16
Finnalpino, 253
Finn-class dinghy, 273–74
Fitch, Frank E. (mate, *Red, White & Blue*), 49–51
folding boats. *See also* kayaks; rowboats
  William Andrews's, 102–**3**, 112, 120–21
Ford, John T. (politician), 54, 56–57
40,000 Miles in a Canoe (Voss), 127
Four Months in a Sneak Box (Bishop), 83
Fox, Richard K. (publisher), 107
Fox, Uffa (boat designer), 261
Fram (Fridjtof Nansen's boat), 105–6
Frobisher, Martin, and contact with Inuit, 17, **18**

gaff cutter, 116–17, **118**
Gallega (Christopher Columbus's boat), 15
Ganga Devi (John Alexander, Hugh Burt, and Adrian Corkill's boat), 229

Garnet (British warship), 65–66
gasbags, inflatable, 149–50
Gavinski, Agathe. *See* Müller, Aga (girlfriend and wife of Paul Müller)
George V, King, 136
Gilboy, Bernard, **90**–91
  Pacific, 91–97, **96**
  quest for purpose as motivation, 6
  A Voyage of Pleasure, 332
Gilboy, Catherine (wife of Bernard Gilboy), 91
Gillet, Ed (Necky Tofino kayak), **298**–99
Giltspur (Tom McClean's capsule boat), **290**–91, 293–94
Gipsy Moth V (Francis Chichester's boat), 268
Giraldi, Fred, 304
Giskø (cargo ship), 132
God's Tear (Wayne Dickinson's capsule boat), **292**–93
Gold, Capt. Charles W. (*John T. Ford*), 54–56
Golondrina (Carlos Aragón's Finn-class dinghy), 273–74
GP-A (General Purpose–Amphibious), 192, **193**, 194–202, **200**
Grace L. Fears (halibut boat), 113–14
Gradely, Gladys, 3–4, 144–45
Great Republic (Howard Blackburn's gaff cutter), **117**–18
Great Western (Howard Blackburn's gaff cutter), 116–17
gunter-gaff rigged boat, 100–102, **103**
Guppy 13, **271**
Guzzwell, John (*Trekka*), 4, 214–17
Gvodev, Eugeny (*Lena*), **320**–21

"Half-Safe": Across the Atlantic by Jeep (Carlin), 200
Half-Safe (Ben Carlin's Seep), 194–202, **200**
Hamburg-America Line (HAPAG), 147
Hanley, Barry (crew, *Half-Safe*), 201
Harbo, George (*Richard K. Fox*), 104–5, 106–12
Hasler, Blondie (*Jester*), 103, 267–68

Hattie I. Phillips (Howard Blackburn's schooner), 116
Hayter, Edward R. W. (crew, *City of Ragusa*), 60
Hermes (David Pyle and David Carrick's open boat), 265–66
Heyerdahl, Thor (*Kon Tiki*), 12, 219
Higgins and Gifford (boatbuilders), 85, 98, 100
Hill, Douglas (*Rag Tag Fleet*), 282
Hippocampe (Jean Lacombe's cutter), 214
Hoare, John (*Puffin*), 244–48, 249, 250, 253–**54**
Honnor Marine, 289
Horie, Kenichi (*Kodoku*), 5, **228**, 229–33
Hudson, John M. (*Red, White & Blue*), 49–51, 52
Hunter Boats Ltd., 267
Hurriane Alma, 249, 250
Hurricane Celia, 252
Hurriane Faith, 253

inflatable boats
  Alain Bombard's, 207–10, **208**
  and Gene Aldrich, Harold Dixon, and Anthony Pastula, 172, **173**, 174–78
  John Mikes's, 51–53, **52**
Ingersoll, O. K. (boatbuilder), 49
Instituto de Pesca (trawler), 143
Inuit
  kayaks, 6, **7**, 17–20, **19**
  kidnapping of, 17–**19**
  in Scotland and Ireland, 1–2, 8–9, 18–20
Island Girl (John Letcher's cutter), 239

Jackson, Frederick (*Windward*), 106
James, Naomi, 325
James L. Caird (Ernest Shackleton's boat), 138–43, **139**, **142**
James Parker (Thomas Crapo's schooner), 81
Jane Crooker (Mr. and Mrs. Bradley's boat), 144–45
Jester (Blondie Hasler's boat), 267–68

J. Laurent Giles (boat design
firm), 204, 214
Johansen, F. Hjalmar (crew,
Fram), 105–**6**
Johnson, Alfred (*Centennial*),
66, **67**, 68–74
Johnstone, David (*Puffin*),
243–48, 249, 250, 253–**54**
John T. Ford (Charles Gold's
ketch), 54–57, **55**

Kaluna (brig), 76
Kashima, Ikuo (*Korassa,
Korassa II*), 256
kayaks
Ed Gillet's, **298**–99
Franz Romer's folding, 103,
148–54, **149, 150**
Fridtjof Nansen's, 105–**6**
Hannes Lindemann's Aerius,
220–24, **223**
of Inuit, 6, **7**, 17–20, **19**
John MacGregor's, **42**,
44–46
Peter Bray's, **327**–28
Kent, 43–44
ketch, 54–57, **55**
Klepper, Johann (tailor/boat-
builder), 148–50, 154
Klepper kayaks
Franz Romer's folding, 103,
148–54, **149, 150**
Hannes Lindemann's Aerius,
220–24, **223**
Kodoku (Kenichi Horie's
sloop), **228**, 230–33
Korassa (Ikuo Kashima's boat),
256
Korassa II (Ikuo Kashima's
boat), 256

Lacombe, Jean (*Hippocampe*),
214
Ladd, Stephen (*Squeak*), **306**,
307–9
La Fougueuse (French patrol
boat), 325
Lalonde, Dayton J. (*Craig*),
229
Lamb, Dana and Ginger
(*Vagabunda*), 170–**71**
lateen-rig boat, 85–88, **87**,
98–99
Laurent Giles Naval Architects
Ltd., 333
Lawlor, Dennison (naval archi-
tect, father of Josiah
Lawlor), 100

Lawlor, Josiah W.
Christopher Columbus, 102,
103
fame as motivation, 3
Neversink, 100
Sea Serpent, 100–101
Lecomte, Ben (transatlantic
swimmer), 323
L'Égaré (Henri Beaudout's
raft), 219
L'Égaré II (Henri Beaudout's
raft), 219–20
le Gouvello, Raphaëla (sailboard), **324**, 325–26
Lehg II (Vito Dumas's boat),
174
Lena (Eugeny Gvodev's boat),
320–21
Letcher, John, Jr.
Island Girl, 239
Self-Steering for Sailing Craft,
239
technical challenge as moti-
vation, 4
L'Hérétique (Alain Bombard's
life raft), 207–10, **208**
Liberia II (Hannes Linde-
mann's dugout canoe),
217–18
Liberia III (Hannes Linde-
mann's Aerius kayak),
220–24, **223**
lifeboats
F. L. Norton's, 100
John Hudson's, 48–51, **49**
Nicolas Primoraz's, 58–61, **60**
Ole Brude's, 128–**32**
life rafts
Alain Bombard's, 207–10,
208
and Fred Ericsson and Ensio
Tiira, 210–14, **213**
and Gene Aldrich, Harold
Dixon, and Anthony
Pastula, 172, **173**, 174–78
John Mikes's, 51–53, **52**
and Poon Lim, 179–83, **180**
Life Saving Raft Co., 51, 52
Lim, Poon, in life raft, 179–83,
180
Lindemann, Hannes
Liberia II, 217–18
Liberia III, 220–24, **223**
Little One (William Willis's
raft), 250, **251**–53, 261
Little Western (Frederick Nor-
man and George Thomas's
cutter), 88–89

lobster-boat style rigged boat,
100–101
Lundin, Olga (wife of Sven
Lundin), on *Bris VI*, 303
Lundin, Sven, 285–**86**
Aluminium-Bris, 286–87,
300
boat designs, **302**, 333
Bris, 286
Bris VI, 300–303, **301**
composite construction tech-
niques, 300–301
Luxton, Norman (journalist/
crew, *Tilikum*), 123–25,
128
Luxton Museum of the Plains
Indians, 128

MacGregor, Maj. Duncan
(father of John MacGre-
gor), 44
MacGregor, John "Rob Roy,"
44–45, **48**
birth of pleasure boating,
47–48
English Channel crossing, 47
Kent disaster, 43–44
opinion of *Red, White & Blue*,
50–51
Rob Roy (1865 kayak), 44–46
Rob Roy (1866 kayak), **42**, 46
Rob Roy (yawl), **47**
The "Rob Roy" on the Baltic, 46
*A Thousand Miles in the "Rob
Roy" Canoe in the Rivers and
Lakes of Europe*, 45–46, 332
tour of Europe in *Rob Roy*
(1865 kayak), 45
*The Voyage Alone in the Yawl
"Rob Roy,"* 47–48
Mallene, Jerry (*Nonpareil*), 52
Manry, Robert
quest for purpose as motiva-
tion, 6
Tinkerbelle, 234–39, **235**
Tinkerbelle (book), 332
Manry, Virginia (wife of
Robert Manry), 234–35,
239
Manson (Thomas Crapo's
brig), 81
Maria Theresa (Nathaniel Bish-
op's paper canoe), 82–**83**
Marichalar, Count Álvaro de,
on Sea-Doo, 328–**29**
marlin, 288
Martinez, Jose (crew, *L'Égaré
II*), 219–20

Marty, Christian (sailboard), 304

Mary, 21–22

McClean, Tom (*Giltspur*), **290**–91, 293–94

McNally, Tom
Big C, **294**
fame as motivation, 3
Vera Hugh I, 314, 315–17
Vera Hugh II, 318, 321–23, **322**

Méndez, Diego (crew for Christopher Columbus), 14–17, **16**

Mermaid (Kenichi Horie's sloop). See *Kodoku* (Kenichi Horie's sloop)

Mermaid (William Andrews's gunter-gaff rigged boat), 100–102

Merriman, Clark S. (inventor), 62

Merriman suit, 62–66, **64**, 174

Mikes, John (*Nonpareil*), 52–53

Miller, George (*Nonpareil*), 52

Miller, Professor (canoe-like shoes), 305

Minter-Kemp, Martin (*Strongbow*), 268

Mitchell, Samuel (boatbuilder), 75

Modena, Marc (crew, *L'Égaré II*), 219–20

money, as motivation for sailing adventures, 2

monocoque, 128–**32**

motivations for sailing adventures, 1–6

Mudie, Colin
boat plans, 333
Puffin, **245**
Small World, 224–27, **225**, **226**
Sopranino, **204**, 205–6

Mudie, Rosemary (wife of Colin Mudie), on *Small World*, 224–27

Müller, Aga (daughter of Paul Müller), on *Berlin*, 189–91

Müller, Aga (girlfriend and wife of Paul Müller), 155, 158–59, 189

Müller, Paul, 154–55
Aga, **155**–58
Aga II, 159–60
Berlin, 189–91
money as motivation, 2

Murphy, Edmund (crew, *John T. Ford*), 54–56

The Mutiny on Board H.M.S. "Bounty" (Bligh), 332

Nansen, Fridtjof (*Fram*), 105–**6**

Natural History: Book II (Pliny the Elder), 9

Nautilus (William Andrews's lateen-rig boat), 85–88, **87**

Navigatio Sancti Brendani Abbatis, 10–12

NCS Challenger (Anthony Steward's open boat), 309–**12**

Necky Tofino kayak, **298**–99

Neversink (F. L. Norton's lifeboat), 100

New Bedford (Thomas Crapo's whaleboat), 75–81, **78**

Newman, Chris (*Spirit of Cleveland*), 312–13

Newman, Stuart (brother of Chris Newman), on *Spirit of Cleveland*, 312–13

Newt (Peter Bray's kayak), **327**–28

New York World (newspaper), 98

Nimbus (George Cadwalader and Duncan Spencer's boat), 263

Nonoalca (Bill Verity's capsule boat), 242–**43**

Nonpareil (John Mikes's life raft), 51–53, **52**

Nor (bark), 99

Norman, Frederick (*Little Western*), 88–89

Norton, F. L., 100

Nova Espero (Stanley Smith's boat), 191–92, 202–4, **203**

Observer Singlehanded Transatlantic Race (OSTAR), 233, 267–68

Okeley, William
folding rowboat, 26–30, **29**
life in Algiers, 22–28
survival as motivation, 2
voyage on *Mary*, 21–22

Olsen (mate, *City of Bath*), 89–90

open boats
Anthony Steward's, 309–**12**
David Pyle and David Carrick's, 265–66
Webb Chiles's, **273**, 288–90, **289**

Orellana (Dana Starkell's dugout canoe), **279**, 283–**85**

Ovando, Gov. Nicolás de (Hispaniola), 13, 16

Pacific (Bernard Gilboy's schooner-rig boat), 91–97, **96**

Pandora, 41

paper canoes, 82–**83**, **84**

passages. *See* sailing routes

Pastula, Anthony, in life raft, 172, **173**, 174–78

Paul Boyton's Water Chutes, 66

Pelican. See Tilikum (John Voss's dugout canoe)

Pen Duick IV (Alain Colas's trimaran), 268

Perry's Monitor Life Raft, 51–53, **52**

personal test, as motivation for sailing adventures, 5

Peters, Eric (*Toniky Nou*), 314

Peyron, Stéphane (sailboard), 304

Phantom Ship (William Andrews's folding boat), 112

Pidgeon, Harry, 169

Pilot Press (Catholic publication), 59–60

Pioneer Minx (American steamer), 233

pleasure boating, birth of, 47–48

Police Gazette (journal), 107

porpoises, 135, 192

Potter 19 Chubby, **333**

Primoraz, Nicolas (*City of Ragusa*), 57, 58–61

Puffin (David Johnstone's surf boat), **245**–48, 249, 250, 253–**54**

Pulitzer, Joseph (newpaper magnate), 98

Pyle, David (*Hermes*), 265–66

Queen (steamer), 62–63

quest for purpose, as motivation for sailing adventures, 5–6

Qui Vive? (Tanneguy de Wogan's paper canoe), **84**

rafts. *See also* life rafts
Henri Beaudout's, 219–20
William Willis's, 219, 250, **251**–53, 261

Rag Tag Fleet (Douglas Hill and Michael Cullinane's catamaran), 282
Randal, John (William Okeley's business partner), 25
reading recommendations, 331–32
Rebell, Fred, 160–62, **163**
  Elaine, 162–70, **166**
  Escape to the Sea (book), 332
  sociopolitical motivation, 3
Red, White & Blue (John Hudson's life boat), 48–51, **49**
Richard K. Fox (George Harbo and Frank Samuelsen's surf boat), 107–11, **108**
Rickenbacker, Eddie, 175
Riddle, Capt. (mate, *John T. Ford*), 54
Ridgway, Capt. John (*English Rose III*), 244–48, **247**, 249, 250, 251, 253
Riding, John (*Sjö Äg*), 4, 233–34, 263, 270
Rob Roy (John MacGregor's 1865 kayak), 44–46
Rob Roy (John MacGregor's 1866 kayak), **42**, 46
Rob Roy (John MacGregor's yawl), **47**
The *"Rob Roy" on the Baltic* (MacGregor), 46
Romer, Franziskus "Franz," **146**–47
  Adler, 147
  Deutscher Sport, 103, 148–54, **149**, **150**
  Hamburg-America Line (HAPAG), 147
Roughing It in Rubber (Boyton), 65
Rougier, Paul (French planter), 167
rowboats. *See also* surf boats
  John Fairfax's, 261–63, **262**
  John Ridgway's, 246–48, **247**, 249, 250, 251, 253
  Stephen Ladd's, **306**, 307–9
  William Okeley's folding, 26–30, **29**

Saga of "Cimba" (Maury), 135, 331
sailboards, 304, **324**, 325–26
sailing adventures. *See also* small boats
  Chay Blyth's Challenge Business, 332

dangers of, 330–31
factors affecting voyages in the 1970s, 280–82
history of, 7–8
motivations for, 1–6
reading recommendations, 331–32
success rate, 331
Sailing Alone Around the World (Slocum), 116, 331
sailing canoes
  Chris and Stuart Newman's, 313
  Fritz Fenger's sailing, 132–35, **133**
  Patrick Ellam's sailing, 204
sailing routes. *See also* boat/craft types
  Acapulco, Mexico, to Nuku Hiva, French Polynesia, 273–74
  Ålesund, Norway, to Gloucester, MA, 130–31
  Amazon delta to Miami, FL, 186–88
  Atlantic City, NJ, to Huelva, Spain, 103
  Baltimore, Ireland, to Saint John's, Newfoundland, 303
  Baltimore, MD, to Ireland, 54–57
  Berlin, Germany, to Bassa, Liberia, 189–91
  Boston, MA, to Coverack, England, 100–101
  Boston, MA, to Gibraltar, 118
  Boston, MA, to Le Havre, France, 86–88
  British Columbia to Hawaii, 90–91
  California to Hawaii, 267
  Cape Espartel, Tangier, to Las Palmas, Canaries, 322–23
  Caribbean to Chicago, IL, 243, 248–50
  Casablanca, Morocco, to Florida, 260
  Castle Garden, NY, to Le Havre, France, 108–11
  Chicago, IL, to Africa, 257–58
  circumnavigation, Brisbane, Australia, start, 295–98
  circumnavigation, Cape Town, South Africa, start, 311–12

circumnavigation, Caspian Sea start, 320–21
circumnavigation, Falmouth, England, start, 269–70, 271–**72**, 278
circumnavigation, Japan start, 266
circumnavigation, Victoria, British Columbia, start, 215–17
Dakar, Senegal, to Chicago, IL, 259
Dakar, Senegal, to Guyana, 304
Dartmouth, England, to City Island, NY, 203–4
Dartmouth, Nova Scotia, to Dartmouth, England, 191–92
Egypt to Las Palmas, Canaries, 289–90
England to Darwin, Australia, 265–66
England to Tahiti, 30–31
English Channel crossing, 47
Falmouth, England, to Bridgetown, Barbados, 205–6
Falmouth, MA, to Falmouth, England, 236–39
Genoa, Italy, to New York, NY, 256
Gibraltar to Saint Vincent, West Indies, 270
Gloucester, MA, to Cowes, Isle of Wight, 88–89
Gloucester, MA, to Lisbon, Portugal, 117–18
Gloucester, MA, to Liverpool, England, 70–74
Gloucester, MA, to Portishead, England, 117
Göteborg, Sweden, to Argentina, 287
Grenada to Saba, Leeward Islands, 134–35
Hamburg, Germany, to America, 156–58
Hawaii to Alaska, 239
Hong Kong to Falmouth, England, 229
Honolulu, HI, to San Pedro, CA, 168–69
Isle of Wight to Kloster, Sweden, 240–42
Las Palmas, Canaries, to Barbados, 207–9

Las Palmas, Canaries, to Miami, FL, 261–63

Las Palmas, Canaries, to Saint Croix, Virgin Islands, 218

Las Palmas, Canaries, to Saint Thomas, Virgin Islands, 151–53, 221–24

Lisbon, Portugal, to Jamaica, 313

Liverpool, England, to Boston, MA, 59

London, England, to Europe to London, England, 45

London, England, to Gloucester, MA, 89

Long Beach, CA, to Sydney, Australia, 287–88

Long Beach, CA, to Yokohama, Japan, 256

Los Angeles, CA, to Hawaii, 239

Los Angeles, CA, to Sydney, Australia, 229

Maine to Falmouth, England, 89–90

Maupiti, French Polynesia, to Tau Island, American Samoa, 233

Milk River, MT, to South America to Miami, FL, 308–9

Monterey, CA, to Hawaii, 298–99

New Bedford, MA, to Newland, England, 77–80

Newfoundland to Falmouth, England, 318

Newfoundland to Oporto, Portugal, 293

New York, NY, to La Rochelle, France, 304

New York, NY, to Liverpool, England, 60

New York, NY, to Southampton, England, 52–53

Nishinomiya, Japan, to San Francisco, CA, 231–33

Norfolk, VA, to Falmouth, England, 276–78

Nova Scotia to Falmouth, England, 219–20

Peru to Australia, 250

Plymouth, England, to Bermuda, 233–34

Plymouth, England, to Newport, RI, 268–69

Port Allerton, MA, to Aranmore Island, Ireland, 292–93

Port Everglades, FL, to Tralee, Ireland, 243

Portland, ME, to Cooks Islands, 294

Portland, ME, to Plymouth, England, 291–92

Portugal to San Juan, Puerto Rico, 317

Puerto Rico to Guadeloupe, 304

Québec to Florida, 82–83

Saint John's, Newfoundland, to Falmouth, England, 290–91

San Diego, CA, to Suva, Fiji, 273

Sandy Hook, NJ, to Deal, England, 48–50

San Francisco, CA, to Australia, 92–97

San Francisco, CA, to Hawaii, 333

Senegal to Martinique, 325

Suva, Fiji, to Rabigh, Saudi Arabia, 288–89

Sydney, Australia, to Honolulu, HI, 163–68

Tenerife to Barbados, 225–27

Tenerife to Trinidad, 304–5

Tofua to East Timor, 35–40

Toulon, France, to New York, NY, 214

Trinidad to Miami, FL, 282

Vancouver, British Columbia, to Auckland, New Zealand, 242

Victoria, British Columbia, to Sydney, Australia, 124–26

Samuelsen, Frank (*Richard K. Fox*), 104–5, 106–12

Santiago de Cuba (steamer), 52

Santiago de Palos (Columbus's ship), 15

Sapolio (William Andrews's folding boat), 102–3

schooner-rig boat, 91–97, **96**

schooners, 81, 97, 116, 143, 268

Schultz, John E. "Jack" (*Sea Fever*), 183–89, **185, 188**

Schultz, Maj. John G. "Dutch" (father of John. E. Schultz), 183

Sea-Doo, 328–**29**

Sea Fever (John E. Schultz's dugout canoe), 184–**88**

Sea Lion Park, 66

Sea Serpent (Josiah Lawlor's boat), 100–101

Seep (seagoing jeep), 192, **193**, 194–202, **200**

Self-Steering for Sailing Craft (Letcher), 239

self-steering techniques, 92–93, 205, 277–78

semicapsule boat, **275**–78, 281, 287–88. *See also* capsule boats

Seven Little Sisters (William Willis's raft), 219, 250

Severin, Tim, in skin-covered boat, 11–12

Shackleton, Ernest
  Endurance, 136–39, 142
  James L. Caird, 138–43, **139, 142**
  Instituto de Pesca, 143
  Southern Sky, 143
  Yelcho, 143

Shackleton's Boat Journey (Worsley), 332

Shaney, John (mate, *John T. Ford*), 54

sharks, 92, 93, 101, 134–35, 152, 166–67, 212, 213, 312, 328

Shering (mate, *John T. Ford*), 54–56

Shrimpy (Shane Acton's Caprice cruiser). See *Super Shrimp* (Shane Acton's Caprice cruiser)

"Shrimpy": A Record Round-the-World Voyage in an Eighteen Foot Yacht (Acton), 272, 332

Sierra Sagrada (Francis Brenton's dugout canoes), 243, 248–**50**
  with balloon, 256–59

Sjö Äg (John Riding's boat), 233–34, 263, 270

skin-covered boats, 10, 11–12

skin-covered kayaks, 6, **7**, 17–20, **19**

Slocum, Joshua
  fame as motivation, 3
  Sailing Alone Around the World, 116, 331
  self-steering techniques, 93
  Spray, 93, 116, 123–24, 331
  Voyage of the "Liberdade," 331

sloop, 162–70, **166, 228**, 230–33

sloop-rigged dinghy, 234–39, **235**

small boats. *See also* boat/craft types; sailing adventures
boatbuilding materials, 281–82
boat design recommendations, 332–33
definition of, 1
motivations for adventures, 1–6
technology advances, 281–82

Small World (Colin Mudie's balloon-boat), 224–27, **225, 226**

Smeeton, Beryl and Miles (*Tzu Hang*), 215–16

Smith, Colin (brother of Stanley Smith), on *Nova Espero*, 191–92

Smith, Stanley
Nova Espero, 191–92, 202–4, **203**
West Wight Potter sailing dinghies, 239–42, **240**

sociopolitical reasons, as motivation for sailing adventures, 3–4

Sopranino (Patrick Ellam's boat), **204**–6, 214, 333

Sorensen, Peder (fisherman), 241

South, Mary C. *See* Andrews, Mary C. (wife of William Andrews)

Southern Sky (Norwegian whaler), 143

Spencer, Duncan (*Nimbus*), 263

Spencer, William (crew, *Vision*), 53

Spiess, Gerry
Alone Against the Atlantic (book), 276, 332
Yankee Girl, **275**–78, 281, 287–88

Spirit of Cleveland (Chris and Stuart Newman's sailing canoe), 313

sponsors, 149–50, 265

Spray (Joshua Slocum's boat), 93, 116, 123–24, 331

Sprogis, Pauls. *See* Rebell, Fred

Squeak (Stephen Ladd's rowboat), **306**, 307–9

Starkell, Dana (son of Don Starkell), on *Orellana*, 278, **279**, 282–**85**

Starkell, Don (*Orellana*), 278, **279**, 282–**85**

Starkell, Jeff (son of Don Starkell), on *Orellana*, 282–83, **285**

Steward, Anthony "Ant" (*NCS Challenger*), 309–**12**

Stewart, Geoffrey (Drascombe Longboat), 270

Stoney, Mayor Thomas Porcher (Charleston, SC), 158–59

Stoy, Mayor Franklin (Atlantic City, NJ), 120, 121

Strange, But True (Crapo), 79, 81

Strongbow (Martin Minter-Kemp's boat), 268

Styff, Joanna. *See* Crapo, Joanna (wife of Thomas Crapo)

success rate for sailing adventures, 331

Super Shrimp (*Shrimpy*) (Shane Acton's Caprice cruiser), 269–70, 271–**72**, 278, 294–95

surf boats. *See also* rowboats
David Johnstone and John Hoare's, **245**–48, 249, 250, 253–**54**
George Harbo and Frank Samuelson's, 107–11, **108**

survival, as motivation for sailing adventures, 1–2

swims, transatlantic, 319, 323

swordfish, 95

technical challenges, as motivation for sailing adventures, 4–5

technology advances, 281–82

Ten Cents War, 65

Tepa, Damanihi, 233

Teplow, Bill (Potter 19 Chubby), **333**

Terlain, Jean-Yves (*Vendredi Trieze*), 268

Testa, Serge (*Acrohc Australis*), 295–98, 321

Theta (Patrick Ellam's sailing canoe), 204

Thomas, George (*Little Western*), 88–89

Thompson, William C. (president, Life Saving Raft Co.), 52

A Thousand Miles in the "Rob Roy" Canoe in the Rivers and Lakes of Europe (MacGregor), 45–46, 332

Thumbelina (Kenneth Weis's boat), 242

Tiira, Ensio, in life raft, 210–14, **213**

Tilikum (John Voss's dugout canoe), **122**–28

Tinkerbelle (book) (Manry), 332

Tinkerbelle (Robert Manry's sloop-rigged dinghy), 234–39, **235**

Toby (dog, *Vision*), 53

Toniky Nou (Eric Peters's boat), 314

transatlantic crossings. *See under* sailing routes

transatlantic swims, 319, 323

transpacific crossings. *See under* sailing routes

Traynor, John (*City of Bath*), 89–90

Trekka (John Guzzwell's boat), 214–17, **215**, 333

Tribulations of a Chinaman (Verne), 65

Tropicvance (barkentine), 93

Truman, Pres. Harry S., 182

Tzu Hang (Miles and Beryl Smeeton's boat), 215–16

umiak (Inuit boat), 8–9

Uræd (Ole Brude's lifeboat), 128–32, **129**

U.S. Navy search policy, 178

Vagabunda (Dana and Ginger Lamb's wood and canvas canoe), 170–**71**

Vanackère, Gaston (crew, *L'Égaré II*), 219–20

Van Ruth, John (West Wight Potter 14), 266–67

Vendredi Trieze (Jean-Yves Terlain's schooner), 268

The Venturesome Voyages of Captain Voss (Voss), 332

Vera Hugh I (Tom McNally's capsule boat), 314, 315–17

Vera Hugh II (Tom McNally's capsule boat), 318, 321–23, **322**

Verity, Bill (*Nonoalca*), 242–**43**

Victoria, Queen, 64

Victoria and Albert (HMY), 64

Vihlen, Dana (son of Hugo Vihlen), 318

Vihlen, Hugo
April Fool, **255**–56, 259–**60**, 314

fame as motivation, 3
Father's Day, 314–18, **315**
Vikings, early explorations of,
9, 10–12
Violet, Charles (mate, *Nova
Espero*), 202–4
Vision (J. C. Donovan's brigan-
tine-rig boat), **53**
Vizcaina (Christopher Colum-
bus's boat), 15, 16
Volunteer (Thomas Crapo's
boat), 81
Voss, John
40,000 Miles in a Canoe
(book), 127
small-boat handling, 127–28
Tilikum, **122**–28
*The Venturesome Voyages of
Captain Voss* (book), 332
*The Voyage Alone in the Yawl
"Rob Roy"* (MacGregor),
47–48
Voyage of the "Liberdade"
(Slocum), 331
The Voyage of the Paper Canoe
(Bishop), 83
A Voyage of Pleasure (Gilboy),
332
*The Voyage of Saint Brendan the
Abbot*, 10–12
Voyages du Canot en Papier (de
Wogan), 84

Wallace, Rev. James, on Inuit
kayakers, 18
Waters, Elisha (boatbuilder),
82
Watkinson, John (English
boatbuilder), 265, 266
Weis, Kenneth (*Thumbelina*),
242
Weisskopf, Gustave. *See*
Whitehead, Gustave
(inventor)
Welch, Tom (doryman, *Grace
L. Fears*), 113–14, **115**
West Wight Potter 14 (John
Van Ruth's boat), 266–67
West Wight Potter sailing
dinghies, 239–42, **240**
whaleboats, 75–81, **78**
whales, 87, 103, 134, 298, 328
Whalon, Catherine. *See*
Gilboy, Catherine (wife of
Bernard Gilboy)
Whitehead, Gustave (inven-
tor), 119
William Tapscott (cargo hauler),
50–51
Willing Griffin (David Blag-
den's boat), **264**, 265,
267–69
Willis, William
Age Unlimited, 250
fame as motivation, 3

Little One, 250, **251**–53, 261
Seven Little Sisters, 219, 250
windmill/water propeller boat,
58–59, **60**
Wind's Will (Bill Dunlop's capsule boat), **291**–92, 294
Windward (Frederick Jackson's
boat), 106
wood and canvas canoe,
170–**71**
Worsley, Frank (skipper,
Endurance), 138–43

Yakaboo (Fritz Fenger's sailing
canoe), 132–35, **133**
Yankee Girl (Gerry Spiess's
semicapsule boat), **275**–78,
281, 287–88
yawl, **47**
Yelcho (Chilean steamer), 143
Yokoyama, Akira (boat design-
er), 230
Young, Harry, 171–72
Young, John L. (amusement
park owner), 119–21, 305
Young's Pier (Atlantic City,
NJ), 119–**21**, 305
Yrvind, Sven. *See* Lundin, Sven